From Frontier Policy to Foreign Policy

From Frontier Policy to Foreign Policy

THE QUESTION OF INDIA
AND THE TRANSFORMATION OF
GEOPOLITICS IN QING CHINA

Matthew W. Mosca

STANFORD UNIVERSITY PRESS
STANFORD, CALIFORNIA

Stanford University Press
Stanford, California

© 2013 by the Board of Trustees of the Leland Stanford Junior University.
All rights reserved.

No part of this book may be reproduced or transmitted in any form or by any means, electronic or mechanical, including photocopying and recording, or in any information storage or retrieval system without the prior written permission of Stanford University Press.

Printed in the United States of America on acid-free, archival-quality paper

Library of Congress Cataloging-in-Publication Data

Mosca, Matthew W., author.
  From frontier policy to foreign policy : the question of India and the transformation of geopolitics in Qing China / Matthew W. Mosca.
     pages cm
  Includes bibliographical references and index.
  ISBN 978-0-8047-8224-1 (cloth : alk. paper)
  ISBN 978-0-8047-9729-0 (pbk. : alk. paper)
     1. China—Foreign relations—1644–1912. 2. Geopolitics—China—History. 3. Geography—China—History. 4. India—History—British occupation, 1765–1947. 5. China—History—Qing dynasty, 1644–1912. 6. China—Foreign relations—Great Britain. 7. Great Britain—Foreign relations—China. I. Title.
  DS754.18.M69 2013
  327.5105409'03—dc23
                                              2012031059

  ISBN 978-0-8047-8538-9 (electronic)

Typeset by Bruce Lundquist in 11/14 Adobe Garamond Pro

Contents

Acknowledgments vii

Reign Period Abbreviations ix

    Introduction 1

PART ONE | THE QING EMPIRE'S VISION OF THE WORLD

1. A Wealth of Indias:
India in Qing Geographic Practice, 1644–1755   25

PART TWO | FORGING A MULTIETHNIC EMPIRE: THE APEX OF A FRONTIER POLICY

2. The Conquest of Xinjiang and the Emergence of "Hindustan," 1756–1790   69

3. Mapping India:
Geographic Agnosticism in a Cartographic Context   101

4. Discovering the "Pileng":
British India Seen from Tibet, 1790–1800   127

PART THREE | THE AGE OF TRANSITION, 1800–1838

5. British India and Qing Strategic Thought in the Early Nineteenth Century   163

6. The Discovery of British India on the Chinese Coast, 1800–1838   199

PART FOUR | FOREIGN POLICY AND ITS LIMITS

7. The Opium War and the British Empire, 1839–1842   237

8. The Emergence of a Foreign Policy: Wei Yuan and the Reinterpretation of India in Qing Strategic Thought, 1842–1860   271

Conclusion:
Between Frontier Policy and Foreign Policy   305

Character List   315
Notes   329
Bibliography   367
Index   389

Acknowledgments

In the course of this project I have incurred many debts. Thanks must go first to Philip A. Kuhn, Mark C. Elliott, and Peter C. Perdue, for offering unflagging support and a lofty standard toward which to aspire. Deep gratitude is due also to Helen F. Siu and Angela K. C. Leung for their timely support for my research.

Friends too numerous to mention have given material and moral support. Particular thanks are due to Dr. Onuma Takahiro and Dr. Brian Vivier for reviewing this entire manuscript with painstaking care. Others who gave unstinting assistance include: David Brophy, Devon Dear, James Fichter, Ying Hu, Loretta Kim, Christopher Leighton, Ben Levey, Li Ren-Yuan, Max Oidtmann, Jonathan Schlesinger, Hoong Teik Toh, and Lawrence Zhang. Errors that remain despite this abundance of help are, of course, the full responsibility of the author. I record my gratitude to the staff of the archives and libraries used in the course of this project, notably the Harvard-Yenching Library, the Asian and African Studies reading room of the British Library, the First Historical Archives and National Library of China in Beijing, the National Palace Museum and the Academia Sinica's Fu Ssu-Nien Library in Taipei, and the Toyo Bunko in Tokyo. Financial support has come from many sources. In its initial stage, research was supported by United States government (FLAS and Fulbright IIE) and Harvard University (Sheldon Traveling, Reischauer, and Whiting) fellowships. The Center for Chinese Studies of the University of California, Berkeley, kindly granted me a fellowship. The Institute for the Humanities and Social Sciences of the University of Hong Kong allowed me to spend three years in stimulating research surroundings. This book would not have been possible without the institute's generous publication subvention. Equally essential has been the wise and patient counsel of Stacy Wager and Carolyn Brown at Stanford University Press, and the thorough and helpful advice of the copyeditor and two anonymous readers.

Above all, thanks are due to the support of the Mosca and O'Reilly families—aunts, uncles, great-aunts, and cousins—and to my brothers Peter and John. This book is dedicated to my beloved parents, Paul and Eileen Mosca.

Reign Period Abbreviations

KX Kangxi (康熙): 1662–1722
YZ Yongzheng (雍正): 1723–1735
QL Qianlong (乾隆): 1736–1795
JQ Jiaqing (嘉慶): 1796–1820
DG Daoguang (道光): 1821–1851
XF Xianfeng (咸豐): 1852–1861
TZ Tongzhi (同治): 1862–1874

Qing empire and its neighbors

Introduction

In 1638, Hong Taiji, the Manchu ruler of a small state on the northeastern fringe of the Asian continent, made a prophetic boast to a visiting envoy. The Mongol Yuan and other earlier dynasties, he declared, had campaigned as far as India, and his own Qing dynasty was now their equal.[1] Almost preposterous at the time, this assertion was realized by the conquests of his successors, who expanded the empire westward far into Inner Asia and ultimately extinguished their tenacious foe, the Junghar Mongols. In July 1757, Amursana, last pretender to the rule of an independent Jungharia, fled pursuing Qing forces into Russia. When the Qianlong emperor fully absorbed Amursana's domain two years later, the Qing realm reached its greatest extent, and its western border in Tibet and Xinjiang indeed abutted the Indian subcontinent. Never had the empire appeared more secure.

Yet the ramifications of another battle, fought far to the south almost at the moment Amursana fled the field, eventually confronted the Qing with a new and more powerful neighbor. In June 1757 the East India Company and its allies routed the nawab of Bengal, making the first in a patchwork of conquests that would in time establish British rule over virtually the whole of India. For the next hundred years, Company forces expanded their dominion to the south of the Himalayas as effectively as the Qing had done to the north. In addition to the established trade between Guangzhou and Indian ports, agents of the East India Company began to appear on a vast arc of the Qing frontier, from the cities of Central Asia to the coast of northern China. This activity aimed at the expansion of trade with China, the revenues of which were necessary to meet the costs of conquest and rule in India. Ultimately, fiscal need required the defense of this trade by force of arms.

The Opium War of 1840–1842, in which Indian resources were heavily deployed, was an unprecedented military disaster for the Qing. A second war with the British empire erupted in 1856, and proved a still greater catastrophe. Only a century after Qianlong forced Amursana to flee, the emperor's great-grandson saw his own representative, Governor-General Ye Mingchen, captured by the British and taken to Calcutta in forced exile. Once perceiving itself as an empire of matchless power that had decisively settled the major threat to its frontier, the Qing state now found itself engaged in a struggle on a far greater scale.

How did Qing rulers, officials, and scholars interpret the rising power of the British in India between 1750 and 1860, and how did this understanding influence the policies that were proposed or implemented to maintain the empire's security? By considering these intertwined questions, this book identifies two major changes that occurred between the start of this period, when the Qianlong emperor brought the empire to the height of its power, and the end of it, when Qing weakness in the face of European empires became starkly evident. One was a shift in the Qing state's external relations, from a "frontier policy" toward a "foreign policy." In the eighteenth century, the empire was conceived by its rulers to be surrounded by a collection of discrete frontier areas, each to be analyzed and managed according to its own political circumstances. The formulation by the emperor and his ministers of segmented, regionally specific strategies to guide Qing relations with the outside world is what is meant here by "frontier policy." This approach, well suited to flexibly governing the far-flung diversity of the empire's borderlands, became less effective when the Qing confronted European empires that operated simultaneously in multiple, noncontiguous areas and could not be managed, or even fully comprehended, on any single frontier. From the late eighteenth century onward, China's geographers and strategists grappled with the implications of this change. One proposed solution, fully articulated for the first time shortly after the Opium War but drawing on ideas that had emerged earlier, can be termed a "foreign policy," which conceived of a single hierarchy of imperial interests framed in reference to a unified outside world. Ultimately, this shift in outlook led to a revolution in how Qing rulers and subjects perceived their position: no longer unique, the Qing empire became one among several large entities locked in competition. Older strategies would have to be adapted by investigating, and perhaps imitating, China's rivals.

Although propelled in part by external events, this turn from a frontier policy to a foreign policy depended on an equally significant internal change in the Qing empire's information order.[2] Before 1800, the Qing realm was an amalgam of diverse conquered peoples united by common subordination to the same ruling house. Although the emperor and a small cohort of high advisors had a panoramic view over the entire domain, on the ground the administration of different regions relied heavily on indigenous power holders following their local political traditions. Reports sent to the capital from these regions reflected the language and culture of the inhabitants. For local governance this multiplicity of viewpoints was unproblematic, indeed necessary. However, where informants from around the empire submitted parallel reports about the same events, no common idiom existed in which to amalgamate them. Because descriptions of the outside world drew heavily on distinct local nomenclature, political conceptions, and cosmologies, the Qing central state had access to a rich and growing stock of data, but not a unifying matrix in which to understand and interpret it.

Around 1800, as the capacities of the Qing court diminished, private Han Chinese scholars began to take more interest in reforming the empire's administration. In the process, they broke the court's monopoly on a panoramic view of the empire's frontiers. Using various sources of official and unofficial information, they too began to survey the realm's non-Chinese frontiers, and the world beyond them. The emerging unofficial sphere of policy discussion was more flexible and unfettered than the confines of the bureaucracy. Already in the eighteenth century, the state had synthesized geographic and geopolitical information on a limited scale. Now, the computing power of individual researchers, communicating in letter or print across a scholarly network, was able to reach conclusions that surpassed the single imperial mainframe. By the middle of the nineteenth century, Chinese scholars had succeeded in creating a standardized lexicon for world geography. Through this, the empire's many localized outlooks were for the first time translated into a single language, producing a new global vision and a fresh reevaluation of its strategic interests.

In perhaps no other case was the need for integrated knowledge so great, the difficulties in constructing such a system so daunting, and the consequences of success so profound as that of China's understanding of British activities in India. Over land and sea, along almost the entire stretch of the Qing empire's southern frontier, commerce and religion sustained contact with India. Through this interaction, much information about India passed from foreign informants to Qing subjects in frontier zones, and then into government documents or private writings. However, because these accounts were filtered through the cultural lenses of those living along the empire's border, activities in India were known to China only in fragments. Among the references to the British conquest of Mughal India received by different arms of the Qing government, for instance, were an oral report from a Kashmiri trader in Yarkand, a petition from Nepal, a letter from a Portuguese Jesuit, and comments from a British envoy in Beijing, each employing different geographic vocabularies and offering contradictory political glosses. Understanding contemporary developments was therefore not a simple matter of passive observation, but an active and sometimes contentious process of analysis and debate. Due to India's wide familiarity and geopolitical relevance for Qing observers, reconstructing these debates offers a glimpse into the empire-wide channels of information circulation, the principles and habits of strategic thought, and the exchange between bureaucratic and scholarly spheres that shaped the geographic and geopolitical worldviews of the entire Qing empire in this period.

As Qing scholars and bureaucrats gained an increasingly clear picture of what was occurring in India, they realized that their own state was vying for power with foes equally formidable. This change is most evident in the field of geography. European maps, which had earlier constituted only a small and controversial niche in the canon of worldviews, came to be accepted as the only valid representation of the world and its constituent parts. Chinese versions of these maps began to use a standardized vocabulary that eliminated the multilingual confusion of names found earlier. As this knowledge became more widespread, the empire's political leaders appreciated for the first time that struggles on a global scale were being carried out on their borders. Instead of dominating and managing a tapestry of small neighbors, the government suddenly had to entertain the possibility of being overcome by larger ones. Together, changes in geographic and strategic thinking allowed a unified foreign policy, which demanded a more active engagement with other states, to emerge as an alternative to a frontier policy. This did not radically alter the conduct of Qing foreign relations after 1840, or even after 1860. The need to accommodate great internal diversity, more than bureaucratic inertia or complacency on the part of traditionally minded officials, preserved the influence of frontier policy. As will be discussed in the Conclusion, the balance between a frontier and foreign policy was closely tied to the internal politics of the Qing empire.

Qing Foreign Relations Reconsidered

Two factors propelled the adjustment in geo-strategic outlook from a frontier policy toward a foreign policy: prevailing conceptions of the outside world—its basic physical shape and the disposition of the Qing empire and other countries within it—and assumptions about how best to ensure the empire's security within the parameters of this geopolitical context. New information about foreign developments could obviously lead to a reconsideration of imperial strategies. Perhaps less obviously, strategic assumptions themselves could greatly influence the fullness and type of information channeled to officials and scholars concerned with formulating policy. In the Qing case, the ways intelligence was gathered, processed, and interpreted were shaped by intellectual legacies, bureaucratic procedures, and estimates of the empire's security. Proceeding from this basis, it is possible to reconcile two contradictory visions of the Qing empire's relationship with the outside world, and the role of information in forming it.

Until recently, imperial China's approach to foreign relations before 1840 was assumed to have been molded chiefly by ideological preconceptions of an ideal world order. According to the pioneering efforts of John K. Fairbank to construct a general framework for interpreting Ming and Qing foreign relations, there existed a "Chinese world order" founded on a Sinocentric ideology and manifested through institutional procedures collectively termed the "tribute system."[3] This world order was essentially "an outward extension of [the imperial government's] administration of China proper" designed to enforce—or appear to enforce—an emperor-centered hierarchy on foreign peoples.[4] Although in theory the emperor claimed universal authority, the main purpose of the system was less to manipulate actual foreign conditions to China's economic or military advantage, than to give domestic audiences proof that foreigners acknowledged and submitted to the emperor's power. Various measures, including trade incentives, religious and cultural pressures, and occasionally outright military force, were used to produce superficial conformity.

In this interpretation, rulers and officials appeared to possess what was in essence an a priori system for categorizing and managing foreign peoples, one that did not require close scrutiny of actual conditions within, or dynamics between, individual tributary states. Consequently, Fairbank argued, China suffered from a dearth of knowledge about foreign powers that produced fundamental misperceptions and poor policy choices, especially in the eighteenth and early nineteenth centuries. In his classic study *Trade and Diplomacy on the China Coast*, he briefly reviewed some major Qing works of geography, only to dismiss the corpus as scant, "irretrievably confused," and effectively useless: "These examples of Chinese folklore, ignorance, and confusion about the Western barbarians do not strike one as representing a distinct set of ideas and evaluation," and were one factor in China's "intellectual unpreparedness for Western contact."[5]

Subsequent studies, particularly those concentrating on China's political interactions with European countries, have continued to see basic elements guiding imperial China's foreign relations as inimical to a realistic view of the world. Although ideology increasingly yielded to domestic politics in the search for the forces driving Qing foreign relations, Chinese diplomacy was still seen as inward-looking and committed to preserving "appearances."[6] John E. Wills, Jr., has suggested that Qing rulers, especially the successors to the Kangxi emperor, defensively concentrated on ceremonial forms rather than external realities, so that "a dangerous reliance on illusion would be a persistent failure of Chinese foreign policy."[7] James Polachek in particular has highlighted the "'court politics' of foreign policy," interpreting commentary about the outside world as a disguised proxy struggle over domestic agendas, particularly in the decades surrounding the Opium War.[8] Major works of geopolitical analysis produced around that time were "not much more than a polemic" written to score points.[9] If Qing officials and scholars seemed oblivious to dangerous external trends, there was little reason to explore the intelligence sources and strategic thinking actually underlying their policy choices.

Similarly, scholarship on the practice of geography in the Qing period has until recently declined to consider its political and strategic implications. Studies of Ming and Qing cartography, by far the largest subfield within the study of Chinese geography, have devoted considerable attention to elucidating the disputed reception of European maps and techniques of "scientific" cartography in China from the standpoint of cultural and intellectual history.[10] How maps and written sources might have influenced the strategic outlook of the state or private scholars has been ignored, and even the very notion that cartographic data could have shifted ideologically entrenched worldviews has been disputed.[11] In current scholarship on the maritime sphere, it is only during and immediately after the Opium War that knowledge about the outside world and the evolution of China's strategic thinking have come to be regarded as two facets of the same topic.[12]

It has long been recognized that Qing policy toward Inner and Central Asia differed significantly from that pursued toward maritime European powers, but only in the past two decades has this coalesced into a major reconsideration of the empire's foreign relations.[13] Unlike the study of the maritime frontier, where defeats after 1840 have loomed largest, research into the court's inland policy has instead emphasized the success of sophisticated, realpolitik strategies in the conquest and rule of Tibet, Qinghai, Muslim eastern Turkestan, and virtually all Mongol territories. With vision unclouded by insular and Sino-centric assumptions, the dynasty's Manchu rulers are shown to have used logistical, technological, and administrative innovations similar to the state-building projects carried out by contemporary European and Russian governments. In Inner Asia, the Qing expanded and defended its interests like other "early modern" states.[14]

Manchu policy in Inner Asia succeeded in part because of its emphasis on using information to organize and execute diplomacy and warfare. Within the central administration, as Beatrice S. Bartlett has pointed out, methods of transmitting and filing correspondence and deliberating policies were reformed to meet the logistical requirements of large-scale campaigns.[15] Superior communications and planning, together with a sophisticated knowledge of Mongol political culture, helped the Qing to pacify the steppe.[16] Maps, collected from foreign sources or drafted within the court, were a "weapon in their struggle for control of central Eurasia."[17] In other words, pragmatism, flexibility, and a judicious mix of force, guile, and diplomacy allowed the empire to dominate Inner Asia, an achievement that merits comparison with the conquests of any other contemporary empire.

Thus, current scholarship describes Qing foreign relations as active and engaged in Inner Asia, and more passive and disengaged on the maritime frontier of China proper. Why did the empire show such dynamism in one theater in the eighteenth century, and yet prove unable to replicate this success elsewhere in the succeeding century? One answer is to break Qing foreign relations into smaller and more manageable units along temporal and spatial fault lines, treating Inner Asia and the maritime sphere as essentially distinct, and the empire's capacities in the nineteenth century as radically diminished from their peak in the eighteenth century. There is validity in these distinctions. It is generally agreed that at the end of the eighteenth century and in the first decades of the nineteenth century, the capabilities of the Qing state were limited by fiscal crisis, a sharp decline in the effectiveness and discipline of the bureaucratic administration, social upheaval, and rebellion.[18] Around the same time, China's place in the global economy entered a major relative decline.[19]

Still, it is misleading to explain changes in the styles of Qing foreign relations solely on the basis of preconceived zones or periods without seeking to understand how Qing rulers and their ministers strategized on the basis of the information available to them. The dynamic and aggressive foreign policy aimed at defeating the Junghars and limiting Russian expansion, in which Qing practices appeared "early modern," was part of a project to secure the Mongol steppe. Although it was between the 1670s and the 1750s, chiefly in the Inner Asian theater, that Qing empire-building appeared most comparable to that undertaken elsewhere in Eurasia, this does not mean that the Qing state reserved a special style of imperialism for that region. Once the Junghar threat was eliminated and control over the Mongols assured, Qing policy there shifted away from aggressive campaigning toward maintaining a stable frontier using techniques of control similar to Fairbank's tributary system. On the western edge of their domain tributary precedents were employed not for ideological reasons, but as "no more, or less, than a diplomatic toolbox . . . replete with a vast range of instruments, all of which had been tried and tested by rulers of China over centuries."[20] In other words, there were no absolute policy differences distinguishing the empire's borderlands. Rather, it was the nature of the threat perceived that guided the empire's foreign policy choices.

This conclusion arises from an examination of policy changes over time as well as space. More than any decline in the capacities of the central state, it was changes in the way rulers and officials understood the empire's geopolitical position that had the most important implications for Qing foreign relations. It is generally agreed that at some point in the late eighteenth century the Qing government turned away from the vigorous empire-building continuing elsewhere in Asia.[21] Here again, the final defeat of the Junghars was of epochal significance, creating an effect not unlike the "end of history" perceived by some American commentators at the close of the Cold War. Although Qianlong would continue to prosecute frontier wars, some protracted and bloody, no neighboring power seemed any longer to imperil the empire itself. Organized to make war, the Qing state had continued to grow and reform under that impetus, so that, as Peter C. Perdue has argued, the "end to military challenges on the frontier let much dynamism ebb out of the bureaucracy." Qing rulers had pursued administrative centralization, intensive resource extraction, and technological innovation to overmatch their foes abroad and maintain social order at home. With no major rivals on the horizon, "weakness, complacency, and rigidity" began to appear.[22]

To recapitulate, after the conquest of China, controlling the military might of the Mongols remained the single most important dimension of the empire's security, and the challenge posed by the Junghars was therefore met with attention, resources, and strategic innovation qualitatively different than that devoted to other neighboring peoples. Strategies the court was unwilling to contemplate elsewhere—unsolicited embassies, formal treaties, preemptive strikes—were adopted to fight this enemy. Even Qianlong's bitter war against Burma was not comparable.[23] It follows that the most important element in interpreting Qing foreign relations is neither regional exceptionalism nor the fluctuating capacities of the central state—significant as these may be—but rather the way emperors, scholars, and officials understood the risks posed by outside forces. If this is so, the connection between intelligence and strategy, what Qing policy-makers learned and what conclusions they drew from it, requires more attention than it has hitherto received. On the basis of this approach, I argue that no political, cultural-ideological, or economic factor fundamentally divided the reasoning of Qing strategists from that of their peers in other contemporary Eurasian empires. Rather, Qing policy diverged from that of its neighbors, ultimately at great cost to its security, because the Qing had a completely different perception of prevailing geopolitical dynamics and the extent of foreign threats after the conquest of the Junghars in 1757.

This raises a second puzzle: Why did the Qing empire believe itself fundamentally secure after the flight of Amursana and slow its competitive state-building just at the time when empires elsewhere on the continent, including some very near the Qing border, began a frenetic struggle for survival in what has been termed the "first age of global imperialism"?[24] The Seven Years War (1756–1763) saw the emergence of the British East India Company as a major territorial power in India, the French Revolutionary and Napoleonic Wars were a worldwide struggle with implications for virtually every corner of Asia, and the Anglo-Russian "Great Game" commenced shortly afterward. Intensifying rivalries were by no means limited to European empires: by 1840, almost every polity surrounding the Qing empire, from Macao through continental Southeast Asia, India, and Nepal to Afghanistan and northward to Russia, was deeply enmeshed in interlocking territorial struggles—struggles in which the British empire, and particularly British India, played a central role. Encircled by intensifying warfare and diplomacy, why did the Qing decline to engage in this almost universal maneuvering for alliances, grand strategic plans, and intensive surveillance—activities at which it had excelled only decades earlier—and, to the contrary, even relax its state-building efforts?[25] Why was its geostrategic analysis so out of alignment with prevailing Eurasian trends?

The key to understanding this difference lies in the empire's geographic and geopolitical thought. The Qing state saw the world differently. Difference does not necessarily imply a lack of sophistication in intelligence gathering or information processing. Archival records reveal that the Qing court was informed of at least the outlines of most of the major military engagements fought in the empire's vicinity, including those in India. In many cases, detailed accounts of current affairs abroad were easily obtained from domestic and foreign informants. Moreover, all of these sources fed into a system of centralized information gathering, filing, retrieval, and publication, designed to guide complex logistical and military operations when a need for them was perceived. Qianlong was as much a paper-shuffling "royal bureaucrat" as any of his European contemporaries, with committed, intelligent, and diligent servants.[26]

The reason the Qing government perceived its strategic environment so differently from other Eurasian empires was due primarily to the reciprocal relationship between geopolitical worldviews and strategic thinking. The operations of the Junghars, though carried out across vast distances from western Tibet to Inner Mongolia, were contiguous and relatively easy to track. The nature and structure of the Junghar polity itself caused few problems for elite Qing Manchu and Mongol military advisors, who were familiar with the means and goals of steppe warfare. Moreover, appreciating the depth of the Junghar threat, the court conducted constant surveillance of enemy activities. Once this threat was eliminated, the Qing court's focus turned to maintaining its enlarged territory. On the Inner Asian frontier, the energy devoted to collecting and analyzing intelligence diminished.[27] The central government's attention was atomized across a range of discrete frontiers, and intelligence gathering was limited to threats in the immediate border area. Although the state largely achieved its goal of keeping the peace without becoming entangled in irrelevant foreign squabbles, it became less able to identify emerging threats even when a substantial amount of information about them was available. British activity in Asia was vastly more challenging to fathom than the Junghar threat had been, requiring noncontiguous military and diplomatic operations to be pieced together and the significance of unfamiliar economic and political institutions to be teased out. The result was mutually reinforcing: only fear of a large-scale threat could justify breaking from frontier policy, but identifying such a threat required the synthesis of information from around the empire, precisely what the frontier-based approach inhibited.

In sum, the most important variable in Qing foreign relations was whether the court and private scholars considered themselves to be facing an assortment of discrete, localized challenges, or a single, integrated crisis involving the empire as a whole. For western European empires in the eighteenth century, it is axiomatic that their rivals would force them to fight on a global scale, so that local contexts could not be viewed in isolation from the interests and goals of the total empire.[28] Recently, scholars of other empires in Europe and Asia have found it useful to identify the "grand strategies" by which rulers determined the overall interests of their large dominions.[29] For most of the period studied in this book, Qing statesmen and scholars never conceived a comprehensive "grand strategy," even at the loosest and most abstract level, one of the reasons their judgments of Qing interests differed so far from the estimations of their neighbors. By reconstructing how Qing rulers and officials saw the world, and the intellectual and political factors that influenced them, these differences are shown to have resulted from responses to external conditions impelled by reasoning not fundamentally different from that guiding the assumptions of their British counterparts. It was not ideology, but the scale of analysis, that set Qing policy-makers apart. Over time, at least some Qing observers shifted from "masterful disengagement" across many small frontiers to a "grand strategy" comparable to that of their major rivals. The trajectory of this change is the story of this book.

Reconstructing Qing Geopolitical Worldviews

The key to the momentous changes described above lies in the worldviews of Qing rulers, ministers, and scholars. To reconstruct their outlooks, it must first be recognized that the worldview underpinning a frontier policy, in which external developments were seen in regionalized fragments rather than a panoramic vision, was reinforced by a complex of procedures and habits of thought. Three are of particular importance: strategic assumptions about the relationship between the Qing government and neighboring rulers, the structure of the Qing bureaucracy in its intelligence gathering and foreign relations, and the intellectual context of geographic scholarship.

Relations with foreign rulers were viewed as fundamentally bilateral, and the Qing government took pains to maintain neutrality in disputes that did not directly concern its own territory. From the imperial standpoint, the statements of submission and overlordship exchanged with tributary rulers were in no sense mutual defense pacts against third parties, still less aggressive alliances, but rather a device for stabilizing a specific stretch of the Qing border. These policies were designed to maintain the status quo, or, in extreme cases, restore it by force. Except in times of exceptional danger, as this book will demonstrate, the Qing government was reluctant even to contemplate drawing third countries into its relations with a foreign state, either as a useful ally or a common enemy. Acutely aware of the dangers of entanglement in its tributaries' internal factional struggles or external quarrels, the empire reacted only when the zone around its immediate border was imperiled. Unless a major campaign was being contemplated, there was no need for a constant and thorough survey of events much beyond the frontier itself. Furthermore, with so lengthy a border to manage, imperial surveillance was crisis-oriented, and a frontier zone that seemed quiet would rarely attract active scrutiny.

The structure and procedures of the Qing bureaucracy dovetailed with this localized approach to strategic planning. Responsibility for a particular stretch of the frontier and the management of relations with specific polities beyond it devolved upon officials administering adjacent provinces or other territories. In times of unrest, it was the responsibility of such an official to submit intelligence to Beijing together with his interpretation and policy proposals, which would then be considered and perhaps modified by the emperor and his ministers. Coordination was possible at the level of the Grand Council, the empire's highest deliberative body, which could potentially draw together information from several regions to shed light on a particular problem, but this was exceptional. Normally, it was assumed that officials on the spot could collect all the information required to address any local disturbance, and the intelligence they forwarded was generally used on its own terms.

The consequences of this structure must be considered in terms of bureaucratic responsibility. Local officials had great power to mold the court's perceptions of the world, and they understandably did so in ways that fit their interests. Generally speaking, this meant ignoring all but the most pressing frontier problems. Emperors normally considered aggressive behavior by foreign states to be prima facie evidence of poor management by local officials, and at the very least would subject them to careful investigation. Since the court expected the frontier to be quiet, neither the central government nor local officials had incentive to scrutinize superficially peaceful border areas. Bureaucrats best placed to study the outside world thus had the most incentive to remain officially ignorant of it. To acknowledge a problem meant proposing a solution and becoming responsible for its implementation. The larger the problem, the less appealing this responsibility became. It would take an especially diligent, capable, and selfless bureaucrat to scan the horizon for emerging threats and draw these to the court's attention. As we shall see, most officials proposed limited solutions to very narrowly defined problems, and even then only when it was impossible to overlook them.

Frontier policy was underpinned by an assumption of minimalism: that the empire's borderlands could be broken down into regions, that their routine management could be handled by nearby officials using local intelligence and resources, and that such management need not involve constant surveillance of the neighboring state's domestic politics or foreign relations. To the extent that these assumptions proved ill-founded, there was a strong onus on individual bureaucrats to protect their careers (if not their lives) by covering up rather than excavating potential problems. This approach, it should be stressed, was well suited to the economical management of many frontiers with very different local circumstances by a limited bureaucracy. In many cases it indeed produced the kind of benign, routine frontier interactions desired by the court, with relatively little attention from the center.

If strategic and bureaucratic factors already tended to divide imperial foreign relations into segmented frontiers, this approach was reinforced by the empire's methods of studying foreign geography. In so diverse a domain, information arriving from each frontier bore the distinct linguistic and cultural stamp of its region of origin, making it hard to recognize when the significance of a report arriving from one frontier overlapped with that from another. Neither officials nor scholars possessed a standardized framework within which to place in mutual relation all available geopolitical knowledge. Under these conditions, it was almost impossible to assemble many threads of local data into a coherent tapestry and identify trends working themselves out across several frontiers.

Just as these three factors reinforced each other, so would change in one sphere induce shifts in the others. The artificially limited fields of concern imposed on, and defensively embraced by, the empire's bureaucrats were gradually broken down by the emergence of a parallel community of private statecraft scholars (see Chapter Seven) who were willing and newly able to issue written considerations of the empire's political problems as a whole. The rising power of European empires in Asia, above all the British in India, led to a growing sense of urgency in policy discussion and increasingly detailed inquiries about foreign conditions. Again, it was private scholars who most forcefully emphasized the need for action. As their inquiries advanced and more raw geopolitical intelligence emerged, it increasingly became possible to build a coherent, panoramic vision of China's place in the world. Collectively, non-bureaucratic channels of policy debate, a new consciousness of strategic challenges, and advances in geography broke the monopoly of frontier policy and led to the formulation of a foreign policy that for the first time treated the imperial frontier as a whole.

Of these three crucial elements, Qing geographic worldviews are the most difficult to reconstruct because they relied on modes of scholarly analysis that are unfamiliar and even counterintuitive today, and were formed by numerous sources of information from different cultural and linguistic backgrounds. Progressively denser networks of information transfer drew together elements from conflicting local perspectives on the outside world into fluctuating and provisional syntheses. Individuals selected from sources of different provenance on the basis of their own judgments of reliability, so that geopolitical worldviews varied widely throughout the empire. In the case of India, where the networks of information collection and interpretation reached all of the empire's frontiers and included contributions not only of private scholars and non-Han imperial elites, but also of sailors, merchants, and a range of foreigners, these outlooks became particularly complex.

Complexity originated in the multitude of apparently incommensurable sources themselves and the genre conventions of the official and unofficial works that circulated them. Linguistic differences meant that the names given to foreign places in one area were often unintelligible in another. Diverging cultural and religious histories had inflected the geographic and political thought of different groups with particular concepts and presumptions. Political loyalties among foreign informants also influenced reports about, for instance, whether rising British power in India was benign or expansionist. Discussions of the outside world could vary even between individual Chinese provinces, where localized factors—proximity to Europeans at Guangzhou and Macao, for instance, or dense networks of overseas migration in Fujian—could also leave imprints on the base of available knowledge.[30] Transmitting coherent geographic understandings across linguistic and cultural boundaries between regional or intellectual communities was extremely difficult.

Diverse outlooks were further complicated by the networks of knowledge transfer within the Qing state and the scholarly world. The career of any given piece of information was difficult to predict. Among the many strands of information about India crossing the Qing border, some circulated widely throughout the empire by attracting the attention of the highest levels of government, being recorded in a popular work of scholarship, or both. Other strands of knowledge, equally familiar in a certain place or among a certain group, might appear only rarely in documents or books and remain virtually unknown to both the central government and subjects elsewhere in the empire.

It is also necessary to consider "ordinary knowledge" circulating among subjects, which (as David Morgan has remarked in the case of medieval Persia) was likely "rather more extensive than the surviving written evidence may lead us to suppose."[31] More imperial subjects, notably merchants, sailors, and returned sojourners, were professionally familiar with foreign conditions than in any previous period of Chinese history. In general, however, their "practical knowledge," like that of other specialized occupational groups, belonged to the "great variety of knowledge traditions that never reached the written or printed page."[32] This was partly because writing about geography or imperial statecraft was seen to require the high degree of literacy obtained only by literati elites, and partly because those living abroad or in close contact with foreigners had incentives not to advertise their knowledge.[33] To be sure, the Qing state and private scholars were aware that subjects of certain backgrounds could be tapped for critical intelligence via official depositions or records taken down by a literati amanuensis. Still, that merchants, sailors, and emigrants rarely propagated their expertise restricted the knowledge base of the empire, especially given that Chinese communities in Southeast Asia (and from the late eighteenth century in India and the eastern Indian Ocean) often lived in close contact with European imperial administrations. Their "ordinary knowledge" of emerging political and economic trends had few channels through which to reach the political or scholarly elite—who were often skeptical of the uncorroborated firsthand accounts that did reach them.

The scope, purpose, and conventions of the genre in which geopolitical information was recorded also mattered. This is most obvious for bureaucratic documents, in which officials were responsible for the facts and proposals they advanced and therefore wrote with great circumspection, including only information directly relevant to the administrative problem at hand. An author might well suppress germane but inconvenient aspects of his knowledge. Similar constraints applied to formal reference works, normally by teams of scholars, which had their own strictures of relevance and authority. Here too, authors might be much better informed about current affairs than the constraints of their format allowed them to reveal. Those writing privately possessed greater freedom to cite any source and offer their own opinions and theories, but even here the genre in question—a comprehensive study, a short essay, a brief note in a jottings book, a letter—influenced the analysis and the evidence used.

Genre determined three major modes of analyzing the outside world in the Qing period. The first, operational geography, was employed in Qing state correspondence. Here, officials relied primarily on living informants with local expertise, and gave little attention to scholarship or even government archives. The second mode, scholastic geography, was undertaken exclusively by literati employing textual modes of analysis, usually in the context of state-sponsored research such as the imperial gazetteer. Rigorous rules of evidence required the use of authoritative written sources, often older official works. Here oral inquiries were almost never made, although compilers might cite official documents based on such inquiries. Finally, there was the sphere of private geography, the personal writings of individual authors, the scale and significance of which differed greatly over time depending on prevailing attitudes among officialdom and within the academic community. When intensively pursued, as after 1800, this was the most dynamic, diverse, and comprehensive form of research, unfettered by rigid conventions or bureaucratic restrictions. However, it was a much more diffuse and varied field of inquiry than scholastic or operational geography, and in practice it was almost impossible for any individual to master the vast corpus of geographic writings.

It should be stressed that no single type of source, or even class of source, was comprehensive or universally preferred. Rather, those interested in

India was not seen as a whole, and the deep anti-British fears common elsewhere in Asia did not come to grip the emperor or his highest ministers.

For a new type of geopolitical worldview to emerge, reciprocal adjustments were required in geographic knowledge, the structure of policy-making, and strategic assumptions. These began to occur after 1800; their emergence is described in Chapters Five and Six. After the Qianlong era, Han Chinese literati were liberated from many of the restraints that had impeded their study of geography and frontier affairs. Free to grapple with an unprecedented range of materials, they increasingly viewed the empire's frontier as an integrated panorama, and came to recognize the ubiquity of British imperial activity. Attention to the opium trade and the fiscal and command structures behind it led them to identify a nearby network of Asian territories ruled by England. Pulling this thread led Chinese scholars to discover that the Indian ports known collectively at Guangzhou as "Gangjiao" were in fact territories historically known as India. Once the concept of "British India" became available, its importance as the financial and military cornerstone of the British empire quickly became apparent.

PART FOUR. FOREIGN POLICY AND ITS LIMITS

For some scholars, this recognition led to a fundamental reconsideration of Qing geographic and strategic practices. Foremost of these was the influential policy analyst Wei Yuan, who argued that the empire's fragmented outlook had fatally hindered its capacity to identify and meet the British threat. The findings of his predecessors and the fruits of wartime intelligence gathering (described in Chapter Seven) constituted a critical mass of information that allowed Wei to integrate the empire's geographic knowledge, a goal that had eluded his predecessors. From his pen emerged a standardized system for referring to foreign place-names, raising some to prominence and casting others into obscurity. For Wei Yuan, the corollary of this revolution in geographic knowledge was a comparable integration of the empire's foreign policy. What had once seemed like discrete frontiers with local concerns, he argued, were in fact fronts in a larger war. Breaking with earlier practice—although he massaged his historical accounts to disguise this fact—Wei argued that the Qing needed to build coalitions against its one major enemy, the British empire. The centerpiece of his plan was to induce Nepal, Burma, and Russia to descend upon India as Qing allies, and together with Indians themselves push the British back into the sea. Bereft of

ies arrived at court. Matching the growing variety of information was the unexampled personal interest of the emperor, as a scholar and patron, in synthesizing geographic knowledge. Multilingual teams were assembled to translate, process, and interpret information that Qianlong's generals had gathered, while Manchu and Chinese officials mapped the terrain beyond the empire's boundaries with the aid of indigenous informants and Jesuit missionaries. Yet even these magnificent labors synthesized only a small part of available information about India.

In the 1750s and 1760s, looking outward from the vantage point of southern Xinjiang, the Qing state encountered India chiefly as "Hindustan." Decades later, during the drive to expel the Nepali Gurkhas from Tibet between 1788 and 1793, part of the territory earlier called Hindustan came to be described in different, Tibetan vocabularies. On the coast, under the influence of European languages and Chinese dialects, still other terms for contemporary India prevailed. Only in the 1790s did the first intimations emerge that localized intelligence gathering was inadequate to understand sprawling British imperialism in Asia. Because the aftermath of war in the Himalayas coincided with the arrival in 1793 of a British envoy, Lord Macartney, the Qing court was forced to address the connection between the country of Yingjili he represented and the tribe of the Pileng (Farangi, European) recently discovered in Bengal. Drawing on various channels of intelligence, the Qianlong court was able to ascertain the apparent kinship of these two groups, but this understanding remained vague and did not influence their foreign relations strategy. For the ensuing five decades, policies toward the Bengali Pileng and the Yingjili at Guangzhou were formulated in isolation.

PART THREE. THE AGE OF TRANSITION, 1800–1838

By the first decades of the nineteenth century the Qing court's fragmented view of the world was increasingly out of step with the strategic and military concerns of its Asian and European neighbors. The British empire became the single most powerful force on the southern Qing frontier. For most foreign observers in contact with the Qing, this constituted a revolution in Asia's balance of power that demanded a proportional response from Beijing. Messages to this effect, together with reports about contact with British India, made their way to the Qing court by various channels, each in the geographic idiom of its regional context. Though seen in its parts, British expansion in

into how these various terms were understood by the author, and often reveals the sources most influential for him. The degree to which an author tried to construct a synthetic worldview is a good proxy for the degree to which Qing officials and scholars saw the world as regional fragments or a larger whole.

Plan of the Book

PART ONE. THE QING EMPIRE'S VISION OF THE WORLD

This book begins by exploring the dense texture of information about India circulating within the empire during the first century of Qing rule and the analysis applied to it. Sources and techniques that dominated the study of foreign geography in the first century of Qing rule are examined in the Chapter One, which concentrates on two issues: the way geographic argument proceeded by proposing connections between bodies of evidence that were hard to commensurate, and the corresponding posture of skepticism that led geographic claims to be considered provisional, which I describe as "geographic agnosticism." In place of a single, dominant worldview there circulated a range of competing perspectives on India, including those of authors from the Han to the Ming dynasties, who left an extensive legacy of diverging sources; of Buddhist, Muslim, and Christian writers, who supplied geographic accounts according to their own intellectual and religious traditions; and of Mongol and Tibetan scholars, who influenced the Manchus and then the Han literati. Although elements in all these geographic worldviews cross-pollinated and influenced each other, they retained fundamental differences in their terminology, cosmologies, and religious and political implications. The result can be conceived as a single field of geographic debate held in tension by centrifugal and centripetal forces, but never congealing into a stable synthesis.

PART TWO. FORGING A MULTIETHNIC EMPIRE: THE APEX OF A FRONTIER POLICY

The next three chapters concern the Qianlong period, a time of intensive military and scholarly efforts, during which these centrifugal and centripetal forces each grew stronger. As imperial armies moved into distant and unfamiliar regions, new reports about India expressed in unfamiliar vocabular-

geography, and with the requisite access, routinely consulted all three types of material to form their worldviews. Thus, although different genres could at times appear to be products of very different mental worlds insulated from each other, they were in fact different faces of a single field of research more tightly connected than might appear at first glance. It was not uncommon for officials or editors writing in one place under tight genre restraints to reveal elsewhere in personal notes or essays information not hinted at in their more formal pieces. However, though scholars read widely, this multitude of specialized genres meant that geographic writings were often only obliquely in dialogue with each other. Ultimately, developments in one genre influenced the others, but in complex and subtle ways.

No single source alone can be taken as a proxy of Qing worldviews. The diversity of raw data, of interpretation, and of genre meant that no two people approached the question of India and its contemporary situation from quite the same basis of information. Rather than seeking the chimera of *the* Qing perspective on India, which did not exist, or undertaking the impossible task of elucidating the nuances of each individual outlook, this study will track major dialogues and debates within the empire, the various positions adopted by important commentators, their interrelations, and the evolution of outlooks over time as different sources rose and fell in influence.

To draw out connections and coherent trends among this range of outlooks, the following study relies heavily on the analysis of something that today might appear insignificant and dryly philological, but for Chinese officials and scholars formed the most important element for formulating arguments and organizing data: geographic vocabularies, place-names above all. As will be explained in Chapter One, Chinese scholars were conditioned to treat place-names as the foundation of geographic analysis. Virtually all of the fragmented regional and cultural views of India were associated with their own lexicon, arising from different languages and canonical sources. Some terms for India were widely familiar; others found only in writings from a particular region or intellectual background; and still others unique to an individual author. This abundance of place-names proved to be a significant and vexing hurdle in the construction of a coherent picture of the world, but it was a difficulty that Chinese scholars confronted explicitly with extensive analysis. It is also a boon for historians, because place-names mentioned in a piece of writing are, as it were, the fingerprints left on it by the sources the author had consulted. They reveal direct and indirect sources of information; the way they were placed in mutual relation offers insight

opium revenues and sepoys, England could pose no threat to China. What he was proposing, in other words, was that the Qing empire menace India using the strategy some English observers feared Russia would deploy in the "Great Game."

To adapt to foreign imperialism, Qing foreign relations became more centralized in the decades after the Opium War, and the drawbacks of fractured policy-making among various territorial officials became obvious. This was part of the reason the Qing government established its first "foreign office," the Zongli Yamen.[34] Nonetheless, Wei Yuan's more radical idea of a tightly integrated empire operating in close alliances with foreign powers was not adopted. One factor was certainly the inherent caution of Qing bureaucrats, who did not wish to risk their careers and possibly their lives to advocate costly measures that could end in disaster. Another was the limitations of the state's military and financial resources and the known unreliability of potential allies. The imperial government recognized Qing weakness more keenly than Wei.

Choices facing the Qing empire after 1840 were not simply a failed but familiar strategic model and one that was effective or "modern." The challenge was how to balance local needs and conditions with the emergence of empire-wide strategic considerations. To maintain control over its frontiers, the Qing state needed the resources and cooperation of local leaders. The logic of the frontier policy, foregrounding local needs, remained a source of strength and stability. Neither a frontier policy nor a foreign policy was tenable in its purest form. Finding the correct balance between them in the face of changing external conditions remained a major problem as the Qing government became a Chinese one.

A Note on "India"

This book uses the word "India" to refer to the region more commonly known in current scholarship as South Asia. I have decided to preserve the former term out of fidelity to the book's Chinese and Manchu sources. As Qing scholars were keenly aware, "Asia" was a European geographic concept. Its validity was controversial, and most were reluctant to adopt it. By contrast, the English word "India" derives from the same etymological root as the most common Chinese terms for that region (as well as comparable terms in Mongolian and Manchu). The felicitous conjunction of English and Chinese usage extends to the word's geographical flexibility. In both languages, in the period under study, the boundaries of "India" were vague. In this sense as well it is a better fit than the misleadingly technical "South Asia."

For many of the decades under study, India was a patchwork of competing powers. How far and on what levels it makes sense to conceive of India as a unified entity in the abstract is a question beyond the scope of this study.[35] For the present study, "India" makes sense as a unit of analysis for two reasons. First, almost all subjects of the Qing empire conceived of India as a coherent geographic concept that did not depend for its existence on political unity. Independent states within its bounds were generally understood to be components of a larger India. Moreover, because this study concentrates on Qing understandings of the process by which the British empire conquered India piece by piece over the course of decades, it is first necessary to study how the areas that would come under British rule were understood in the period before their conquest. For this reason, the "India" that is the target of this study more or less conforms to the territory under direct or indirect British rule on the subcontinent by 1860 (excluding Burma). Comparatively little attention is given to southern India since, certain ports excepted, it had little contact with the Qing empire. Occasionally other territories not under direct British control by 1860—chiefly Nepal, Kashmir, and eastern Afghanistan—will form part of our analysis due to the crucial role they played as intermediaries between the Qing empire and India. Needless to say, the term "India" as used in this study bears no anachronistic relation to the borders of the current Republic of India.

PART ONE

The Qing Empire's Vision of the World

ONE

A Wealth of Indias
India in Qing Geographic Practice, 1644–1755

The Practice of Foreign Geography in Early Qing China

How did Qing officials and scholars understand the physical and political disposition of the outside world? Geography is among the most empirical of sciences, and it is natural to turn at once to the abundant descriptions of foreign lands available to them, including military intelligence, travelers' reports, religious and historical writings, and maps. Yet this material contained a range of conflicting accounts and interpretations. Studying the world in this context meant not passively consuming a transparent body of evidence, but struggling to put the available data in order. Before turning to the empirical basis informing Qing worldviews, and the constructions placed on it by individual scholars, it is therefore necessary to begin with the practice of geographic scholarship itself: the modes of reasoning and debate in which variegated worldviews coexisted and evolved, and the attitudes engendered by these methods.

Scholars of foreign geography in the Qing period were aware that their knowledge was limited, uncertain, and provisional.[1] This was due not to a lack of information, for centuries of interaction with the outside world had brought to China a great volume of data about foreign geography, but rather to the manifest incommensurability of those data. The corpus had accumulated over time via informants with different linguistic, regional, intellectual, and religious backgrounds, whose reports could not easily be amalgamated into one coherent account. Generations of scholars recognized and responded to this challenge by reading broadly, on the basis of which they ventured theories about how seemingly contradictory reports might be harmonized. Such theorizing relied on methods of exegesis and argument inculcated by formal schooling, above all the aggregation and juxtaposition of citations. Textual research and debate profoundly shaped the study of geography by concentrating attention on philological questions of nomenclature. With precise spatial data sparse or lacking altogether, maps—which could only present one image of the world—were far less useful than written geographic studies for reasoning through a thicket of contradictory sources. Before the late Qing, foreign geography was studied almost entirely through word rather than image.

Conscious of the impediments to certain knowledge about the outside world, and possessing a textual methodology tolerant of conflicting opinions and deferred judgment, Chinese scholars generally approached foreign geography with an attitude that can be termed geographic agnosticism. Some claims might be preferred and others doubted, but none could be absolutely endorsed or eliminated. No single conception of the world displaced all others, and judgments on the value of geographic evidence remained provisional.

ELEMENTS OF INCOMMENSURABILITY: DESCRIPTIONS OF THE WORLD BEFORE THE EARLY QING

By the early Qing, Chinese geographers had too much information about the outside world. Informants of various backgrounds, whose testimonies ranged from comprehensive accounts of the universe to fragmentary jottings on a single journey, had over time deposited many strata in the geographic record. Cosmologies available to scholars in 1644 posited seas and continents differing in number, size, and shape. The same regions were often described in different ways using inconsistent names. As scholars of geography read diligently in all these accounts and tried to construct theories that synthesized them, there emerged a range of hybrid outlooks at least as numerous as the original sources themselves. Even a simplified typology of pre-Qing sources and synthetic arguments lies beyond the scope of this study, but it is useful briefly to review this process in order to demonstrate why the body of geographic evidence remained incommensurable despite dogged and skillful attempts to reconcile it.

One of the earliest and most influential descriptions of the world in the Chinese intellectual tradition is found in the "Yu gong" chapter of the *Shangshu*. After describing the nine regions (*zhou*ᵃ) of China, it concluded vaguely: "On the east reaching to the sea; on the west extending to the moving sands; to the utmost limits of the north and south:—[Yu's] fame and influence filled up all within the four seas."[2] In the Warring States and early Han periods, more elaborate models of the world emerged. The *Shanhai jing* conceived of a central rectangle surrounded on each side by sea, beyond which lay a "great wilderness" (*dahuang*).[3] Alternatively, Zou Yan (ca. 250 BC) proposed that the world was composed of nine continents (*zhou*ᵃ), and that China as described in the canonical *Shangshu* was simply one ninth of a single continent. Each of these continents was surrounded by a "lesser sea" (*pihai*), while a vast "ocean" (*yinghai*) encircled the nine continents collectively.[4]

Competing worldviews provoked scholarly debates, often with political subtexts. Supporters of Zou's model argued that it described the vastness of the world better than the "Yu gong," while its detractors retorted that it was unfounded and denigrated China. As Mark Edward Lewis has pointed out, the "Yu gong" was upheld by those inclined to venerate the words of the sages, Zou's worldview by those who believed that state policies could innovate effectively beyond the classical heritage.[5] Ideological implications could intrude into empirical arguments.

Beginning in the Western Han period (206 BC–AD 25), the new genre of standard histories brought readers more details about the outside world. Its prototype, Sima Qian's *Shi ji*, included descriptions of the nomadic Xiongnu and other foreign peoples, and subsequent works in this pattern continued to chronicle the political relations of foreign states with Chinese dynasties. Gazetteers, the geographic counterparts to standard histories, added descriptions of foreign peoples when the locality in question bordered the outside world.[6]

Even in the most canonical of these sources, the "Yu gong" and standard histories, inconsistencies were obvious. For example, debate persisted over whether "four seas" really surrounded a central landmass, and if so, how they corresponded to known locations. The Song scholar Cheng Dachang (1123–1195), finding that the "Yu gong" did not specify the location of the

West and North Seas, turned to historical evidence. A Han envoy, he noted, had reached a sea beyond Tiaozhi (the Seleucid empire), which Cheng took to be the West Sea, and other travelers reported a sea to the north.[7] A more cautious contemporary, Hong Mai (1123–1202), was only willing to certify the existence of North, East, and South Seas. He believed that there was no evidence of a West Sea, the ocean beyond Tiaozhi being simply the western shores of the South Sea. Reference in the *Shangshu* to "four seas" was "probably a statement based on extrapolation" (*gai yinlei er yan zhi*).[8] However, the Ming scholars Qiu Jun (1420–1495) and Yang Shen (1488–1559) believed that the West Sea indeed existed, based on rumors of a large body of water beyond Yunnan in the extreme west.[9] All of these arguments were duly recorded in a commentary by Zhu Heling (1606–1683), who advanced no opinion of his own. Later, the Qing geographer and classicist Hu Wei (1633–1714) registered a radical dissent. The *Erya*, an early dictionary or thesaurus, defined "four seas" as the foreign peoples in each direction, a definition given moreover in the category for words concerning land (*di*) rather than water (*shui*). On this basis Hu denied that the "Yu gong" referred to oceans at all. Places described in subsequent histories as "West Sea" and "North Sea" did indeed exist as real bodies of water, Hu conceded, but at such vast distances as to be irrelevant to the cosmological schema of the classical text.[10]

All of these scholars tackled geographic research using their deep familiarity with classical and historical works and associated commentaries. They arrived at diverging conclusions despite applying similar textual methods to a similar range of orthodox sources. Significantly, none of them believed that one particular source could alone be considered comprehensive, and each found it necessary to reconcile, or at least to grapple with, apparently conflicting information from different works.

Around the end of the Han period, Chinese scholars began to confront a new and unfamiliar vision of the world presented by Buddhist sources. These claimed that the world revolved around a central axis formed by Meru (Sumeru), a mountain of supernatural height surrounded by four major continents (*dvipa*) within a salt sea.[11] Humans occupied only the southern continent of Jambudvipa, which in its form resembled the Indian subcontinent and Tibet, being narrow at the bottom and wider near the top, split in the middle by the mountain chain of Himavat (the Himalayas). North of those peaks lay Anavatapta, a sacred lake usually identified with Lake Manasarowar in western Tibet, from which was said to emerge the Indus, Ganges, Oxus (Amu Darya), and Śita (Tarim) Rivers.[12]

First propagated in Chinese by translated scripture around AD 300, Buddhist cosmology was also described in detail by pilgrims.[13] Two monk-authored accounts, the *Foguo ji* of Faxian (ca. 337–422), who between 399 and 414 journeyed overland to India and returned by sea, and the (*Da Tang*) *Xiyu ji* of Xuanzang (596–664), whose journey was made entirely by land, were particularly influential. Claims made in Buddhist-derived sources could not easily be reconciled with other accounts. Cosmologically, the theory of four continents around Mt. Sumeru had no Chinese parallel. Even if ocean-enveloped Jambudvipa could be equated to the lands within the "four seas," this Buddhist continent still contained unknown features bearing unfamiliar names. Moreover, Buddhist worldviews had strong Indo-philic biases, presenting northern India, and particularly Bodh Gaya, as the center of the world.[14] Although scholars preferring orthodox Confucian works denounced this bias, Buddhist sources gradually cross-pollinated with older ideas into a variety of synthesized positions. Anavatapta, lodged within high mountains at the center of Jambudvipa, began to be conflated by some authors with Kunlun, a legendary peak regarded in pre-Buddhist Chinese sources as a central pillar supporting the heavens.[15] Such syntheses extended to riverine geography. Pre-Buddhist sources differed over the source of the Yellow River, producing complex theories—often with ideological implications—of multiple sources connected by underground streams.[16] In time Kunlun and Anavatapta, both considered to be the origin of major rivers, began to be associated with each other. Xuanzang, for instance, cautiously asserted that according to some people the Śita River, which Buddhist sources claimed to flow from Lake Anavatapta, ran underground and emerged elsewhere as the source of the Yellow River.[17] This remained a live question: in the Qing period the Kangxi emperor used Chinese histories, Buddhist scripture, and his own survey maps to analyze the Anavatapta-Kunlun relationship (see below). Synthetic trends also emerged in cartography. Maps of Jambudvipa prepared in the Tang or Song period for devotional purposes concentrated at first almost exclusively on India, but ultimately evolved into world maps that placed other countries within the Jambudvipa framework. Intermediate stages show evidence that monks had trouble reconciling Buddhist statements of India's geographic centrality with an impulse to give China prominence. By the late Ming, however, integral maps of Jambudvipa, centered on Lake Anavatapta, gave China and India roughly equal space.[18]

Ideological factors continued to shape interpretations of incommensurable data. A Buddhist work, the *Shijia fang zhi*, raised the ire of the Yuan-period scholar Wu Lai (1297–1340) by offering an effusive description of India's size and centrality. For Wu, the authority of monk-pilgrims paled before that of standard histories like the *Han shu*, which gave far more modest descriptions of India. Wu attracted a critic of his own, the Buddhist sympathizer Qian Qianyi (1582–1664). At issue, Qian believed, was China's centrality: "[Wu] Lai means to say that India is a small country west of the Pamirs, that the family of the Buddha was scattered, moving around irregularly, not resembling what the [*Shijia*] *fang zhi* called 'a central land and great country' (*zhongtu daguo*)." By contrast, Qian credited Buddhist sources: "Within the realm of Central India the *Xiyu ji* records that [Xuanzang] passed altogether through 29 countries. [Wu] Lai cites words in the 'Biography of Zhang Zai' to make the arbitrary judgment 'it is simply one country.' The 29 countries he passed through, were they phantom nations?"[19] Geographic reasoning reflected religious and ideological preferences.

Islam too introduced new geographic conceptions into China. Under Mongol rule, several Muslim scholars are known to have transmitted their knowledge to indigenous researchers, notably Zhu Siben (ca. 1273–1337), who prepared a map reaching to Malacca and Central Asia between 1311 and 1320, and Li Zemin, whose map (ca. 1330) used Islamic sources to depict Europe and Africa.[20] In later centuries, Chinese Muslims continued to draw on Arabic and Persian geographic knowledge. Some became deeply enmeshed in the elite literary and philosophic culture of the Ming and Qing periods, occasionally translating Islamic geographic worldviews.[21] These were, of course, Mecca-centric: Ma Zhu (1640–1711), for instance, informed his imaginary non-Muslim interlocutor that "The *ka'aba* is located at the center of the world."[22]

From the Song period onward, travel accounts became particularly influential. Some were by scholars in frontier areas who recorded second-hand information, others by voyagers describing their own experiences abroad. Early Ming diplomacy significantly enlarged this corpus.[23] By the late Ming, many such writings had been digested into comprehensive geographic works aspiring to treat the entire known world, so that early Qing scholars had at their disposal eyewitness accounts of many parts of Asia.

Unlike works associated with foreign religions, travel accounts tended to offer piecemeal descriptions of the outside world that did not systematically challenge existing cosmologies. Yet, as new information accumulated it could trigger major conceptual innovations, for instance in maritime divisions and terminology. By the Tang, the term "Southern Sea" (Nanhai) had come to indicate all the foreign peoples of Southeast Asia and the Indian Ocean, necessitating a more precise lexicon. The *Lingwai daida* by Zhou Qufei (ca. 1135–1189) divided foreign countries between the Southeast and Southwest Seas, based on a boundary running from Srivijaya to Quanzhou. In time the word *yang* (conventionally translated as "ocean") also began to appear in this usage, and by the Yuan-era *Daoyi zhilüe*, the Southeast and Southwest Seas had respectively transformed into the Eastern and Western Oceans, a conceptual framework popularized by chroniclers of the Zheng He (1371–1433) voyages.[24] Although the dividing line between the two oceans shifted, they remained the major divisions within the maritime sphere.[25]

Contemporary European worldviews were introduced between 1584 and 1608 on a series of Chinese-language maps composed and circulated by the Jesuit Matteo Ricci (1552–1610).[26] A further step was made in 1623, when Giulio Aleni (1582–1649) elaborated on geographic notes left by his predecessors to compose the *Zhifang wai ji*, the first book to outline European geography systematically. Justly called "much more important than Ricci's maps in spreading information about the non-Chinese world," Aleni's work continued to be widely consulted in the Qing period.[27] Along with the later *Kunyu tushuo* of Ferdinand Verbiest (1623–1688), it represented the definitive account of Jesuit geography for Chinese scholars.

When the Jesuits reached China, they encountered geographic concepts with heterogeneous origins making conflicting claims. To popularize their own views, including the novel theory that the world was composed of five water-bound continents, they had to borrow from existing vocabularies to make their description intelligible and persuasive, "encoding" their claims by "wrapping an unfamiliar idea in an acceptable format."[28] Jesuit geographers like Ricci, Aleni, and Martino Martini (1614–1661) consulted Ming-era sources extensively.[29] Thus, even in their own writings these missionaries synthesized European and Chinese concepts. For Chinese scholars, most of whom were unwilling to swallow their claims in toto, it was still more necessary to consider European assertions in the context of older geographic traditions. A five-continent world reminded some of the theories of Zou Yan, although the inferences drawn from this similarity differed.[30] Some late Ming scholars repudiated Ricci's maps because they appeared either to denigrate China's position in the world, or to mislead viewers about Europe's actual proximity and aggressive intent.[31] A Buddhist critic argued that the Christian God was simply the deity Indra who dwelt on Mt. Sumeru, proving that the Jesuits were unfamiliar with the whole (Buddhist) cosmos. The Christian polemicist Xu Guangqi (1562–1633) replied that, to the contrary, the narrow Buddhist view of four continents had now been superseded by the wider experience of Europeans. Indeed, Xu went so far as to claim that Chinese Buddhist cosmological views were unknown in India (according to Jesuit discussions with scholars there), probably indicating that Chinese Buddhists had plagiarized Zou Yan.[32]

This cursory review illustrates a paradox in the study of foreign geography in China. New sources constantly emerged, giving more raw information about little-known parts of the outside world, but at the same time increasing the number of names and concepts with which geographers had to wrestle. As the numbers of variables increased within an intellectual environment that valued wide reading, there emerged a cacophony of conflicting opinions rather than a coherent synthesis. Under these conditions, any single firsthand source had little intrinsic authority; far greater weight was carried by the judgment of scholarly interpreters who could determine its authority by reference to many others. The process by which this scholarly assessment was made therefore requires close scrutiny.

TECHNIQUES OF GEOGRAPHIC SCHOLARSHIP

Textual research methods shaped the study of foreign geography. An overwhelming majority of descriptions about the outside world were unmapped, and even the minority that did supply maps paired them with voluminous written description. Maps not forming part of a book normally bore extensive textual glosses.[33] Compared to the far larger written corpus, maps had a marginal role in shaping the worldviews of Qing scholars and officials. This dominance was self-reinforcing: textual sources begat textual commentary, because maps were inadequate to set out and debate the nuanced contradictions of documentary evidence.

The dominance of text-based research into foreign geography had several important implications. First, anyone with a standard elite education could conduct geographic research at the highest level, as China had no class of practitioners exclusively trained in and devoted to that subject. With so many scholars offering opinions with prima facie claims to consideration, idiosyncratic outlooks proliferated. Second, geographic reasoning was strongly influenced by common practices of textual scholarship. Although geographic arguments were ultimately built on descriptions claiming firsthand knowledge, the validity of any one description had to be evaluated within a wider matrix of corroboration. If newer and older accounts conflicted, the authority of competing claims became a matter of debate, so that any one record of empirical experience yielded to the greater authority of the textual criticism that was applied to it. The effect of collecting textual evidence in compendia, as Benjamin A. Elman has observed apropos late Ming natural studies, meant that "in time, words as glosses, that is, the textual lives of things, took precedence over any analysis of the things signified."[34] No new and revolutionary set of claims, even the comprehensive systems brought by the Jesuits, could overturn, or even stand outside, the total matrix of available geographic sources.

Textual research became particularly dominant in the Qing period through the rise of the *kaozheng* or "evidential research" movement, which emphasized "exacting research, rigorous analysis, and the collection of impartial evidence drawn from ancient artifacts and historical documents and texts."[35] In this environment, those studying foreign geography were influenced by what John B. Henderson has termed the "commentarial assumption," derived from classical studies, that the canon of sources should represent an underlying philosophical unity, so that scholars ought to apply their acumen to reconciling apparent conflicts between accounts.[36] Geographic researchers, like classicists, sought to reconcile conflicting claims about what they regarded as a single coherent reality. Moreover, commentaries tended to become open-ended repositories of knowledge that grew steadily in size and complexity as different interpretations accumulated over time.[37] Hallowed earlier opinions were not expunged when new views were advanced, and the corpus of geographical theories grew progressively denser.

Because most geographic descriptions existed as words rather than images, names were the primary units of analysis. When applied to domestic Chinese territory, this approach caused few difficulties because records clarified the historical emergence and evolution of proper names and the units of administration to which they referred. Normally, the etymology of Chinese place-names, drawn from nearby topographical features (especially rivers), local flora or fauna, auspicious characters, past kingdoms in the area, or important political events, was transparent.[38] By the Ming and Qing periods, sophisticated specialist books on domestic place-names began to appear.[39] Central to this research was the method of *yan'ge*: the convenient listing, in tabular or textual format, of the successive names applied to particular administrative units as well as remarks on their changing boundaries.

Understandably, these finely honed methods also guided research into foreign geography. Yet an approach that was successful within China itself was treacherous when applied to changes in names, regimes, and boundaries abroad. One major problem was the deceptively simple matter of transcription. As a Qing geographer complained,

> Foreign place-names are most difficult to decipher: if ten people transcribe them ten versions will result—one man may himself use more than one transcription. Now in foreign languages one sound has only one spelling, but in Chinese scores of characters are homophones, and moreover foreign countries have consonant clusters lacking in Chinese. Thus, when using Chinese to render foreign sounds, seventy to eighty percent of it does not match. Plus, Westerners who study Chinese all live in Guangdong, where the local dialect is not the standard Chinese pronunciation (*Hanwen zhengyin*). Garbled in transmission, it becomes indecipherable.[40]

Another Qing scholar identified no fewer than eighteen separate characters used at various times in transcriptions of "Russia."[41] Problems of transcription were compounded by different informants using different names for a single group. If a new name emerged, did this mean that the original people been supplanted by another? That a revolution had brought a new regime to power? Or was the informant simply using an alternate name? It was easy—as Qing scholars recognized—for relevant references to a foreign country to pass unnoticed, or for two different places to be conflated.

As a concrete example of how place-names could influence geographic conceptions, consider the case of Ceylon (modern Sri Lanka). Early Chinese sources called it Shizi-guo, Sengqieluo, and additional variants, but during the Zheng He voyages of the early Ming it had come to be known as Xilan(shan). When Qing editors of comprehensive reference works prepared entries on Ceylon's geography, they relied on place-names to gather and organize geographic knowledge. Sometime after 1736, the court editor Qi Shaonan (1706–1768) was assigned to compose accounts of foreign peoples for the empire's comprehensive gazetteer (*Da Qing yitong zhi*). His entry for Ceylon began by stating that Xilanshan "had no contact with China from ancient times," but this categorical statement was modified by a note adding that "some say" it was identical to an ancient country called Langyaxiu in contact with the Liang dynasty (502–557).[42] Whether "Langyaxiu" (and "Langyaxu") referred to Sri Lanka, ancient Langkasuka on the Malay Peninsula, or both at different times is a question not yet settled even in current scholarship.⁴³ However, for present purposes it is more interesting to ask why Qi came to note a possible link between Xilanshan and Langyaxiu, while ambivalent about its validity.

Qi drew in part on the *Ming shi*, a history of the preceding dynasty just completed by fellow bureaucrats. The *Ming shi* itself had gone through several drafts. The earliest of these stated: "Xilan is across the straits from Cochin [Kezhi]. . . .In the indigenous speech a high mountain is termed *xilan*, hence its name. Some say it is the ancient country of Langyaxiu. It lies in the Southern Sea."⁴⁴ The author of this passage was You Tong (1618–1704), a noted playwright who had passed a special exam and been appointed as a court editor.⁴⁵ Elsewhere in his writings You explained that his knowledge of external geography came from "examining what was recorded in the [*Ming*] *Huidian* and [*Ming*] *Yitong zhi*, as well as various books such as the *Xiyu ji*, [*Huang Ming*] *Xiangxu lu, Xingcha* [*shenglan*], and *Yingya shenglan*."⁴⁶ In other words, he had read the major geographical sources—themselves, it might be added, often products of similarly wide reading. Indeed, You's description of Xilan's etymology and location is very similar to that found in the *Huang Ming xiangxu lu* (preface 1629), which in turn closely resembled the earlier *Shuyu zhouzi lu* (preface 1583).⁴⁷ The author of that work, Yan Congjian, derived his own information from archival and textual research.⁴⁸

These authors recognized that the claims they repeated were uncertain. Yan Congjian, for instance, began his entry by stating "The country of Xilan is the ancient Langyaxiu," but a few lines later clarifies that although "in former times [Xilan] had no contact with China, some say it is Langyaxiu, which had contact in the Liang period."⁴⁹ Such ambiguity remained in the final version of the *Ming shi*: "Xilanshan. Some say it was the ancient Langyaxiu that once had contact with China in the Liang period." In short, Qi's entry in the *Da Qing yitong zhi* was torn between two models. Its direct predecessor, the *Ming yitong zhi*, flatly stated that "there is no evidence [about Xilanshan] in former dynasties."⁵⁰ On the other hand, the *Ming shi* opened by stating the possible link with Langyaxiu. Qi's ambiguity, evidently an attempt to conform to both authorities, was not the last word. Misgivings were expressed by Zhang Zongying, who was ordered to check the accuracy of the *Ming shi* decades later. He dutifully reread the *Liang shu*, which he noted placed Langyaxiu "in the Southern Sea, whereas here [Ceylon] is said to be in the Western Ocean."⁵¹ Zhang evidently did not realize that in the Liang period "Western Ocean" did not yet exist as a geographic concept, and what later became the "Western Ocean" was then still subsumed within one "Southern Sea."

Yan'ge judgments of this type directly influenced the organization and classification of geographic knowledge. The editors of the *Gujin tushu jicheng*, a massive early Qing encyclopedia, accepted the view that Langyaxiu was indeed the ancient name for Xilanshan. Anyone wishing to read about Ceylon in the Ming period therefore had to search for it under the heading for Langkasuka.[52] The same editors, however, did not recognize that "Shizi-guo," recorded by the Tang-era pilgrim Xuanzang, was also an ancient name for Ming "Xilanshan," and thus accorded it a separate entry.

Interpretations of place-names also influenced the reception of new geographic knowledge. Although he followed prevailing Chinese nomenclature for many other Asian place-names, Giulio Aleni described Ceylon in his world geography as Zeyilan, a new transcription that he did not connect to Xilanshan or earlier names.[53] For Chinese scholars to evaluate this account, however, new Jesuit names had to be converted back into terms commensurate with the broader matrix of existing sources. One early Qing scholar who took up this challenge, Lu Ciyun (fl. 1662–1683), was well aware of the pitfalls that awaited him. As he explained in his editorial principles, there were cases "when one country, seen in two books, has a different name in each." Lu was optimistic that his "detailed evidentiary analysis" had "standardized these in a single form." In fact, however, he failed to spot that Xilan and Zeyilan referred to the same place.[54] Later Qing authors also coined new terms for Ceylon, such as "Xilun," without acknowledging a link to older terminology.

In short, when geographic information was arranged by words, place-names served as the principal tool for ordering that information, and thus as the elemental building blocks for constructing a conception of foreign geography. How names were connected to each other had a material impact on how external conditions were understood. Scholars who grappled with this question naturally consulted earlier authorities, and the authority their own accounts would come to possess depended in large part on the breadth of their reading and the acuity of their insights. Writings by Tang pilgrims, Ming sailors, or Jesuit missionaries were of little use until they had passed through the editorial gauntlet and been appropriately collected, juxtaposed, and interpreted into a composite form. That composite form, given the difficulties and complexities of its construction, was provisional and often retained obvious contradictions. Reading the same body of works, scholars would notice different details or give weight to different sources, prompting very different conclusions. As the case of Ceylon shows, constant reinterpretation left uncertain fundamental aspects of a country's identity, history, and location.

SPATIAL WORLDVIEWS IN TEXT-CENTERED GEOGRAPHY

Descriptions of spatial location were also overwhelmingly textual, and places could find themselves relocated from source to source. For instance, utterly conflicting viewpoints existed concerning the position of Bengal within India. The *Xingcha shenglan* of Fei Xin (ca. 1388–1436), who accompanied the Zheng He voyages, stated of Bengal that "its location is said to be the territory of West India" (*xi Yindu*). A contradictory position was taken by the *Ming yitong zhi*, which remarked: "India has five parts, this is East India" (*dong Yindu*).[55] The late Ming *Shuyu zhouzi lu* hedged its bets, offering the following definition: "Bengal . . . that is, India of the west (*xi Tianzhu*). India has five parts, this is a country of East India, though some say this is a country of West India."[56]

Written sources also made it difficult to settle relative locations in such a way that they could easily be translated into a schematic image. Comprehensive geographies of the late Ming attempted to categorize all foreign countries using cardinal directions as a master organizing principle. Although at first glance this appears to be a system arranging geographic information on a spatial basis, closer inspection reveals that non-spatial considerations could be more important than physical location when making these assignments. As categories, "south," "west," "north," and "east" had implications beyond simple cardinal directions. For instance, most states on the Indian Ocean littoral visited during the Zheng He voyages were placed by late Ming geographers in the "southern" category regardless of their latitude. Some, however, were perceived as belonging to the Western Regions (Xiyu) and therefore assigned to the "western" territories. Bengal, identified as part of India (conventionally a component of the Western Regions) was normally listed in the "western" category, which stretched across Central Asia from Mecca to Hami, rather than among "southern" locations, which included proximate maritime sites on the Indian subcontinent such as the Coromandel Coast (Suoli).

The priority of cultural-historical factors over physical proximity in assigning countries to the four directions becomes even more obvious if we examine the relative position assigned to Hormuz (Ch., Hulumosi), just off the southern coast of modern Iran at the entrance to the Persian Gulf, Aden (Ch., Adan), on the Arabian Peninsula near the entrance to the Red Sea, and Mecca (Ch., Tianfang), near the Red Sea coast. Early Ming works placed all three countries in the same "Western Ocean" (Xiyang) region, but the late Ming shift toward universal geographies separated them into different categories. For example, Yan Congjian placed Hormuz among the "Nanman" ("southern peoples"), together with Java, Ceylon, and other maritime sites. Mecca, by contrast, was located in the "Xirong" ("western peoples") category, alongside Hami and Samarkand—although these were nearer to Hormuz than Mecca.[57] The *Xianbin lu* placed both Mecca and Aden in its *Xiyizhi* (Treatise on Western Peoples) but Hormuz (to their north) in its *Nanyizhi* (Treatise on Southern Peoples).[58] The early Qing *Gujin tushu jicheng* placed Mecca among the countries of the west, but Aden among those of the south. Hormuz (east of Aden) was placed in the "western" category, but for reasons that show the influence of textual over spatial factors: the editors of the work confused Ming-era Hormuz (Hulumosi) with the Tang-era country of Hulumo (probably near the Wakhan region of modern Afghanistan).[59] In short, conceptual schemes were quasi-spatial, often assigning countries to spatial categories on the basis of loose conventions rather than precise physical location.

Maps were handicapped relative to textual sources because they could not evade or finesse difficult riddles of spatial arrangement. Mapmakers faced the same incommensurable body of sources as other scholars, but had to produce one unambiguous interpretation of the shape of the world and the location of sites within it. This led to a range of conflicting images, often by the same author or in the same collection. The influential *Guang yutu* atlas by Luo Hongxian (1504–1564) drew on Yuan and Ming antecedents to show Burma as entirely landlocked in one map and coastal in a second.[60] Centuries later the Qing scholar Ma Junliang (granted the *jinshi* degree in 1761) placed three conflicting maps on one sheet, and gave a fourth interpretation in another work.[61] Clearly, Luo and Ma were putting forward various potentially valid renderings for the viewer's consideration, and some mapmakers frankly acknowledged that their representation was conjectural, giving the reader "epistemological choice."[62]

Under the intellectual conditions of the early Qing, maps had the obvious weakness that no single image could adequately reconcile all available information. Ultimately, maps could not form complete, autonomous renderings of the world because they were unable to convey the incommensurability of the evidence on which they were based. In Qing textual geography, the process of reasoning was more important than the provisional conclusion, and it was precisely this reasoning that a map could not illustrate. At best, maps were abbreviated (and thus intrinsically subordinate) sketches of a complex worldview derived from written sources. Given this limitation, it is not surprising that official works universally refrained from supplying maps to their sections on foreign geography, even when they were provided for domestic territory.

EVIDENCE AND GEOGRAPHIC AGNOSTICISM

The textual methods described above resulted in what can be termed the kaozheng paradox of Chinese geography: the more assiduously new, firsthand evidence was sought, the more authority fell into the hands of the scholar rather than the eyewitness. For new evidence led to a more complex and incommensurable corpus of sources; corroboration was the only method by which to judge among them; and only a scholar had the necessary training to make arguments based on reference to earlier accounts. Older sources, crucial as corroborative evidence, did not become obsolete, and so an ever more intractable mass of information accumulated. In this context even the most totalizing geographic system, forcefully presented, could not become authoritative enough to displace rival interpretations. To the contrary, systems like Jesuit geography were themselves cannibalized and subsumed into the total body of available evidence, a grab-bag from which individual Qing geographers drew as they saw fit.

Early Qing geography resembles the "pre-paradigmatic science" outlined by Thomas Kuhn in *The Structure of Scientific Revolutions*. Kuhn identified, in the period before the emergence of paradigms or "coherent traditions of scientific research," a "pre-paradigmatic science" characterized by a wide variety of competing viewpoints and disagreement over very basic questions. Under these circumstances,

> though the field's practitioners were scientists, the net result of their activity was something less than science. Being able to take no common body of belief for granted, each writer . . . felt forced to build his field anew from its foundations. In doing so, his choice of supporting observation and experiment was relatively free, for there was no standard set of methods or of phenomena that every . . . writer felt forced to employ and explain.[63]

Without agreed criteria by which to winnow relevant from irrelevant facts, individual researchers faced a "morass" of data. Movement toward a broadly accepted paradigm required not just new discoveries, but the elimination of some older claims. An emerging paradigm "emphasized only some special part of the too sizable and inchoate pool of information."[64] Without a shared foundation for research, scholars talked past each other instead of contributing to a common enterprise.

Although early Qing scholarship on foreign geography was in a pre-paradigmatic state, domestic research was moving toward a clearer consensus. Within the Qing realm official research expeditions, most famously the general cartographic surveys of the empire, allowed one dominant spatial understanding to emerge. Domestically, direct observation cut through millennia of textual argument. Court authors claimed that a mission had reached "the true source" of the Yellow River, which "since ancient times, searches have failed to reach."[65] Likewise, after Qing armies had made the Western Regions accessible, "the truth was obtained in all that was heard and seen," and ancient errors were corrected.[66] Even in private accounts, the rhetoric of direct observation was used to confer authority on certain descriptions and to dismiss others as rumor or hearsay.[67]

The question of trust made eyewitness evidence influential within the empire, but less authoritative for regions beyond Qing control. As Steven Shapin has noted of the Scientific Revolution, the evaluation of evidence had a social dimension: judgments on the veracity of reported experience were tied to broader notions of personal reliability.[68] Chinese scholars likewise paid attention to the trustworthiness of their informants. Authoritative (fully corroborated, imperially endorsed, and potentially replicable) accounts could be gained for domestic but not foreign territory. Though many Qing subjects crossed the empire's borders, these were rarely elite literati informants perceived to be educated, disinterested, and trustworthy. Rather, they were merchants, sojourners, and sailors considered prone to exaggeration and credulousness. Foreigners, and those associated with them, could even be suspected of deliberately providing false information.

Direct observations of foreign conditions could therefore not be taken at face value, and corroboration was needed. The researches of the Kangxi-period geographer Lu Ciyun, who wished to describe the entire world comprehensively and reliably, show this method in action. Lu found that unimpeachable sources like standard histories were not comprehensive, while sources that claimed to describe the most distant lands were not reliable. For instance, the *Shanhai jing* was "equal to tales of the strange, with no way to confirm its veracity." Even late Ming universal geographies like the *Xianbin lu*, while "greatly complete," did "not yet utterly cover all directions." To see further, Lu was willing to use Aleni's *Zhifang wai ji*, based on the missionary's "personal experience" (*qinli*).[69] However, Lu did not simply transcribe Jesuit writings into his own book, but as a scholar was obliged to "examine them" against a host of major Chinese reference works. By blending all available sources, adjusted for their seeming veracity, he hoped to arrive at an approximation of the truth. Lu was wary of categorically rejecting even dubious claims: "Given the size of the universe, there is nothing that does not exist." Even standard histories recorded marvels, and these he "preserved in order to await evidential inquiry" (*cun zhi yi si kaozheng*). Yet it was Lu and not his sources which determined validity and admissibility. Even the Jesuits, otherwise accepted as "remarkable men of the Western Regions" who could "cause men to hear of things not heard of before," seemed unreliable when their religious faith clouded their judgment.[70]

The balancing of comprehensiveness with accuracy found its fullest expression a century later in the *Siku quanshu zongmu tiyao*, a concise evaluation of important writings compiled under imperial auspices into a single collection late in the eighteenth century. Here elite, self-consciously orthodox scholars were required to weigh the reference value of individual sources. Especially for private writings, the authority of a geographic claim depended on the perceived reliability of its author. Works by earlier Chinese scholars and officials, whose social and intellectual background was comparatively similar to that of the *Zongmu tiyao*'s editors, were treated gently, with attention concentrating on how the author obtained information. The editors struck a cautious note about the descriptions of distant India and Arabia in the writings of a Song official, but concluded that since his statements derived from personal inquiries among men who had been to those regions, "historians may rely on it."[71] When the *Haiyu* of the Ming-era official Huang Zhong (1474–1553) was found to conflict with that in the *Ming shi*, the compilers concluded that as the former was composed nearer to the events in question and used testimony from maritime merchants with a clearer view of events, "it seems it should not be in error" and could be used to "correct discrepancies among histories and accounts."[72] When travelers or geographers from literati backgrounds were censured, it was for credulity rather than bias or deceptive intent. A Yuan-era envoy to Cambodia was chided for attributing a marvelous event to the Buddha rather than natural causes, evidence that "his experience was extremely narrow."[73] Likewise, the Qing official Chen Lunjiong's *Haiguo wenjian lu* was lauded for being based on direct experience, and praised on certain matters as "sufficient to decide long-standing doubtful points arising from credulity." However, the editors challenged his claim that Siamese "devils" had engaged Zheng He in a contest of skill. Foreigners credulously believed in devils, the editors reasoned, and Chen's failure to spot and refute this falsehood was a "minor lapse."[74]

When, however, the author of a geographic work came from a religious or intellectual background the compilers of the *Zongmu tiyao* found uncongenial, their skepticism became pronounced. Buddhist and Jesuit accounts came in for particular scrutiny. Faxian's *Foguo ji* was criticized for Buddhist Indo-philia: "This book takes India to be the Central Country (Zhongguo) and China to be a peripheral land, which is probably the Buddha boasting of his own religion—its absurdities are not worth arguing with."[75] Of Xuanzang's *Da Tang Xiyu ji*, they likewise commented that it "recklessly relates miracles, and is extremely inadequate for investigation."[76] Jesuit authors were portrayed as having impaired critical faculties. Aleni's *Zhifang wai ji* was said to contain "many oddities that cannot be cross-examined, and it seems that much exaggeration cannot be avoided." A similar charge was leveled at Ferdinand Verbiest's *Kunyu tushuo*.[77]

Yet despite doubting Buddhist and Christian authors, the editors of the *Zongmu tiyao* nonetheless preserved and propagated the very works they criticized. The duty to consider and transmit even implausible accounts was explicitly noted. Despite its shortcomings, Faxian's work was observed to be ancient and had certain virtues, so that "there is no harm in preserving it to broaden different accounts" (*cun guang yiwen, yi wu buke ye*). Xuanzang's work also contained information that could be useful for mutual comparisons, so that "for the time being we record and preserve it, to supply material for evidentiary examination" (*gu lu cun zhi, bei cankao yan*). Similar latitude was extended to European-authored works. Aleni's outlandish claims prompted the comment that "given the vastness of heaven and earth, what does not exist? Recording and preserving it is also sufficient to broaden different accounts" (*tiandi zhi da, he suo bu you; lu er cun zhi, yi zu yi guang wenyi ye*). Verbiest was also treated leniently: "But if it is verified according to what is recorded in various books and what is transmitted by merchant vessels, it also contains things which are clearly not falsehoods. . . . [It is] not a total fabrication. Truly there is no harm in preserving it in order to broaden different accounts" (*cun guang yiwen*). Although some accounts were more trustworthy than others, the editors did not deem themselves competent to judge an account absolutely false, and erred on the side of preserving geographic descriptions.

This led to a conception of perfection quite different from the ideal of one accurate, mathematically based visual rendering of the earth pursued by contemporary mapmakers in Europe. The compilers of the *Zongmu tiyao* praised works that sought to verify knowledge using an array of sources critically analyzed.[78] The particular virtue often identified by Qing scholars in geographic works was *bei*, "completeness." A work was deemed to be "complete" (*gaibei*) or "complete and detailed" (*beixiang*) when it made full and judicious citations from all relevant textual knowledge. *Bei* indicated a specific type of completeness: that within a range of necessary items, "everything that should be there is present."[79] Ideally, accounts assembled in "complete" works would clarify each other and coalesce into a lucid worldview. In reality, however, such works often contained "diverging accounts" (*yiwen*), some clearly erring through reliance on unverified "hearsay" (*chuanwen*), exaggeration, or distorting allegiance to a foreign agenda. Yet without being able to decisively judge any claim true or false, it was best to "preserve" (*cun*ª) them all, allowing future scholars to have the full range of evidence at their disposal.

This critical posture of geographic agnosticism constituted a middle ground between absolute faith in any single description of the outside world and an atheistic denial that the outside world had a knowable form.[80] In principle, Chinese geographers sought a coherent vision of external reality that made sense of all available sources. Like religious agnostics, however, they were aware of the limits of their knowledge. Scholars had great latitude to propose new interpretations of intractable issues, but their interpretations would not be the last word on the subject.[81]

EUROPEAN AND CHINESE
WORLD GEOGRAPHY IN COMPARISON

The distinctive epistemology of Qing world geography becomes clearer when contrasted to the methods prevailing in contemporary Europe. When Matteo Ricci drew his first Chinese world map in the 1580s, he presented Chinese readers not only a new picture of the world, but a new methodology. Although the details remained in flux, his depiction of the globe reflected a rough consensus accepted by almost every educated European of his time: cartography had become a science with a paradigm, its findings commanding broad agreement. A century earlier, this had not been the case. In the fifteenth century, Chinese and European geographers had confronted similar problems with similar "pre-paradigmatic" methods. Why did European scholars reach a consensus about the outline of the world, and Chinese scholars did not?

Around 1400, European geographers of the early Renaissance faced contradictory claims about the shape of the world, put forth in classical sources (which of course did not entirely agree with each other), scripture and medieval Jerusalem-centered *mappaemundi*, navigational portolan maps, and reports by real or putative travelers and sailors such as Marco Polo. European scholars in the late fifteenth century tried to harmonize these incommensurable accounts. As in China, geographers engaged in complex debates over the form and number of continents and the size and outline of surrounding oceans, taxing their ingenuity to reconcile conflicting claims, only to have their idiosyncratic conclusions disputed and reformulated by their successors.[82] Some European scholars, like their Chinese counterparts, simply listed a range of diverging opinions without attempting to select among them.[83] As in the works of Luo Hongxian or Ma Junliang, a 1436 book of maps by a Venetian mapmaker presented three distinctive and not obviously compatible geographic outlooks.[84] Renaissance scholars were familiar with conflicting worldviews.

Ultimately, voyages of discovery and the reintroduction of mathematical cartography via the translation of Ptolemy's *Geography* into Latin revolutionized geographic practice. To be sure, there was no immediate and fundamental break from methodologies and assumptions also common in China. Ptolemy's reintroduction actually strengthened the influence of classical models: "Between the diverging opinions of a Pliny and some modern traveler, the Renaissance scholar did not hesitate: he trusted *auctoritas*."[85] Maritime explorers also gave weight to traditional textual sources. Christopher Columbus (1451–1506), as Valerie Flint has demonstrated, read widely in all available materials—classical, biblical, and medieval. He "annotated avidly," drawing parallels between incommensurable accounts. His understanding was shaped by interpreting these heterogeneous sources: "The part played by the coastlines he actually explored in the texturing of his expressed convictions was a very small one; and that played by the richly colored realms of his imagination was a very large one indeed."[86] Long after European navigators reached America and the Indian Ocean, controversies raged among explorers and geographers. New information circulated unevenly, and scholarly humanists were slower to abandon older sources than statesmen and soldiers. Although the ideal of mathematical cartography theoretically permitted the physical and political contours of the world to be described purely as coordinates on a universal grid of latitude and longitude, in reality even accessible locations yielded astronomical data only with difficulty.[87] Though aspiring to more precise evidence, Mercator (1512–1590) continued to consult Marco Polo, as would his successors centuries later.[88] Europe still contained a range of geographic opinion.

Thus, it was not access to perfect and homogeneous geographic data that set European and Chinese geographic practices on a diverging path. Western scholars still had to grapple with texts. However, Europe found in mathematical cartography a research method that brought all geographic data into competition on a unified field of debate. Once it was accepted that the world formed a sphere divided into three hundred and sixty degrees, cartographers could argue over exact points within a finite space. They were forced to translate elements drawn from diverse sources into a standardized language. Sources could no longer be accepted on their own terms, because adopting one claim had direct implications for all others.[89] Moreover, there emerged a hierarchy for evaluating evidence, with an astronomically or mathematically derived location expressed on a grid of latitude and longitude at the apex. This greatly narrowed what Thomas Kuhn calls the "latitude of expectation"—the extent to which practitioners might plausibly differ with the findings of their peers.[90] By making increasingly minor adjustments within a unified body of accepted data, cartography appeared to be a field making linear progress toward absolute accuracy.

To epitomize the difference between Chinese text-centered geography and European map-centered geography we can juxtapose the methods and assumptions of two major scholars of the late eighteenth century, the French geographer Jean-Baptiste d'Anville (1697–1782) and the Qing scholar Ji Yun (1724–1805). D'Anville had access to the latest exploration reports, but like Ji also made use of a variety of texts, including classical, medieval, and Arabic sources. In constructing his maps he relied heavily on source criticism, trying to form a balanced synthesis between diverse and conflicting descriptions. For d'Anville, however, the completed map was an end in itself: the conventions of mathematical cartography allowed him to fully express his partly textual conclusions in a single image, and there was no need to publish the manuscript notes and extracts he had written in the course of constructing it.⁹¹ For an elite Chinese scholar like Ji Yun, the importance of these two elements was inverted. Like d'Anville, Ji assiduously gathered different sources and critically analyzed them. Rather than settling on a single image of the world, however, Ji was alerted by his approach to the unreliability of many geographic sources and the provisionality of geographic knowledge. From a lifetime of collecting information, Ji realized that ancient and contemporary sources, foreign and Chinese informants, all appeared to contradict each other. If Buddhist and Muslim sources were problematic, Ji surmised, then the European map presented in Ferdinand Verbiest's *Kunyu tushuo* was also presumably exaggerated or misleading.⁹² Only textual commentary, rather than a single, seamless image of the world, could adequately address the conflicting pieces of evidence available to Ji, and his nuanced considerations of their worth.

From the mid-eighteenth to the mid-nineteenth centuries, Chinese geographic practice moved slowly from text-oriented geographic agnosticism toward a single, standardized worldview framed against a roughly agreed-upon cartographic background. Tracking the factors contributing to this change, using the case study of India, is one of the major aims of this book. To do so, we must follow Qing geographers in not permitting any single type of source or method to dominate our analysis, nor let any be excluded. Geographic scholarship was a dialogue between many sources, and must be studied as a totality.

Early Qing Perspectives on India, 1644–1755

Against the intellectual background of early Qing world geography, we turn to the question of how India was understood in the century or so between the Manchu capture of Beijing in 1644 and the launch of Qianlong's massive military campaign against the Junghars in 1755. Any examination of this subject must consider not only the empirical information available but also the methods of reasoning used to interpret it, particularly the circulation and interaction of competing worldviews.

Compared to the last century of Ming rule, the hundred years after 1644 saw an explosion in the diversity of available geographic information. This was due in part to the continued exertions of groups active before the Qing conquest—mariners and coastal officials, Jesuits, scholars in China's major cities—and in part to new Inner Asian dominions, where military expansion and the concomitant appetite for intelligence increased the stock of data. Geography in this period was a loosely integrated field of inquiry. Although the Qing frontier was much closer to India in 1755 than it had been in 1644, and the first reports of British activity there had already reached Qing officials, there was little pressure, politically or intellectually, to systematically weave the disparate strands of information about India into a coherent form.

Though loosely integrated, the entire Qing empire must be approached as a single field of geographic debate. Certainly, no individual, not even the emperor, had access to all the geographic information circulating within the empire's boundaries, nor was any single conception of foreign geography shared by all, or even most, imperial subjects. Still, officials and private geographers encountered worldviews originating from multiple sources and regions. Artificially disentangling them offers a misleading picture of how the empire's inhabitants encountered the outside world. Rather than individual threads, it is necessary to show the fabric of connections that circulated information among all corners of the Qing domain, allowing the intersection of knowledge originating in areas and groups that at first glance appear widely separated. In keeping with the concerns and methods of Qing observers, this section pays particular attention to place-names, as it was in the encounter between these basic building blocks of geographic knowledge that conflicting worldviews collided and were reconciled, partially merged, or remained in tension.

NAMES FOR INDIA IN CHINESE
AT THE START OF THE QING PERIOD

By 1644, China possessed a rich lexicon for India and its component cities, states, and natural features. An exhaustive survey of these terms would require a study in itself; this section will only briefly review the most influential vocabulary bequeathed to Qing geographers from earlier periods.

In Chinese, as in Arabic, Persian, and European languages, the most common words for India derived ultimately from the Sanskrit term *Sindhu*, "river" (indicating the Indus).[93] Sima Qian's *Shi ji*, the first Chinese work to refer to India, termed it "Shendu," but this was soon superseded in popularity by "Tianzhu."[94] With the introduction of Buddhism, India became better known through sutras and pilgrimage accounts. One of these, the famous *Xiyu ji* of the monk-pilgrim Xuanzang, coined the toponym "Yindu."[95]

Although it did not replace "Tianzhu," "Yindu" also came into common use, particularly in reference to the "five Indias" (*wu Yindu*, i.e., North, South, East, West, and Central), a division that became conventional.[96] By the Tang period many other less prominent names for India and its constituent regions occurred in Buddhist and secular writing; it would be otiose to devise a comprehensive list.[97] The Mongol name for India, "Enedkeg," later adapted into Manchu as "Enetkek," shared a common etymological origin with these Chinese words.[98]

During the Song dynasty (960–1279), "the pursuit of commercial profits had replaced the transmission of Buddhist doctrines as the underlying stimulant to Sino-Indian exchanges."[99] As maritime trade supplanted overland contact, India, especially the flourishing kingdom of Bengal, came to the notice of geographers on the coast. In the succeeding Yuan period new names for India emerged, notably "Xindu" and "Xindusi," which were occasionally found in Qing sources.[100] More intensive contact with India began in the early Ming. The dynasty's first ruler dispatched the monk Zongle (1318–1391) there by land to seek Buddhist sutras.[101] Maritime expeditions between 1405 and 1433 carried Chinese military and diplomatic influence to the coast of India, with envoys traveling as far inland as Delhi.[102] By the end of the fifteenth century, however, contact between India and China had dwindled. After the return of the last official seaborne mission, private Chinese traders rarely went west of Malacca.[103]

In the late Ming, Jesuits became an important conduit of information about India. Missionaries introduced their own terms, including a Chinese version of the Latin *India*, rendered *Yingdiya* by Ricci and *Yindiya* by Aleni. As Aleni explained, however, this meant simply "India, the five Indias" (*Tianzhu wu Yindu*), and other late Ming Jesuits simply retained "Yindu" and "Tianzhu."[104] A second Jesuit innovation, the term "Mughal," had no Chinese equivalent. In Persian, *Mughul* meant "Mongol," referring to the fact that Babur (1483–1530), the dynasty's founder, was a distaff descendant of Chinggis Khan. Mughals themselves did not adopt this usage, which had pejorative overtones, but Portuguese called the ruler of that empire *o grão Mogor*, or "great Mughal," and thus *Mogol* and *Mogor* became conventional in Europe for the dynasty and its territories.[105] This empire, founded almost a century after the last Ming official voyage to India, was unknown to Chinese geographers before the Jesuits introduced it in the Chinese form "Mowo'er." To explain this neologism they referred to existing Chinese conventions: "There are five Indias, only South India remains as it was before, the other four Indias have all been absorbed by the Mughal empire."[106] Together with new terms, Jesuits retained much existing Chinese vocabulary, excluding only specifically Buddhist geographic terms and concepts.[107] Ricci situated the older names "Banggela" and "Xi Tianzhu-guo" alongside "Yingdiya" and "Mughal empire."[108]

By 1644, then, Chinese geographers had many terms for India at their disposal. In some cases, the same etymological root had generated apparently distinct names (e.g. "Shendu," "Tianzhu")—divergences compounded when the root was filtered through a foreign language into forms like "Enetkek" or "Yingdiya." In others, certain regions or political formations (e.g. Bengal, the Mughal empire) had come to prominence. As the Qing engaged intensively with the outside world after 1644, the stock of terms for India multiplied further.

DELIMITING THE "WESTERN OCEAN" (XIYANG)

In textual geography, the evolving interplay between terms from different regional or cultural backgrounds greatly influenced understandings of India. As emerging terms were aligned with existing usages, both could change their nuances. Individual authors frequently used the same toponym somewhat differently. This phenomenon, and the impact of fluctuating meanings on geographic worldviews among elite scholars and coastal informants, is particularly vivid in the case of "Xiyang," or "Western Ocean."

In the Yuan and Ming periods, "Xiyang" had emerged to indicate a region roughly corresponding to the modern Indian Ocean, a significance later complicated by Jesuit attempts to overhaul Chinese understandings of the "West." Initially, neither Ricci nor his colleague Michele Ruggiero stressed European distinctiveness. Rather, in the early 1580s they stated that they had come from India (Tianzhu-guo)—not wholly inaccurately, since the Jesuits' Asian operations were based in Goa. Ruggiero justified this on the grounds that India was esteemed in China as a civilized and holy country, and the name could therefore appropriately be borrowed to describe his own homeland. Until 1594 Jesuit missionaries dressed as, and were called, "Buddhist priests" (*seng*).[109]

Ultimately, Ricci changed course and began "creating an image of Europe for China," a project that required him to disassociate the Jesuits from India.[110] For Ming geographers, west of China lay the Western Regions (Xiyu) reached overland, and the maritime Western Ocean (Xiyang). These two zones, thought to be primarily Buddhist and Muslim, extended to the west of the known world. Jesuits wished to relegate this amorphous West (particularly India) to secondary status, in contrast to a distinct and more significant Christian Europe. Aleni, as Bernard H. K. Luk has pointed out, wished to present Europe as "unrivalled in the non-Chinese world. This would imply a playing down of the splendour and might of the Muslim and Indian countries."[111] Chinese allies took up this polemical agenda. Zhang Chao, in his preface to the 1669 Jesuit-authored *Xifang yao ji*, contrasted the "two Wests" (*liang Xifang*) of Europe and India, to the detriment of the latter.[112] As noted above, scholars hostile to the Catholic agenda recognized its pro-European bias, and denounced Jesuit works as false or exaggerated.[113]

At the heart of the project to distinguish Europe from India lay Xiyang. Aware that Chinese sources called the Indian Ocean the Western Ocean, and perhaps also that the Ptolemaic system called the North Atlantic the Oceanus Occidentalis, Ricci created two distinct Western Oceans. In his 1602 map, he labeled the sea off the west coast of India the "Small Western Ocean" (Xiao Xiyang), while terming the North Atlantic the "Great Western Ocean" (Da Xiyang). Aleni explained: "The general name of the land is Europe. It is situated in the extreme west of China; hence it is called the Great West, Far West, or Extreme West. With reference to the ocean, it is also called the Great Western Ocean (Country)."[114] Nonetheless, Great Western Ocean certainly implied superiority, in size if not culture, over the Small Western Ocean. Hostile Chinese critics even considered the use of "great" (*da*) a presumptuous attempt to equate Europe with China, whose ruling dynasties also used this prefix.[115]

Although Ricci explained on his map that "India (Yingdiya) is a general name, what in China is called the Small Western Ocean," India does not seem to have been so called before his arrival.[116] Rather, Ricci added the term "small" to the normal use of Western Ocean to indicate maritime India.[117] The *Ming shi* remarked that "Great Western Ocean" came into use with Ricci, which suggests that its counterpart, "Small Western Ocean," had been similarly unfamiliar to scholars.[118] More conclusively, a Portuguese-Chinese dictionary compiled by Ricci and Ruggiero stated that the Portuguese *India* was equivalent to the Chinese Western Ocean (Xiyang), not Small Western Ocean as we would expect if the term were in prior indigenous use.[119] Whether India in this context meant the subcontinent or the wider Indies, calling the Indian Ocean the Small Western Ocean was Ricci's personal innovation.

If adopted consistently, the creation of two distinct Western Oceans was not necessarily confusing. However, Qing geographers found the Jesuit system less familiar and authoritative than older sources in which "Xiyang" already possessed a well-established meaning. Most were reluctant to christen the Western Ocean the "Small Western Ocean," or to call the Jesuits' homeland "Great Western Ocean," an adjustment that implied acceptance of their geographic claims, and perhaps sympathy with their political and religious ones. Yet, as the editors of the *Ming shi* remarked, "people from this country fill up China, so their land must indeed exist, and cannot be a lie"—and therefore had to have a name.[120] With no Chinese words for this unknown Jesuit homeland, it was necessary to judiciously borrow a minimal number of Western concepts. There followed various hybrid compromises with confusing implications.

Court editors disagreed over how to incorporate Jesuit information. You Tong, who first drafted the section in the *Ming shi* on foreign countries, largely accepted the Jesuits' terminology and referred to their homeland as "Europe" (Ouluoba). Another Kangxi-era bureaucrat-editor referred to "the country of the Western Ocean," but followed Aleni in explaining that its "general name was Europe." He elaborated that there existed a Great Western Ocean in the "extreme west" and also a "Small West, the country of India."[121] Ultimately, however, the final draft of the *Ming shi* expunged "Europe" and substituted "Italia" (Yidaliya), said to be in the Great Western Ocean, presumably because using "Europe" was tantamount to accepting the controversial Jesuit theory of five continents, which the editors called "preposterous and unverified" (*huangmiao mokao*).[122] Italy, simply the name of Ricci's home country, was uncontroversial.

When Qi Shaonan began to compose an equivalent section about Portugal, the Vatican, and the Jesuits for the imperial gazetteer, he headed the entry neither "Europe" nor "Italy," but "Xiyang." Qi knew that Jesuits preferred "Great Western Ocean" but instead called them "men of the Western Ocean," and attributed a 1670 Portuguese embassy to "the country of the Western Ocean" (Xiyang-guo). Holland was also said to be in the Western Ocean. However, Qi also continued to use "Western Ocean" for regions visited by Zheng He in the early Ming. Indeed, since he located the Western Ocean within the "Southwestern Sea" (Xi'nanhai), near Sumatra and Champa, he seems to have conflated these two regions.[123] In a more explicit instance of this, the Yongzheng-era edition of the Guangdong provincial gazetteer blended in its entry on the Western Ocean country (Xiyang-guo) information about the Ming-era Indian Ocean state of "Guli" (sometimes called Xiyang Guli) with accounts of embassies from Europe in the Qing period, apparently not recognizing that two different countries were involved.[124]

Epitomizing the reluctance of Qing officials to adopt the Jesuit innovation of Great and Small Western Oceans is the dynastic Veritable Records (*Qing shi lu*). For the Kangxi, Yongzheng, and Qianlong reign periods (1662–1796), the term "Great Western Ocean" appeared only three times and "Small Western Ocean" but twice. Three of these cases occurred when quoting memorials sent up from officials on the coast, suggesting that this distinction survived primarily in the coastal vernacular. In a fourth instance a Portuguese embassy was attributed to the "Great Western Ocean," but other references to the same embassy used only "Western Ocean." By contrast, there were scores of instances in which Jesuits and Western countries were termed "Western Ocean" without any modification.[125] In official records, then, "Western Ocean" could be applied with equal propriety to the Indian Ocean or to the homeland of European missionaries.

Some early Qing scholars, such as Mei Wending (1633–1721), had a clearer understanding of the complexities entangled in the term. As a mathematical and astronomical expert familiar with Jesuit writings, he was aware of the ambiguity inherent in the term "Xiyang":

> Note: The Muslim area (Huihui) was anciently known as the Western Regions (Xiyu). Since the time when Zheng He of the Ming put to sea on his mission, because they were more than one country they were collectively called the Western Ocean. Subsequently, Europeans (Ouluoba) entered China, and called themselves Great Western Ocean, which is to say they were further west than the Muslim area. Now their calendrical book is entitled "New Method of the Western Ocean," which probably means simply that the Muslim calendar is the old method of the Western Ocean. In these essays when I mention the new method I will always say "Europe" and dare not conflate them both together [under the name] Western Ocean, in order to distinguish them (*bu gan huncheng Xiyang, suoyi bie zhi ye*).[126]

For Mei, "Xiyang" alone would ambiguously refer to both the Muslim maritime sphere and to Europeans. His decision not to simply adopt the Jesuit solution of distinguishing the Great and Small Western Oceans may perhaps suggest that he found this a biased European self-reference to their homeland, unsuitable for a Qing scholar.

In the late Ming and Qing periods, what any particular writer meant by Western Ocean depended on the geographic traditions familiar to him and his attitude toward them. In general, Chinese scholars were reluctant to swallow Jesuit innovations whole but could not ignore them when discussing Europe or Europeans. Even scholars skeptical of Jesuit terminology were familiar with missionary claims. Under these circumstances, geographic lexicons formed neither distinct schools nor harmonized blends. Instead, scholars idiosyncratically drew features from different traditions, investing "Xiyang" with a subtle array of meanings.

INDIA AND "XIYANG" ON THE CHINA COAST

Xiyang was of interest not only to elite scholars working at court on the basis of written evidence. By 1684, having conquered Taiwan, the Qing court controlled the entire length of China's long and busy coast. From then on, much geographic information arrived from maritime informants, primarily local officials and merchants in trading ports. Such men, though comparatively familiar with foreign conditions, very rarely volunteered their knowledge in writing, doing so only when the state (or, less commonly, a private scholar) wished to interrogate them about external events. Whatever their origins, coastal accounts generated new geographic terms, as the narrator introduced vernacular place-names not found in reference works. In this regional context, names like "Xiyang" gained further implications.

By 1698, Muslim traders from Surat and elsewhere in India had begun to arrive at Guangzhou.[127] The French Jesuit Antoine Gaubil, outlining in 1725 the scope of Qing foreign relations, stated that "Europeans and Muslims of the Indies (*les Mores des Indes*) can go to the ports of Guangzhou and Fujian."[128] Chinese records are more reticent, but Kangxi received memorials about vessels arriving from the "Muslims of Surat" (*Sula huizi*) and Bombay (*Pengbai-guo*).[129] These Indian merchants seem to have kept a low profile and had little contact with Qing officials, who conducted no formal inquiries about Indian conditions in this period.

In Beijing, however, the Kangxi emperor was more active in questioning informants about foreign conditions. Jesuits in Qing service continued to propagate European worldviews, most famously Verbiest's map and companion written description of the world, the *Kunyu tushuo*, written early in the Kangxi period.[130] Later, Kangxi received a world map and maps of Asia, Europe, Africa and the Americas, printed by the French Academy of Sciences, with attached Chinese commentaries and place-names.[131] Kangxi also personally questioned Fan Shouyi (1682–1753), a

Chinese Jesuit who had been to Europe, and instructed him to write an account of his travels.[132]

Another figure questioned about maritime conditions by Kangxi was the surrendered pirate Chen Shangyi. Using information from Chen and possibly other informants, the emperor offered a commentary on contemporary world affairs, including Central Eurasian politics. In his account, Kangxi mentioned Hindustan among the Muslim nations and also remarked that "the Muslims of the northwest are most numerous in their variety, they are all descendants of Yuan Taizu, and there is also a branch in the Small Western Ocean."[133] This seems to be an oblique reference to the Mughal empire in India, but there is no evidence that Kangxi recognized a connection between these Mongols and the "Mughal" (Mowo'er) on Jesuit maps. Coastal informants were also available to court officials like Cai Xin (1707–1799), who in 1740 approached Cheng Xunwo (1709–1749), a man from his home district in Fujian who had sojourned in Java, to write an account of that island. The resulting work summarized the maritime world as seen from Dutch territory. Cheng used distinctive geographic terms for India: Ceylon, called "Xilong," was mentioned as one of the islands belonging to Holland, while the presence of Bengalis (Wangjiaola[a]) in Java was also noted.[134]

The most influential maritime geography of the early Qing period, the *Haiguo wenjian lu*, stood somewhere between works written by imperial command and those composed under individual impetus. Its author, Chen Lunjiong, was a major source of maritime intelligence for the Kangxi court.[135] He was the son of Chen Mao, a maritime merchant recruited as an advisor during the Qing conquest of Taiwan for his thorough knowledge of the coast.[136] Thereafter, he had traveled for five years in the Eastern and Western Oceans on an official mission to track the remnants of the Zheng regime.[137] Resuming his career as a military official, Chen Mao attained the high post of Guangdong Vice Commander-in-Chief (*fu dutong*). He was known for his uncommonly systematic observations of the physical layout of foreign countries, and this knowledge was transmitted to his son.[138]

Chen Lunjiong built on his father's legacy. While a licentiate he had read widely, becoming proficient in foreign conditions, customs, and navigation. Later he joined the imperial bodyguard, where Kangxi questioned him about maritime affairs, apparently by comparing Chen's local knowledge with other Chinese and Jesuit materials. Chen himself recalled that the emperor "personally instructed me, showing me a Complete Map of the Coast and Foreign Countries (*yanhai-waiguo quantu*)."[139] For his advice during the 1721 Zhu Yigui rebellion on Taiwan, Chen was appointed to coastal military posts in Fujian, Guangdong, and Zhejiang, reaching the rank of Provincial Commander. He continued to research overseas geography. In Guangdong, Chen recalled, he "would daily see merchants from various places in the Western Ocean; I inquired about their customs and examined their maps and books." These maps agreed with those that Kangxi had drawn and shown him while he was at court. As a coastal governor-general commented in 1748: "Among naval commandery officers, it is difficult to find one very familiar with the maritime situation and who is an expert in foreigners and foreign conditions (*daoyi fanqing*). . . .There is nothing [Chen] is unacquainted with concerning the circumstances of foreigners or naval training."[140]

Chen's stock of information was distilled into his account of the maritime world, the *Haiguo wenjian lu* (completed 1730; published 1744), a work unique in both its detail and the scale of its circulation and influence. In writing his magnum opus, Chen displayed a conflicted relationship with European sources. He seems to have regarded European maps as basically accurate, and included a Western-style one of Europe, Asia, and Africa in his own work, possibly based on Jesuit maps shown to him at court.[141] However, Chen largely ignored Jesuit writings and naming conventions. Catholic authors took pains to capture the exact sound of European names in Chinese. Chen, presumably using oral informants, gave shorter and more idiomatic forms, for instance, "Shibanya" (Hispania) rather than Aleni's "Yixibaniya." While missionaries tried to describe the entire world, Chen made no reference to the "five continents" theory, and excluded the Western Hemisphere from consideration.[142] Chen's reluctance to rely on Jesuit materials may have derived simply from his preference for direct inquiry to bookish learning, but an inherited hostility to Catholicism is also a strong possibility. His father was one of the first officials to call for measures against Christian missionaries toward the end of the Kangxi reign, and his son may have shared his skepticism.[143]

Chen's *Haiguo wenjian lu* was the first Qing account to describe European imperial activity in India. Chen divided the maritime world into five regions named after "oceans"; India belonged to the "Small Western Ocean" (Xiao Xiyang) zone, which extended from Bengal to the eastern Mediterranean and encompassed all of Central Asia. Within the Small Western Ocean he first described Persia (Baoshe), also named the "Great White-turbaned Country" (Da Baitou), and its eastern neighbor the "Small

White-turbaned Country." The latter, whose people were said to resemble those from the Western Regions, evidently refers to Afghanistan and northern India. East of those countries lay Bengal (Minya), whose people were dark but otherwise resembled neighboring "turbaned" peoples. Here the English, Dutch and French gathered for trade. Beside Bengal Chen placed "India (Tianzhu), the Buddhist Country," perhaps a reference to holy sites in eastern India.¹⁴⁴ Peninsular southern India was called "Geshita" (probably from the Portuguese *costa*, "coast," for the Coromandel Coast), also mentioned as a place of trade in a roughly contemporary work from Macao.¹⁴⁵ Major ports in India were also listed: on the east coast lay English Bengal (now transcribed "Wangjiaola^b"),¹⁴⁶ French Pondicherry (Fangdizheli), and Dutch Negapatam (Niyanbada). On the west coast the English held Surat (Sula) and Bombay (Wangmai). These ports, Chen noted, were "all built by the Hongmao [i.e., Europeans] to facilitate trade."

The *Haiguo wenjian lu* was a seminal work in several respects. Whether Chen was gathering totally new information, or simply writing down knowledge already familiar to Chinese mariners, he introduced a range of terms unknown in earlier geographic texts. Moreover, his work was the first to outline the European ports on the Indian coast. Precisely because it was sui generis, later Chinese geographers found it hard to collate it with other works.

Chen's reference to the Great and Small Western Oceans despite an aversion to other Jesuit terminology suggests that these words had become part of the coastal vernacular. Coastal officials would have been more familiar than their court counterparts with patterns of European movement within Asia, and had more need to distinguish Europe proper from its colonies. However, even on the coast "Small Western Ocean" proved a slippery term, used in at least two distinct senses. Broadly, it referred to the entire Indian Ocean–Central Asian region, the usage followed by Chen, but it also had a narrower meaning. As the *Aomen jilüe*, a description of Macao first printed in 1751, put it: "The Great Western Ocean is far from China, and it takes three years to reach there. Not so far west is called the Small Western Ocean; it is ten thousand *li* from China and the Great Western Ocean sends a leader to supervise it. The leaders of Macao seek orders from the Small Western Ocean in all things."¹⁴⁷ This clearly describes the administrative structure linking Portugal to Goa, and Goa to Macao; indeed, in their glossary of Portuguese words the authors equated the Small Western Ocean with the Portuguese word "Woya" (Cantonese, "Ngo-a"), Goa.¹⁴⁸

Where one stood on the Qing frontier determined the apparent contours of the outside world, and the appropriate vocabulary in which to describe them. At least some administrators and military officers on the coasts of Fujian and Guangdong knew of India's major ports, and the names for them in the regional patois. Words like "Geshita" and "Wangmai" could emerge under the influence of foreign usage, and terms like "Xiao Xiyang" could take on localized meanings not found elsewhere. This was a living vocabulary, fluctuating as new terms emerged and older names faded. Through memorials and books, local perspectives could reach a wider audience, but how such information was to be reconciled with other sources remained an open question.

CHINESE MUSLIM SOURCES

Religion, intellectual training, and communal ties could influence the perception of foreign geography as much as regional vantage. Within China, Muslim subjects (Hui) were among the best placed to understand recent developments in India, which by 1644 had for centuries been partly incorporated into the wider Muslim world. Through meeting foreign coreligionists in China, reading books in Persian and Arabic, or themselves participating in the hajj pilgrimage to Mecca, Chinese Muslims also remained connected to the Islamic ecumene in the Qing period.[149] Indeed, by then Chinese Muslims were more likely than Chinese Buddhists to travel to India for religious reasons: for instance, the influential religious teacher Ma Laichi (1681–1766) may have passed through India on his way back to China from Mecca, and studied under an Indian shaykh.[150] One hajji, Ma Dexin (1794–1874), traveled in 1841 through Calcutta on his way from Yunnan to Mecca.[151]

Islamic scholarship gave Chinese Muslims, like Chinese Buddhists or Christians, a distinctive understanding of the outside world, but in general Hui made little attempt to circulate this knowledge beyond their own communities, and often turned away from Chinese scholarship to learning in Arabic and Persian.[152] For instance, the travel account of the hajji Ma Dexin was written in Arabic and only later translated into Chinese. The principal exception occurred in Jiangnan, the intellectual heartland of China, where an elite Muslim educational network studied Islamic writings (and often Persian and Arabic) while remaining "in constant contact with the mainstream Chinese intellectual trends of the period."[153] A major figure in this movement was the Nanjing native Liu Zhi (ca. 1655–1745), whose commentaries on geography blended Chinese sources with Islamic texts through the deft use of glosses to create a hybrid description of India. This he viewed as the powerful Muslim state of Hindustan, leading him to modify Chinese works that he otherwise relied upon heavily.

Liu's most extensive description of India is found in his *Tianfang zhisheng shilu*, completed in 1724 and printed twice in the Qianlong era.[154] In dividing and naming the countries of the world, Liu closely followed non-Muslim Chinese sources, such as the early Qing *Bahong yishi* of Lu Ciyun and Ming-era writings (along with those of Jesuits),[155] thus offering descriptions of the "five Indias" (*wu Yindu*) and Bengal. However, his entry on the "five Indias" bears a distinctly Islamic imprint. Although he quoted Lu's statements, Liu expurgated passages unpalatable for his Muslim audience. For example, Lu's original text notes that Yuan Taizu (Chinggis Khan) "destroyed the Huihui, entered and camped in West India, and encountered a large, one-horned beast"—Liu retained the episode but omitted the destruction of Muslims.[156]

In addition to his mainstream Chinese source, Liu also translated a passage from an Islamic geographic text, whose title he put into Chinese as the *Tianfang yudi*:

> According to the *Tianfang yudi*, in the southeast there are the Five Xindu. Now, Hindustan (Xindusitang) is one region divided into five *du* ["metropolis," but perhaps short for "Xindu"]. The center is called Hindustan, and like the Western Metropolis and the Northern Metropolis the king and people are all Muslims. The Southern Metropolis is the Country of the Buddha (Foguo), also named Tianzhu, where Sakyamuni was born. Eastern Xindu is also called Banggala. The king and people are all Muslim, but there are Buddhist Chinese and Cangji people who live interspersed. Emperor Ming of Han sought Buddhism here.[157]

In this translated work, and in a second translated hajj record by another author, India is referred to following Persian usage as Hindustan, not as Yindu, with its Buddhist heritage.[158]

Liu's text was unique in describing the full extent of Muslim rule in India. The *Ming shi* described Bengal as Muslim, but not Jaunpur or Delhi. Many other works still depicted India, especially Central India, as primarily Buddhist. The Jesuits described the scale of Mughal rule but discreetly failed to identify its rulers as Muslims. Verbiest mentioned Buddhism in India and added that "now, the various countries along the coast are all followers of the correct Christian religion," but said nothing about Islam there.¹⁵⁹ Only Liu made clear that all but the south of India was under Muslim rule, and probably for this reason located the birthplace of the Buddha in South India, not the conventional Central India.

In another work, the *Tianfang xingli*, Liu reviewed for Chinese readers a common Islamic mode of dividing the world, the Persian *kishwar* system of seven major regions or climes. He diagrammed a spherical earth containing Europe (Ouriba), Sudan (Suodang, i.e., Africa), Syria (Xi'eryang, i.e., the Levant), Arabia (A'erbi), Persia (Fa'erxi), China (Chini), and Hindustan (Xindusitang). Liu consulted several Arabic geographic texts, and this description certainly derives from one of them.¹⁶⁰ Nonetheless, he did not dogmatically assert this system over mainstream Chinese perspectives, and in most of his geographic scholarship presented the world in a manner almost indistinguishable from a non-Muslim literatus.

Once again, "Western Ocean" demonstrates how an author could put distinctive nuances on a term in widespread use. Ma Zhu, a contemporary of Liu Zhi, explained dimensions of Muslim geography in his *Guide to Islam* (*Qingzhen zhinan*), noting that the world had seven seas, and that the Western Ocean was only one of them. With a nod toward Chinese geography, however, he explained that what were called the Four Seas were the "origin" (*faliu*) of the Western Ocean, evidently an attempt to reconcile Islamic and Chinese conceptions of the world. Further data about the Western Ocean were provided from the journal of an anonymous Chinese hajji, entitled *Record of an Ocean Traveler* (*Piaoyang keji*). Setting out from Fujian, the pilgrim had passed through the Western Ocean, including Portuguese and Dutch colonies, before arriving in the Great Western Ocean. Although this would imply that he reached Europe, the record presents the world to the west as entirely Muslim: "As we gradually drew further from China, everyone came to be of our [Muslim] religion," and within this vast region, all of the rulers were said to follow Islam.¹⁶¹ For Muslims, the Western Ocean referred to their western ancestral homeland. In 1816 a member of the British Amherst embassy encountered a Muslim merchant near Beijing who described his ancestors as coming from "Se-yang, 'The Western ocean.'"¹⁶²

In sum, access to Arabic and Persian sources led Chinese Muslim authors to a distinctive view of India. Although their geographic worldview did not circulate as widely as Buddhist and Christian counterparts, the conquest of the Western Regions after 1755 soon brought new scholarly prominence to India as the Muslim land of Hindustan.

INNER ASIAN UNDERSTANDINGS OF INDIA

Inner Asian peoples under Qing rule possessed their own vocabularies for India. Subsequent chapters will detail how Qianlong's military activities in Tibet and Xinjiang influenced understandings of India throughout the empire, and this section will concentrate on the influence of information from Inner Asian sources before 1755. In this earliest stage, Mongol views of India were prominent within the Qing empire. By 1750, however, these had been supplemented by a crop of private geographies written by Chinese officials serving in Tibet, which touched upon that territory's neighbors below the Himalayas.

By the Qing period, India was central to the religious and historical thought of the Mongols. Over the course of the sixteenth century most Mongolian-speaking peoples had converted to Buddhism, and their subsequent intellectual life was profoundly influenced by Tibetan scholarship.[163] For learned Tibetans, India was viewed chiefly through the lens of imported Buddhist texts.[164] Under this influence, even secular works traced the origins of the Mongols back to India. For example, the chronicle *Altan tobči*, likely completed during the rule of Ligdan Khan (1604–1634), traced the lineage of the Mongol khans back through Tibet to "Maha Samadi . . . the first king of India."[165] Johan Elverskog has observed that this perception of genealogical ties to India continued to strengthen over the course of the Qing period, and by the end of the Yongzheng period it was made known to Chinese readers.[166] Mongol authors also adopted Buddhist geographical concepts such as Jambudvipa.

The Manchus encountered Tibetan Buddhism much later than the Mongols and, certain individuals aside, were not overwhelmingly influenced by its genealogical or geographic outlooks. In terminology and historical scholarship, however, Mongol influence ran much deeper. "Enetkek" (and its variant form "Enethe"), the Manchu word for India, was derived from the Mongolian "Enedkeg."[167] Although the semantic range of "Enetkek" was similar to "Tianzhu" and other generic Chinese names for India, it was often transcribed rather than translated into Chinese. Tulišen, member of a 1712–1715 embassy across Russia to the Torghud Mongols, included the "country of Enetkek" (Enatehe-guo) on his map of countries to the west.[168] It thus became another word for India that Chinese geographers were required to digest.

Early Manchu perspectives on India were influenced by histories of the Mongol empire. Both Mongolian chronicles and the Chinese *Yuan shi* (translated into Manchu before the conquest of Beijing) recorded that Chinggis Khan had led his troops as far as India before turning back.[169] India appears to have represented for the second Qing ruler Hong Taiji (1592–1643)—no doubt very vaguely—the western end of the known world and the limit of his political aspirations. As he boasted to a lama emissary from a Khalkha Mongol khan, "Of old, in the days when the khans of the three nations of the Great Liao, the Great Yuan, and the Jin were fighting, they got as far as India in the west. . . . These men, these horses are [capable of] the same."[170] Indeed, Hong Taiji apparently considered India a tributary state. According to the *Waiguo ji*, a chronological list of early Qing tributaries compiled by Zhang Yushu, the tribe of Enetkek (*Eneitehei buluo*), defined as "India Major of the extreme west" (*jixi Da Xitian*) had "submitted" (*fu*) to the dynasty in the Tiancong period (1626–1636).[171] What this indicates is unclear.

Babur was a descendant through his mother of Chinggis's son Chaghatai (d. 1242). By the time he reached India, however, virtually no connections existed between the Mongols living in their original homeland (later to become Buddhist Qing subjects) and their distant western cousins, already Turkic-speaking Muslims. Still, in the eighteenth century at least some Mongol officials at the Qing court were vaguely aware that a descendent of Chaghatai now ruled India. Gombojab (fl. 1692–1749) wrote in a 1725 genealogy that Chaghatai's third son, "Adaramamad," became khan of India, ruling from the city of "Balaša." The identity of Adaramamad, probably a later Muslim ruler, has not been established.[172] Whether or not Kangxi himself was aware of this claim of a Mongol tie to India, he acknowledged that a branch of the Mongols lived in the Small Western Ocean and was generally aware that many Muslim rulers in Central Asia claimed Mongol heritage.[173] In the Qianlong reign the influence of such Inner Asian political intelligence increased at court and passed more extensively into Chinese sources.

Inner Asian warfare also exposed Chinese scholars to Tibetan geographic vocabulary and conceptions. Although Qing operations in Tibet were led by Manchu and Mongol generals and high officials, in times of crisis a number of ordinary Chinese civil officials were deputed to the frontier to manage grain transport, secretarial duties, or other tasks. Despite their brief postings and lower rank, they composed the great majority of geographic accounts of Tibet, giving their readers fresh information about the world beyond the empire's boundaries.

The Junghar invasion of Tibet in 1717 was the first episode of Inner Asian warfare that brought new information about India into the Qing empire.

Kangxi fought back vigorously and expelled the Junghars from Lhasa in 1720, marking the beginning of direct Qing supervision over Tibetan affairs.[174] Yansin, a Qing general presiding over postwar administration, numbered India (Enong'ake) among the "tribes" (*ayimagh*) surrounding Tibet, and placed it on a list of correspondents to be notified of the Qing victory.[175]

In the ensuing decades, several more officials left records about the Himalayas and the lands beyond. Because the southern frontiers of Tibet were of little strategic significance for the wars with the Junghars, and because few Chinese officials passed beyond Lhasa, descriptions of India in this period were extremely terse compared to those that appeared later in the century. The *Xizang zhi*, for instance, mentioned only that a month south of Bhutan was "the frontier of the country of India" (*Tianzhu-guo jie*).[176] The first edition of the *Da Qing yitong zhi*, printed in 1744, also noted that over 2,000 *li* south of western Tibet lay Enetkek (Eneteke-guo), and added that the border of ancient India (*gu Tianzhu*) was southwest of that region.[177]

In addition to the Manchu "Enetkek" and the Chinese "Tianzhu," some Tibetan words for India were already appearing in the writings of Chinese authors. Zhang Hai, who served in Tibet in the Yongzheng and early Qianlong period, mentioned a place called "Jiaga'er" to the southwest of Tibet.[178] This was a Chinese rendering of the Tibetan "Rgya-gar," meaning India, but Zhang supplied no gloss. He also mentioned that the far west of Tibet bordered on the "turbaned Muslim Kashmiris and Bacha" (*chantou Huihui Kaqi Bacha*). As will be discussed below, in the late eighteenth century the term *Ti-ling pa-ca* was used in Tibetan as a transliteration of *Delhi Padshah*, the Delhi (i.e., Mughal) emperor. Zhang's "Bacha" may therefore have referred to the Mughal empire, of which Kashmir was then a part.

Even in Inner Asia, the Western Ocean was mentioned by Chinese authors. The *Xizang jianwen lu* of Xiao Tenglin, from the early Qianlong period, stated that southwest of the Salween River the land bordered "such places as Bhutan, Nepal, and Xiyang," adding that a month south of Bhutan lay India (Tianzhu).[179] Similarly, the early Qing encyclopedia *Gujin tushu jicheng* placed the "Western Ocean-sea" (Xiyanghai) on the southwest border of Yunnan.[180] Geographically the Indian Ocean should be indicated, but a roughly contemporary description of Tibet noted that merchants from the Western Ocean—distinct from "turbaned peoples" (*chantou*), Muslims, and Eluo'elesu (Russians?)—sojourned there and mentioned the presence of Western Ocean medicines there.[181] This may refer to the presence of Catholic missionaries in Lhasa in the first half of the eighteenth century. Even in the Tibetan context, then, "Xiyang" seems to have referred ambiguously to both Europe and India, a fact that would cause confusion in the 1790s.

Before 1757, the East India Company did not wield political authority in Bengal and was not noticed by Chinese geographers in Tibet. One possible exception may be the 1753 *Xiyu yiwen* of Chen Kesheng, which described below Tibet a country called Piluo-guo, ten thousand *li* in size and with a circumference requiring five months to travel. This land, almost certainly Bengal, was said to resemble Tianzhu, "the country of the Buddha," as described in official histories.[182] Chen added that it "has sea routes that reach to Guangdong" (*hang hai zhi Yue*). Given that seaborne trade between Bengal and China was dominated in this period by European vessels, this is possibly an oblique reference to English settlements.

Kangxi had sent two expeditions to map Tibet, but also consulted Buddhist sutras for further information about western Tibet, where the Ganges was said to originate. He quoted a statement in the *Yinben jing* that the major rivers arising from Lake Anavatapta flowed out of the mouths of four animals, and commented that in reality these rivers emerged from mountains that somewhat resembled those animals in shape. He elaborated:

> *Mabujia kababu* [Tib., *rma bya kha 'bab*] translates as "The Peacock's Mouth." Its waters flow southward . . . join the waters flowing eastward, and flow southeastward until they reach India [Enetkek] and become the Gangga mulun River [Tib., *Gang-ga*, Ganges; Mong., *mören*, "river"], what is called in [Chinese] Buddhist teachings the Heng River. The *Foguo ji* records that Faxian of the Wei dynasty followed the Heng River to the Southern Ocean, and [from there] entered Bohai in Shandong.[183]

This shows not only the emperor's wide reading, but also his attempt to reconcile sources from different languages and cultures.

From Tibet Hindu mendicants entered China in the seventeenth and eighteenth centuries for religious and commercial purposes, some travelling as far as Guangdong, Beijing, and even Mongolia. Some of these men were recorded as speaking Chinese, and referred to their homeland as "Da Xitian" (Great Western Heaven), recognized by Qing interlocutors as a reference to India. Despite encountering bureaucrats and occasionally entering state custody, they do not seem to have formed a significant conduit of information about contemporary Indian affairs, at least outside Tibet, and their interesting careers will therefore not be addressed in this study.[184]

After 1750, Inner Asia became the single largest source of new information about India reaching readers of Chinese. Although its influence was not yet dominant in the Kangxi and Yongzheng reigns, when there were fewer avenues for translating and circulating intelligence from Mongol, Tibetan, and Turkic sources, it was already contributing substantially to the empire's perspectives on India. Sometimes new terms, like "Jiaga'er," appeared in Qing sources for the first time. In other cases, authors gave new significance to already familiar names and concepts, like Tianzhu and Xiyang. Readers had to decipher the mix of local and general terminology found in the lexicons of specific authors.

BLAME THE MESSENGER: THE ORIGINS AND PERSISTENCE OF GEOGRAPHIC COMPLEXITY

Geographic outlooks in the first century or so of Qing rule, both scholarly and political, form a benchmark against which subsequent developments can be measured. This early period was defined by a decentralized and multifarious range of perspectives recorded in scholarly compendia, bureaucratic correspondence, and private writings. Some of the incommensurability among these accounts of India arose simply from India's diversity. However, the principal source of conflicting claims about India's names, political situation, religious orientation, and geographical position found in Chinese and Manchu sources before 1755 was the amplification of that diversity through the increasing complexity of Qing intellectual life. Information about India reached China after being encoded in different languages and intellectual traditions, and adjusted to meet the needs of competing religious and political loyalties. Once across the Qing frontier, it was captured, decoded, and circulated by an equally diverse array of Qing subjects. Depending on whether, and in what spirit, one read Muslim, Catholic, or Buddhist sources, whether those sources were used alone or in relation to a mass of materials, and whether one was privy to the latest reports from Fujian or Tibet, India and its regions took on very different guises.

Chinese readers, in the methods and assumptions guiding their geographic analysis, expected and accommodated this diversity. Wide and careful reading was a hallmark of good scholarship in all fields, and while not every source became widely known, researchers assiduously gathered materials. Few authors addressed Indian geography without drawing information from multiple linguistic, regional, or religious backgrounds. Yan'ge logic led them to expect variant references to the same place, but the sheer scale and incommensurability of the material precluded a synthesized outlook from emerging. No one author, nor even the state itself, came close to elaborating the connections between Jiaga'er, Da Xitian, Enetkek, Yindu, Tianzhu, Xindusitang, or Xiao Xiyang, or even between single regions of India like Bengal, known as Banggela, Wangjiaoliao, Minya, and Piluo. In a research tradition dominated by textual argument and infused with a spirit of geographic agnosticism this raised little anxiety; in a political tradition that considered frontiers separately, it raised few difficulties. The ideal of comprehensively ordering geographic data did not fade between 1644 and 1755, but the wisdom of refraining from overly ambitious judgments was apparent.

"Western Ocean" highlights the simultaneous interdependence and idiosyncrasy of Qing geographic thought in this period. At first glance, it formed a common point of reference for orthodox court editors like Qi Shaonan, Jesuits like Aleni and Verbiest, the Muslim scholar Ma Zhu, the Fujianese maritime expert Chen Lunjiong, and Xiao Tenglin on assignment in Tibet. Upon closer examination, the Western Oceans, Great Western Oceans, and Small Western Oceans mentioned by these authors varied in significance. Each author nestled his Western Ocean within a particular cosmological framework, and often assigned the region (or regions) unique political or religious nuances. Still, these applications of Western Ocean and its variants were in dialogue. Chen Lunjiong's usage was linked to Ricci's innovations, and Ricci borrowed from existing Ming-era geographies. Ma Zhu and Xiao Tenglin were also influenced by other writers, though in ways now less apparent. The fluctuating meanings assigned to "Western Ocean" emerged not from competition between dogmas, but from interaction between hybrid positions. Because commentators were often talking past each other using descriptions rife with ambiguity, speculation could persist indefinitely without coalescing into a common, standardized geographic outlook. For a century to come, the relationship between India and Europe, and between the vast overland region to the west and the vast maritime region to the south, remained hotly debated.

Politics reinforced this tolerance for unharmonized outlooks. Before 1755, there was no pressing need for the Qing state to track developments in any part of India. In the northwest, the empire's frontier did not yet encompass cities in the Tarim Basin trading with the subcontinent. In Tibet, the court's attention was riveted on the north to guard against Junghar invasion, not developments south beyond the Himalayas. On the coast, European and native traders arrived from India, but in small numbers and largely without the provocative commodity of opium. None of the European powers then possessed in India more than ports and narrow hinterlands, and even in Southeast Asia their territorial control remained very limited. Current events provided no impetus for either the state or private scholars to coordinate intelligence gathering across multiple frontiers and build an integrated picture of the relationship between India and the Qing empire in a global context.

These conditions changed when the Qianlong emperor marshaled his forces in 1755 to crush the Junghars and incorporate their lands. Under his energetic rule, the movement toward geographic standardization quickened, but it was confronted by the challenge of digesting new intelligence from previously inaccessible regions. The intensifying struggle between order and incommensurability is discussed in the following chapters.

PART TWO

Forging a Multiethnic Empire: The Apex of a Frontier Policy

TWO

The Conquest of Xinjiang and the Emergence of "Hindustan," 1756–1790

Between 1644 and 1755 the heterogeneous perspectives on India circulating within the empire overwhelmed efforts to commensurate them. As the Qianlong emperor took the throne and brought the capacities of the Qing central government to their highest pitch, there was reason to think that this balance would be recalibrated. Bureaucratic agencies in the capital had always been a clearinghouse for information from all corners of the empire. In the decades after 1755, as the empire's armies pushed into regions hitherto virtually unknown, the court's understanding of the surrounding world deepened. A bonanza of fresh intelligence was placed at the disposal of an administrative and scholarly apparatus that surpassed in its manpower and expertise any previously assembled in China. The Grand Council, an elite cabinet of statesmen and talented clerks, was at the peak of its efficiency. A growing number of sophisticated academic projects employed many of the empire's leading scholars. To elucidate points of political or intellectual significance the court could draw on learned elites from Mongol, Tibetan, and Turkic backgrounds, as well as European missionaries, and could command territorial officials to inquire among merchants and foreigners.

Qianlong devoted his enormous resources to correcting and standardizing knowledge. Well aware of the linguistic roots of geographic confusion, he made sure that the polyglot experts he employed took pains to address precisely this problem. One of the major goals of both the intensive research into newly conquered territory and the careful re-editing of older scholarly works was to remove ambiguity and clarify the geographic record by assigning each place a standardized name and historical pedigree. Many of these definitive judgments were fruit of the imperial brain itself. Qianlong estimated his own scholarly opinions highly, particularly because he commanded several of the major languages of his empire. With India as with other topics, he believed that his findings surpassed existing views. Nor did he hesitate to amplify and propagate his beliefs in the court's copious literary output. Under Qianlong, one might have predicted, the kaleidoscope of perspectives on India would be reassembled by immense labor into a single coherent image.

Immense labor there was, and yet at the end of Qianlong's reign Qing perspectives on India were perhaps even more complex and fragmented than they had been at the beginning. The reasons for this are explored here and in the following two chapters. As Qing forces pressed outward, they encountered unfamiliar geographic terminology. For the purposes of campaigning, the court accepted local usage on its own terms, and did not see a need to scrutinize how the words used by local informants might be connected to geographic lexicons used elsewhere. When this intelligence was subjected to scholarly scrutiny at the end of the campaign, analysis was circumscribed by Qianlong's own interests: terms and sources connected with Inner Asia were eagerly sifted, but to the neglect of potential avenues of inquiry leading to other regions or intellectual traditions. The result was only a partial and incomplete synthesis: the centrifugal force of an influx of new terminology and information overpowered even the centripetal pull of the court's ordering efforts.

Also blunting the influence of Qianlong's projects was the place of the imperial court in the empire's intellectual life. Incoming political intelligence was kept in great secrecy in the Grand Council, while the latest scholarly discoveries were often recorded in manuscripts open only to a thin stratum of elite officials. Although the emperor took pains to make sure court scholarship was correct, he took less care to ensure that the larger scholarly community was apprised of advances in research. Thus, rather than dominating and guiding the empire's geographic understandings, the perspectives of Qianlong and his staff were little more than another voice added to the chorus of scholarly opinion.

The present chapter concentrates on the case of "Hindustan" to examine evolving understandings of India in the middle of the Qianlong reign. Between 1758 and the early 1760s, during the conquest of eastern Turkestan, local and foreign informants drew the court's attention to this massive but little known territory lying below newly captured Yarkand. Sustained intelligence gathering unearthed a detailed picture of northern India and the chaotic state of late Mughal politics. For Qianlong, already familiar with India as it was represented in Chinese and Tibetan Buddhism as well as in standard histories, the integration of this land into his conception of contemporary and historical geography proved a compelling but challenging puzzle. Although superficially the questions he grappled with were philological, the subtext of his theories about Indian geography had obvious significance for the comparison of his achievements with those of earlier Chinese and Mongol rulers. His findings, the result of sophisticated textual inquiry and multilingual reasoning, were duly incorporated into several works of court scholarship. However, by ignoring various classes of sources, especially those concerning the maritime sphere, the precise identity of Hindustan and its relationship with India remained a question that would be revisited in the following decades.

The Elements of Scholarship at the Qianlong Court

Active in devising, supervising, and correcting scholarly projects carried out by his court officials, and himself the author of a prodigious output ranging from scholarly essays to poems, the Qianlong emperor had a greater influence on the intellectual life of his age than any other Qing ruler.[1] Earlier, his father and grandfather had positioned themselves as intellectual and moral arbiters as well as rulers, and close imperial supervision of official compilations meant that Qing rulers became "the highest authoritative standard in historical discussions," monopolizing the right to make legitimate pronouncements.[2] Qianlong, convinced of his unerring judgment and with little patience for dissenting viewpoints, further expanded the prerogatives of imperial scholarship and enforced his own opinions on official works at will.[3]

Qianlong's single greatest influence on the direction of official scholarship was his passion for translation, transcription, and polyglot research. Translation had always been a crucial activity for the Qing government. Early

Manchu rulers pursued it systematically even before they seized Beijing in 1644, and Kangxi and Yongzheng later sponsored multilingual dictionaries and ambitious translations of Confucian works and Tibetan Buddhist scriptures, employing Manchu, Chinese, Mongolian, and Tibetan personnel.[4] Qianlong, expanding the scope of such projects, distinguished himself by an unprecedented concern for etymologies and the correct transcription of foreign sounds. This interest, which would deeply influence his scholarship on India, had several roots. His polyglot education—growing up bilingual in Manchu and Chinese, mastering Mongol upon taking the throne, and by his own report studying Tibetan and Chaghatai Turki—doubtless sensitized him to the phonetic subtleties of languages.[5] A more specific root was his interest in Buddhist *dharani*, ritual incantations that were credited with magical effects provided their pronunciation exactly matched the original Sanskrit. In earlier periods Chinese monks had sometimes read the dharani in an Indian script, but more commonly sacrificed accuracy for the convenience of Chinese transliteration.[6] Qianlong's tutor in Buddhism, the Lcang-skya khutughtu Rol-pa'i-rdo-rje, led him to the opinion that Chinese monks consequently mispronounced dharani.[7]

To the problem of transcribing foreign words into Chinese, the solution was Qianlong's beloved alphabetic Manchu script. The idea of using the Manchu language specifically in the service of phonology seems to date back to the compilation of the *Yinyun chanwei*. This piece of court-sponsored research, commenced in the late Kangxi period and concluded under Yongzheng, took Manchu letters as a model for reforming the study of Chinese phonology.[8] Qianlong also regarded the Manchu script as the benchmark of phonetic accuracy in his own polyglot projects. Early in his reign he commissioned the foundation for all later official systems of standardized multilingual transcription, the *Tongwen yuntong*. Using tables and glosses, the book systematically gave Chinese equivalents to letter combinations found in Tibetan and Sanskrit (*Tianzhu zimu*, written in the Lan-tsha script common in Tibet).[9] Since Chinese characters, as single syllables, could not precisely represent the complex consonant clusters found in Tibetan and Sanskrit, the book's editors devised a system of combining up to three Chinese characters into a single compound "character" that, if pronounced as a single syllable according to certain rules, would theoretically mimic the multi-consonant syllables of other languages. The attempt to shoehorn Chinese into an alphabetic mold in the pursuit of phonetic correctness, without attention to the difficulties these innovations would pose for all but a trained elite, is characteristic of Qianlong's uncompromising pursuit of perfection over popularization. This pursuit extended beyond Chinese: Qianlong created new letters in Manchu expressly to capture Sanskrit sounds, allowing direct Sanskrit transcriptions in the Manchu translation of the Buddhist canon.[10] All of these efforts seem to have been influenced by the revival of Sanskrit studies among scholars in Tibet.[11]

These grapplings with Sanskrit and Tibetan in Chinese and Manchu symbolize the fact that Qianlong first encountered India as the birthplace of Buddhism, a perspective that would later color his perception of it from the vantage point of Islamic Central Asia. In an appropriate coincidence, the phonological techniques pioneered to transcribe Sanskrit and Tibetan later influenced the analysis of Muslim-ruled Hindustan. This was because Qianlong quickly came to appreciate that correct transcriptions, first devised for phonological and religious purposes, were useful also for political control and historical inquiry. When military campaigns between 1755 and 1759 suddenly brought vast new territories under Qing rule, it was necessary to prevent confusion by ensuring that a person or place have only one standard name in each of the empire's major languages. This new name had to be "correct"—that is, its form in the original language had to be ascertained and then used as a basis for all transcriptions. Etymology consequently flourished under imperial patronage. For the first time in Chinese history there was an attempt to explain systematically—for certain regions, exhaustively—the precise meaning of a wide range of non-Chinese toponyms. Given the logic of yan'ge theory, it is not surprising that research into current names was expected to yield new and valuable insights into historical geography, especially the relationship among alternate names for the same place. "Hindustan" soon bore the brunt of the court's analytical rigor.

"Hindustan" and Its Strategic Significance, 1758–1764

THE POLITICAL AND COMMERCIAL BACKGROUND

Between 1755 and 1757, the Qing government conquered the Junghars and laid claim to their territories. These included cities in eastern Turkestan, most notably Yarkand, that were trading centers with ties reaching across the Pamir and Karakoram Mountains to India, Afghanistan, and Central Asia. Through these new possessions, the Qing empire was linked to India by a network of routes.[12] The most direct and politically stable route ran southeast from Yarkand, plunged south into the Kunlun range, crossed the

Karakoram Mountains by a series of arduous passes, and reached Leh, the capital of Ladakh. From there, a gentler track led to the Vale of Kashmir and on into the Punjab. It was also possible to cross from Qing territory due west over the Pamirs, pass through Afghanistan, and enter the Punjab and Sindh regions from the west.[13] Between these two major routes were commercially viable but less-frequented caravan tracks passing through smaller polities in the valleys of the Pamir and Karakoram ranges.

Various communities of traders, including natives of Kashmir and Central Asia, transited these routes. Indian merchants also arrived regularly in Xinjiang, and a few hundred probably resided there in the eighteenth and nineteenth centuries.[14] They formed part of the Indian merchant diaspora active in the Central Asian trade linking Russia, Persia, Afghanistan, Bukhara, Tibet, and Xinjiang. Individual traders often belonged to coordinated firms, in touch with merchants elsewhere, so few events in northern India of major political or commercial significance were unknown to them. In acquiring these territories, the Qing empire had gained a pool of political intelligence.

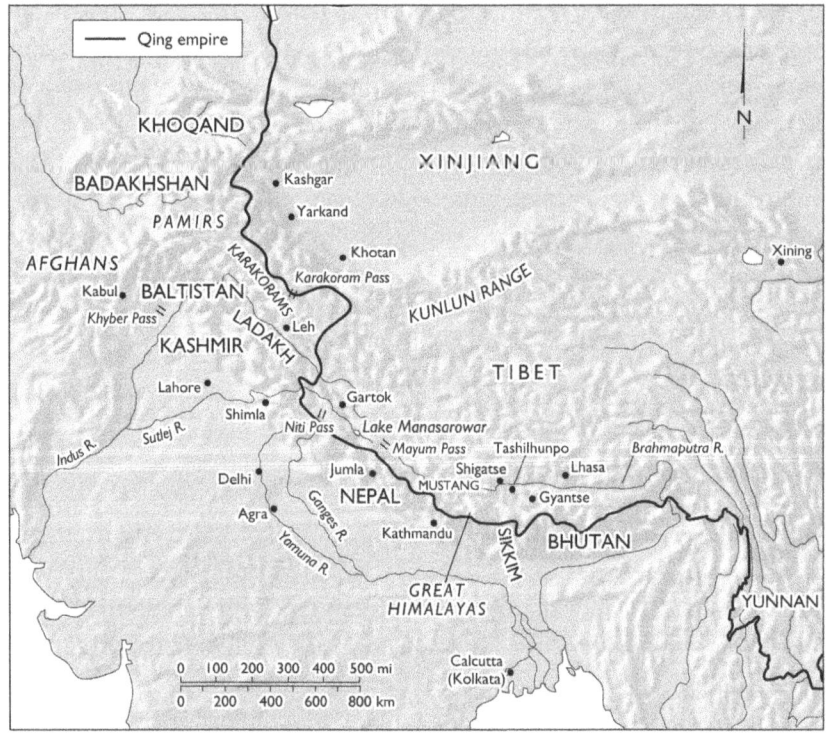

Southwestern frontier of the Qing empire

The formidable mountains lying west and south of Yarkand were a fault line of political authority. In the century before the Qing conquest, powers on various sides of them—Junghars to the northeast, Uzbeks to the northwest, Afghans to the west, and Mughals to the south and southwest—had temporarily asserted suzerainty over small valley states, but difficulties of access meant that conquest rarely produced effective, stable control. At the height of their power, Mughal emperors claimed most of the principalities in and around this mountainous region, from Badakhshan in the northwest to Ladakh in the southeast, but their authority was tenuous and often short-lived.[15] Later, in the first half of the eighteenth century, the Junghars became active in this zone, sending envoys to Ladakh and engaging in military operations across the Pamirs in Badakhshan and Chitral.[16] When the Qing in turn made contact with rulers in this region, they did so as only one of several competing empires.

Qing expansion westward in the eighteenth century coincided with a decline in Mughal unity and power, conventionally considered to have begun after the 1707 death of the last powerful emperor, Awrangzib. Regional powers fragmented the empire, although the authority of the Mughal ruler in Delhi continued to receive nominal recognition. Invasions from the northwest, beginning with the sack of Delhi by the Persian ruler Nadir Shah in 1739, further eroded the resources of the Mughal central state. When Nadir was killed in 1747, one of his subordinates, Ahmad Shah Durrani, emerged to carve out his own empire in Afghanistan. Not only did Ahmad Shah dominate northern India, invading it five times between 1748 and 1761, he also extended his authority into the mountainous regions east and northeast of Afghanistan. From about 1750, his forces reached Badakhshan, which he then claimed as his own territory.[17] His troops also took Kashmir from the Mughals.[18] Although his control of these territories was contested and often precarious, he was by far the strongest regional force when the Qing conquered eastern Turkestan, and his activities received close scrutiny in Beijing.

Before the conquest of Kashgar and Yarkand in 1759, the Qing government had only limited contact with the mountainous regions beyond them. The one major exception was Ladakh, a small state nestled in the western Himalayas between Tibet and Kashmir. In 1720, soon after Qing forces retook Tibet from the Junghars, Ladakh had sent an embassy to Beijing. Because Ladakh was situated where the main trade route running southward from Junghar-held Yarkand met that crossing Qing-held Tibet, its value as a secure listening post was recognized.[19] Before 1758, however, the Qing had little reason to seek out news about Kashmir or India.[20] This changed when it was decided to take the Tarim Basin. The Junghars, from whom it was conquered, had initially ruled this area through a line of Naqshbandi sufis, known as Afaqi khwajas, but they had rebelled and were subsequently kept as hostages at the Junghar capital of Ili. In 1755, in the first stages of the Qing campaign, two brothers in this line, Burhan al-Din and Khwaja-i Jahan, were dispatched back to their ancestral homeland with the support of Qianlong, who hoped to rule Altishahr (Kashgaria, southern Xinjiang) through their mediation. Soon, however, they turned against Qianlong and attempted to govern independently. In the course of the campaign to conquer them, officials encountered Hindustan for the first time.

FLIGHT OF THE KHWAJAS AND
RELATIONS WITH BADAKHSHAN

As Qing forces began to close in upon Burhan al-Din and Khwaja-i Jahan, the Qianlong emperor plotted to ensure they could not flee abroad and foment unrest from beyond the Qing frontier. In an edict of October 1758, he alerted his general Jaohūi to the possibility that upon the capture of Yarkand, Khwaja-i Jahan might "flee into such tribes as Burut [i.e., the Kirghiz] and Hindustan."[21] It is unclear who drew Qianlong's attention to Hindustan as a possible refuge for his foes, but this was a reasonable fear, for anyone who managed to flee through Ladakh to Kashmir would have been effectively beyond Qing reach.

As he closed in on Yarkand toward the end of 1758, Jaohūi informed the emperor that "I calculate that if the rebels flee, they will head only toward Hindustan, Badakhshan, Kala Tubote [i.e., Ladakh] and other places along the southern route."[22] He later proposed to "send troops to such places as Hindustan, Badakhshan, and Tumote to patrol the rebels' routes of flight."[23] Checked in his progress, Jaohūi withdrew and began a second advance the following year. Hindustan was still perceived to be the most likely destination of their flight, and Qianlong ordered Fude, the general in charge of the southernmost pincer movement against Yarkand, to proceed first to the relief of Khotan, where he could block any attempted escape southward across the Kunlun range toward Ladakh and India.[24]

With the final advance on Yarkand and Kashgar underway, Jaohūi memorialized that he had learned of approaches made by the rebels to the rulers of both Khoqand and Badakhshan, with a response arriving from the latter.[25] A Muslim associate of the brothers captured around this time reported that they had conferred and concluded that the route to Ladakh was now cut off by Qing forces. Because permission had not arrived for them to flee to Khoqand, "they desire to go to Hindustan via the Badakhshan route."²⁶ Although other reported routes of escape existed, Qianlong concluded that "it appears comparatively accurate that they will flee via Badakhshan to Hindustan."²⁷ Taking no chances, he ordered the Lcang-skya khutughtu, then on a mission to Tibet, to command Ladakh and Mnga'-ris in western Tibet to capture the khwaja brothers if they somehow escaped southward.²⁸

Blocked by Qing troops to the east, Burhan al-Din and Khwaja-i Jahan fled southwest across the Pamir range into Badakhshan, where the ruler Sultan Shah had them killed. His motives for doing so remain unclear, but according to some accounts it was because neighboring tribes were already plotting to rescue them.²⁹ According to the most immediate official reports, the two states implicated in this rescue attempt were nearby Qunduz and Darwaz. Other sources, however, name Hindustan as the origin of this plot. The *Huangchao wenxian tongkao*, composed from official records, remarked that south of Bolor, a territory in the Karakoram range southeast of Badakhshan, "there was a small tribe called Hindustan. . . . When Khwaja-i Jahan fled to Badakhshan, Hindustan then attacked it with its troops, intending to rescue him, but did not succeed. Subsequently, this tribe was annexed by the Afghans."³⁰ The *Qing shi gao* reiterates that when Fude was pressuring Badakhshan to extradite the captives, Hindustan brought troops intending to save Khwaja-i Jahan and his brother.³¹ A later Qing historian stated that after the ruler of Badakhshan killed Khwaja-i Jahan, his country was besieged by a combined Afghan-Hindustan force, until the Afghans were persuaded to join with Badakhshan in repelling the Hindustani assault.³² For a brief period, then, "Hindustan" appeared to be a protector or avenger of Burhan al-Din and Khwaja-i Jahan, although exactly what power is indicated by this term remains unclear.³³

Qing forces did not engage these "Hindustani" troops, if indeed they existed, but Qianlong took note of Hindustan as a major country. Badakhshan had sent a tribute embassy to the Qing court, and when it was about to depart for home in March 1760, Qianlong ordered that some of the Qing officials deputed to escort it and a Khoqandi counterpart were afterward to proceed to Hindustan and present an imperial edict and gifts.³⁴ One officially edited Qing source records that "Hindustan formerly traded in Yarkand of the Muslim Regions (Huibu). In 1760 it was issued an edict and bestowed gifts, and now it trades as before."³⁵ Apart from commerce, the emperor may have had diplomatic ends in view. When Badakhshan handed Khwaja-i Jahan's body over to the Qing, its leader, Sultan Shah, made clear that this was strongly opposed by local religious leaders and other Muslim rulers, and asked for military aid to block reprisals. Early in 1760 he asked the Qing grand minister consultant (*canzan dachen*) at Yarkand, Arigūn, for 20,000 troops to attack the Uzbeks, and his envoy to Beijing also requested major military aid. Qianlong doubted Sultan Shah's motives and declined, but it is possible that Hindustan was named as a potential threat and that the Qing ruler wished to get in touch with it for that reason.[36]

Just as the Qing were taking control over Xinjiang and contemplating a mission to Hindustan, the situation in India rapidly deteriorated into chaos. Early in 1757 Ahmed Shah had taken and plundered Delhi. Not wishing to seat himself on the Mughal throne, he withdrew to Afghanistan. To counterbalance Afghan influence, the Mughal emperor Alamgir II's influential vizier Imad al-Mulk then concluded an alliance with the Marathas, a powerful Hindu confederacy based at Pune, not far from Bombay. Moving northward, the Marathas retook Delhi and drove Ahmed Shah's son Timur from his Punjabi base in Lahore. To restore his influence, Ahmed Shah entered India again in 1759. At this point Imad al-Mulk murdered Alamgir II and placed a puppet emperor on the throne. Alamgir's son Ali Gawhar, already in exile, declared himself emperor as Shah Alam II. In 1760, the Marathas sent a massive army northward, forcing a decisive clash with Ahmed Shah.[37]

In Kashmir the situation was equally complex. Ahmed Shah, having seized the Punjab from Mughal control, was induced in 1753 to invade Kashmir as well. The administrator he left behind was soon killed by his own chief advisor, Sukh Jiwan, who in 1754 declared himself ruler of Kashmir. Although at first putatively acting as Ahmad Shah's viceroy, he eventually shifted his nominal allegiance to the Mughals. He maintained his position throughout the 1750s, but Kashmir experienced considerable turmoil, and it was clear that if Ahmad Shah recouped his fortunes he would attempt once again to seize the valley.[38]

Qing officials were aware of this turmoil even before Qianlong ordered an embassy to Hindustan, for as early as 1759 Ladakh was apprising them of developments in India.[39] By the spring of 1760, the Qing government was making inquiries about the outcome of events, which they perceived to be a war between "Hindustan" (the Mughal empire) and the Afghans.[40] Kashmiris arriving in Qing territory were also able to provide succinct, albeit garbled, accounts of Indian affairs. A certain Hojiya Asam explained that in 1756 Ahmed Shah had seized Lahore and proceeded to Jahanabad (Shahjahanabad or Delhi), clashed with the "Lord of Hindustan" (Ma., *Undustan i noyan*), and returned to his territory. The following year Ghalib Jang (Galibjang), son of "Nizam al-Mulk, ruler of the Deccan in Hindustan" (Ma., *Undustan-i harangga Dakiyan i akim Nadzamuluk*) consulted with "Alamgir, lord of Hindustan" and drove out the remaining Afghans.[41] His report continued, misleadingly, that Sukh Jiwan (Sekjiguwan), as Afghan-appointed ruler of Kashmir, had then raised an army and besieged Delhi, at which time Alamgir died. The vizier Ghazi ud-Din (Wedzer Gadzatan; i.e., Imad al-Mulk) fled to the Deccan with Alamgir's sons, and now a major force was once more coming north led by Ghalib Jang.[42]

Qing officials in Yarkand commented on this report, pointing out that the emperor of Hindustan was dead and his son was apparently soon to clash with the Afghans. Moreover, the intended embassy would have to pass through war-torn Kashmir and Lahore. It was agreed to suspend the mission pending further news from Ladakh.[43] Instead, it proceeded to Badakhshan, reaching Sultan Shan in October 1760, and presenting him with Qianlong's edict. In the ensuing conversation, Sultan Shah remarked that he was threatened by Hindustan, and again requested Qing aid. Ming Žen, the ranking envoy, believed that Badakhshan's true goal was protection in petty local squabbles, not against major enemies. As a Qing tributary, he informed Sultan Shah, Hindustan and other countries would not dare attack him.[44] Departing from Badakhshan, the Qing return embassy headed southeast to the Yarkhun valley, reaching Bolor in what is now northwestern Pakistan.[45] Given that it met Bolor's ruler, Shah Khoshomat, on December 1 and was back in Yarkand by December 26, there is no possibility that it made an unplanned trip to Hindustan, nor was such a journey mentioned in the final report.[46] A decade and a half later, in 1775, the Panchen Lama informed George Bogle, a British envoy to Tibet, that "many years ago he [i.e., Qianlong] had some thoughts of sending some Ambassadors in a friendly manner into Hindostan; but his people dissuaded him from it."[47] Geographically, however, Qianlong continued to believe that the primary route from his territory to Hindustan ran through Badakhshan and Kashmir, the originally proposed itinerary of the embassy.[48]

Hindustan's ruler, the Qing court anticipated, might also attempt an embassy of his own to Beijing. In 1760, officials in Yarkand inquired of Ladakh whether news of one was current, and ordered that any such mission be received and reported at once to Xinjiang, a point reiterated later in the year.[49] No Hindustani embassy seems to have materialized, but curiously the *Baxun wanshou shengdian*, composed to commemorate Qianlong's eightieth birthday in 1790, unambiguously recorded that Hindustan had sent an envoy to present tribute, claiming in one passage that Hindustan "asked to be a servant of the court" (i.e., a tributary), and in another that it "presented tribute." In one of his later poems, Qianlong lists Hindustan as a country that "sent an agent to the court to present a tributary memorial and tribute."[50] What episode the Qing side had in mind in making these claims is unclear.

HINDUSTAN IN THE CONTEXT OF QING-AFGHAN DIPLOMACY

By 1761 Qianlong was familiar with Hindustan as an important regional power, possibly hostile and certainly in political chaos. Attention to Hindustan peaked in the following year, when an embassy from the Afghan ruler arrived at court. Before turning to examine this episode, and the Qing government's interpretation of it on the basis of its intelligence gathering, it will be useful quickly to return to the political and military situation in northwestern India at this time.

Despite sending a large force against the Afghans, the Maratha army remained for some time in a fortified camp, where it was first pinned down and then crushed in the battle fought at Panipat, near Delhi, on January 14, 1761. Destroying his enemies, Ahmad Shah recognized Shah Alam II as Mughal emperor and returned toward Kandahar in March of that year. Subsequently, his military action in India was limited to checking the rising Sikh power in the Punjab.[51] In the years immediately after 1762, however, it seemed to observers in Xinjiang that Hindustan now belonged to the Afghans.

Given Ahmad Shah's claims over Badakhshan, and his interest in Central Asian territories north of Afghanistan, the Qing conquest of eastern Turkestan required his attention. Apart from any perceived military rivalry, Ahmad Shah also had reason to resent the Qing as a non-Muslim power conquering Muslim subjects (although, it should be noted, the Qing were replacing another non-Muslim power, the Junghars, who had long held sway over Yarkand and Kashgar without provoking a retaliatory holy war). After his withdrawal from India in the spring of 1761, the Afghan ruler was free to respond to Qing expansion. His intentions at this point remain unclear. Non-Chinese sources suggest that he sent a letter to the Qing court in 1762 demanding it withdraw from Muslim territories, and, when this ultimatum was rejected, began to assemble a huge invasion force. An attack never materialized, and it seems that Ahmed Shah's endeavor to build a united front against the Qing ultimately collapsed.⁵²

On April 30, 1762, the Qing court received an intelligence report from a certain Molosabir, a Yarkandi trader who had visited Ladakh. He explained that Ahmad Shah had killed the khan of Hindustan, Alamgir (Aliyamgir), whose son Ali Gawhar (Aliyag'owar) had fled to Bengal. Ahmad Shah established the grandson of Alamgir on the throne, and returned to his nomadic territory. According to the latest reports, Ali Gawhar had assembled an army in Bengal, while Ahmed Shah had returned and reached Gujrat, from where he tried to induce Kashmir to surrender to him.⁵³ This seems to have been a garbled and somewhat stale account of the events of 1759–1760. In September 1762, a messenger named Tsewang was sent by the ruler of Ladakh to report that the Afghans had taken Kashmir and "the entire territory of Hindustan" (Ma., *Undustan i gubci nukte*). An accompanying letter explained that in the face of recalcitrance from Sukh Jiwan, Ahmed Shah had sent an army under Nur-ud-din Khan (Urding han) and defeated him at Tusimer (Tosamaidan Pass?), taking Kashmir. The tone of the letter was extremely favorable to Ahmed Shah, presumably a ploy by the ruler of Ladakh to curry favor with the powerful new suzerain of Kashmir.⁵⁴

Shortly thereafter, Qianlong received an overture to cross the Karakorams himself and dip his toe into troubled Mughal politics by establishing his own rule in Kashmir. On November 30 an associate of a certain Niyas (Niyaz) Bek arrived at Yarkand. His master, he explained, was a Kashmiri who had held a military post in Delhi before abandoning the city when it fell into chaos and retreating back to his home. There he found hundreds of households that had earlier fled the cities of the Tarim Basin but now, having heard of Qianlong's merciful rule, wished to migrate back. Niyas proposed to lead them into Xinjiang. After his arrival, "having left his household behind in Yarkand, if we gave him a few troops, he would like to consult with the ruler of Ladakh (Tubet) and the people of Kashmir, and take Kashmir and offer it to the emperor." Niyas Bek's own letter elaborated on this proposal, explaining that after his return from Delhi to Kashmir he had served as an officer under Sukh Jiwan until the latter's destruction by the Afghans. According to Niyas Bek, although Kashmir had come into Ahmad Shah's possession, Hindustan itself had no ruler. Under the present unsettled circumstances, he suggested, the loan of only a few troops would allow him to seize Kashmir and offer it up to the Qing emperor.⁵⁵

By this time, Qianlong and his officials were well aware that Kashmir was in the possession of Ahmad Shah. Sinju and Amin Khwaja, in charge at Yarkand, explained to Beijing why this offer was best ignored. First, news had arrived that Ahmad Shah had already dispatched an embassy to the Qing court in order (in their view) to submit, so that "his lands have all become our lands, his Hindustan and Kashmir have also become ours." Second, since Ahmad Shah had shown decorous restraint and declined to seize Hindustan directly, instead restoring it to the line of its original rulers, his behavior was hard to fault, and the Qing would have difficulty justifying the invasion of Kashmir. More pragmatically, they pointed out, Kashmir and Delhi were far away, and would be hard to administer. Finally, they observed the obvious danger that Niyas Bek might be secretly plotting to have Qing forces take Kashmir on his behalf, only to eject them and rule it himself. The whole enterprise, they argued, was simply not worthwhile. Qianlong agreed, and the matter was dropped.[56]

By this time, as noted, Sinju was aware that Ahmed Shah had dispatched an embassy toward Beijing.[57] Sultan Khwaja, who had played an important role in Qing-Badakhshan relations and once visited Hindustan, was ordered to Badakhshan to welcome the envoy.[58] About a month later he was ordered to go to Afghanistan to "conduct matters," although the aim of his mission is unclear.[59] Qianlong considered Ahmed Shah's envoys a tribute mission, or chose to make known that he did so in the Chinese historical record. He quoted the Afghan ruler's own letter, which purportedly expressed delight that Qianlong had defeated the Junghars and opened the way for direct Qing-Afghan contact. In the official Qing view, Ahmad Shah's embassy was the result of the Afghan's "long desiring the transformative effects of [imperial] benevolence." Beneath this gloss, however, it is clear that Ahmad Shah's letter was intended to boast of his military prowess and that Qianlong recognized this. Ahmad Shah's embassy was dispatched less than two years after the battle of Panipat, and gave an account of his victory. The Afghan's letter stated that the Maratha khan (Ma'erta han) Nabalachi (probably the Maratha peshwa or chief minister, Balaji Bajirao) had amassed a force of several hundred thousand troops to respond to his own seizure of Delhi. When they heard that he was approaching, however, they fled into the fortress of Panipat (*Panipate cheng*). After a six-month siege Ahmad Shah defeated them, killing over a hundred thousand. This had overtones of a veiled threat, and Qianlong's reply downplayed Ahmad's victory: "Nabalachi had been able to gather a certain number of followers, and yet entered a fortified city without joining battle, sitting and waiting for his execution. This matter is quite unfathomable!" It also recounted his own recent victories, justified his conquest of Xinjiang, and described the grim fate of those who had opposed him. He stated that Ili and Yarkand were now Qing territory, and that Khoqand and the Kirghiz were his tributaries.[60] This should probably be read as the official Qing diplomatic position concerning its sphere of influence in Central Asia, or, as one scholar puts it, its "expectations of the new Central Asian order."[61]

After the rapid succession of events between 1758 and the early 1760s, relative calm returned to the mountainous zone between Qing territory and India. Ahmad Shah died in 1773, and his son and successor proved much less aggressive. The Punjab, the part of India closest to Xinjiang, fell increasingly under the domination of the Sikhs, who were not yet active in extending their power toward Ladakh and north into the Karakoram range. The British, although they began to take an interest in the eastern parts of the Himalayas as early as the 1760s, were still decades away from exploring their western reaches. Under these conditions, the interest of local Qing officials in the politics of Hindustan diminished considerably.

INFORMATION ABOUT HINDUSTAN
IN THE CONTEXT OF TRADE

After the early 1760s, Hindustan was no longer of great political or strategic interest to the Qing government, but many Indian traders continued to reach Kashgar and Yarkand, and Qing officials stationed in those cities remained aware of Hindustan's size and economic importance. The earliest description of India by one of these officials, probably Yunggui, who served in Kashgar from 1761–1762, described the route from Badakhshan to Lahore, the nearest major city in Hindustan. It proceeded to describe that land, the southernmost place in the "Muslim Regions." The size of the territory was difficult to determine, the author explained, because even traders long acquainted with it had never fully circumambulated its boundaries. It had three provinces, and the capital of the foremost province was Jahanabad. The region was dominated by mountains to the northwest, northeast, and southeast, and to the southwest more than twenty large rivers flowed into the ocean. This suggests a description primarily of the Punjab.[62]

In the 1770s, two more Qing officials made personal inquiries about Hindustan. Wu-cheng-ge, serving in Kashgar, used an interpreter to speak with major Muslim merchants about their travels, recording the results. Hindustan he located over three month's journey due south of Kashgar, placing it about twenty days southeast of Kashmir. For his account of it, Wu-cheng-ge seems to have relied to some extent on Yunggui's manuscript, because he made many of the same points: its capital was Jahanabad, which ruled a vast and populous country; even merchants who had long resided there had never visited all its parts; its rivers all flowed west into the Western Sea.[63]

By far the most influential description of the region, however, was that contained in an account of Xinjiang by another Manchu official, Cišii. Most of his information about Hindustan, it would appear, derived from a Hindustani *qalandar* (Ch., *hailanda'er*), or Muslim mendicant, whom he interviewed in 1775.[64] Cišii located Hindustan as being over forty days southwest of Kashmir. He gave a detailed description of Indian people and customs, and emphasized Hindustan's size—over 370 cities were said to be ruled from its capital—wealth, and distinctive language. Indian goods were ubiquitous throughout the Western Regions, he explained, and there was even a trade in which Chinese porcelain, valued in India, was exchanged for Hindustani jade cups and bowls.[65]

Some editions of Cišii's work also refer to a land called Yindi, said to be over sixty days by horse from Yarkand. The merchants of that country were said to trade jewels, jade, and other precious objects in Yarkand, returning with porcelain, tea, and rhubarb. They spoke a different language, so Muslims had to use an interpreter to converse with them. The bulk of the entry described how men from Yindi venerated cows, prayed to them for assistance, and bitterly reviled cow-killing among Muslims in the Western Regions. Cišii professed himself unable to understand this custom.[66] It seems likely that at this time Yindi did not refer to a distinct country, but simply to the Hindu merchants from various places who traded in Yarkand and were described in Persian as *Hindī*. Because Cišii saw Hindustan as an Islamic country, he may have had difficulty accounting for non-Muslim Indians and assigned them an independent and distinct homeland.

Cišii's account dealt with northwestern India, the last part of the subcontinent to have significant engagement with the British, and his work makes no direct reference to Europeans there. Nonetheless, he recognized that there was maritime trade between Hindustan and China. As he explained, "From time to time, ocean-going vessels from Fujian and Guangdong arrive and moor there, many of them having those who wish to profit from [the sale of] rhubarb. In consequence, goods from Guangdong and Fujian are frequently found there, and some come again to Yarkand, where they are transferred into China." As evidence, he noted that "a Muslim in Kashgar purchased a bolt of Zhangzhou wool, which bore the Chinese brand Tianshun, and was certainly a Fujianese product." It seems likely that the products Cišii described were imported from Guangzhou on British ships as part of the "country trade" (see Chapter Five). Cišii's conversation with his *qalandar* informant may nonetheless contain a subtle reference to Europeans. The Muslim holy man informed him that at a vast distance southwest of his country there were countries inhabited by men "as white as snow" and as "black as lacquer," presumably a reference to Europe and Africa. Cišii added, "Might these not be the so-called 'black devils' and 'white devils' of Guangdong?"[67]

THE EMERGENCE OF A FRONTIER POLICY ON THE XINJIANG FRONTIER

As we have seen, the immediate result of the conquest of eastern Turkestan was to plunge the court into complex, interlocking diplomacy with a number of Central Asian states. As late as 1763 the Qing central government continued to receive detailed reports about conditions in Hindustan, but in the following decades the sphere of official surveillance shrank, and the empire gradually disentangled itself from the turbulent politics beyond the Pamir and Karakoram ranges. This was not instinctive isolationism, but a deliberate policy to preserve the empire's strength and security. Notwithstanding the lofty terminological conventions in official records, the documentary records makes clear that Qianlong and his ministers recognized that their neighbors viewed diplomacy as a quid pro quo, hoping to wheedle the Qing government into helping them realize their own ambitions. Avoiding such commitments was a key principle in Qing foreign relations.

In many cases, foreign interests lay not in trade, but in conquest. Before their defeat, the Junghars had been a major power in Central Asia whose influence radiated far beyond the boundaries of what would become Qing territory. In smashing them, the Qing displayed resources that interested ambitious local power holders, especially those wishing to counter Ahmed Shah. Some overtures for further military adventures were easily ignored, such as those by Niyas Bek, but things became more complicated when the Qing were obligated to the supplicant. This was the case with Badakhshan, which after killing the khwaja brothers repeatedly troubled the court for assistance. Although this was couched as requests for protection against powers who resented Badakhshan's loyalty to Beijing, the Qing court soon realized that Sultan Shah had ambitions of his own. In the 1740s, an earlier ruler of his state had concluded an agreement with the Junghar leader Galdan Tsereng to jointly campaign against the Uzbeks, and it seemed that Sultan Shah now wished to reestablish a similar mutually profitable agreement with the Qing.[68]

Qianlong soon ran out of patience with these overtures. In 1764, Sultan Shah earned a sharp rebuke for suggesting, inter alia, that the Qing take his side in his ongoing struggle with another Qing tributary, Bolor, and grant him military aid against the Afghans. In reply, the emperor showed that he had no illusions about the unsentimental motives that had originally led Badakhshan to hand over the remains of Khwaja-i Jahan, attributing the act to fear of the imperial army and greed for the rebel's possessions. Any disputes with his neighbors were blamed on Sultan Shah's own misdeeds, and he could not expect Qing partiality.[69] When Badakhshan mediated a tribute mission from Bukhara, an equally pragmatic assessment was made by Eldengge, the highest ranking Qing official at Yarkand. By imposing himself as an intermediary, he argued, Sultan Shah was certainly fishing for further rewards, and possibly even trying to intimidate Bukhara by presenting himself as a close agent and associate of the Qing. As for Bukhara itself, it might be responding to news of imperial benevolence, or just scheming to use Qing prestige to ward off attacks by foreign tribes.[70]

Qianlong saw nothing to be gained by getting involved in the fluid and intricate politics of Central Asia. His officials were instructed to concentrate on the security of the Qing frontier itself rather than tracking chimerical rumors abroad. When officials in Kashgar relayed intelligence suggesting that Ahmad Shah might be contemplating an invasion in alliance with Khoqand, the emperor refused to sanction a thorough investigation: "If indeed there is an alliance [by Khoqand] with the Afghans to spy upon conditions in the Muslim Regions [of the Qing empire], it will certainly be difficult to cover up, and, fundamentally, it can be dealt with directly. At present, it is profitless to ponder the matter in advance."[71] If the frontier defense itself was solid, officials could safely ignore labyrinthine intrigues beyond it. When two tributaries quarreled, Qianlong at first acted as a reluctant referee, forcing Badakhshan to call off its invasion of Chitral and Khoqand to relinquish Kirghiz territory.[72] Very quickly, however, he switched to counseling, but not enforcing, peace. Even the imminent destruction of Sultan Shah by the Afghans did not stir the Qing to action. Although the Badakhshi ruler asked for help in 1769 against a reported anti-Qing coalition between Ahmad Shah and the son of Burhan al-Din, Qianlong refused. He monitored the situation in

Badakhshan, but did not intervene to save Sultan Shah from the Afghans.[73] In regard to the Kazakhs, Onuma Takahiro has also identified a pronounced change in Qing policy in the 1770s. Over the course of that decade, in the face of increased importuning for military aid, which began as early as 1767, Qianlong settled on a policy of absolute noninterference in Kazakh affairs. This policy persisted into the following century, and the Qing court made no countermoves as the Kazakh steppe was taken over by Russia.[74]

After the conquest of eastern Turkestan, as Laura Newby has observed, "the Qing authorities in Altishahr quickly concluded that hostility among the various tribes and polities of Central Asia was endemic. . . . They resolutely avoided military intervention and grew increasingly resigned to constant squabbles. . . . The court's concern was only that the status quo should be maintained."[75] This posture reflected a cost-benefit analysis. The Qianlong emperor was aware of the theoretical benefits of using states like Badakhshan in the empire's defense, but also aware that foreign rulers might manipulatively channel Qing power and wealth toward their own ends. Rather than joining a complex system of alliances that defined foreign states as friend and foe, with all the expense, vigilant diplomacy, and constant mobilization this would entail, Qianlong preferred to take a more passive stance, defending his empire on its frontier where the situation was relatively clear and Qing interests manifestly at stake. Provided that foreign powers respected this boundary, he had no desire to supervise their mutual relationships or internal governance. This policy orientation, as we shall see, prevailed on every Qing frontier.

Attempts to Synthesize Knowledge of India in the Qianlong Period

QIANLONG'S PERSONAL UNDERSTANDING OF HINDUSTAN

To guide its military operations and diplomacy, the Qing court conducted vigorous intelligence gathering. Especially in the years immediately after the conquest of Xinjiang, when the surrounding environment was unfamiliar, research extended into India and Central Asia. The fruits of these inquiries, however, bore a regional stamp. Official reports to Beijing about Hindustan relied on the accounts of Muslims in state service, the testimony of merchants or mendicants, and correspondence with foreign rulers. Off-duty geographic inquiries by Qing officials were equally reliant on reports by foreign merchants and travelers, mostly Muslim. In both cases, the terms used by these sources to describe India's geography and political players were virtually unknown elsewhere in the empire.

In the context of "operational geography," research intended to guide policy in a local theater, regionally inflected reports could be accepted on their own terms without further analysis. From the standpoint of scholarly geography, however, novel accounts of "Hindustan" raised questions about how to incorporate it into established frameworks. This line of inquiry was one strand in a much larger project at the court. From the earliest stages of his conquest of the Junghars, the Qianlong emperor had been eager to analyze the historical geography of his new possessions, determining the ancient names of contemporary sites and thus comparing his own conquests (favorably) with those of his predecessors on the throne of China. To do so, he undertook a polyglot version of the standard mode of analysis in Chinese historical geography: yan'ge, the construction of an historical sequence of names for a given place. That is, he sought to translate the local usage outlined in operational documents into a geographic language consonant with other strands of scholarship, whether standard Chinese histories, Buddhist sutras, or famous travel accounts. Within this analytical framework, "Hindustan" and its tantalizing connection to "India" proved a riddle that for decades attracted imperial interest.

A name originating in Persian geography, "Hindustan" had two broad meanings in the eighteenth century: it could refer either to all of India, or more commonly to India north of the Deccan and excluding Bengal. Politically, it was a name for the Mughal empire.[76] Within the Qing empire before 1758 it occurred only rarely, in some Chinese Islamic and Jesuit writings. In present terms, we can define the "Hindustan" mentioned in Qing documents from Xinjiang as referring to the territories of northern India that were then, or had recently been, ruled from Delhi by the Mughal emperor, with the Punjab being particularly prominent. This explanation would not have been intelligible to Qianlong, for whom the "Mughal empire" was unfamiliar by that or any other name. For him, the meaning of "Hindustan" had to be analyzed with reference to three distinct fields of knowledge at his disposal. First, he was aware of India as it was depicted in the Buddhist scholarship pursued at his court. The names Qianlong used for this Buddhist India, as found in a 1758 tetraglot preface to a collection of revised dharani, were "Enetkek" in the Manchu text, "Enedkeg" in the Mongolian, "Rgya-gar" in the Tibetan, and in Chinese various synonyms including "Yindu" and "Qianzhu."[77] Second, Qianlong knew of India as it was outlined in Chinese and Mongol historical geography, fields that played a prominent role in court scholarship designed to analyze his new conquests. Finally, he had access to a large pool of raw military intelligence about the lands to the west of his empire.

The chief difficulty in reconciling these three approaches to Indian geography, which Qianlong seems not to have fully appreciated, lay in relating Muslim Hindustan to Buddhist Tianzhu. Apart from Muslim-authored geographies in Chinese, which had limited circulation, no Chinese source indicated that Central India—the place of the Buddha's enlightenment and the most sacred territory of Indian Buddhism—had fallen under Muslim rule. Qianlong was aware that Buddhism no longer flourished in India, but evidently did not know that Muslim rulers held sway over its place of origin. His geographic writings were therefore colored by a presumed separation between Muslim and formerly Buddhist territory. This was not simply a scholarly matter, but also had obvious political implications: most preceding dynasties had reported receiving Indian envoys at their courts, and both the Mongols and the Ming had projected their military power to India itself. For a ruler like Qianlong who wished to compare his own power with that of earlier dynasties, spinning his own contact with India (or the lack thereof) could burnish the glory of his rule.

These two issues were foremost in Qianlong's mind when in 1768 he composed an essay setting forth his views on the historical and contemporary geography of India, "An Examination into Mistakes Concerning India" ("Tianzhu wu Yindu kao'e").[78] Classified as an "examination" (*kao*), this was in Qianlong's view a work of serious evidential scholarship that drew on his polyglot learning for information to correct errors in the historical record. As such, it offers a lucid explanation of how the emperor synthesized and reconciled the scholarship and strategic intelligence concerning India assembled in the early decades of his reign.

Qianlong began with Buddhist cosmology, pointing out that "[according to] the Buddhist canon, Mt. Sumeru is the center of this realm of desire; on its four sides there are four continents, and that on the south is Jambudvipa." Jambudvipa, in his view, could be divided into three "Great Countries" (*da guo*) ranged around Kunlun: China, India (Tianzhu), and the Ottoman empire (Honghuo'er).[79] India was further divided into regions, the so-called "five Indias" (*wu Yindu*). It could also be called Enetkek, a word Qianlong believed to derive from the Tibetan, but as noted above was in fact borrowed from Mongolian.[80] Later in the essay Qianlong advanced the (incorrect) hypothesis that the word ultimately derived from E're'nang, the name of a small country once visited by a Song pilgrim.

Qianlong believed that Enetkek, or India, was located south of Hindustan. Thus his geographical theories were based from the outset on the idea that India and Hindustan were two separate entities. India, the emperor acknowledged, was no longer an important Buddhist country. In his essay on India he pointed out that, "Since East India is near Tibet, therefore Tibet from time to time hears of Indian affairs. According to Tibetan monks, although India is the land where the Buddha became manifest and preached the Dharma, yet in fact India does not today cause the Buddhist Law to flourish, but rather a heterodox teaching (*yijiao*)." Although the nature of the Buddhist collapse in India is not specified, it is clear that in the emperor's mind India continued to exist as a coherent geographic entity, no longer vigorously Buddhist but certainly distinct from Muslim Hindustan. Qianlong was willing to admit that his posited boundary between Hindustan and North India represented something of a fluid cultural frontier. He remarked, "Although Hindustan is a Muslim land, yet according to what is transmitted by Muslims, it contains Buddhist remnants (*Fo yiji*). Thus, still more [clearly] do we know that it either borders with North India, or was formerly subject to India and later subject to the Muslim Regions." However, Qianlong did not make the leap to concluding that Hindustan, although now under Muslim rule, contained territory that was once the heartland of Buddhism.

Philologically, Qianlong acknowledged a phonetic link between the names Hindustan and India, but nonetheless maintained they were two different places. As he observed, "Wendusitan is now called Hendusitan in Tibet and the Muslim language [i.e., Chaghatai Turki]. Probably, transliterators distorted the sound *hen* into *wen*. Now, these two words are similar in sound to Yindu. This is further evidence that North India is near Hindustan." He added that there was little point in quibbling over the accuracy of *hen, wen, yin*, or *shen*, since these were "not the original Indian sounds."

If Hindustan was not India, then Qianlong faced a political challenge. He acknowledged the awkward fact that "since ancient times, the prestige and moral force of China (Zhonghua) has never been greater than in the present dynasty, yet in over a century India has never dispatched an envoy to pay tribute." Qianlong dismissed envoys from Utg'ali Bargišuwara Khan (probably the ruler of Khurda in Orissa) as representing "East India, merely a small state near our Tibet—not Central India."[81] The *Da Qing yitong zhi* stated that Yuan Taizu (Chinggis Khan) had reached East India, and the

Ming Yongle emperor had received tribute from it.[82] By dismissing his own envoy from East India as insignificant, Qianlong was implicitly denigrating the achievements of his predecessors—they too had not had contact with the core of Central India. Qianlong went further in questioning the achievements of his predecessors. Records of Indians paying tribute found in the histories of the Tang and Song periods were largely false, he claimed. The main target of his skepticism, however, was Chinggis Khan's supposed journey to India. First, Qianlong bluntly observed: "the *Yuan shi* states that Yuan Taizu saw *jiaoduan* [mythic beasts] in India. I suspect this was also the border between North India and the Muslim Regions in today's Hindustan, not Central India." His second observation cited the *Menggu yuanliu* (the Chinese name for the Mongolian chronicle *Erdeni-yin tobči*) as recording that "Yuan Taizu advanced his army to Enetkek, where he encountered three one-horned beasts that seemed to be kowtowing. Yuan Taizu said, 'This seems to be Heaven showing me that from here to the Woqi'ertu suolin [Mong., *očirtu sayurin*] the way is far and most difficult.' He then brought back his army." Qianlong noted that "Woqi'ertu suolin is Mongol for the Vajra Throne [in Bodh Gaya], that is to say Central India where the Buddha became manifest and preached the Dharma," further proof that Chinggis Khan had never reached that region. Qianlong simply ignored embassies to India from Yongle, even though the *Ming shi* identified Jaunpur, reached by his envoys, as Central India.

Qianlong was equally careful to justify his own lack of contact with India. He immodestly observed that "with the strength of China (Zhongguo) today, what difficulty would there be in taking passage through the Pamirs and Kashmir to reach Central India, like the Tang and Song? But since this is not the perfection of virtue, supposing I were to scheme further to reach this end, even if I attracted people from far-off lands, what connection would this have to true government? Therefore I have not done this." That is, direct contact with Central India would be superficially glorious but contribute nothing substantial to his rule. The presence of Afghan forces in Hindustan passed unmentioned.

Qianlong used an enormous breadth of evidence in his scholarship, drawing upon Buddhist scriptures, Chinese official histories and pilgrimage accounts, Mongol chronicles, news reported by Tibetan monks, and the latest intelligence from newly conquered Xinjiang. Polyglot sources, coupled with his own inclinations, led him to dwell on questions of etymology, transliteration, and translation. Yet the sources and arguments he omits are equally telling. Completely ignored were the voyages of Zheng He, information contained in Jesuit writings and world maps such as the *Kunyu quantu*, and the coastal perspective outlined by Chen Lunjiong. Qianlong does not seem to have realized that as a polity Hindustan was present on European world maps in his possession under the name Mowo'er. Overall, Qianlong's scholarship reveals an overwhelming interest in the Western Regions and Mongol, Tibetan, and Muslim sources at the expense of other materials. Jesuit and maritime sources were preserved in the *Siku quanshu* manuscript library, but it was Inner Asian–oriented scholarship that guided Qianlong's scholarly outlook.

In addition to his research essay, Qianlong's delight in "Hindustani jade" (*Hendusitan yu*) led him to produce numerous poems that illustrate his evolving geographic views. "Hindustani jade" was transported from the Kunlun mountains southward into India, fashioned into objects in the Mughal style, and exported back to China via Xinjiang.[83] Qianlong had a clear idea of its origin and mode of import, remarking in one note: "Hindustan is even further to the southwest of Badakhshan, and since the Muslim Regions were pacified in the *jimao* year [1759], merchants from that place have from time to time brought jade objects to sell on the Muslim Frontier (Huijiang), and then at intervals these have been purchased and submitted to court; probably this is something that did not exist forty years ago." He had a special fondness for its intricate carving and the extreme thinness of its objects, and praised the quality of its workmanship: "Hindustan jade-workers use water polishing to treat the jade. This saves work, yet the manufacture is delicate and marvelous, far beyond the reach of jade craftsmen of Suzhou."[84] Altogether he composed seventy-four poems describing its beauty. Fortunately for the historian, if not the connoisseur of verse, Qianlong's poems often alluded to his geographic or historical theories and included footnotes to explicate his meaning. Using them, it is possible to track his evolving opinions.

Qianlong first referred to "Hindustan jade" in a poem dated to 1768, at the same time as his kaozheng essay concerning India, and his odes show how his view of this toponym evolved. The conceits he played with in his writing exacerbated contradictions in the original essay. As we have seen, he clearly distinguished Hindustan from India. At the same time, he argued that the initial sound of the word Hindustan, in his opinion best rendered with the character *hen*, had in the past also been variously rendered by *wen*, *yin*, and *shen*. In other words, Qianlong believed that "Hendu" was simply another and more correct way of saying "Yindu." This is significant because in Qianlong's poetry he reserved the cumbersome full name "Hendusitan" for his titles, invariably abbreviating it for prosodic reasons to "Hendu" in the text of the poem itself. His use of the term "Hendu" in poetry led him to elaborate on his phonetic theory. A poem of 1778 included the line "The pronunciation of 'Yindu' differs in each dialect" (*fangyan Yindu yin ge shu*), appended to which is the note: "'Hendu' is a phonetic variant of 'Yindu'" (*Hendu ji Yindu zhi zhuanyin*). In a slightly later note he gave this insight a more extreme form, suggesting that "Hendu" was the original sound from which "Yindu" derived: "'Yindu' in Chinese is a transliteration of the two characters 'Hendu'; it has long been fixed in this form."[85] This notion is probably a logical extension of his opinion that "Hendusitan" was in fact a Sanskrit (*Fanwen*) word. How he acquired this opinion is uncertain, but a Tibetan informant seems probable, since a Tibetan traveler to India in 1752 was using "Hen du" to refer to non-Muslim Indians he believed to be Buddhist.[86] Qianlong's comment seems to be implicitly one-upping another eminent scholar of Sanskrit-Chinese equivalence, the Tang monk Xuanzang, who had asserted that "Yindu" (not "Hendu") was the most accurate Chinese phonetic equivalent to the Sanskrit term for India.

Qianlong's phonological dabbling had important geographic implications, for if "Hendusitan" could be abbreviated to "Hendu," and if "Hendu" was a variant of "Yindu," then might not Hindustan actually be India itself? There are hints in his poetry that Qianlong was tending toward this view, for at least twice he used the name "Yindu" in reference to a piece of jade that the title refers to as Hindustani. In one line he remarks: "The unworked jade is harbored in the Kunlun Mountains, for carving it is transmitted to India (Yindu)," and in a second he writes "In India (Yindu), skilled workers are numerous" (*Yindu lianggong huo*). In exercising poetic license, Qianlong had already blurred nearly to extinction the line between Hindustan and India that was clearly outlined in his earlier essay. As we shall see, new intelligence near the end of his reign would lead him to reverse his opinion and come to view Hindustan and India as one and the same place.[87]

THE INFLUENCE OF QIANLONG ON THE CONTENT OF COURT SCHOLARSHIP

Although Qianlong had a vantage on the world unparalleled in the empire, he cannot stand for the empire. We must now move outward by degrees from the imperial person and examine the views of India offered elsewhere, beginning with the scholarly projects that Qianlong sponsored but did not author.

In 1772, Qianlong initiated the compilation of the *Siku quanshu*, intended as a manuscript collection containing all important writings in the four major genres recognized by Chinese bibliographers (classics, histories, philosophical masters, and collected writings), including new court-sponsored works. Naturally, Qianlong exercised great influence over this project. All who worked on it were sensitive to his wishes, and he reviewed and corrected the writings of his compilers. However, gathering and evaluating a multitude of works composed over millennia made it impossible for a single viewpoint to assert itself to the exclusion of others. As R. Kent Guy has observed, the compilation of the *Siku quanshu* was "above all an exercise in coordination and compromise" by the court and scholarly community.[88] Here we will examine three cases involving Hindustan to determine the influence of Qianlong's personal scholarly judgments on works included in the *Siku quanshu* and the limits of his influence.

The most obvious and successful manifestation of Qianlong's influence on the *Siku quanshu* project was its standardization of place-names.[89] This was intended to span the entire historical record, and the "corrected" toponyms generated by the multilingual philology of the court were retrospectively inserted into the Liao, Jin, Yuan, and Ming official histories and many other titles. Qianlong's decision that "Hendusitan" rather than "Wendusitan" was the proper transcription of the place-name formed part of this standardization. In the second edition of the *Da Qing yitong zhi* the entry for "Hindustan" states, "In the past it was called Wendusitan. Now, examining the Sanskrit, it has been corrected to Hendusitan."[90] Another Qianlong court work was more specific, observing that it was properly written in Chinese as *Hendusitan* (痕都斯坦), the small *si* indicating that it was not to be read as a full syllable. Qianlong's specially formulated three-character-compound syllables were written alongside.[91] "Hendusitan" was used consistently throughout the *Siku quanshu*, for instance replacing all older transliterations such as Xindusi, Xundusi, and Xindu in the *Yuan shi*.[92]

Beyond the mechanical replacement of one set of names with another, the chains of reasoning involved become more complex and evidence of the successful percolation of Qianlong's ideas through the project becomes more equivocal. Reconstructions of historical geography fit together in interlocking patterns, so that a judgment on one point had ramifications for many others. When a new element was introduced it was very difficult to adjust all existing sources to fit, even within so centralized a project as the *Siku quanshu*. We can see this by examining how one mid-ranking editor, Fang

Wei, sought to apply Qianlong's ideas. Fang was assigned to the cohort making "evidentiary evaluations" (kaozheng) on the biographies of the famous eunuch-admirals Zheng He and Hou Xian in the *Ming shi*. He began with the observation, "Your servant Fang Wei notes that in regard to the names of the Five Indias, recorded in books from the Ming and earlier, there developed differing accounts due to hearsay transmission. It was not possible to examine them in detail." Fang then described how he had read Qianlong's essay about India, and summarized the emperor's theory that it was reached overland, through the Pamirs and Hindustan. He continued, obsequiously, "the imperial instruction and analysis is sufficient to smash the errors transmitted over a thousand years. This biography states: 'The [Yongle] Emperor wished to make contact with Bengal and other countries, and once more ordered Hou Xian to command a fleet of ships to make the journey. This country [i.e., Bengal] is East India.' It also states: 'West of Bengal there is a country called Jaunpur. Its territory is located within the Five Indias, and is the ancient Country of the Buddha.'" Fang then added his own critical observation, "Since Hou was leading a fleet of ships he could not reach the territory of the Five Indias. The text below also states that he traveled comprehensively throughout Tibet and other countries and returned. This also contradicts what is recorded above."[93] Fang apparently believed that because India was reached overland via Xinjiang, a Ming official could not have reached it by sea.

Presumably Fang intended to flatter Qianlong by valuing his revisionist insights above the authority of the Ming historical record and by casting doubt on the claim (already studiously ignored by the emperor) that a Ming envoy had reached Central India. There is also no way to know whether Qianlong reviewed and approved Fang's judgments, or whether this statement simply passed unnoticed. Yet even if Qianlong approved this note, the claim seems to have reflected Fang's own personal judgment rather than a systematic campaign to enforce Qianlong's conclusions on the *Ming shi*. The geographical account of Jaunpur itself, in a different volume, contained no similar denial that it was Central India, nor did the kaozheng review of that account composed by one of Fang's colleagues. Statements that Jaunpur was Central India contained in other works included in the *Siku quanshu*, for example the *Da Qing yitong zhi*, likewise passed uncontested. The description of Faxian's famous return from India by sea aroused no skepticism from the editors of the *Siku quanshu zongmu*, although they were quick to identify other problematic points in the work (see Chapter One).

The historical identity of Hindustan was another problem. If it was not India, then with what earlier state was it to be identified? This difficulty was taken up in the *Huangyu Xiyu tuzhi* (Illustrated Gazetteer of the Western Regions in the Imperial Domain), a gazetteer intended to match the geography of the contemporary Western Regions to the Chinese historical record, using the yan'ge method of establishing the succession of names dynasty by dynasty. To this end, chronological tables were added to the work. According to these, Hindustan in the Western Han and Tang periods was not India, but Jibin.[94] The rationale for this identification derived from Qianlong's determination that Hindustan was not India, but its neighbor: "The *Tang shu* stated that Jibin was located south of the Pamirs, neighboring India. It guided Tang envoys to reach India, so it may be known that this country was on the border of India." The author of this entry then justified his conclusion by citing Qianlong's assertion that Hindustan neighbors India.[95] Similar reasoning appeared in other texts. The *Da Qing yitong zhi* was even more emphatic in making the connection: "The *Tang shu* also says that Jibin is south of the Pamirs and neighbors Tianzhu. Today, Hindustan neighbors Yindu. Yindu is Tianzhu. Thus, Jibin is Hindustan without doubt."[96] In this instance, Qianlong's conclusions were accepted unquestioningly by those composing reference books to be inserted into the *Siku quanshu* project, and the imperial perspective had a direct impact on historical geography.

However, the view that Hindustan was Jibin was not universal. It will be recalled that Qianlong's own essay quoted by Fang Wei had nothing to say about the location of Jibin, and the idea that Jibin was Hindustan was extrapolated by scholars working on the *Xiyu tuzhi* and other works. Thus, when Fang Wei wrote the kaozheng evaluation of the entry for Samarkand in the *Ming shi* he allowed the statement that Samarkand was called Jibin in the Han and Tang to pass without comment, even though it was elsewhere identified with Hindustan.[97] Ultimately, it was impossible to adequately supervise all the speculation involved in the sprawling *Siku quanshu* project and ensure complete consistency in every detail.

In short, insights from Qianlong's personal scholarship influenced the committees of scholars composing or reviewing works for inclusion in the *Siku quanshu*. In this sense, the vast compilation project was a vehicle for reproducing and amplifying imperial opinions. However, the implications of Qianlong's writings were interpreted differently by different editors, leading to conflicting judgments even within the manuscript collection itself.

Aiming to remove inconsistencies and integrate various sources, Qianlong inadvertently introduced new puzzles and discrepancies. That this should be true for a work compiled under tight bureaucratic control by a centralized scholarly apparatus closely supervised by an emperor obsessed with standardization gives some indication of the difficulties involved in homogenizing the entire discourse on geography and geopolitics within the empire.

THE INFLUENCE OF QIANLONG'S SCHOLARLY THEORIES BEYOND THE COURT

To what extent did Qianlong's new style of polyglot scholarship, his concern for philological correctness, and his specific judgments influence the geographic understandings of Qing subjects? Both during Qianlong's lifetime and in subsequent decades, the influence of his integrated geographic worldview was surprisingly limited. Despite his monumental projects, his opinions did not evolve into a consensus among the empire's scholars. There were two major reasons for this, both involving access. One was access to the results of court scholarship. The editors at the court were a tiny and elite fragment of the empire's community of scholars. Although they were sensitive to imperial whims, the works they produced did not circulate widely. Some were printed, but these were circulated chiefly among provincial yamens and well-connected bibliophiles. The *Siku quanshu* manuscript collection, the only available source for certain titles that were not printed, was available within China only in Beijing, Shengjing, Jehol, and in three cities in the Yangzi delta, Yangzhou, Hangzhou, and Zhenjiang. Copies in the Yangzi region were not completely installed until 1790, close to the end of Qianlong's reign.[98]

A second reason involved the accessibility and intelligibility of the techniques and ideas animating Qianlong's scholarship. Particularly in the fields of historical geography and phonology, Qianlong relied heavily on his own polyglot erudition and displayed an uncompromising concern for "correctness" at the expense of all other considerations. Court writings were not user friendly. For someone who did not know Manchu, let alone Tibetan or Mongolian, the emperor's phonological arguments, to say nothing of his cumbersome "tripartite formation" (*sanhe*) system for expressing foreign syllables, would have been difficult to grasp. If this scholarship was hard to fathom outside of its court context, it was impossible to replicate. Only at court could Tibetan, Mongolian, European, Manchu, and Chinese scholars be brought together in a single working environment. Even wealthy and accomplished scholars in other centers of the empire could not have hoped to reproduce similar conditions. Like a flower that could only grow in the artificial ecology of a greenhouse, historical geographic research involving five languages and six scripts could survive only in Beijing, and even there only with vigorous imperial patronage.

An illustrative counterpoint to Qianlong court scholarship is the *Yiyu suotan* (commonly called the *Xiyu wenjian lu*) prepared by Cišii. By imperial standards this was a frivolous work, providing virtually no worthwhile philological or historical geographic commentary, and relying chiefly on hearsay rather than kaozheng textual studies. Most obviously in its naming conventions, where it used "Wendusitan" instead of "Hendusitan," but also in its method and spirit, it was untouched by the scholarly aims of the Qing state. Nonetheless, it circulated in numerous manuscript and print editions, even finding an audience among the elite editors of Qianlong's court. Its circulation did not diminish in the nineteenth century, and one modern reference work lists 17 different titles for the entire work or excerpts, with an even larger number of individual editions.[99] As we shall see, "Wendusitan" remained a far more popular and influential name for Hindustan than Qianlong's candidate, "Hendusitan," even though the latter was promoted with all the resources of the imperial state. Ultimately, although Qianlong's personal writings and those he sponsored remained familiar and influential geographic works in their own day and in the following century, they never formed more than one strand in the empire's geographic debates.

Conclusion

From the standpoint of geographic knowledge, the Qianlong emperor's two great achievements worked at cross purposes: his military campaigns piled up reams of new geographic and geopolitical data, which his scholarly campaigns sought to digest and synthesize. This was not an equal contest, and at the end of his reign the empire contained more conflicting ideas about Indian politics and geography than it had when he took the throne in 1735. Although in part this reflected the unevenness and idiosyncrasies of court-sponsored research, the main cause lay in the structure of the empire's approach to external affairs and foreign intelligence.

One consequence of the military operations of the Qianlong reign was the need to master quickly the geography and politics of regions that had hitherto been little known. Each campaign demanded the immediate elucidation of conditions along the relevant portion of the empire's frontier. Here the Qing state relied almost entirely on local informants: indigenous elites given new ranks and co-opted into service, knowledgeable subjects who could be questioned by military officers, or merchants and others arriving from abroad. To inquiries about the outside world, replies were formulated according to regional conditions, reflecting not simply local languages, cultures, and religions, but the trade routes and political contacts running beyond the empire's borders.

For several reasons, evident in the case of Hindustan, such information proved difficult to reconcile with other strands of geographic knowledge. In warfare and diplomacy, Hindustan was most relevant for southern Xinjiang, and less so for Tibet, let alone more distant regions. In the Qing bureaucracy, it was pertinent only for the axis linking the Grand Council in Beijing to Yarkand and Kashgar. This absence of multi-frontier coordination was compounded by the basic principles of Qing strategic thought and the seriality of frontier crises. Because of the emperor's reluctance to contemplate long-distance alliances or maneuvers, there were few compelling practical uses for a fuller knowledge of conditions in Hindustan: whatever happened there seemed unlikely to affect Qing security. As new problems on the frontier emerged, first in Burma and then elsewhere, the court became even more committed to preserving the status quo, diverting its intelligence and military resources—and finite imperial attention—to a site of greater danger.

This does not mean Qing geographers were satisfied with so fragmented a view. To the contrary, they appreciated that although terms like "Hindustan" were unfamiliar in the forms used in Xinjiang, they were nonetheless connected to, if not identical with, older terminology from Buddhist or historical sources. Although this was an academic rather than strategic problem, it was tackled vigorously. Compared to the historical and geographic productions of earlier reigns, for instance the encyclopedic *Gujin tushu jicheng*, those of the Qianlong court were far more synthesized. For the first time evidence from languages other than Chinese was widely exploited in official geographic compendia, and the emperor's confidence in his own opinions reduced the caution and evasive ambiguity in earlier official reference works. Qianlong believed he had solved most of the riddles in this new intelligence, and his theories were duly incorporated into court works.

Even in court scholarship, however, the synthesis was at best partial. Certain languages and cultures captured imperial interest, others did not. Russian and Korean received very little attention, European and Southeast

Asian languages virtually none at all. This was for a lack of interest, not of experts: early in his reign Qianlong was presented with a manuscript entitled *Huayi yiyu*, which gave categorized translations into Chinese of words in English, French, German, Latin, Portuguese, Italian, Burmese, Sanskrit (*Xitian*), Tibetan, and many others.[100] The emperor would have found no shortage of potential guides to these languages and cultures, but they interested him much less than Inner Asia. Even in regard to India, he neglected pertinent information from Jesuit writings, Chen Lunjiong, and even the *Ming shi*, sources he certainly knew about. Not only did Qianlong's synthesizing aims produce only partial results, but even within the carefully organized *Siku quanshu* project attempts to enforce his judgments generated new contradictions. More importantly, the emperor did not have a monopoly on the description of Hindustan. Many scholars, even at court, were probably more familiar with Cišii's account than Qianlong's. For all of these reasons, the overall effect of the scholarship of the Qianlong reign was to increase rather than reduce the variety and complexity of the empire's data on India, spreading new information without decisively solving older puzzles.

In short, despite the skillful intelligence gathering and great scholarly accomplishments of the Qianlong period, there was no revolution in the empire's views of India. Geographic scholarship was still dominated by incommensurable outlooks emerging from different regional or intellectual environments. The adequacy of geographic scholarship in the Qianlong period cannot be judged in absolute terms, but only in light of the standards and aspirations of Qing strategists and geographers themselves. From this perspective, the crucial issue is the degree to which they confronted questions that their methodologies of investigation could not easily solve. The emergence of such intractable questions depended in turn on the degree to which external events were becoming coordinated across multiple frontiers and could only be sorted out by a more integrated and panoramic worldview. Above all, it was the British conquest of India, commencing in 1757, that established these conditions. By the end of the Qianlong period, as we shall see, an even more integrated understanding of the lands surrounding the empire was beginning to appear necessary.

THREE

Mapping India

Geographic Agnosticism in a Cartographic Context

Operational documents and textual scholarship were not the only formats in which the Qing court analyzed and organized intelligence gathered during the conquest of Xinjiang. Elsewhere in the capital a largely separate staff was at work under imperial orders to expand an enormous map, begun during the previous Kangxi and Yongzheng reigns, to chart not only newly conquered Qing territory but also Arabia, Persia, and India. Where archives and libraries offered the Qing court many diverging accounts of India, this map presented a single, detailed picture. Moreover, its graticule of longitude and latitude was compatible with the European-style world maps imported or prepared locally by Jesuits. This giant map carried the emperor's personal endorsement in the form of a preface and was distributed by the palace press. How we understand its preparation and reception therefore affects how we interpret all geographic research in the Qing period. Did it remain simply one among many competing versions of Indian geography, or gain unique authority in shaping how Qianlong and his subjects saw the world? Had the empire's segmented geographic understandings, at least for the court elite, been harmonized definitively in one brilliant synthesis?

Cartography has dominated Western research into Qing-era geographic scholarship and the surveying behind these court maps has dominated the study of Qing cartography. Research into court-sponsored mapping has concentrated on two historiographical debates: over the relationship between "scientific" and "traditional" cartography, and over that between mapping and empire-building. Rather than reopen these questions directly, the present chapter will approach them obliquely by addressing two neglected ones. First, how and why did these court survey maps come to include India? Qianlong famously commanded Qing technicians and court Jesuits to map his newly conquered territories in Xinjiang, but most territory added to the map lay outside Qing frontiers, beyond the reach of his survey parties. This chapter reconstructs the sources of information and cartographic methods that allowed a rendering of northern India.

A second question concerns the map's reception by the emperor himself, his high ministers, and officials and subjects without privileged access. Before and after the completion of this map, many other cartographic conceptions of the world circulated in China. This reflected the geographic agnosticism of Chinese scholars, who believed that no claim to have captured the world's true image had unrivaled authority. Did the official survey map signal an end to geographic agnosticism at court and, if so, was this judgment accepted by the empire's scholarly readership?

Although the historical record does not yet permit unequivocal answers, this chapter argues that geographic agnosticism influenced the creation and reception of the court survey map. In the Qing period, Chapter One argued, there was an epistemological rupture between domestic territory, which could be directly examined by trusted informants, and foreign lands, which could not. This distinction applied likewise to court cartography. For lands ruled by the Qing empire, imperial survey maps were widely acknowledged as a benchmark of geographic accuracy. For lands beyond, however, maps had to be patched together piecemeal from a variety of elements, particularly reports by local informants and maps from Europe. As we shall see, the findings of Western cartography were relegated to the lowest rung of authority, used *faute de mieux* for lands not described elsewhere. Furthermore, whereas Qianlong endorsed the results of the survey of his own territory and tried to make older palace maps conform to them, he tolerated diverging cartographic representations of the outside world. Under Qianlong, in regard to India and other non-Qing territory, the court survey map remained only one among many competing authorities.

To avoid ambiguity in the following pages, the editions of the map produced within the precincts of the palace on imperial orders and plotted on a graticule of latitude and longitude are here termed "court survey maps," although as we shall see much of their content was drawn from sources other than surveys. A word must also be said on the challenges of studying Qing cartography. At present scholars can consult many (though not all) of the finished court survey maps, but access to what survives of the materials on which they were based—survey drafts made in the field, ad hoc military maps sketched by Qing generals, European world maps possessed by the palace—is restricted. Compounding this difficulty, the agencies working on these maps, and the individual scholars employed there for their technical skill, have left a much scantier documentary legacy than their counterparts working in other fields of Qing geography. Much work remains to be done, and revisions of the findings presented here will likely become necessary as new evidence comes to light, but I believe the preponderance of evidence supports the conclusions outlined below.

The Kangxi and Yongzheng Period Court Surveys

Before Qianlong's court survey maps depicted northern India, his grandfather Kangxi and father, Yongzheng, had supervised the creation of several earlier editions that had not. These earlier maps do not directly concern us, but a short review of their origins, methods, and personnel is indispensible for interpreting official cartography in the Qianlong period. In particular, it is necessary to clarify the transition from the Kangxi map, which included very little territory not actually surveyed, to the Yongzheng map, which depicted vast swathes of land beyond the scope of direct observation. This change helps explain how elements from European world maps came to be used in official surveys.

In the second half of his reign, the Kangxi emperor sponsored a survey of his realm using mathematical and astronomical principles introduced to him by Jesuit missionaries in Qing service, a decision reflecting administrative needs and his informed confidence in European cartography.[1] By 1692, Kangxi had received rigorous lessons in mathematics and astronomy from French Jesuits, and came to believe that advances in these fields would allow maps of unprecedented precision.[2] Jesuit technical expertise, however, was carefully scrutinized by the emperor, who launched a survey of his entire realm only after comparing his own firsthand knowledge with the results of limited trials. Even then, the resulting map was restricted to areas where Qing officials could personally verify the accuracy of the results.[3]

Kangxi also maximized control over the project by training Qing subjects to cooperate in surveying work, establishing palace schools that did not rely on Jesuit teachers, and even personally instructing some promising young scholars like He Guozong (d. 1766) and Mingghatu.[4] These measures, as Catherine Jami has noted, were designed to insulate Qing students from direct intellectual exchange with Jesuits outside imperial supervision.[5] In certain places, as in Tibet, staff from these institutions conducted surveys independent of Jesuits. In the following decades mapping remained among the duties of court specialists in mathematics and astronomy, alongside calendar-making and writing compendia on natural science.

For Kangxi and his officials, then, the court survey map remained completely separate from the European world maps proffered by the Jesuits, even though both types were technically compatible. This outlook contrasted with that of the French Jesuits who played a predominant role in Kangxi's surveys, for whom mapping the Qing realm was only one facet of a larger Paris-based project to create a new and more accurate map the world.[6] Kangxi was aware that the cartographic principles he now endorsed were claimed by the Jesuits to make European world maps uniquely comprehensive and precise. Specimens of such maps entered his hands, first those prepared by Verbiest early in his reign, and later samples printed in Paris. Chinese notes were pasted onto those of French origin, and some were redrawn in Chinese and Manchu versions.[7] Chen Lunjiong reported that Kangxi consulted European-style maps when discussing world affairs (see Chapter One). Nonetheless, the emperor limited official survey maps to his own lands; nothing was included solely on the strength of unverified European maps. Kangxi did not trust the Jesuits implicitly, and distinguished their unverifiable worldviews from his own empirically tested surveys that could legitimately receive imperial endorsement. Still, even the first Kangxi maps did not rely entirely on surveying. Within China, Jesuits and their Qing partners turned to local informants for essential information.[8] In places where Beijing's control was not absolute, notably parts of Tibet, Korea, and the territories of the Junghar Mongols, a few survey readings were combined with data from informants and older maps.[9] The 641 points actually fixed by surveying formed a spatial skeleton on which a large corpus of data from existing records and other geographic materials took shape.[10]

On the basis of draft maps sent in from the field, maps of the whole empire were prepared in Beijing. A woodblock atlas (formed from 28 component maps) was made in 1717 and presented to the emperor in 1718 under the title *Huangyu quanlan tu*. Fr. Matteo Ripa also made an early copperplate test map in 1717, divided into horizontal strips (*paitu*). In 1719 a new manuscript version (32 sheets) was completed, which was printed in a copperplate edition (47 plates) by Ripa under the title *Yuqin Da Qing yitong quantu*. In 1721 a "definitive" woodblock edition was made in 32 plates, an emendation of the 1719 edition.[11]

In contrast to the attention lavished on the Kangxi-era survey maps, their Yongzheng successors have largely been overlooked. Yet for present purposes the second generation of court survey maps is more significant, for these began to extend beyond the Qing empire itself. By the 1720s, strategic planning required a clear picture of the Junghar homeland and its neighbors. Since Beijing could not dispatch surveyors to these lands, another approach was found. The first 1717 edition of the Kangxi survey had already included a chart entitled "Map of [the territory of] Tsewang Araptan" (*Zawang A'erbutan tu*), while the 1719 strip-format map reached beyond Kashgar to Andijan.[12] In this period there is no evidence that actual surveys were made beyond Hami, nor did these mapped territories lie on the route of the famous embassy to the Volga Torghuts between 1712 and 1715.[13] Presumably, then, the Kangxi survey maps drew intelligence from Mongol informants or Manchu officers—a source employed for later maps as well.[14]

International politics drew Qing interest westward beyond the Junghars. Before his death in 1722, Kangxi had ordered the Jesuits to make a map based on reports about the lands between his territory and the Caspian Sea. On the orders of the Yongzheng court, Frs. Régis (1663–1738) and Fridelli (1673–1743) prepared in 1725 a new map extending to the Caspian based on information from Torghuts in Qing service.[15] That is, the Jesuits continued their role of giving cartographic shape to raw geographic data, only now without the help of direct surveying. In January 1727, during the visit of the Russian envoy Sava Vladislavich, Yongzheng's brother Yin-xiang (1686–1730) interrogated the Jesuits about several Asian kingdoms and viewed a European atlas and maps of Asia, Europe, Africa, and America. He then commissioned a further map of the region between the Amur and the "North" and "East" Seas, giving Fr. Gaubil (1689–1759) and others access to the map made two years earlier by Régis and a German atlas presented by the Russians. Yongzheng soon expanded the project to cover all of Russia up to St. Petersburg; the results were completed in less than a month and later printed.[16] These maps of Russia and Central Asia were stand-alone works. To increase their utility, it was decided to merge them into the court survey maps prepared under Kangxi. Part of the resulting map would be based on actual surveys under Qing supervision, part on the testimony of informants, and part on Western maps and atlases. Research by Yu Fushun and other Chinese scholars has established that during or after the autumn of 1727 a woodblock version of the map was prepared in ten strips.[17] Presumably work began on this version after the Jesuits finished their stand-alone map of Russia and Central Asia at the end of February 1727.[18] Sometime after the seventh month of Yongzheng 7 (July 26–August 23, 1729), an updated version of the official survey map was prepared, first as a colored manuscript designed for military planning against the Junghars, and later as an identical woodblock print edition.[19] Today the first, 1727, version of the map has been reissued in facsimile, but the revised 1729 editions are not available in high resolution.[20]

From its representation of the Caspian Sea, it can be seen that this map was based on the most recent European data. Before Peter the Great commissioned a survey of it in 1715, European, Russian, and Qing maps did not capture that sea's true shape. These Russian findings were printed in 1720, and a copy sent to Paris in 1721.[21] These data may have reached Beijing through the atlas of the German cartographer Johann Homann presented by Sava Vladislavich to Yongzheng.[22] It is also possible that the new depiction of the Caspian was present on a map given to the Qing court by Peter the Great in 1721.[23] It seems most probable, however, that the Jesuits used a "new" map of the Caspian made in Paris by their compatriot and collaborator Guillaume de l'Isle (or Delisle; 1675–1726), which had reached Beijing by November 1725.[24] Whatever European map they used for the rough outline of Eurasia, however, the Jesuits still had to rely heavily on informants when naming and plotting locations in Inner and Central Asia.

Although the enlarged Yongzheng court survey map included Central Asia and all of Russia to the Gulf of Finland and the Black Sea, it excluded the Pamirs, Afghanistan, Persia, and India.[25] Already by the end of the Yongzheng period there were hints that this scope was no longer adequate to the empire's strategic needs. Yin-xiang interviewed Muslims in Beijing, and then questioned Gaubil, including about the routes linking Tibet and the Mughal empire.[26] Because no Indian territory was marked on the survey map, a European work had to be consulted. According to Gaubil, Yin-xiang also noticed with concern the proximity of Yunnan to the Mughal frontier, and wanted better maps of that area.[27] However, his premature death in 1730 temporarily stalled the impetus for extending the Jesuit-Qing mapping efforts. Although the geographic interest of the court was slowly creeping toward Mughal India, it became pronounced only after Qianlong conquered the Tarim Basin.

Genesis of the Qianlong Court Survey Map

Under Qianlong, the Yongzheng-era court map was expanded to cover India, Afghanistan, Persia, and Arabia.[28] In part, this new edition drew on the well-known surveys ordered by the emperor between 1755 and 1759 as a result of his victories over the Junghars and khwajas. In its final form, however, it also used materials from European world maps and local informants in Xinjiang. This section addresses the neglected question of how these elements were woven together into a single cartographic tapestry.

As early as the spring of 1755, even before his initial victory over the Junghar ruler Dawachi, Qianlong was already making preparations to have his new territories surveyed, and by July he had ordered an update of the court survey map.[29] A team, supervised by He Guozong and including Mingghatu and Fude (d. 1776), "two lamas deeply versed in mathematics," and the Portuguese Jesuits Felix da Rocha (1713–1781) and Joseph d'Espinha (1722–1788), departed Beijing in March 1756.[30] It submitted results in November or December of that year. When renewed warfare led to further conquests, a second survey party, including Mingghatu, the two Jesuits, and Deboo (1719–1789) left Beijing in May–June 1759 (QL24/5), and returned with a survey of southern Xinjiang and some of the lands beyond.[31]

Survey maps were not the only maps the court used. During the fighting itself, ad hoc military maps had been prepared, largely on the basis of local informants. On April 4, 1758, Qianlong referred to a map sent in by his general Arigūn based on the testimony of the Qing ally Amin Khwaja and corrected by an informant who had visited the Muslim Regions (Huibu).[32] Qianlong almost certainly had this map in mind when he observed nearly a year later that, "We, by means of consulting a map, see that Khotan is quite near Yarkand." In the same entry he noted, "Again viewing what is arranged on the map, all the region northwest of Kashgar is the pastureland of the Burut [i.e., Kirghiz] and Kazakhs."[33] Twice in June–July 1759 (QL24/6) Qianlong mentioned a map submitted by Fude, then campaigning, and also ordered his generals to "make maps and memorialize them" (*huitu juzou*).

Local informants supplied maps throughout the campaign. Khosh Kopek Beg (Hošik) of Khotan, who had submitted to the Qing in 1759, sketched out for the Qing general Jaohūi the probable flight routes of Khwaja-i Jahan.[34] In the same year a certain Khwaja Sir Beg (Huo-ji-si) presented a map outlining strategic routes.[35] A former Oirat official provided testimony regarding the routes from Qing territory to Badakhshan and Khoqand, on which a map was based.[36] Evidently, these rough maps were cross-checked against each other and oral testimony from other informants.[37] As the postface to the first court catalog of maps in 1761 remarked of the new frontier maps, "At that time we questioned prisoners and asked troops, in order to know the strategic situation and distances to aid in our planning."[38]

How much territory was covered by ad hoc campaign maps before the second survey party began its work late in 1759 cannot now be determined, but there is reason to think that some specimens extended toward Hindustan. In May–June 1759 (QL24/5), just as Mingghatu's party was setting out from Beijing, Qianlong was already in a position to remark that "again looking at the map, the Hindustan route seems to pass through Keriya."[39] As noted above, interest in this route derived from the emperor's anxiety that Khwaja-i Jahan and Burhan al-Din might escape to India. Around the same time, intelligence about the Western Regions and the situation in western Tibet was forthcoming from Qianlong's close clerical confidant the Lcang-skya khutughtu, although it is unclear whether he discussed routes from Yarkand to Hindustan.[40]

These ad hoc military maps were incorporated into the civilian surveys. An entry in the *Qing shi lu* dated to July–August 1759 (QL24/IC6), records Qianlong's orders that Jaohūi and Fude give their maps of Yarkand, Kashgar, and other places, already submitted to the throne, to Mingghatu and Deboo when they reached the Muslim Regions. The surveying party would then make astronomical and other observations and correct the maps.[41] Qianlong's own comments suggest that this occurred, because the completed survey map shows a route connecting Keriya with Hindustan (by way of Yarkand and Afghanistan), a feature Qianlong had already noted on the ad hoc maps. In short, the Jesuits and Qing surveyors were responsible for giving the map its shape by determining the latitude and longitude of certain sites and plotting them on the projection; local informants were responsible for much of the actual content, especially in regions that surveyors could not reach.

When new surveys were launched in 1755 it was already anticipated that European maps would play a role in the finished product. The first survey team was ordered to take along a map termed the *Kunyu quantu* (Complete Map of the Earth), a generic title given to European world maps.⁴² The most famous map of that name was Ferdinand Verbiest's 1674 work, and some scholars have assumed that this was the work consulted.⁴³ However, the same title was also given to the maps of Asia and the world presented to the court by French Jesuits around the turn of the eighteenth century.⁴⁴ Given that Verbiest's map was older and less detailed than other maps available in the palace, it seems unlikely that his was indicated.

In contrast to the informants, ad hoc military maps, and Jesuit world maps, actual survey data had a very limited role, if any, in the way the completed Qianlong court edition depicted non-Qing territory. A later Jesuit account published the coordinates of such places as Tashkent, Margilan, and Andijan, attributing them to the survey of 1759–1760, and this has been taken as evidence that the second surveying mission penetrated far into Central Asia.⁴⁵ In fact, the survey party does not seem to have left Qing-held territory. It set out in June 1759 (QL24/5), and, as Manchu archives now make clear, surveyed only the southern parts of Xinjiang. Reaching Yarkand on December 6 of that year, it viewed Fude's map and "made inquiries of a person knowing the distances to places, did calculations, and drew in such places as Bolor, Badakhshan, Wakhan, and Sariqol."⁴⁶ The crucial word here is *bodombi*, to calculate, which suggests that the team converted the oral report of their informant into locations plotted on the map. A second memorial reveals that this method was applied also to Andijan and Khoqand.⁴⁷ The team left Yarkand on December 14 heading toward Khotan, and was back in Aqsu by January 4, 1760, with the finished map, so there is no possibility that it moved beyond Qing territory. In other words, the research team "surveyed" these Central Asian areas only in the sense that they plotted their location based on the testimony of an informant. There is no evidence that even this imprecise method was used to probe the geography of Hindustan; indeed we do not know if India was included on the draft survey map prepared in Xinjiang and submitted to the court.

When the survey team returned with its draft map of southern Xinjiang and the lands beyond, it had to blend its findings with other material and integrate both into a revised edition of the survey map last updated in the Yongzheng period. To reconstruct this process, the government agencies involved must first be considered. Actual field surveying, as a form of applied mathematics and astronomy, was undertaken largely by the staff of the Directorate of Astronomy (Qintian jian). The leader of the second survey group, Mingghatu, served as its director. Prince Yun-lu (1695–1767), the member of the royal family most closely involved in Qianlong-era cartography, was not formally attached to the directorate, but had been editor-in-chief of the final version of the *Lüli yuanyuan* project, a major astronomical, mathematical, and musical compendia on which He Guozong and Mingghatu had also worked.[48] In short, court cartography was a subfield of employment for specialist officials trained in the late Kangxi period and working together under Yongzheng and Qianlong.

Jesuits worked in the technical core of official mapmaking by taking observations and drafting locations on a mathematical projection. In the Kangxi period, missionaries had dominated mapmaking, presumably training their coworkers from the Qing bureaucracy in the course of their labors. In 1755 most of these trained Qing specialists were still active, but their Jesuit teachers had largely passed away: Jartoux in 1720, Régis in 1738, Parrenin in 1741, Fridelli in 1743, and de Mailla in 1748. Gaubil died in 1759, before the Qianlong map was completed, and was not involved in the work. Under Qianlong, Qing officials requiring help with cartography consulted their Jesuit colleagues in the Directorate of Astronomy, Frs. Kögler (1680–1746) and Pereira (1689–1743) early in the reign, and their successors afterwards. In 1749, this agency had dispatched Frs. Hallerstein and da Rocha to make a map of the Mulan hunting area for Qianlong, an experience that probably determined da Rocha's participation in the two later surveys of Xinjiang.[49] When Qianlong wanted further surveys made in 1755 he naturally turned to his most senior officials with the appropriate experience, He Guozong and Mingghatu. Ordered to take along two Jesuits, they recruited da Rocha and d'Espinha from the Directorate of Astronomy.

How much influence did the Jesuits have over the finished form of the Qianlong survey map? Missionaries continued to supply technical skills that others in the Qing empire could not provide—Qianlong would not have employed them unless this had been the case, and he himself remarked that "Westerners are much more skilled in surveying than domestic personnel."[50] Nonetheless, one scholar has recently claimed, "In the Qianlong period Chinese were in charge, and foreign missionaries were only their assistants," a circumstance attributed to the technical proficiency of available non-European staff.[51] Based on the available documentary record, it appears that Jesuits served in a consulting capacity, brought in as technical advisors for particularly challenging tasks. As proposed in the memorial drafting the parameters of the project, "In regard to points where it is appropriate to work in conjunction with Westerners, we will transmit our inquiry to them and manage it together."[52] What role Jesuits played in day-to-day map drafting remains unclear: Qing documents may downplay the role of European staff; Jesuit accounts certainly do the reverse. However, as we shall see when we turn to examine the finished maps, court Jesuits unquestionably lacked full executive control over their final form.

In addition to the Directorate of Astronomy, other palace and capital agencies were involved in the project. It had an archival dimension, because older specimens of the court survey map from the Kangxi and Yongzheng periods had to serve as the foundation for the new drafts. Some editions were on display in various palaces, but the main archive for maps and their printing blocks was the Map Bureau (Yutu fang), subject to the Imperial Workshop (Zaoban chu) of the Imperial Household Department (Neiwufu), which had been established to store and track the court's large collection of maps and illustrations.[53]

The first concrete step toward preparing a new edition of the court survey map was taken on May 21, 1756, while the initial survey party was still in the field. Orders were passed down to inventory the holdings of the Map Bureau in search of earlier editions. This turned up a set of 47 copperplates (Matteo Ripa's 1719 edition); a set of 32 wooden plates attributed to Jiang Tingxi (presumably either the 1718 or 1721 edition); and a wooden version in 105 sheets.[54] Although officials at the time believed all of these maps to date from the Kangxi period, the map in 105 sheets was actually a Yongzheng-era work.[55] The map in 32 parts was an atlas in which each province and territory received an individual plate (*fentu*), while the other two were integral maps cut into horizontal strips (*paitu*). Since the *fentu* format had become obsolete after the Kangxi period, only the other two maps were taken as models for the new edition. Of these two, the Yongzheng maps had been made on a square grid of latitude and longitude (*fangge*), while the 1719 copperplate was made on a trapezoidal projection (*xiege* in Chinese, for its slanting lines of longitude). New Qianlong editions were made on both projections.

Work on editing the new survey map began in September 1757. The editing was referred to as "augmenting and correcting" (*zenggai*), indicating that two tasks were involved: updating and improving the existing maps, including major changes to the earlier depiction of Central Asia—the *gai*; and drawing in completely new territories—the *zeng*. One major source for this revision was of course the first survey of newly conquered lands, which had become available at court by January 12, 1757, when Qianlong commented,

"Now, for the most part (*daduan*) the land has been mapped, and the remaining places can be revisited at leisure."⁵⁶ Updating also required the map to reflect recent changes in names and administrative boundaries within China, necessitating the use of state archives. For this reason, staff were seconded from the Grand Council, Grand Secretariat, and Imperial Household Department to work within the Office of Military Archives (Fanglüe guan), an agency closely connected to the Grand Council and charged with documenting the history of the Junghar wars.⁵⁷

Work on a new version of the court survey accelerated when, sometime between mid-April and mid-June of 1760, the second survey team returned to Beijing (although the results of its survey were couriered back more quickly, arriving at the end of February).⁵⁸ In late June, Fuheng and Prince Yun-lu, the two high-ranking ministers in charge of the project, stated that in the Inner Court (Neiting) there were wooden and copperplate maps with lacunae and discrepancies. They proposed leading a team of He Guozong and Mingghatu, as well as four Jesuits—Hallerstein, Anton Gogeisl, da Rocha, and d'Espinha— to inspect the maps, consulting on doubtful points, if necessary, with officers who had served in Xinjiang.⁵⁹ Sometime thereafter, the Office of Military Archives had sent d'Espinha and others to examine and correct a copperplate map of 2.5 inch (*cun*ᵇ) grid segments on a slanted projection, and a wooden map of 2 inch segments on a square projection, both in the Inner Court. Presumably these two maps derived from the wooden and copperplate editions mentioned earlier.

On September 6, the Office of Military Archives reported that it was first necessary to await the completion of a "new map," and then use this to correct the two maps viewed by d'Espinha. On January 29, 1761, Prince Yun-lu and Fuheng reported that this "new map"—a woodblock version with a trapezoidal projection and 1.8 inch grids—had been completed. This had been compared to the two maps "drawn by the Office of Military Archives," which now conformed to it in all points. Once certain features of Kazakh territory had been corrected on the maps, the 2.5 inch copperplate version was to be printed by the Imperial Workshop, and the woodblock versions by the Wuyingdian printery.⁶⁰ On July 19, 1761, the Grand Councilor Liu Tongxun and He Guozong were ordered to hand the *Xiyu tuzhi* over to the Office of Military Archives. While the title *Xiyu tuzhi* should properly indicate a gazetteer not a map, Qin Guojing and Liu Ruofang suggest that this date also marked the final completion of the new survey map of the Western Regions.⁶¹

Mystery clouds the subsequent history of the map. It seems that Fr. Michel Benoist completed the copperplate printing of the 1761 edition of the Qianlong survey map around 1769–1770.[62] Surveying continued after that: when the Torghuts were resettled in Xinjiang, Qianlong sent d'Espinha and others to the frontier to take new surveys, and issued orders to modify and reprint the existing copperplate and woodblock maps.[63] During the second Jinchuan war in 1774 he ordered Jesuits to make survey readings, and in August 1776, commanded them to help draft a map of the area around Mukden.[64] It is widely assumed that the version of the Qianlong map now reprinted is Benoist's 1769–1770 work, but whether its presentation of India was updated after 1761 is unknown. Certainly, by the late 1770s the court's interest in cartography was on the wane. Wang Qianjin has found that the survey map was not changed to reflect the newer and more accurate coordinates presented in the revised 1782 *Xiyu tuzhi*.[65] Corroborating the likelihood of neglect by 1780 is the fact that the published map used the "old" terminology (e.g., Wendusitan instead of Hendusitan) that Qianlong took such care to banish from the *Siku quanshu*. It is also significant that Burma, the site of Qianlong's next war, in the late 1760s, was never added to the survey map even though it could easily have been charted by the same blend of informants and European maps used for India and Central Asia.

This timeline is peculiar, because other areas of Qianlong-era official scholarship and publishing remained vigorous at least through the mid-1780s. Several hypotheses may explain the court's declining cartographic output. Surveying and mapmaking had always required technically proficient officials to supervise their Jesuit coworkers, and those active during the surveying in the 1750s, all students in the Kangxi period, were by then old: He Guozong died in 1766 and Prince Yun-lu in 1767, Mingghatu sometime between 1763 and 1769.[66] In short, by around 1770 none of the key technical advisors who had supervised the new Qianlong surveys survived, nor did they have obvious successors. Of the Jesuits in the project, Benoist and Hallerstein both died in 1774. Da Rocha (d. 1781) and d'Espinha (d. 1788) lived somewhat longer, but overall the expertise needed for cartographic collaboration was no longer available. This would explain a rapid drop-off in court mapping by the first half of the 1770s, even as other projects were lavishly patronized. It may also be that there was no pressing propagandistic or strategic need for a new edition. For Qianlong, expanding the map after the Junghar campaigns was an attractive way of illustrating his own conquests, but no later war led to significant territorial gains. For military purposes, Qianlong continued to rely on ad hoc maps prepared by commanders in the field, not surveys. Unless new evidence comes to light, it appears that Qianlong had by the mid 1770s abandoned the goal of keeping updated court survey maps in constant preparation.

India's Composite Image on the Court Survey Map

We now turn to how India is represented on the finished court survey map. Neither Chinese nor Western sources explain the editorial principles, debates, and compromises that allowed data from Qing surveys, local accounts, and European maps to be integrated. Studying the form and content of the map reveals that, while European maps were certainly consulted and partly followed, their evidentiary authority was subordinate to both earlier surveys and local informants. Moreover, distinctive characteristics of Jesuit cartography were systematically eliminated from the finished map. Western conceptions of the world had limited influence when different strands of information were woven into a cartographic image of India.

Only a glance is needed to see that the completed Qianlong court survey map was partly based on a European world map. The clear delineation of major geographical features—the northern part of the Deccan and the Kathiawar Peninsula in India, the Persian Gulf and Arabia—take the shape found in contemporary Western maps but in no other source available in the Qing empire. In this, the makers of the Qianlong court survey were following the precedent of the Yongzheng map, which had drawn heavily on European data for the representation of the Caspian and Black Seas and European Russia.

Although individually these features have a familiar shape, their arrangement and relative positions deviate considerably from contemporary European cartography. To establish this, I have compared the distances between several locations given on both the Qianlong survey and a 1751 map of Asia by J. B. d'Anville, probably the most recent European map available to the Jesuits in Beijing.[67] Below is a list of several major points where the Qianlong map diverges from the most recent European work, with the discrepancy between them, expressed in approximate degrees of longitude, in brackets: 1) the Persian Gulf on the Qianlong map is located below the eastern Black Sea and the Caucasus Mountains [discrepancy of 9 degrees]; 2) Multan, in modern Pakistan, is south of the Caspian Sea [discrepancy of 18.5 degrees]; 3) the Indian Ocean between the mouth of the Persian Gulf and the western tip of the Kathiawar Peninsula covers only five degrees of longitude on the Qianlong map [discrepancy of 9 degrees]; 4) Dhaka, in modern Bangladesh, is immediately below Lake Manasarowar in western Tibet [discrepancy of 8.5 degrees].[68]

Discrepancies of this magnitude cannot be attributed to oversight or carelessness. Nor is it conceivable that the Jesuit cartographers, had they been free to represent Asia as they wished, would have presented a map deviating so far from contemporary European knowledge. Other factors were constraining their ability to reproduce features of recent European world maps in the survey map. That is, the court survey map contained elements to which the latest European data had to yield. One such element was Tibet. In the Kangxi period Tibet had been surveyed in haste, but this rendering was preserved intact on the Yongzheng versions; by the Qianlong period its imperially endorsed shape had become canonical. When the Kangxi and Yongzheng editions were made the basis for the Qianlong revisions, the shape of Tibet was preserved. European cartographers too had drawn heavily on the Kangxi survey for their rendering of Tibet, but had adjusted it to fit known coordinates for places in India, thereby significantly modifying the original Qing survey data. By contrast, pre-Qianlong editions of the Qing court survey map had been prepared without reference to India. Thus, when it become necessary to draw India onto the court survey map, an epistemological problem arose: would the imperially approved image of Tibet, made by trusted Qing surveyors, yield to the latest European data? It would not.

A concrete example of the contortions required for the mapmakers to fit the latest European maps of India around Qing maps of Tibet is the location of the Ganges River. The Kangxi survey map has the Ganges originating in Lake Manasarowar in western Tibet, and the Qianlong map shows it entering India just below that lake and then flowing almost due south to its delta. To accomplish this, Dhaka in Bengal had to be placed below the western Himalayas. When the Ganges delta is depicted below western Tibet, it becomes impossible to place Delhi and Agra south of the Himalayas. Exacerbating this problem, the original Kangxi survey shows the Himalayas running approximately east-west, and then abruptly curving north at a 90 degree angle below Ladakh, whereas European maps had modified this into a gradual slope to the northwest. To conform European data to the official Qing rendering of Tibet, then, Delhi and Agra had to be placed west rather than south of the Himalayas. Because those cities lay on the Yamuna River, in reality a tributary of the Ganges, the makers of the Qianlong survey map had to sever the Yamuna from the Ganges and give it a separate delta west of the Himalayas. This had the effect of placing Agra only one degree south of Ladakh and two degrees west of it, where the d'Anville map showed Agra as six degrees south of Ladakh, and two degrees *east* of it. In short, those making the map were prepared to do violence to the most up-to-date European conceptions of India's geography in order to preserve the precedent inherited from earlier survey maps. Unquestionably, the Jesuits advising the Qianlong court did not have carte blanche to present the version they themselves must have considered more accurate.[69]

The map's boundaries offer further evidence that the Jesuits and European world maps had limited influence on the final survey map. Under Qianlong the map added the Arabian Peninsula, Persia, Afghanistan, and northern India, but excluded most of southern India, peninsular Southeast Asia, and most of Europe. This can be explained on aesthetic grounds: the Yongzheng edition of the map, which extended south to Qiongzhou (modern Hainan) and west to St. Petersburg, had a conspicuous blank space in its southwest quadrant, and the Qianlong expansion filled in precisely this zone.[70] A political explanation can also be advanced: between 1759 and 1762 the Qing court was especially interested in the Muslim Regions (*Huibu*), and Qianlong spoke in particular of the "great countries" of India and the Ottoman empire. By showing both, it might be argued that the survey map satisfied the court's operational needs as of 1760. Yet the map's limits bear closer analysis on two points. First, it seems unlikely that the Jesuits would have elected to give a comprehensive picture of Muslim Asia but not of their European homeland, further evidence that the Jesuits' role in drafting the map was limited. Second, as we have seen above in official compendia compiled around the time the survey map was being prepared, Jesuit claims that the globe held five continents remained controversial in the Qianlong period. A conception of the world as one inhabited continent surrounded by water—whether the traditional land within the "four seas" in China, or Buddhist Jambudvipa—remained influential. If the court survey map had added the distinctive peninsulas found on Western maps, this would be striking visual evidence that the court was accepting Jesuit renderings of the world. By instead showing a square chunk of territory, surrounded by water or land that trailed off into blank space, its implied cosmology was not distinctively Western, and Qing advocates of rival worldviews would have found nothing that explicitly contradicted other theories of the world's shape. Indeed, nothing on the map invalidated Qianlong's 1768 claim that the world was water-encircled Jambudvipa. The map was cosmologically neutral, not a vindication of Jesuit theories.

Geographic nomenclature also indicates that when the court survey came to cover lands beyond Qing territory, the Jesuits had little influence over the place-names used. On their own maps, a standardized set of names had been employed consistently since the time of Matteo Ricci and Giulio Aleni, but on the court survey map an entirely different vocabulary appears. Limiting our examples to India, there is no trace of standard Jesuit terms like Mughal empire (Mowo'er), India (Yindiya), Delhi (Deli), or Western Ocean (Xiao Xiyang), to say nothing of higher-level concepts like "Asia." All oceans on the map are labeled generically as "sea" (Ma., *mederi*; Ch., *hai*), sidestepping the issue of competing maritime naming systems. Rather, Qing court mapmakers showed a preference for the vocabulary of local informants. This was evident as early as the Yongzheng edition, where the spatial rendering of the Caspian Sea came from a Russian or European map but the lake itself was called Tenggis Omo, a combination of Mongolian and Manchu terminology. This was the name used by the Torghut Mongol informants living on its shores, and adopted by Tulišen.[71] A similar preference for local informants can also be seen on the Qianlong survey map. There, for instance, the names for the tributaries of the Indus are rendered differently from the terminology on contemporary European maps. The Sutlej River, for instance, was called the Ludhiana River (Ma., Ludi yana bira), the upper reaches of the Indus the Attock River (Ma., Atak bira), and a third tributary of the Indus the Kundu wal River, all names not used on contemporary European sources. In several cases, as when Delhi was referred to as Jahanabad (Ma., Jahal rabat), or the Mughal empire as Hindustan, the map's terminology followed that in current use in Kashgar and Yarkand.[72]

Finally, the density of place-names in India also shows that the needs of the court and perhaps the availability of local informants led European maps to be adapted and altered. On the court survey map populous Bengal was granted only three cities, while approximately nine appeared between Bengal and Surat. Other areas on the map, such as Persia, had a similarly low density. Northwestern India, by contrast, was depicted in great detail: the tributaries of the Indus embraced over fifty settlements. Particular attention to this region doubtless reflects the court's interest in Hindustan after 1758 as a potential bolthole for its enemies, and probably also the familiarity of informants in Yarkand and Kashgar with northwest India. The Qing court, in other words, created a Xinjiang-centric map of India.

Assistance from Jesuit staff and European world maps allowed the outline of India (as well as Persia and Arabia) to be placed onto the court survey map within the framework of latitude and longitude that already embraced Russia, Central Asia, and the Qing empire itself. Their contribution, however, was only one element in a blend that included local informants and older survey maps. Although the principles and methods behind this blending remain frustratingly opaque, evidence suggests that recent European cartography yielded place to other sources. In itself, that the Qianlong court cartographers modified or disregarded European maps need not imply that they doubted their veracity. For the parts of Inner and Central Asia actually surveyed or otherwise investigated, it was clear that the Qing court possessed information surpassing that possessed by any European cartographer. Well into the nineteenth century, as Enoki Kazuo has pointed out, European cartographers acknowledged the Qianlong survey map as the best available source for these regions.[73] However, the limits imposed on evidence from European maps ran deeper. Their depiction of the world had to be reformed to fit around earlier imperially endorsed depictions of Qing territory, the authority of which was nonnegotiable. Even the hallmarks of Jesuit world maps that did not contradict earlier surveys but nonetheless were unmistakable components of controversial European cosmology—characteristic place-names, continents, and prominent peninsulas—were eliminated as far as possible from the completed map. In short, the survey map's depiction of India was a unique and distinctive medley of information, and one that no European cartographer could endorse. How was this gap with recent European world maps regarded by the producers and consumers of the court survey?

The Evidentiary Status of Court Surveys and Jesuit World Maps

Regardless of how the court survey map was created, upon its completion did its depiction of India and other territories represent for the Qianlong emperor and his ministers the most authoritative spatial rendering of the outside world? Was it a criterion against which to test the accuracy of other representations? If the answers are "yes," then 1760 not only marks the end of geographic agnosticism (at least in regard to India), but also of the influence of localized worldviews tied to particular frontiers. To address this issue, the following section examines the reception of a world map presented to the throne in 1760 by the Jesuit Michel Benoist (1715–1774), just as the survey map was being prepared. Qianlong's degree of tolerance for discrepancies between two renderings of India's geography is a good proxy for his perception of the definitiveness of the court survey map for non-Qing territory.

First, we must clarify Benoist's connection to the court survey project. Here, internal Jesuit politics intersected with Qing institutional structures. In the Kangxi period, French Jesuits had taken the lead in official cartography, but this cohort had largely died off by the early Qianlong period. By 1755, as noted, court cartography was aided by missionaries attached to the Directorate of Astronomy, primarily Portuguese and German Jesuits under Portuguese religious patronage. French Jesuits, from the moment they reached China in the late seventeenth century, had been national and scientific rivals of the Portuguese-sponsored mission, functioning under separate church hierarchies and dwelling in separate residences.[74] All of the Jesuits named in official documents in connection with official surveying or mapmaking in the period between 1755 and 1762—da Rocha, d'Espinha, Hallerstein, and Gogeisl—were associated with the Portuguese mission. I have discovered no Qing document that connects Benoist to work on the survey map, and in the late 1750s, Fr. Gaubil, a French Jesuit, was unable even to obtain a copy of the results of the Qianlong-era surveys from his Portuguese colleagues.[75] Benoist was also institutionally separated from the project, employed not at the Directorate of Astronomy, but from the time of his arrival in China in 1744 in architectural and engineering projects at the Yuanming yuan palace outside Beijing.

Nonetheless, Benoist has consistently been regarded as the figure most directly concerned with the preparation of the court survey maps. This is on the strength of a letter in which he stated, "Long before, His Majesty had caused new maps of different sizes to be made of his whole empire and of bordering countries. . . . I was charged with the direction of this work."[76] It is unclear when and in what capacity Benoist began to carry out these duties. Copperplate printing of the map, which Benoist certainly directed, began around 1769, long after the drafting of the survey map between 1755 and 1761. The only Chinese reference I have found to Benoist's involvement in surveying dates to 1774, when Šuhede was ordered to determine which Jesuit, Benoist or d'Espinha, was more skilled in the technique (even here, the task in view was military rather than cartographic).[77] Given that Benoist is not mentioned earlier in connection to the creation of the court map, that engraving the map onto copper plates is the only specific duty he acknowledges, and other circumstantial evidence introduced below, it seems likely that he was involved only in preparing the maps for printing in the late 1760s, rather than in the actual drafting of their content before 1761.[78]

Whatever his role in the survey project itself, Benoit sought to produce maps and discuss geography with Qianlong. The missionary recorded in a letter of 1766 that he had made "terrestrial globes" for the emperor.[79] By 1760, Benoist had begun work on a new European-style map of the world meant to gratify Qianlong. According to an account written after Benoist's death, it was the emperor's frequent questions about Chinese geography that led the missionary to plan this work. One of his Chinese friends informed him that such a map would be a suitable gift for the emperor's upcoming fiftieth birthday, and Benoist accordingly decided to make an enormous world map in two hemispheres, each five feet in diameter.[80]

Benoist's map, entitled (like Verbiest's and the Chinese translation of the French world map given to Kangxi) the *Kunyu quantu*, was the only Chinese-language Western-style map known to have been given to Qianlong, and remained the most up-to-date map of that type possessed by the Qing court until after the Opium War.[81] The Qing record of this gift is relatively complete. On September 10, 1760, Qianlong issued an edict about the map and its companion book. According to a Jesuit source, Qianlong was delighted, praised the work, and had it sent to his private apartments. Still, this first version was incomplete. Benoist had left blank the region of the new Qing conquests, to be filled in later. He also asked Qianlong to have his text vetted for stylistic errors.[82]

Benoist thus presented his world map to the throne before the draft of the official survey was complete, and in doing so, moreover, he emphasized that it represented the very latest advances in European geographic knowledge (he was relying on d'Anville's maps from the early 1750s)—claims also made explicit in its companion work, the *Diqiu tushuo*.[83] His claims certainly caught the emperor's attention, but Qing and Jesuit sources differ on how they were received. Writing in 1775, Benoist's obituarist claimed that he was ordered to report to the "bureau des cartes" (Benoist himself refers to the "tribunal intérieur," probably the Office of Military Archives) and defend his innovations, where he generally won the support of Prince Yun-lu, Qianlong's uncle.[84] In his own letter, Benoist affirms that Yun-lu wrote a memorial in his support, leading Qianlong to request a second copy of the map, supply Benoist with assistants to polish his writing, and order that to the different globes in the royal palaces "will be added the new discoveries as I have drawn them on my map."[85] The obituarist claims that "[the emperor] invited him to examine and review the general map of the empire that was going to be made in 100 leaves."[86] In other words, the Jesuit position is that Benoist persuaded the emperor and his ministers of the value of his map. Why, then, does the court survey differ so significantly from Benoist's world map regarding India?

Qing documents reveal a similar but more nuanced picture. Qianlong recognized that the map departed from older depictions of the world, and indeed ordered Prince Yun-lu and He Guozong, simultaneously working on the survey map, to inspect the works for "errors" (*budui zhi chu*). They responded in January 1761. For their inspection, they had first compared Benoist's map with earlier specimens in the same style, including a globe in the Inner Court and a copy of Verbiest's *Kunyu quantu* in one of Beijing's Catholic churches. All three maps were "broadly similar," they found, but Benoist now extended Russia over 40 degrees further east, and America over 50 degrees further west. Benoist justified this on the grounds that in 1741 the Westerner Li-le had surveyed these areas and his new contributions had necessitated changes to Verbiest's older map, an explanation corroborated by Hallerstein and others.[87] While preparing for his mission, Benoist had studied partly under the direction of the eminent French astronomer Joseph-Nicolas de l'Isle (1688–1768).[88] De l'Isle had sojourned in Russia, where he had for a time directed a project to map that empire.[89] Although we do not know if Benoist and de l'Isle kept in contact, both were in touch with Gaubil in Beijing in the 1750s.[90] Li-le is therefore J.-N. de l'Isle, and the date 1741 probably refers to Bering's second expedition to that region, to the results of which de l'Isle had access.[91] Yun-lu and He Guozong added that, stylistic changes apart, Benoist's world map required alteration only in its depiction of some parts of Inner Asia: Benoist had followed the "old map of Ili" (*Yili jiu tu*) and not the "new map drawn by Mingghatu and da Rocha." This may mean that Benoist had used the first survey of Jungharia by He Guozong but had left blank the area surveyed more recently under Mingghatu, or that the "old map" referred to a still earlier work. The points requiring correction were pasted on the map, and when Qianlong approved them a new version was to be ordered.

In sum, Qing sources confirm that Benoist and other Jesuits were required to justify the new geographic depiction and largely satisfied Yun-lu and his colleagues. However, it is clear that the encounter between Benoist's world map and the draft court survey was the opposite of what Jesuit letters suggested: Qianlong wanted to make sure Benoist's world map exactly matched his own survey in its depiction of Xinjiang, not use the world map to correct the shortcomings of the survey he had commissioned. This was part of the standardization underway at court. In late June 1760 Fuheng and Prince Yun-lu memorialized that Yun-lu had once supervised the construction of a globe for Kangxi. The conquest of the Junghars had now made this globe obsolete, and the two men proposed to "draw a supplement for the newly opened lands" (*tianhua xinpi tuyu*) so that the globe would reflect the new imperial achievements. They wished to expand this revision to other maps at court, presenting their results for imperial inspection.[92] Qianlong took his European-style world maps seriously enough to keep them up to date—up to date with his new surveys, not the latest world maps.

By contrast, that Benoist's depiction of India, based on d'Anville's latest maps, differed profoundly from the rendering on the court survey map seems to have attracted no attention. Although the only reproductions of Benoist's world map available to me are of too low a resolution to permit detailed analysis, it diverges from the survey map in approximately the same ways as the d'Anville map outlined above. Specifically regarding India, the depiction of the Indus and Ganges-Yamuna River systems and of the Himalayas reveals striking differences. For instance, Benoist has the Yamuna merge into the Ganges, and the entire system flows south of, rather than west of, the Himalayan range, which itself slopes markedly toward the northwest. Such differences were unlikely to have passed unnoticed, since Qianlong himself, several other court Jesuits, and the most senior Qing astronomical and cartographic experts, Yun-lu and He Guozong, had all examined both maps, seemingly with care. Even though Benoit's world map was presented to the emperor months before the definitive "new" survey map was completed (in January 1761), and years before the last printing of the survey map (in or shortly after 1770), there was no attempt to standardize their renderings of non-Qing Asia.

Evidently, the emperor and his ministers were not concerned that the court survey map did not conform to what in the Jesuits' opinion was the best and most recent geographic data. Qianlong was apparently content that the court survey and Benoist's world map contradicted each other on key points of Indian geography. Thus, the emperor's attitude toward cartographic discrepancies manifestly differed depending on whether the lands in question fell within or beyond his domain. For the Qing empire itself there was only one valid image, at least for maps framed within a grid of latitude and longitude. Not only older globes but also Benoist's recent map had to conform to the official surveys. For the outside world, however, the official survey does not seem to have possessed the same definitive authority. Benoist was not ordered to change his mapping of the Indus or Ganges (or even the southern slopes of the Himalayas) to fit the survey, nor was the survey made to fit him. Among various conceptions of the outside world, Qianlong did not pass judgment.

To understand his attitude it is necessary to return to the inception of the survey project. Kangxi had included only findings verified by the supervision of Qing officials, relying somewhat on local informants but totally excluding unverifiable European cartographic sources. As the strategic horizon of the Qing empire extended westward, the Yongzheng and Qianlong emperors felt the need to have a map of Russia, Central Asia, India, and other lands. Still, although invisible on the survey map itself, the distinction between court-verified results and less reliable European-derived cartographic data seems to have been preserved; the authority of the map differed in regard to Qing and foreign territory. Qing rulers were not hostile to the Jesuits' data, but neither did they accept their maps as the best available image of the world. In the spirit of geographic agnosticism they were preserved, even admired and displayed, but only as one among many competing theories.

The Qianlong emperor's ambivalence toward European geographic knowledge is amply demonstrated by other evidence. His writings used the Buddhist concept of Jambudvipa but never, as far as I can determine, did he refer to "Asia." When writing about India after 1760 he prominently cited information from Mongol, Islamic, and Tibetan sources, but never Benoist's map nor its terminology, such as India (Yindiya) or the Mughal empire (Mowo'er).[93] Indeed, I have not been able to find a single geographic or philological note or essay by Qianlong in which he used distinctively Jesuit geographic terms, or cited a European book or map to support his argument. Kangxi's geographic commentaries sometimes referred to latitude and longitude, and there is proof that he consulted world maps in discussing world affairs, but no such evidence seems to exist for Qianlong.

As with the editors of the *Siku quanshu zongmu tiyao* described in Chapter One, it is misleading to describe Qianlong's engagement with European cartographic evidence or methods in absolute terms, whether positive or negative. Neither a proponent nor an opponent, the emperor simply wished to know more about one of the many theories concerning the outside world circulating in his empire. Fr. Benoist's letters reveal that he discussed geography and astronomy with Qianlong frequently and at length. By 1766 he was able to inform a correspondent that "five or six times, in addition to the terrestrial globes I have directed and the world maps that I have traced, the Emperor has questioned me about different countries, and in great detail about Russia."[94] Elsewhere he described a long conversation in which the emperor posed numerous questions across a range of subjects: the role of Europeans in Russia, Burma, and Java; the methods of European colonial governments; Western techniques of mapping and the problem of charting remote or uninhabited regions; and other matters.[95] Perhaps the most telling moment of the conversation came when Qianlong asked, "In your world maps you draw all the realms of the world; you have not been in all these countries, how can you draw them on the map?" and, "It is commonly said that the world contains ten thousand realms, that is to say, an infinity. There are countries by themselves inaccessible, which are uninhabited, and where by consequence you have not been able to penetrate. . . . You will lack, at least, a map of these countries?"[96] The subtext of these last two comments is significant, because it hints that the emperor believed the Jesuits to be exaggerating their claims to have mapped the world definitively. Surely they should share the modest agnosticism of Qing scholars? The content of European world maps and the scientific rationales behind survey mapping were familiar at the Qing court, but these did not acquire an exclusive or even predominant hold over the study of foreign geography. As we can see from Qianlong's writings discussed in Chapter Two, though he paid close attention to a wide range of geographic conceptions drawn from the empire's languages and cultures, he relied in his textual arguments on written sources and oral informants, not map evidence.

From around 1800, elite private Han Chinese geographers specializing in the study of historical geography and the Western Regions began to make extensive use of the court survey maps in their own research. Like Qing emperors and their palace staff, these scholars prized their mathematical precision and consulted them carefully for research on domestic geography. Although some scholars had access to the Qianlong editions that covered virtually all of Asia, these maps were cited only very rarely on points of foreign geography. Regarding India, the court survey map had virtually no impact on scholars. Like the court, then, these users regarded these maps as the best possible rendering of domestic territory, but of limited value for depicting foreign lands.[97]

Conclusion

Qing geographic sources, the preceding two chapters have argued, cannot be interpreted in isolation from their context. Contemporary scholars researching geography ranged widely through conflicting materials and drew conclusions that synthesized, warily and provisionally, seemingly incommensurable elements. No source could stand outside or above this matrix of evidence, and this was true also of the Jesuit world maps. Their authors hoped they would be received as a complete and authoritative system, rendering earlier worldviews obsolete; for their Qing readers, they were one source among many.

Was this also true of the court survey map itself? It was produced at great expense by a large staff of technicians after years of labor and the close supervision of the emperor and his highest officials. And indeed, insofar as the maps were the product of actual surveying guaranteed by Qing functionaries—that is, to the extent they mapped territory under direct imperial control—their claim to offer an unprecedentedly clear image of the empire's territory that superseded all earlier sources appears to have been widely accepted at court and among elite private scholars. This was particularly true of Qing holdings in Inner Asia that had hitherto been poorly understood in China. Among officials and private scholars with good court connections, the survey maps began in time to rival textual sources as a reservoir of authoritative evidence guiding research into the historical and contemporary geography of Qing territory.

For foreign geography, this was not the case. Neither the emperor nor his high ministers seem to have placed much weight on the map's evidence regarding territory beyond Qing control, nor did Han literati in the early nineteenth century. This was because for non-imperial territory the map was enmeshed in the matrix of corroboration described in earlier chapters, its rendering formed by weaving together strands from various sources (including European maps widely regarded as dubious) without firsthand evidence from a trusted observer in the Qing elite. Certainly, its composition implied a measure of confidence in European cartography greater than the skeptical evaluations of Aleni and Verbiest offered by textual editors evaluating books for the *Siku quanshu*. Presumably He Guozong, Mingghatu, and Prince Yun-lu, long acquainted with Jesuits and their writings, trusted European world maps more than others in the Qing state. Still, even within the process of composition the authority of the latest maps imported from the West gave place to other evidence.

The survey map's utility in regard to foreign territory was also limited by its regional origin on a single frontier. Its Qianlong-era recension highlighted the newly proximate "Muslim Regions" and, within that wide area, charted in greatest detail territory nearest to Xinjiang. In choosing geographic nomenclature, the map's authors showed a clear preference for the local lexicons of Inner and Central Asian informants. In no sense was the court survey a universal geographic instrument that transcended the perspective of a limited set of informants. Operationally, it was of no use for warfare or diplomacy along other parts of the frontier with India, such as the eastern Himalayas. Bengal was left almost entirely blank, its river systems grossly distorted to fit the needs of reconciling the Kangxi survey of western Tibet with European maps. Calcutta was excluded, as were most other major European ports in India trading to China. Officials wishing to get a purchase on Indian geography from the vantage point of Lhasa or Guangzhou, and the emperor and Grand Council supervising them, could get no help from the survey map. Not surprisingly, it does not seem to have been consulted in subsequent military operations or diplomatic crises. Academically, the map was of equally limited use. It gave its users little guidance about how it could be reconciled with other worldviews circulating at Qianlong's court. Whether to the viewer's eye it represented Jesuit Asia, Buddhist Jambudvipa, or the sea-hemmed central landmass described in the "Yu gong," the map offered only one set of nomenclature (transcribed from French or Asian sources) that could not easily be reconciled even with names found on Jesuit world maps in Chinese, let alone those of Chen Lunjiong or the geographic lexicons in use in Guangzhou and Tibet. For instance, its name for Bengal, "Ban'gala," seems never to have been adopted (or even noted) by any Qing geographer after 1760. In short, scholars would have gained little aid from the survey map when they confronted intractable problems in their textual sources, and it is not surprising that it was rarely cited as a source of foreign geography. Far from becoming a universal criterion for research, the map remained only one version of the outside world, with limited influence.

FOUR

Discovering the "Pileng"
British India Seen from Tibet, 1790–1800

As Qing officials and geographers contemplated Hindustan and its invasion from the northwest by Ahmad Shah, another power was less dramatically but more durably establishing itself elsewhere on the subcontinent. In 1757 the East India Company defeated the young nawab of Bengal at Plassey and replaced him with its own candidate, later defeating another nawab and his allies at Buxar in 1764. In the following year the Company was invested by the Mughal emperor with the *diwani*, or right to collect and administer the revenues, of Bengal, Bihar, and Orissa. In fact, though not in name, Bengal was firmly under its control. Though not yet paramount in India, the British had become a major regional player. Their rise, however, does not seem to have attracted great notice in the Punjab and Kashmir, where its relevance paled beside the activities of Ahmad Shah; it was not reported to Yarkand in the eighteenth century.

But Yarkand was not the Qing territory nearest British India. Bengal and central Tibet were linked by commercial routes less arduous than those further west, and Bengali affairs were known to Indian merchants in Tibet and some Buddhist clerics. Supervising both groups were Qing officials (*ambans*) in Lhasa, who formed another conduit for both the central state and Chinese scholars to learn about Indian affairs. Measured by volume of trade, an even more significant channel between Bengal and Qing territory was the sea route to Guangzhou. In the foreign factories near Guangzhou, and in Macao, sojourning Europeans and Indians were familiar with what was passing in India and served as another potential avenue of inquiry.

War and politics shaped the circulation of intelligence about Indian affairs. In 1788, the expanding Gurkha state decided to settle a dispute with Tibetan authorities by force. Faced with a second invasion in 1791, Qianlong, confident of his empire's might, resolved to strike back deep into the Himalayas. Never before had the Qing military been interested in the eastern part of these mountains, and intensive reconnaissance and diplomacy were necessary. Eventually, exigencies of war placed Qing generals in contact with the British governor-general in Calcutta. Soon afterward George III's envoy Lord Macartney (1737–1806) arrived in China. Already anticipating that the Company's expansion in India would worry the Qing state, he found evidence to support this assumption. By 1794, the Qing court had connected the Company's newly discovered activity in Bengal to its trade at Guangzhou.

What the English considered a straightforward connection proved, in the context of Qing intelligence gathering and geographic research, to be anything but. Manchu generals were guided by local informants, and their reports to the throne described India through a Tibetan lens. The names they used in describing the geopolitics of Nepal and its neighbors bore little resemblance to those found elsewhere. At times, this lexicon collided with the equally unique terms for British India emerging in Guangdong. The Qing state was thus forced in the Qianlong period to juggle three new sets of terms for India from Yarkand, Lhasa, and Guangzhou, in addition to Jesuit and Manchu terms, and a plethora of older Chinese names. Events in Tibet in the 1780s and 1790s show the earliest attempt at trans-frontier coordination in Qing intelligence gathering, then still uncongenial to the empire's bureaucratic structure, strategic assumptions, and geographic scholarship.

Qing Views of the Trans-Himalayan Region before 1790

Before 1757, Qing officials detected threats to Tibet only from the Junghars to the north; to Beijing, its peaceful southern and western frontiers near India appeared strategically irrelevant. Tibetan leaders conducted their own relations with peoples beyond the Himalayan frontier with little central oversight, and only episodes of particular turmoil drew Qing officials into trans-Himalayan diplomacy. In 1730 the secular ruler of Tibet, Pho-lha-nas (1689–1747), fought a war without Qing assistance to impose Tibetan suzerainty on Bhutan, and Yongzheng then granted some Bhutanese leaders ceremonial titles.[1] In 1734 the three *han* of Nepal (Ch., Balebu; Tib., Bal-po) opened contact with Yongzheng.[2]

After the Qing had eliminated the Junghars, seemingly the last major threat to their rule, strategic and political interest in Tibet diminished. In this period of benign neglect, the Gurkha ruler Prithvi Narayan Shah (1723–1775) captured the Kathmandu valley in 1769, an event unrecorded in Qing official sources even though the states he extinguished were nominally Qing tributaries. By implication, virtually no news reached the court from the Himalayas, let alone distant Bengal, in this period.

In contrast, by the 1760s the British government in Calcutta began to eye the Himalayas as a potential route of trade with China. When the Gurkhas conquered the most convenient trans-Himalayan route through the Kathmandu valley from its Newari rulers, the British tried to repel them. Hindu mendicant traders, or *gosains*, were then banned from Nepali territory along with Britons, and the transit of Kashmiri Muslim merchants based in Patna and Varanasi was restricted. Bhutan offered an alternative route into Tibet. In 1772 it clashed with the East India Company over control of Kuch Bihar, a small principality near the foot of the Himalayas. When the Panchen Lama wrote to the British in 1774 on behalf of Bhutan, Governor-General Warren Hastings (1732–1818) had a pretext to seek direct Anglo-Tibetan diplomatic relations.[3]

The third Panchen Lama (1738–1780) was uniquely placed to mediate trans-Himalayan diplomacy. During the minority of the Dalai Lama between 1758 and 1776 he had unparalleled influence in the world of Tibetan Buddhism. He also had a "strong leaning for politics and diplomacy" and vigorously pursued a range of international connections, aided by the fact that no Qing official was appointed to his seat of Tashilhunpo.[4] The Panchen Lama was one of the chief proponents of a reviving Tibetan religious interest in India, dispatching his first pilgrim to Bodh Gaya in 1771 and several more thereafter.[5] Reportedly he had learned Hindustani from his mother, and conversed in it with the retinue of 150 Hindu gosains and 30 Muslim "fakirs" whom he supported.[6] The Panchen Lama followed Indian affairs, and was willing to dispatch representatives to the subcontinent.[7]

By the time Hasting's emissary George Bogle (1746–1781) reached Tashilhunpo in 1774, the Panchen Lama had reason to cultivate the British. According to Bogle he was interested in promoting trade with India, and his frosty relations with the Gurkhas may have led him to wish for a vague "connection" with the British to keep them in check.[8] Above all, however, he wanted the Company to support a permanent Tibetan Buddhist presence in Bengal.[9] The Panchen Lama was therefore willing to receive Bogle, but tried to keep this from the attention of the Qing court. Both the ruler of Bhutan and the Panchen Lama himself told Bogle that the Qing authorities would not approve of his entry into Tibet, leading him to try to elude Beijing's notice.[10] The regent to the minor Dalai Lama at Lhasa counseled the Panchen Lama against admitting Bogle, but thereafter seems to have colluded to keep the secret: he enjoined a Nepali in Lhasa for an audience with the ambans that if asked about Bogle, "to give them an evasive answer, and not to let them know that I [Bogle] was a Fringy [European]." In the event he was not asked.[11] If the ambans did learn of Bogle's arrival, it seems likely that they considered him an ordinary pilgrim. At this time the amban supervision of Tibetan activities was, as Ruohong Li has noted, lax.[12] In a memorial concerning regulations for postwar Tibet, Grand Councilors commented that "in the past it was not prohibited for foreigners to come to Tibet to present religious donations or to discuss matters (*jianglun shiwu*), or for the Dalai Lama to send letters. But over the course of time, there being no inspections whatsoever [of these interactions], it came to the point where urgent matters in Tibet were not reported to the ambans."[13] Although this referred largely to the Tibet-Gurkha diplomacy preceding the invasion of 1788, Bogle's visit was also effectively beyond amban supervision.

For the British, one of the Panchen Lama's major assets was his close relationship with Qianlong. They hoped that, in exchange for favors, he would intercede on behalf of the Company. The Panchen Lama evidently agreed to bring British India to the emperor's attention, telling Bogle that he would begin by urging the "Changay Lama," Qianlong's close religious advisor the Lcang-skya khutughtu, to send his own agent to Bengal. Once he too had proof of Hastings' obliging tolerance, the Panchen Lama was confident that his counterpart in Beijing would share his eagerness to access Buddhist holy sites. The Panchen Lama even suggested that he might be able to gain permission for Bogle to visit Beijing. Still, Bogle was asked to keep the Panchen Lama's planned consultation with the Lcang-skya khutughtu secret.[14] An apt moment to raise the matter was the Panchen Lama's 1780 visit to Jehol and Beijing to celebrate the seventieth birthday of the Qianlong emperor.

Events during this trip remain obscure. From its inception, contact between Tibet and British India relied on the principal go-between Purangir (d. 1795), a gosain trusted in both Tashilhunpo and Calcutta.[15] By the time the Panchen Lama set off for Beijing, Purangir was abbot and co-owner of the monastery near Calcutta built for the Panchen Lama by Hastings in 1776.[16] In the early 1780s he informed the British authorities that he had assisted the Panchen Lama's attempt to establish relations between the Company and the Qianlong emperor during a recent sojourn at the Qing court. According to Purangir's testimony, the Panchen Lama had mentioned at a banquet, through the mediation of the Lcang-skya khutughtu, that "in the country of Hindostan, which lies on the borders of my country, there resides a great prince, or ruler, for whom I have the greatest friendship." Purangir was summoned to answer Qianlong's questions about this territory, and gave a tactful but positive appraisal of its size and power. Qianlong agreed to write to its ruler, and it was determined that his letter would be given to the Panchen Lama upon his departure for Tibet, to be forwarded by Purangir to Warren Hastings.[17] Not long afterward, the Panchen Lama died in Beijing.

Unfortunately, this testimony cannot be corroborated. Bogle believed in 1775 that the Panchen Lama would commend Hastings to Qianlong via the Lcang-skya khutughtu. Several years later the Panchen Lama sent a message to Bogle promising to try to gain him admittance to Beijing during his approaching visit.[18] Samuel Turner (1759–1802), sent in 1783 to establish relations with the succeeding Panchen Lama, was assured by the child's regent that the previous incarnation "had even begun to open his mind to the Emperor of China upon this subject [his high regard for Warren Hastings], confident of his sanction and encouragement of the connection."[19] But Chinese-, Manchu-, and, evidently, Tibetan-language sources are silent on this matter.[20] Chinese-language records about the visit were extremely scant, not even listing each meeting between the emperor and the Panchen Lama, let alone details of them.[21] Tibetan records, concerned above all with spiritual matters, might also have omitted the political small talk Purangir describes, at a banquet and over "refreshments of fruit" during a moment of leisure.[22]

Understandably, opinions differ on the veracity of Purangir's report. Objections have been made that Purangir's chronology does not at times match the Chinese record, that for the Panchen Lama to have attempted to cultivate the British in this way would have been risky and improper, that Qianlong would never genuinely have agreed to correspond with a mere trading company, and that no allusion to this episode was made during later Anglo-Qing encounters in Tibet.[23] Errors of chronology do not in themselves invalidate Purangir's account, especially if he testified from memory.[24]

Since the Panchen Lama's primary interest was in arranging pilgrimage to India, raising the issue with Qianlong was not necessarily improper. Whether Qianlong would have agreed to correspondence, and whether this episode would have seemed relevant to the later Himalayan crisis, depends largely on what the emperor thought was being described to him. Purangir's report to the British invariably has him describing Hastings as the ruler of "Hindostan." If Purangir indeed referred to Hindustan, Qianlong would have understood him to mean a Muslim state north of India with no known link to Europeans. The Panchen Lama would also have described the British in largely Indian terms, to judge by his 1775 description of their conquest of India:

> At the time . . . Maduśa [?] lived, there appeared in the land of Priyangudvipa, a frontier area of Jambudvipa, the lords of Aryadeśa [India], the Enlēchi, that one also calls the Pherengi. . . . Engeraichi, Holandhaisai, Parsisi, Bikanda, Hurmuju, Sirkodhana, Rukma, and Purabma belong to their region. These Engeraichi—the most eminent of all that there are, including the land of the Urusu [Russia?]—arrived. Because they were great merchants and requested a region, Maduśa thus gave them a merchant house in the place called Calcutta in east Bengal. While they were peaceful because they had mercantile profits as they wished, the Mlecchas [i.e., the Mughal empire] collapsed due to inner dissensions. Therefore, measures to guard Bengal for the protection of the "Company"-House [Tib., *ka sam li khang*] by the commander [i.e., nawab] receiving orders from Delhi could not be carried out. Because, being the most eminent, they might fall under "murderous daggers" if they were unprotected, the above-mentioned merchants brought soldiers from their [own] countries. From Varendra [northern Bengal] and Bengal they subjugated everything up to Varanasi and brought it under their protection. And today they are also rulers of Srivajrasana [Bodh Gaya]. Their hereditary king lives on an island in the sea, he descends from the family of the Pandavas [heroes of the Hindu epic *Mahabharata*] and therefore himself belongs to the people of Aryadeśa. These people are evidently opposed to both orthodox and heretical teachers (*tirthikas*), and uniquely treat people, whatever religion they might have, even that of the Mlecchas, in a just regime of a purely secular character.[25]

If these were the terms used by the Panchen Lama to Qianlong, he may not have gained a clear sense that the Panchen Lama was describing the English known at Guangzhou. Indeed, Qianlong would likely have believed that an Indian ruler was being described, one that a decade later perhaps did not seem relevant to the events of the Gurkha Wars.

Whatever the truth, Hastings received no letter from the emperor. Suzuki Chūsei, who largely accepts Purangir's account, proposes that Qianlong let the matter drop after the Panchen Lama's death.²⁶ Certainly, their views of India were at odds. The Panchen Lama wished to give Tibetan pilgrims access to India's Buddhist holy sites.²⁷ However, contemporary India seems to have had no religious significance for the Qing emperor (even though, according to the Panchen Lama, Qianlong had lived there in a previous incarnation as Prasenajit, a royal supporter of Sakyamuni Buddha).²⁸ For Qianlong, Tibet was currently the true home of Buddhism. As he commented in an edict of 1792 defending a prohibition on Tibetan pilgrimage to Nepal and India:

> In the Buddhist scriptures I have read, it is indicated that the place where Sakyamuni Buddha achieved nirvana is in the territory of the tribe of Enetkek, extremely far from Tibet. Furthermore, I have heard that all of the common people of this place no longer have faith in Buddhism. Consequently, my view is this: enshrined in the Jo-khang temple [in Lhasa] is an image of Sakyamuni Buddha. If these lamas and Tibetans worship sincerely, then they can constantly show the utmost veneration to the religion passed down by the Buddha.... Why should it be that one can only worship when one has made a far journey into a foreign country, to the place where the Buddha achieved nirvana?²⁹

In short, Qianlong outlawed exactly the type of pilgrimage to Indian holy sites that the Panchen Lama was so enthusiastic in promoting.

Until more evidence comes to light, it is impossible to say whether the Panchen Lama indeed recommended Hastings to Qianlong as an enlightened ruler, and if he did, what the emperor made of this and what actions he took in response. It seems safe to conclude that even if the topic was broached, it was discussed in such a way that it seemed to have no bearing on other parts of the empire or on later events in the Himalayas. Not for another decade was direct and unambiguous contact made between Calcutta and Beijing.

A more tangible legacy of early Anglo-Tibetan diplomacy was its influence on Tibetan terminology for British India, later translated into Chinese and Manchu. Persian was the medium of written communication between Tibet and Bengal at this time, supplemented by discussions in Hindustani between the Panchen Lama and Bogle and occasional Tibetan-language reports to Lhasa from Bhutan or Tibetans sent to India. Within this linguistic context, the British in India were described in Tibet by the following terms:

Farangi. This Persian term, deriving from an Arabic name for the Franks, was widely used in India to refer to Europeans, with mildly derogatory overtones.³⁰ Hostile accounts of the British from Nepal and Bhutan before Bogle's arrival seem to have called them Farangi exclusively, and Bogle found the word widely used in Tibet.³¹ Farangi took the Tibetanized form *Phe-rang*. Luciano Petech speculates that "Farangi" was first carried into Tibet by gosains early in the eighteenth century, and finds its first use attested in a 1741 reference to Capuchin missionaries in Lhasa, where *Phe-rang* was equivalent to the Italian word *Europei*. Variants such as *Phe-reng* then appeared, and ultimately the word seems to have become conflated with the native Tibetan term *phyi-gling*, meaning foreigner.³² In his own Tibetan-language geographic writing, the Panchen Lama used the terms *Phe-reng* and *Phe-reng-gi* to describe the British in India.³³

Indians. For the Panchen Lama, the East India Company was important only insofar as it ruled Bengal, and Tibetan references describe the English as Indian rulers. Warren Hastings was referred to in the autobiography of the Panchen Lama as the "lord of Bhan-gha-la [Bengal]." His autobiography referred to Bogle and Hastings almost exclusively in terms that represented them as Indians. Bogle was "Āchārya Bho-gol," Acharya being "normally applied to every man of parts coming from India" and applied likewise to the gosain Purangir. Bogle was also termed "Bho-gol Sa-heb of the land Bhan-gha-la in India," and was noted to speak in the language of Magadha (*yul-dbus*) and the Nagara language, both referring to Hindustani.³⁴ Elsewhere Bogle records the Panchen Lama referring to "the [East India] Company who is the King of Hindustan." Told by Bogle that the English had been granted rule of Bengal by the Mughal emperor, the Panchen Lama believed "the Empire of Hindustan is now gone to ruin and I am told that the present King of Delhi is raised and supported only by the Fringies."³⁵

English per se. Bogle informed the Panchen Lama about the history and identity of the English. Much of his brief account of Europe, translated into Tibetan, was devoted to that country.³⁶ Bogle also explained that the English had been forced to conquer Bengal, presumably the basis for the Panchen Lama's recent political history cited above. In one conversation, "[the Panchen Lama] made me repeat England two or three times."³⁷ In his writings the Panchen Lama referred to En-lē-chi as another name for Phe-reng.³⁸ He was also aware that the English traded at Guangzhou, but did not know what term was used for them in China.³⁹

The Tibetan scholar 'Jigs-med-gling-pa's 1789 *Discourse on India* further illustrates contemporary views of British India. It was based mainly on the account of a Bhutanese monk-diplomat who had spent three years in India, mostly Calcutta, probably from 1775.[40] In this work the British were usually termed "Phe-reng-pa," with the port city of Ka-li-ka-ta specified as the home of a British chief and his council. 'Jigs-med-gling-pa did not use terminology that conflated the British with Indians, perhaps because he was better acquainted with Indian affairs. Rather, the British are said to have come from outside and conquered Bengali cities. They offered tribute to the Delhi Padshah (i.e., Mughal emperor; Tib., *Ṭi-ling pa-ca*), but also seized lands from him. He recorded the "real home" of the English as an island called "Blighty" (*Bhi-la-ti*), and also remarked upon their maritime trade with China.[41]

In sum, after their conquest of Bengal the English began to become known in Tibet, but through a composite of overlapping identities. They were a political and economic power as the rulers of Bengal, or even all Hindustan, and therefore sometimes accorded labels normally applied to Indians; they were also an island people who had established a base in Calcutta, in a complex relationship with the Marathas and Mughal court, ruled by a "Governor Sahib" and trading with China. In Tibet, as in India, they were most commonly called Farangi. This Tibetan view of British India strongly influenced official Qing terminology during the Gurkha Wars.

The First Stage of Anglo-Qing Contact: The Gurkha Wars

ORIGINS OF THE QING-GURKHA CONFLICT AND THE FIRST GURKHA INVASION OF TIBET

The first direct contact between British India and the Qing court took place in 1793, a consequence of the decision to send an expeditionary force to expel the Gurkhas from Tibet. The war itself has been admirably chronicled elsewhere, and only a sketch of events will be given here.[42] This section will concentrate on Qing knowledge of developments and conditions in India, and the insight this knowledge gives us into intelligence gathering and geographic scholarship.

Before the first Gurkha invasion, the Qing intelligence-gathering apparatus in Lhasa conveyed to the court little of the geopolitical knowledge about India circulating in Tibet. Between 1760 and 1790, successive ambans seem to have fully appreciated neither the complex dynamics of Himalayan diplomacy nor the breadth of the diplomatic contacts of the Panchen Lama. The disparity in knowledge between Tibet and Beijing stemmed in part, as Bogle clearly described, from a conscious effort by Tibetan clerics to avoid the scrutiny of the Qing court. Nor did the ambans themselves necessarily possess the ability to gather and interpret news of events in Nepal, Bhutan, or India. When the Gurkhas crossed into Qing territory in 1788 their rise, motives, and strategic situation were tolerably well understood in Lhasa, which had communicated with them since the 1760s, but even their very name was unknown in Beijing, where the Qing government believed that the Bal-po states still ruled in the Kathmandu valley.

Why the Gurkhas invaded Tibet in the summer of 1788 remains open to debate. Modern scholars emphasize disputes over coinage and trade, while Qing officials placed greater weight on the malignant presence in Kathmandu of the Tibetan cleric Zhwa dmar, whom they believed had fomented the conflict.[43] Whatever the immediate cause, the entry of Gurkha forces led the ambans to request aid, and the court dispatched Chengdu General Ohūi and the Sichuan provincial commander Cheng-de to repel the invasion. When a Gurkha advance toward the Panchen Lama's seat of Tashilhunpo made the invasion appear more critical, Qianlong sent in Bajong, an official familiar with Tibet's language and affairs. Qing forces were not put to the test, however, as the Gurkhas began to retreat by early October after preliminary peace talks.

Faced with the Gurkha invasion, the Panchen Lama solicited British aid. In a letter of October 31, 1788, he requested that the British attack Nepal on his behalf, or at least reject any Gurkha requests for help, at the same time asking that Qianlong not be informed of this communication "for this will bring down ruin and Destruction on me."[44] Beijing had taken a harder line than Lhasa. Whereas the ambans and Tibetan authorities sent an envoy to the Gurkhas on October 19 seeking a truce, Qianlong wished to make peace only after winning a military victory. Thus, when Cheng-de arrived in Lhasa from Sichuan on October 20, he informed the ambans and the Dalai Lama of Qianlong's orders and criticized their decision to open negotiations.[45] In this context the Panchen Lama's letter to Cornwallis, governor-general of British India, dated shortly after Cheng-de's rebuke, was an attempt to secure peace before a massive Qing force arrived. As he admitted, "God knows what will happen to the Ryotts [peasants] when the [Qing] Troops arrive," and later explained that he wished for secrecy "because we will write to the Emperor of China that a Peace has been concluded with the Ghourkhary, and that he will decline sending troops."[46]

That letter was the last act of diplomacy between the Panchen Lama and British India uncoordinated with Beijing or Lhasa. In reply, the British tactfully declined to attack Nepal. The Company would certainly win, Cornwallis acknowledged, yet the expense would be great, and the Gurkhas had not directly provoked its retaliation. Given the large maritime trade between the Company and Qing territory, he observed, it would be "highly improper in me to afford the Emperor any cause of displeasure by an Interference which he has not requested." He added, perhaps alluding to the failure of Tashilhunpo to secure Qianlong's favorable opinion of British India, that the emperor "is probably not informed of the extent of the Company's dominions in Hindostan and of their power in this part of the World." Cornwallis speculated that Qianlong would be delighted to discover intimate relations between Tibet and Bengal, and would open direct contact with India across the Himalayas.[47]

By April 1789 Qianlong was informed that the Gurkhas had repented from fear of Qing armies, accepted Bajong's settlement of their grievances, and agreed to send a tribute embassy to Beijing. In truth, however, the Gurkhas had won favorable terms and promises of a large annual indemnity from the Tibetan government. Qing officials in Tibet were not party to these negotiations and scrupulously ignored the indemnity in their reports.[48] The quick end to the first invasion rendered moot Cornwallis's letter to the Panchen Lama. Indeed, had a larger second invasion not taken place there is no reason to think the Qing government in Beijing would have gained any knowledge of the British presence in Bengal in this period.

THE IMPACT OF THE SECOND GURKHA WAR

Only during the second Gurkha War, for reasons to be explored, did the Qing court gain an unprecedented knowledge of conditions below Tibet. Its researches between 1791 and 1793 were extraordinarily important for the subsequent development of Qing perspectives on British India, for it was then that the Qing first encountered the British presence in Bengal. Through the process of discovery, we can trace the collection, interpretation, and diffusion of information within the Qing empire's official and scholarly circles and the ways intelligence did, and did not, influence the strategy of the Qing government.

The second campaign against the Gurkhas was a much grander endeavor than the first. It was directed by Fuk'anggan (d. 1796), son of the eminent statesman Fuheng (d. 1770) and brother of the grand councilor Fucanggan (d. 1817), one of the best-connected members of the Manchu elite. Having recently put down uprisings in Taiwan and Gansu, he had a reputation as one of the empire's foremost commanders. Among his staff were He-lin (d. 1796), the younger brother of the influential grand councilor Hešen (d. 1799), and Sun Shiyi (1720–1796), a Chinese official with high-level experience in several earlier campaigns. This, combined with Qianlong's attention, ensured that conditions at the front were carefully watched in Beijing. The need to campaign deep into the Himalayas, where no Qing army had gone before, against a government almost unknown, made intelligence particularly crucial. The Qing government and its expeditionary force exerted themselves to find out as much as possible about the rise of Gurkha power and the geography of Nepal and its neighbors. Intelligence could be gleaned by accessing knowledge current in Tibet but unknown to the central state, and by seeking out testimony from Qing subjects and others who had experience in Nepal.

At the start of the second campaign virtually no Qing officials had visited the Gurkha capital of Kathmandu. One of the few who had was the Brigade Vice Commander Yan Tingliang, a Green Standard soldier who had been sent into Tibet from Sichuan during the first Gurkha War. Evidently a confidant of Bajong, he visited Kathmandu in the summer of 1789 to prepare the tribute mission that followed the conclusion of the war, which he then escorted to and from Beijing, returning in late 1790.[49] At the end of 1791, under interrogation by Sun Shiyi about the disastrous peace that ended the first war, Yan mentioned that five or six days from Kathmandu lay the country of the Hongmao (Hongmao-guo), beyond which lay the Western Ocean (Xiyang). Although the Western Ocean was geographically ambiguous, and could be construed to mean the Indian Ocean, Europe, or both, Hongmao ("red hair") normally referred only to Europeans. When this report was received in Beijing, the Qing court turned for clarification to the Jesuit Louis de Poirot. Without knowing the exact question put to him and the information made available, his testimony is difficult to interpret. He told the Qing court that his homeland (identified as Italy in Chinese documents) was northwest of, and politically separate from, the country of the Hongmao. He added that "trade between the country of the Hongmao and China proper (*neidi*) is conducted directly by sea to Guangdong, a journey of four months."[50] From his testimony it is unclear whether he intended to describe European colonies in India or Europe proper, nor can it be determined if Qing authorities thought that Kathmandu was near *the* country of the Hongmao (i.e., in Europe) or *a* Hongmao country (i.e., a colony), or whether they even recognized this distinction.

The proximity of Europeans to Nepal did not attract particular attention. Qianlong's only comment was that "although the country of the Hongmao is quite near the Gurkhas, yet it has long traded with China. We may surmise that it will not necessarily assist the Gurkhas or ally with them." This observation was made against a backdrop of Qing attempts to predict and manipulate the response of countries neighboring its enemy. Yan had observed that the Gurkhas were surrounded by over twenty smaller states. Qianlong assumed that many of these harbored enmity toward the predatory Gurkhas, and he authorized Fuk'anggan to try to draw them in to complement the Qing attack, speculating that to revenge themselves for past humiliations and gain imperial reward they would side with the Qing, or at least remain neutral.[51]

It was the policy of courting assistance from Nepal's neighbors that led Fuk'anggan into direct contact with the British governor-general at Calcutta. Fuk'anggan arrived in Lhasa on February 16, 1792, and two days later summarized his diplomatic agenda in a memorial. The three tribes of Jumla, Bhutan, and Pileng, he observed, had presented "religious donations" (*bushi*) to the Dalai and Panchen Lamas. He had now sent them a request for assistance in the fight against Nepal, together with supporting letters from the Panchen and Dalai Lamas, via Tibetan messengers.[52] This was the first appearance in Chinese of the name *Pileng*, derived from a Tibetan form of the Persian *Farangi*.[53] Among Tibetans only the Panchen Lama and his retinue had previously communicated with the British, and they may have encouraged Fuk'anggan to include the Pileng in his correspondence. At this point, as the memorial makes explicit, Fuk'anggan regarded the Pileng as a Buddhist tribe like Bhutan that recognized the religious authority of the Dalai and Panchen Lamas. If he knew of the earlier Bogle or Turner missions, he probably construed them as religious pilgrimages. Nothing suggests that Fuk'anggan was aware of the anti-European sentiment encountered by Bogle, still less of the connection between the Pileng and Europeans at Guangzhou. Moreover, he posited no link between the putatively Buddhist Pileng tribe and the country of the Hongmao mentioned by Yan Tingliang. Indeed, nothing in this report distinguished the Pileng from other regional tribes and potential allies.

A reply from the Pileng took almost a year to arrive, and in the interim Qing officials learned more about Bengal. In a memorial of early March 1792, just over two weeks after his arrival in Lhasa, Fuk'anggan observed that to the south of Nepal lay "India of the South" (*nan Jiaga'er*), where the Pileng and other tribes resided.⁵⁴ More extensive inquiries were soon made of a range of informants: merchants from Nepal (Balebu), Xilinaga (Srinagar?), and Bhutan, and gosains (*Aza'er lama*). Their testimony was cross-checked with several Gurkha prisoners of war. By this means it was learned that south of Nepal lay "Varanasi (Walanaxi) of India," and that "beyond Jagannath temple (Zhaga'nata) one reaches the ocean's shore." Fuk'anggan and his co-memorialists commented that "it is heard that these places are all controlled by the Pileng. They are extremely far from the Hongmao country in the Great Western Ocean."⁵⁵ Fuk'anggan understood Yan's Hongmao to mean Europe, and in refuting this claim he seems also to have dismissed for the time being a connection between the Pileng and Europeans.

Curiously, during the fighting the Gurkha government presented its own view of Indian conditions. While advancing into Nepal, Fuk'anggan memorialized that he had received a communication from his foes claiming that Tibet was in imminent danger from the tribe of "Delhi Padshah of India of the south" (*nan Jiaga'er zhi Dili bacha buluo*). According to the Gurkhas, only their own efforts had hitherto prevented this, but if the Qing did not grant them aid they would no longer be able to resist. Fuk'anggan considered these claims a deliberate misrepresentation of earlier efforts by the Delhi Padshah to aid Jumla in its fight with the Gurkhas. This was probably a reference, gleaned by Fuk'anggan from Indian informants, to the late 1791 battle in which the ruler of Awadh (nominally vizier to the Mughal emperor) fought with the Gurkhas over the western Himalayan regions of Kumaon, Almora, and Srinagar.⁵⁶ The Qing commander responded to his foes that "Delhi Padshah is extremely far from Tibet. Not only do they have no quarrel with Tibet, they do not even communicate with each other, so how could they desire to occupy Tibetan land?"⁵⁷

The reply finally received from the Pileng must be interpreted in light of Anglo-Nepali relations. From the 1780s the British authorities in Bengal had tried with little success to conciliate the Gurkhas and regain access to the Kathmandu route to Tibet closed to them since the late 1760s. In 1791, however, the Gurkhas hinted to Jonathan Duncan (ca. 1756–1811), the Resident at Varanasi, that they would be willing to grant this access. This sudden reversal in policy had the ultimate goal of securing British military aid or materiel for their war in Tibet. However, when a treaty between the two powers was signed on March 1, 1792, the British authorities in Calcutta were not fully aware of the impending Qing invasion of Nepal, though Duncan had perhaps understood that the Gurkhas were angling to secure British help.[58] British authorities were therefore put in an awkward position when they received the Dalai Lama's first letter to the Pileng on August 3, 1792. The Persian translation that accompanied the original informed them that Qing forces were about to conquer the Gurkhas, but that the recipients had nothing to fear, notwithstanding whatever "artful" claims Nepal might make to secure British aid. It asked that Gurkhas who fled into their territory be delivered to the Qing or held prisoner. The Dalai Lama made clear that his correspondence was condoned by the Qing generals in Tibet and that cooperation would gratify the emperor.[59] Complicating the British response was the raja of Nepal's request, just over two weeks later, for ten guns and European gunners to fight off the Qing advance. On September 5 he wrote again asking to rent two battalions each of European and Indian troops, with arms and supplies; in a letter to Duncan he observed that he hoped his request would be granted because "you and the English in general endeavour at the successful issue of the affairs of those with whom you enter into Engagements." Clearly the Gurkhas believed that their commercial treaty implied that the English would be willing to lend them military assistance. A report of September 4 by a Company agent revealed that Qing forces were on the cusp of taking Nepal and that the raja had fled Kathmandu.[60]

The Company was hamstrung by its diplomatic success. It had urged two successive Panchen Lamas to report well of it to Beijing, and now the Dalai Lama promised to reward cooperation with a favorable report from the Qing general to Qianlong. Yet large-scale trade through the Himalayas with Tibet and perhaps China required access to the superior Kathmandu route, and after decades of hostility the Gurkhas were finally agreeing to allow this. These opportunities were of little use individually, but to seize one meant jeopardizing the other. It is not surprising, then, that the British offered to mediate a settlement. Cornwallis felt that this would please both sides: the harried Gurkhas would welcome British intercession, and the exhausted Qing forces were probably also ready for peace.[61] In the event this policy failed. Because of communication delays, peace terms were being finalized in Nepal even as the British authorities deliberated their response, and the mediation mission was superfluous before it even departed. None of this was foreseen when Cornwallis wrote to the Dalai Lama in a Persian letter of September 25, stating that he had refused a Gurkha request for aid on the grounds that the British used arms only in self-defense. Observing that the British "have for many years carried on commercial concerns with the subjects of the Emperor and have actually a Factory established in his dominions," Cornwallis added that he was sending a "Gentleman" with a small retinue who would endeavor to restore peace between Tibet and Nepal.[62]

By the time he learned of this letter, Fuk'anggan was already aware that the Pileng were in contact with Nepal. Early in 1792 a British agent, Abd al-Qadir Khan, had gone to Kathmandu to negotiate the commercial treaty. Although this did not concern military assistance, Duncan or Khan may have used such a possibility as leverage, given that the Gurkhas certainly hoped for British aid.[63] The Tibetan official Bstan-'dzin-dpal-'byor was a captive in Kathmandu during these negotiations and upon his release he was asked whether the Gurkhas and Pileng were in contact. He replied that a large party had arrived in that city, which Zhwa dmar, the Tibetan cleric believed by the Qing to have instigated the war, had identified to him as an embassy from the Pileng, a large and distant tribe coming to give presents to the Gurkhas. Bstan-'dzin-dpal-'byor viewed this reference to cordial Gurkha-Pileng relations as a tactic to intimidate the Tibetans, but he made no judgment about whether it was true.[64] His report does not appear to have greatly influenced Fuk'anggan's view of the Pileng. In a memorial of September 5, 1792, the Qing general reported to Beijing that because the Pileng tribe was far to the south of Nepal the commands sent over half a year earlier were still unanswered. He mentioned an uncorroborated report that they had sent an agent to the Gurkhas to reproach them (*zewen*) for invading Tibet, indicating that he did not perceive a Pileng-Gurkha military alliance.[65]

It was not until almost six months after the conclusion of peace between the Qing and the Gurkhas, on February 23, 1793, that Lord Cornwallis's letter finally reached Lhasa and came into Fuk'anggan's hands. The bearer of this reply, Daljit Gir (d. 1836), reported that Purangir (whose Tibetan companion had perished en route) had eventually reached the Pileng via Bhutan.[66] Because Purangir was too ill to carry the reply, the task was deputed to himself, Purangir's "nephew" (actually his *chela* or disciple).[67] He claimed that gosains ("Acharya lamas") served daily at the "official fort" (i.e., Fort William in Calcutta) and that what he was relating derived from an eyewitness account of Pileng diplomacy with Nepal. This relation was very favorable to the British, as one might expect from Purangir's disciple.

Daljit Gir's report contributed to geographic knowledge about India and outlined an interpretation of British policy toward the Qing-Gurkha war. He equated the Pileng tribe with Calcutta (Galigada), the former name used by other tribes and the latter by its members themselves. Its chieftain (*buzhang*), called governor (*guo'erna'er*), was deputed by the Delhi Padshah (as the British governor-general was, de jure) and was neither a Muslim like his subjects nor a Buddhist. Calcutta traded in Guangdong, something that Fuk'anggan found puzzling given that he and Sun Shiyi had both recently served there as governor-general yet had never heard of the Pileng. He suspected that some sort of discrepancy between the names used in both places was to blame. Earlier, Fuk'anggan had dismissed Yan's report and argued that the Great Western Ocean was far from the region below Nepal. But since the Pileng traded at Guangzhou he was forced to concede that "it would seem they are a place near the Western Ocean." As we have seen, however, Western Ocean is a geographically ambiguous term, and it is unclear whether Fuk'anggan was suggesting (as Yan had done) that Bengal was close to Europe.

To summarize, on the basis of Daljit Gir's report and earlier information Fuk'anggan now understood that the territory below Nepal was known by the generic name India (Jiaga'er), and that the largest state in that region, bordering the Gurkha empire, was that of the Delhi Padshah, which ruled Calcutta (also called Pileng) and through it traded at Guangzhou. Because of its participation in the Guangzhou trade it was somehow associated with the Western Ocean, but its precise relationship could not be defined.

Cornwallis's reply, carried by Daljit Gir, explained that the British had refused Gurkha requests for assistance but still maintained friendly relations with them; that they also traded frequently with China and had a factory in Qing territory; and that they therefore hoped to act as "Friend and mediator" and return peace to the region through the "amicable Interference" of an agent sent to Nepal.[68] In short, Cornwallis's tone was friendly but neutral. In Manchu and Chinese translation, however, he became a loyal servant of the Qing, a change perhaps introduced into the translation as a matter of course, probably with the complicity of Daljit Gir. In the Manchu version, the Gurkha request caused Cornwallis to recall that "the people of our tribe have constantly traded in a place subject to the Qing empire, and we are both very grateful that the emperor has bestowed grace upon us for many years, and clearly aware of the empire's majesty and strength."[69] In this translated version the governor, identified as the *Dili fatša harangga G'arig'ada aiman-i da* ("head of the tribe of Calcutta subject to the Delhi Padshah") had condemned the Gurkhas and urged them to surrender before they were destroyed, offering to write on their behalf to Fuk'anggan begging for mercy. Furthermore, Cornwallis intended to send an agent to urge peace between Tibet and Nepal, and to subsequently pay his respects to Fuk'anggan.[70]

Fuk'anggan's memorial placed greatest weight on the testimony of Daljit Gir, whom he could personally interrogate, and mentioned the letter only for corroboration. Since Daljit Gir claimed to have seen the British governor berate a Gurkha envoy for transgressing against Qing-protected Tibet and refuse him all assistance about a month before Fuk'anggan's letter had arrived, this showed the Pileng to be spontaneously loyal to the Qing. The Pileng governor, Daljit Gir claimed, had been delighted to receive a communication from Fuk'anggan, which gave him an opportunity to intercede on behalf of Nepal as he had promised. Thus, Fuk'anggan's memorial described the Pileng reply as "very respectful," and the Pileng claim to be repaying imperial grace at Guangzhou by exhorting the Gurkhas to peace as "most reasonable."[71]

A potential source of discord was Cornwallis's offer of mediation. Had the full implications of this offer been understood, it would certainly have struck Fuk'anggan and his emperor as insolent. However, the Qing general took an indulgent view, explaining it as simply the "long-standing custom of mediation of Tibetan peoples" (*fanyi jianghe guxi*). Since the Pileng had putatively recognized the awesome might and grace of the Qing court and chastised the Gurkhas, the nature of their offer of adjudication was obscured. Fuk'anggan speculated that because of their great distance the Pileng had not yet heard of the Qing victory in Nepal.[72] He sent back an account of his triumphs and added that "there is after all no need for you to send someone to come from afar and undertake a laborious journey in vain." Their good behavior, he concluded, would be reported to the emperor, and if future correspondence were necessary it should be sent to the new amban in Lhasa, He-lin.[73] Shortly thereafter he left Tibet.

In light of subsequent events, it should be noted that there is no evidence that Fuk'anggan was hostile to the Pileng tribe during his time in Tibet. Although they did not give him concrete assistance, they were not alone in this. Fuk'anggan reported to the throne at the end of the war that Bhutan, at first professedly eager to help, now only temporized, while none of the other rulers approached had ended up dispatching troops.[74] Later, he remarked that Bhutan, Sikkim, and Gro-mo had all declined to send troops due to the summer heat and their own military weakness. Still, Fuk'anggan had achieved his goal of keeping other countries from aiding the Gurkhas. Nothing Cornwallis had done singled him out for disapprobation. Fuk'anggan also seems to have discounted rumors that the Pileng were on cordial terms with the Gurkhas, and in fact reported that the Pileng had rebuked them. Around the time of the Anglo-Gurkha commercial treaty he had learned that the Gurkha ruler was sending a trusted agent to India (Jiaga'er) on an unspecified mission.[75] Since the Gurkhas themselves had denounced the Delhi Padshah to Qing officials as their enemy, it is very unlikely that Fuk'anggan would have considered the Padshah's subordinate, the Pileng chieftain, a possible ally of Nepal.[76] Finally, he pronounced himself well satisfied with the letter sent from Calcutta.

As Fuk'anggan dealt with Cornwallis's letter in Lhasa, the postwar Gurkha tribute mission reached Beijing. To the Qing court they painted a very different picture of trans-Himalayan affairs. As Leo Rose has pointed out, the Gurkhas were attempting to "balance the Chinese against the British."[77] In practice, this meant trying to persuade the Qing government to ally with them against other powers, particularly British India, just as they solicited aid from the British in an attempt to balance the Qing invasion. It is difficult to determine when this strategy began. In early 1790, at the time of their first tribute mission to the Qing court, the Gurkha ambassadors had informed Qianlong that the "tribes of Jiaga'er and Pula [identity unclear]" had dispatched troops toward them, but these had been "intercepted" by the Gurkhas and gone back, a phraseology that may imply these groups were intending to attack Tibet.[78] Around the same time the Gurkhas had come to believe that their status as tributaries entitled them to a grant of "salary or territory" from the Qing court, and vainly requested this of the ambans at Lhasa.[79] What use they intended for these grants is unclear, but over the next half century they frequently solicited monetary aid from the Qing for use against the British in India. By April 1792 they began representing themselves openly as a buffer for Tibet against the Delhi Padshah.

Now, in 1793, their tributary envoys took advantage of their time in Beijing to inform the Qing court about their conflicts with Hindustan, Europeans, and Borgi (Ba'erji) and asked for assistance if they were attacked by another country.[80] The response was blunt: the Qing government would on no account send troops beyond Tibet. If their new tributary was forced into a fight and emerged victorious this would please the court, but even if the Gurkha state was pressed to destruction the most aid it could expect was exile within Tibet for the royal house.[81] In short, the Gurkhas failed to alarm Qianlong about the possibility of an invasion of Tibet from India.

Qianlong acknowledged that Nepal was near Hindustan, but did not explain how he understood the geographic relationship between the two. As discussed in Chapter Two, Qianlong had earlier believed that Hindustan was a neighbor to India, not India itself. On the other hand, he also knew that the lands below the Himalayas were part of India.[82] A poem he wrote soon after the arrival of their first tribute mission described the Gurkhas as a "distinct tribe of Hendu." He added the gloss that the Gurkhas are a "distinct tribe of Enetkek and Hindustan."[83] In an essay entitled "On Lamas" ("Lama shuo"), written after the second war, Qianlong became more explicit, writing that "Buddhism began in India (Tianzhu), that is to say Enetkek; its territory is called Hindustan."[84] Despite making this connection, Qianlong seems never to have systematically reconsidered the relationship between places south of Nepal mentioned during the Gurkha Wars and locations that had been examined in the earlier Junghar campaigns.[85]

While the Gurkha embassy was asking for assistance in Beijing, diplomacy continued on the Himalayan frontier. Cornwallis's mediator, Captain William Kirkpatrick (1754–1812), entered Nepal in February 1793, and in March became the first Briton to reach Kathmandu. He failed to secure any further concrete benefits for the Company, but both sides testified publicly to their satisfaction with the recent improvement in their relations.[86] The Gurkhas immediately reported to the Qing the mission of "Kirkpatrick (Jilibadi), sent by the leader of Calcutta, who is subject to the Delhi Padshah," along with that of another, from Lucknow (Lakanawo), capital of the nawab of Awadh. In his report the Gurkha ruler corroborated the British version of Anglo-Nepali relations. His country, he recounted, had indeed asked the Pileng for military assistance, but had instead received advice to sue for peace. Kirkpatrick's mission expressed Calcutta's pleasure at the end of hostilities, and urged the Gurkhas to submit to Qing authority. He-lin, who had taken charge of Tibetan affairs after the departure of Fuk'anggan, passed on this communication on May 21, expressing no suspicions about the behavior or intentions of the Pileng. On May 2, the Gurkhas had sent a letter to their envoys in China. This letter, translated by the Qing, painted a less rosy picture of Anglo-Nepali relations, stating that Kirkpatrick was admitted with reluctance and only to obey Qing commands to live at peace with their neighbors.[87]

Kirkpatrick seems to have mentioned to the Nepali government that the British were preparing their own mission to China, and this was duly reported to Lhasa. He-lin was informed that the Pileng envoy had stated: "We have dispatched Lada [Lord, i.e., Lord Macartney] to go by sea from Bilayi to present tribute to the emperor." Bilayi probably refers to England, termed "Blighty" (*Bhi-la-ti*) in 'Jigs-med-gling-pa's 1789 geographic work.[88] The May 2 letter to the Gurkha envoys also mentioned news about a Pileng mission, and asked if they had heard anything about it while in Beijing. He-lin's memorial reached the Grand Council on July 3, 1793, likely the last memorial on the Pileng received before Macartney's reception.[89]

The Influence of the Gurkha War on the Macartney Mission

Although the mission of Lord Macartney to China in 1793–1794 ranks among the most studied episodes in Anglo-Qing relations, little of this voluminous body of scholarship explores the important role played by Indian affairs. To Macartney and his suite, the Qing-Gurkha war and China's contact with British India appeared to play a critical part in determining the outcome of his mission. Macartney believed Qing statesmen received his requests unfavorably because they unjustly saw the British as a rapacious and expanding power in India. Discussions among the Qing court's Manchu grandees in this period remain something of a black box, and a definitive judgment about whether Fuk'anggan and other high ministers did anything to sabotage Macartney's mission is impossible. More significant than the court politics involved, however, is the diverging structures of the Qing and British empires revealed in this encounter. Macartney, briefed on maritime and overland contact between the two empires, took it for granted that the Qing court also had an integrated perspective. In fact, the Qing state was not designed to coordinate between frontiers, and only with the greatest effort could it even begin to reconcile Inner Asian and maritime intelligence. This tendency to treat each frontier separately easily survived the discoveries attending the first major diplomatic encounter with Britain.

Several clues might have led the Qing court to associate Macartney's maritime mission with events below the Tibetan frontier. For Qing observers he had been sent by the English, usually called the Yingjili in Chinese, a maritime people with a steadily increasing portion of the Guangzhou trade. As Europeans, they were classified along with the Dutch as belonging to the Hongmao type, and also placed in certain contexts within the (Great) Western Ocean classification. Contemporary documents remark, for instance, that England "is a Hongmao country" (*ji xi Hongmao-guo*).[90] Thus, England was a candidate to match Yan Tingliang's "Hongmao country" below Tibet that bordered on the Western Ocean, and Fuk'anggan's description of a Western Ocean country that traded at Guangzhou.

There was, of course, countervailing evidence militating against the identification of England with the Pileng. Most obviously, they had different names: the English had never mentioned any term that sounded like Pileng or Galigada, nor had the Pileng alluded to the Yingjili. Second, the Macartney mission was first announced to the Qing at Guangzhou as a belated response to the emperor's eightieth birthday, with no mention of events in Tibet, which a Pileng embassy would surely have made. This was for the simple reason that prior to Macartney's arrival in China neither he nor the East India Company Select Committee at Guangzhou were aware of the role played by British authorities in Bengal during the recent Qing-Gurkha war.

Thus, the Yingjili-Pileng relationship remained an open question in Beijing at the time of Macartney's arrival: no evidence conclusively linked them, but the possibility of a link was clear. Still, even if such a connection was proven, there was no reason to expect dramatic results. Yan's early report that the Hongmao neighbored Tibet had left the emperor unconcerned. Indeed, he assumed that the Hongmao trade at Guangzhou would prevent them from siding with the Gurkhas. Fuk'anggan found this to be so: the Pileng had recorded their gratitude for the Guangzhou trade and refused to aid Qing enemies. Nor had reports from Tibet cast the Pileng in a sinister light. Based on Qing sources, there is no reason to think Lord Macartney's mission would have been harmed by establishing a Pileng-Yingjili connection. For the British themselves, the situation was even more clear-cut: their behavior in the recent war had been exemplary and could positively help Macartney's mission. The Company government in Bengal acted on precisely this view. On July 26, 1793, after the return of Kirkpatrick to Calcutta, the governor-general sent a dispatch to Macartney relating recent events and including copies of correspondence with Fuk'anggan and the Dalai Lama, with passages "acknowledging their obligation to us for declining to interfere in support of the Rajah [of Nepal] at that period."[91] The Select Committee at Guangzhou, which received news of Himalayan events via a private letter on September 11, a month after Macartney landed near Beijing, felt that materials "which may be so successfully employed by the Ambassador, in his Negotiations at Pekin" should reach him at once, and attempted to forward the correspondence, although logistics prevented this.[92]

Yet, in Beijing Lord Macartney was starting to suspect that Himalayan events lay behind a malignant influence in high government circles he felt was working against his embassy. When he left England, neither he nor his principals in London were aware of contact between Fuk'anggan and Cornwallis. However, his instructions dealt with the question of India more generally. Now that Britain had extensive territories there, it was proper to establish "sufficient means of representation and transaction of business" with "principal neighbours" such as the Qing. In such interactions it was necessary to "obviate any prejudice which may arise from the argument of our present dominions in India" by explaining British expansion as self-defense. This last point was necessary because "it is the great object of other European Nations to inspire . . . the Emperor and Ministers of China with an idea of danger in countenancing the Subjects of Great Britain, as if it were the intention of this Country to aim at extending its territory in every quarter."[93] In short, Macartney was instructed to assume that the Qing knew of developments in India and might be swayed by them.

Macartney came ashore on August 5, 1793. He was attended upon his arrival by Regional Vice Commander Wang Wenxiong and the Circuit Intendant Qiao Renjie.[94] At some point before August 16, in Tongzhou on his way to Beijing, Macartney reported that these men "turned the discourse upon our dominions in Bengal, and affirmed that some British troops from thence had lately given assistance to the insurgents in Tibet." Ignorant of recent events in Bengal, Macartney "instantly told them that the thing was impossible, and that I could take upon me to contradict it in the most decisive manner." Qing forces, the men asserted, had unexpectedly "met with a check" that could only be explained by European aid to their enemies, and claimed that "several persons with hats" had been seen among their enemies. Macartney thought this assertion might be "merely a feint or artifice to sift me and try to discover our force or our vicinity to their frontiers." One or two days later the men asked if the English in Bengal would aid the Qing emperor "against the rebels in those parts." Macartney suspected a ploy to get him to contradict his earlier assertions. He again protested that British possessions were too far from Qing territory to be of aid.[95] This seems to have been the only occasion during the entire embassy in which the Qing side explicitly referred to the events of the Gurkha War. However, when Macartney first met Fuk'anggan on September 15 he found him "formal and repulsive," with an "indisposition" toward the English. Another high official later confirmed to Macartney that Fuk'anggan in particular held "prejudices" against the English. Macartney at first assumed this to stem from his tenure administering Guangzhou as governor-general of Liang-Guang. Soon, however, he was to impute it a different origin.[96]

On November 9, at Hangzhou on his return journey, Macartney wrote a report to Henry Dundas (1742–1811), the minister supervising his embassy.

His dispatch is worth quoting at length. According to his understanding, the Qing army in Tibet

> suffered greater losses than were foreseen from such an enemy.... Some of the Chinese Officers immediately fancied, that they perceived European Troops.... These, it was concluded, could be only English. The Report put forward among the People was that on the contrary, we had given assistance. Tho' I take for granted, neither fact to be true, yet the persuasion of the former was sufficient to alienate from us the Administration of China.... The Ministers, coupling it with our supposed hostility, and our real strength on the side of India, were disposed to suspect some sinister intention latent under our present proffer of gifts and Friendship.⁹⁷

In other words, Macartney believed that the Qing reaction to his embassy was conditioned by the court's knowledge of British power in India. This reception was not entirely unexpected:

> In the instructions ... you were perfectly aware of the prejudices ... as to [our] ambitious views from the circumstance of our acquisition of Bengal, and you pointed out the judicious method I was to follow in order to allay any suspicions arising from a Dominion, so accidental and so little sought for, but it was impossible to foresee or prepare against the imputation of an interference with the Chinese Arms, which has really never taken place.⁹⁸

To counteract these anti-British views, Macartney resorted to subtle diplomacy. His information on events in Bengal was "collected in secret and distant hints" from Wang and Qiao, whom he considered friendly. However, only their superior, the hostile official Zheng-rui (fl. 1762–1814), was authorized to report directly to the court. The English ambassador therefore

> took opportunities of conveying [to Zheng-rui] information of the great distance of our Chief Settlements [in India] from Thibet, and our little connection with that Country; of the occupation of all our Troops in Hindostan till lately in the Southern Parts of it against Tippoo, as well as of the Instructions given constantly to our Governors of Bengal particularly to respect such of its neighbours, as were amicably connected with, or under the Protection of the Chinese Empire—⁹⁹

During a private audience in Jehol, Macartney spoke directly to Hešen, the most influential minister, about the circumstances of the British in India:

> In the course of Conversation I took occasion to mention as matters of information ... that upon the Dissolution of the Mogul Empire, in consequence of internal dissensions, some of the Maritime Powers claimed the

protection of our Arms, which was granted without removing the native tributary Princes, who are to this hour in possession of their dignities, as well as of security by our means, which is effected chiefly by our not consenting to any interference in the Contests of the neighbouring Countries. He avoided giving me an opening to be more particular in the Disavowal of aid to the People of Thibet, and I found it necessary to use great tenderness, and many qualified expressions, in conveying any idea that a connection between Great Britain and this Country could be of any importance to the latter.¹⁰⁰

Not until Macartney arrived at Guangzhou and read reports from British India, including correspondence between Fuk'anggan and Cornwallis, did his view of events solidify. The Qing had been fighting not rebel Tibetans but the ruler of Nepal. The blameless actions of the East India Company had for some reason been misrepresented to the Qing throne. Probably to justify military setbacks, Macartney believed, Fuk'anggan was claiming that the British had sided with Nepal against the Qing.¹⁰¹

Is Macartney's interpretation of events corroborated by the Qing record? Two items provide insight into the connection the court perceived between the Macartney embassy and events in India. The first is purely geographic, the translations by missionaries of references in the letter of King George III to Qianlong. The original stated that the British had made peace in India "by engaging Our Allies in Hindostan to put an end to hostilities occasioned by an attack of an ambitious Neighbour." This was translated into Chinese as "a person from a neighboring Hongmao country of the Small Western Ocean (*Xiao Xiyang Hongmao linguo de ren*) unreasonably fought us, but this also has all been pacified." The reference is to the Third Mysore War (1790–1792) against Tipu Sultan, but apparently the missionary translators, unfamiliar with recent events, assumed that a European rival in India was indicated. Discussing Macartney's qualifications, King George referred to his envoy as being "appointed to the Government General of Bengal," a post Macartney had been offered but declined. This was translated as "he had gone to such colonies as Bengal in the Small Western Ocean (*Xiao Xiyang Bengala dengchu shuguo difang*) where he had managed affairs." Finally, it stated that Sir George Leonard Staunton (1737–1801) "exercised with ability and success the Office of Commissioner for treating and making Peace with Tippoo Sultaun, one of the most considerable Princes of Hindostan." This was rendered in Chinese as "He had gone to the country of Hindustan in the Small Western Ocean (*Xiao Xiyang Hendusitan-guo*) to mediate a peace with the king Dibo Suwo'erdang."¹⁰²

This translation is rife with ambiguity. Jesuit translators distinguished the Great and Small Western Oceans, while Qianlong and his ministers referred to Europe throughout the embassy simply as the Western Ocean. Although "Small Western Ocean" would have alerted Qing readers that a smaller and nearer European branch polity was being invoked, "a neighboring Hongmao country" had the opposite implication. In the letter it indicated a state in India, but around the same time the Jesuits described England proper as *the* or *a* Hongmao country, located "in the north of the Western Ocean, northwest of the Qing empire."[103] "Hendusitan" made clear that the British were politically active in the vicinity of Nepal, since Qianlong now recognized the Gurkhas as an "independent tribe of Hindustan." On the other hand, references to "Bengal of the Small Western Ocean" bore no obvious link to the equivalent terms for that area used in Tibet, such as Pileng, Galigada, or Acharya. In short, this letter would have shown the Qing court that British power reached close to Nepal and Tibet, but little else.

Only later in the embassy did the Qing court pinpoint a direct connection between the English and the Pileng. Their source was the Gurkha informant Gang-ga-le-ta-ze-xi, who had once served in the royal palace. Captured by Tibetan forces in September 1791, very early in the second war, he developed a reputation among the Qing commanders as a reliable informant, exposing Gurkha spies, advising them on routes in Nepal, and identifying both live prisoners and severed heads. At the end of the war he was afraid of retribution and the Qing government agreed to let him remain in China with the Scouting Brigade (*Jianrui ying*), based in the Western Hills just outside Beijing.[104] On October 18, 1793, after Macartney had departed from Beijing, a Qing official was dispatched to ask him a series of questions: Are the English the Pileng? What are the customs of that place? How large is its territory? How far is it from Nepal? Are there intervening countries? How far is it from Guangdong and Macao?[105]

Gang-ga-le-ta-ze-xi's remarks were illuminating. First, he asserted that Nepal neighbored Calcutta. Pileng, strictly speaking, was not a geographic but a pejorative name: men of Calcutta were hated for their violent behavior and called Pileng, Farangi, which is "like saying 'villain' (*you yan e'ren*)." On its northwest "Calcutta" (i.e., Bengal and Bihar) bordered Nepal, and Kathmandu was over thirty days' journey from this frontier. To the north it bordered Bhutan and to the south Chaibasa (Zhebusa), both around twenty days from Calcutta; to the east it bordered many small states, and to the west the territories of the Mughal empire (Dili Bacha, i.e., Awadh), both about one month's journey. Gurkha and Calcutta were mutually independent, he testified, though the Gurkha king propitiated Calcutta with gifts. Never having been to Calcutta, he could not tell how far it was from Guangdong and Macao. However, he had seen men from Calcutta who had visited Nepal, and Macartney resembled them in his appearance and garb. It is unclear whether this Nepali informant had seen Macartney in person, or merely a drawing of him, but he judged on the basis of their physical similarity that "probably, Calcutta is England" (*dayue Galigada ji xi Yingjili*). Here again there is ambiguity: were England and Calcutta identical, or just part of the same political structure? His phraseology supports the former interpretation, although a Nepali must have known that the English were not native to Calcutta.

Thus, the Qing court knew by the end of the Macartney embassy that he represented a country active near Tibet. However, the Qing documentary record either fails to corroborate or contradicts much of Macartney's interpretation of how this influenced his reception. There is no evidence that Wang and Qiao were ordered by the court to "sift" Macartney about the proximity of Bengal to Tibet, nor that Fuk'anggan had misrepresented the Pileng role in the Gurkha War in the way Macartney suggested. To the contrary, his recorded attitude toward that country was favorable and his reports to Beijing reflected the actual content of the British letter, albeit with a tributary gloss. Still, Macartney's account cannot be dismissed out of hand. He surely did not invent Wang and Qiao's references to British India or Fuk'anggan's hostility. Moreover, Macartney broached the subject of British India with both Zheng-rui and Hešen, although given his "many qualified expressions" one can assume much miscommunication and misapprehension on the topic. At present it is unclear why Wang and Qiao inquired about British activity near Tibet, and what geographic names they used in their inquiries. Did they actually mention "Bengal"? Would a Qing commander in 1792 really judge European arms to be so superior, or does that reflect Macartney's own assumptions?

There is no sure answer these questions. If we accept Macartney's view that Fuk'anggan was particularly hostile to him, and that this hostility derived from events during the Qing-Gurkha war, then Qing documents suggest that it emerged not in Tibet but after Macartney's arrival. Fuk'anggan had taken the Pileng seriously. Hearing that a "Pileng envoy" was on his way, Fuk'anggan asked to remain in Tibet and met Daljit Gir.[106] He was informed that the Pileng planned to send a mediator. Fuk'anggan stated that this was unnecessary and soon thereafter left Tibet. When he returned to Beijing he learned that an English embassy was on its way, and probably learned from He-lin's reports that a maritime mission from the Pileng was also coming to China. To conjecture, it seems likely that Fuk'anggan would have had a hunch that Macartney was tied to the Pileng, and this might have concerned him. Since he had ordered Cornwallis to send any future correspondence via Tibet, why would the Pileng now send a mission right to Beijing, bypassing field officials? This might suggest that the Pileng-English were trying to use their role in the war to bargain for special commercial considerations—which is exactly what Macartney would have done if he had received the reports from India in time. Qianlong had already rebuked Fuk'anggan for relying too heavily on the aid of other tribes. If the Pileng-English now clamored for a reward, this might cause problems for Fuk'anggan. This interpretation, although purely conjectural, would explain why Fuk'anggan showed no aversion to the Pileng in Tibet yet was ill-disposed toward Macartney in Beijing. Perhaps the questions posed to Macartney upon his arrival by Wang and Qiao were a private attempt by Fuk'anggan or his allies to discover the exact ties between Macartney and the Pileng.

Repercussions of the Macartney Mission

Macartney left China convinced Fuk'anggan's false reports had poisoned the Qing court against British India. Still, he optimistically speculated that a more accurate picture of Britain's benevolent intentions and recent intervention would persuade Qianlong to abandon his "jealousy" of its power in Bengal and possibly even grant it expanded trading rights.[107] To smooth relations and correct the falsehoods ostensibly circulated by Fuk'anggan, a letter signed by King George III was sent in June 1795 as a reply to Qianlong's edict. The British monarch tried to set the record straight about his governor-general's conduct during the war, which Macartney had been unable to do in person:

> We have given particular instructions to our Chief Governor in India, to hold the most friendly & attentive conduct towards such of your Imperial Majesty's Troops or other subjects who may approach that neighbourhood. In consequence of which, upon application some time ago from one of your Generals then commanding in Thibet, our Governor interposed in such a manner as to be of material service. Our Embassador at your Court not hav-

ing during his stay there, any communication with our Territories in Hindostan, could not know or mention to your Majesty, the circumstances that occurred on that occasion, & thereby evince the sincerity of our regard.[108]

Once again the Qing empire's highest ministers would have to consider an English reference to British India.

Geopolitical commentary expressed in English might be translated into Chinese by many paths, and the reception of George III's letter at Guangzhou reveals another. The English original was sent together with a Chinese translation by George Thomas Staunton (1781–1859), son of Macartney's principal secretary. Staunton the younger had learned Chinese during that mission, and was perhaps the only Englishman then capable of writing in it. He translated this passage in an extremely vague way, possibly because of his limited Chinese geographic vocabulary: "India" and "Hindustan" were both translated as "Small Western Ocean," and "one of your Generals then commanding in Tibet" was translated as "an imperial general at that time not far from the Small Western Ocean." When this translation was perused in Guangzhou it was found to be "mistaken in its literary arrangement, and difficult to punctuate," leading Liang-Guang Governor-General Zhu Gui (1731–1807) to have a local translator collate the English original and Staunton's attempt into a fresh Chinese version.

The result demonstrates how far local geographic usage in Cantonese departed from that in Beijing. The translator rendered "Chief Governor in India" as "officials in such places as Gangjiao" (*Gangjiao deng chu difang guanyuan*).[109] The English "Thibet" was rendered "Dimi" (possibly "Ti-bi" in the translator's dialect), while Hindostan was translated as "Yandushidan."[110] Puzzled by the name Dimi (which of course bore no relation to Chinese terms for Tibet such as Xizang or Wei-Zang), Zhu consulted the head of the English factory, who described it as "a place in northwest China adjoining the sea route to his own [home] country" (*zai Zhonghua xibei difang, yu benguo haidao pilian*). Some miscommunication must have occurred, since this can hardly be a description of landlocked Tibet. Zhu remarked that Dimi "seems to be Gurkhas," so he clearly got the gist if not the details of the letter.

The British government had adopted the delicate phraseology "our Governor interposed in such a manner as to be of material service." This reference to Cornwallis's benevolent neutrality and proffered mediation was difficult to interpret and translate. Staunton rendered it very colloquially as "he [the governor-general] did a good deed for the Chinese forces" (*ta zuole haoshi yu Zhongguo junzhen*). Zhu's translator adopted the more straightforward term "helped" (*xiangzhu*). Zhu assumed this to mean military assistance and memorialized that the British claimed to have "dispatched troops to help" (*fabing xiangzhu*).[111] Qianlong replied to George III with an account of Fuk'anggan's victory, adding that the Qing "had not troubled your country's military force." He also remarked in this reply that "your king sent an emissary to Tibet" (*er guowang qian shi qianfu Wei-Zang*), showing that he recognized Daljit Gir from the Pileng and Macartney from the English to serve the same ruler.[112] Perhaps Qianlong identified the English king with the guo'erna'er or his overlord the Dili bacha. This would follow logically from the testimony of Gang-ga-le-ta-ze-xi that "probably, Calcutta is England." Whatever the Qing court's conception of the precise relationship between the English at Guangzhou and the Pileng, it is clear that by 1796 they were recognized to be the same. How far did this knowledge, and other aspects of Indian geography gleaned during the war, circulate beyond the highest echelons of the Qing court?

Strategy, Geography, and the Flow of Information

Qianlong's war with the Gurkhas was the last of his "Ten Great Victories." By the time his armies returned, the great scholarly projects of his reign had largely been completed, and there was no appetite to launch more. Whereas intelligence brought back from the Junghar campaigns was subject to minute philological and historical examination, the equally distinctive local geographic lexicon found in the Himalayas received little analysis. During the war, intelligence had been analyzed at two levels: the localized explanations given in Tibet on the basis of regional knowledge, and more extensive examinations made at the court using a wide variety of informants. These local Tibetan inquiries circulated widely after the war, but the fact that the Pileng were connected to the British does not seem to have passed beyond the Grand Council into the broader scholarly world and quickly became obscure even at the court.

The discovery that the Pileng were the English had been made in stages, mostly on the pages of secret memorials and court letters containing imperial edicts, sources open only to commanders in the field, the Grand Councilors and council clerks, and the emperor himself. Qianlong's reign is often seen as the apex of Qing involvement in, and influence over, Tibetan politics. Yet the last decade of the eighteenth century was not kind to the men who had learned the cumulative geographic and strategic lessons of the Gurkha campaigns. Fuk'anggan, Sun Shiyi, and He-lin, the highest field officials overseeing the war, all died in 1796 while putting down a Miao rebellion. Qianlong and Hešen both died in 1799, the influential Grand Councilor Agūi predeceased them, and Fucanggan was permanently demoted away from court upon the ascension of Qianlong's son Jiaqing, who himself played no role in the pre-1799 administration.[113] Other officials with a more tangential involvement in the war and the Macartney embassy remained, but after 1799 the connection between the Pileng and the English was primarily stored in archival files rather than the memory of serving ministers. The impact of this sudden loss of expertise will be considered in the next chapter.

Seven new works about Tibet came to circulate among scholars between 1790 and 1800. One of these, the *Xizang zhi*, was simply the first printing of a much older work dating to around 1741 and therefore silent on recent developments.[114] Two Chinese officials had composed a book of annotated maps, ethnographic drawings, and brief essays entitled the *Wei-Zang tuzhi*. The printed preface bears a date of QL57/4 (April 21–May 20, 1792), not long after Fuk'anggan reached Lhasa, so it is not surprising to find in it no mention of the Pileng, Galigada, or related geographic concepts that emerged during the second campaign.[115]

Five other works, composed by officials, did refer to wartime events. A gazetteer of Tibet, the *Wei-Zang tongzhi* (conventionally attributed to He-lin), consisted mostly of wartime memorials and other documents. It circulated in manuscript until 1895. This work included an entry on the Delhi Padshah, which He-lin defined as "a large tribe to the southwest, subject to which are Calcutta, Pileng, Acharya, and such places." The entry is simply a reproduction of Fuk'anggan's memorial on the report of Daljit Gir, with no further annotation or explanation.[116] Sungyūn (1752–1835), who served as amban in Tibet after seeing off Macartney, later composed a series of essays on Tibetan administration with appended maps, the *Xizhao tushuo*. These maps depicted "Calcutta, a tribe of the Western Ocean," which was located beside "East India, that is, Acharya" (*dong Jiaga'er ji Azanla*).[117] Neither map nor text described the relationship between the Pileng and the English. Another amban, He-ning (1740–1821), composed an annotated prose poem about Tibet, the *Xizang fu*, published in 1797. This poem mentioned the Pileng and Calcutta as outlined in Fuk'anggan's memorials. The official campaign history, the *Kuo'erka jilüe*, was printed in 1795, but mentions the

Pileng only as they were known to Fuk'anggan in Tibet. A new edition of the *Sichuan tongzhi* (printed 1816) also appeared, containing entries for the Pileng and the Delhi Padshah as foreign countries, but these again were simply excerpts from the original memorial of Fuk'anggan's interview with Daljit Gir, with no further explanation.[118]

Another, more intriguing work was written by Zhou Ailian, who between 1791 and 1793 served in Tibet and Sichuan as an unofficial consultant assisting Sun Shiyi with campaign logistics. In 1798 he completed a manuscript describing his experiences, the *Zhuguo jiyou*, which was not published in the Qing period. In his manuscript he remarked on the proximity of the Gurkhas to the country of the Hongmao, and the proximity of the latter to the Western Ocean. All of this could easily have been gleaned from wartime correspondence passing through Sun's headquarters. However, Zhou also had the chance to interview a Kashmiri merchant, who told him about India (Jiaga'er) based on his personal experience:

> "It is extremely rich . . . also, its king is a *Kha-che* [Muslim] but now holds only an empty position. Two people with very great offices take general charge of affairs. They are of the Christian (*Tianzhu jiao*) religion, and all matters of revenue are under their control. They only use this country's original ruler and dynastic name to subdue the various tribes.[119] They also have one or two Cantonese people there who serve as interpreters, and some Cantonese silk and porcelain is taken to India by sea and sold onward into Tibet". . . . By this we may know that it is no falsehood that Christians plot secretly to invade territories, coming on gradually.[120]

Even Zhou, however, does not seem to have recognized that the Christians were specifically English, still less that the English were close affiliates of the Pileng tribe in Bengal.

Conclusion: Success or Failure at the End of the Qianlong Period?

More geographic information often produced not a clearer understanding of the world but, in an irony already noted, greater ambiguity and uncertainty. Under Qianlong, the Qing state's meticulous and expansive intelligence gathering brought into its net reports of virtually irreconcilable complexity. Setting aside information about India already present by 1790, Qing observers following the Gurkha campaign encountered a torrent of new and puzzling terms. Some—Farangi, Delhi Padshah, Calcutta, Acharya, Borgi—had entered from India and taken on a Tibetanized form. Others, notably

Rgya-gar, were indigenous to Tibet. Fuk'anggan's reports to the capital reproduced this Tibetan perspective in Chinese transcription. Key words for India used by the geographer 'Jigs-med-gling-pa in 1789 are familiar in Qing documents by 1793: *Rgya-gar* became *Jiaga'er*, *Phe-reng(-ba)* became *Pileng*, *Ṭi-ling pa-ca* became *Dili bacha*, and *Ka-li-ka-ta* became *Galigada*.[121]

When such a local micro-system of geographic usage was transcribed into Chinese or Manchu, it had no intrinsic meaning for officials in Beijing. It could be deciphered only when related to other geographic vocabularies. With the arrival of Macartney this task gained political urgency: how did the Pileng connect to the Yingjili or to Gangjiao? Such questions were addressed in secret memorials available to a tiny group of high officials; others could learn about the Pileng only as they appeared from a purely Tibetan vantage. At the very top, an elite cohort used a sophisticated intelligence operation to gather various strands of information, from Chinese, Jesuits, Indians, Gurkha ambassadors and prisoners, and Britons, and partially solved this puzzle. Clues suggested that Yarkand's Hindustan, Tibet's Rgya-gar, Guangzhou's Gangjiao, and Europe's Small Western Ocean all overlapped with the Manchu Enetkek and the Chinese Yindu. Yet many details remained to be worked out: How did the Delhi Padshah (alias the khan of Hindustan, Kha-che king, and Mowo'er) connect to the Pileng guo'erna'er, the "official in Gangjiao," or the king of England? How did England itself relate to the Western Ocean and the country of the Hongmao below Tibet? That the court made headway shows its skill in battling through cosmological agnosticism, linguistic multiplicity, the administrative complexity of British imperialism, and the political and religious bias inherent in all testimony.

Yet to expect at this juncture a eureka moment, a fundamental revolution in Qing worldviews, is to misunderstand the Qing state and scholarly world. Frontier policy relied on much more than the persistence of confusion over geographic identity. Even geographically, Qing observers were not particularly surprised to find Westerners in India. The failure of the Pileng-English connection to attract more notice had deeper roots. Strategically, the details of that tie remained cloudy, and the court was reluctant to make major decisions on the basis of very conjectural evidence. For all Qianlong knew, the English had always quietly traded in India. Certainly, the Pileng lived far from the Himalayas, and seemingly would not have come to the attention of the Qing except for the anomalous conditions of the Gurkha War. Now, it was hoped that Tibet could return to the quiet status quo.

Unless the Pileng-English link was viewed in light of a trajectory of massive British expansion, of a scale that seemed to approach the Junghar threat, there was no obvious reason why the Qing had to change its strategic thinking and coordinate policy across multiple frontiers.

Continuity in strategic thinking was buttressed by the structure of the Qing state. The Pileng-English identification could not have been made on any single frontier; it depended on the central coordination of intelligence. This had occurred in 1793 because of the coincidence of the Gurkha War and the Macartney embassy, both exceptional events demanding careful scrutiny. Normally, the Grand Council was less active in interpreting the raw intelligence passed up from the frontier. Indeed, since such interpretation in Beijing generally produced only conjecture, it was safer to rely purely on local intelligence. In planning its operations, then, the Qing state had good reason to rely only on regional informants, accepted on their own terms, and reason on this comparatively sure footing. After 1793, events in Tibet or on the coast would continue to be met by such localized analysis—only the very gravest matters would attract sustained high-level attempts at coordination by the Grand Council. In this way, geographic, strategic, and bureaucratic methods and assumptions stabilized each other, and the Qing state passed through the turbulent 1790s without fundamental changes to its geostrategic worldview.

PART THREE

The Age of Transition, 1800–1838

FIVE

British India and Qing Strategic Thought in the Early Nineteenth Century

When Macartney left China, British power in Asia was already formidable; two decades later it had become overwhelming. Impelled by local and global motives, it pushed forward in all directions from its Indian epicenter. At the outbreak of war with revolutionary France in 1793, Bengal and Bihar were the only major portions of Indian territory directly controlled by the East India Company. Between 1798 and 1805, under the governor-generalship of Richard Wellesley (1760–1842), it achieved military hegemony on the subcontinent by defeating its major opponent, the Marathas. During the fighting, Delhi was taken and the Mughal emperor Shah Alam II (1728–1806) entered British custody. Tough regional rivals remained, but thereafter no Indian power enjoyed anything approaching the Company's reach and resources.[1]

From this strengthened position, British power pushed closer to the Qing frontier. Eastward, Malacca was captured from the Dutch in 1795, Java temporarily seized in 1811, Macao briefly occupied by British troops in 1808, and Singapore founded in 1819. Well before Napoleon's defeat, Britain had no naval equal in the Indian Ocean or China Seas. Westward, Company territory was extended to the Sutlej River, facing the Punjab. In 1814 war broke out with Nepal, allowing the seizure of a strip of the Himalayas bordering Tibet. By 1820, an Englishman was in Ladakh asking to travel across the Karakorams to Yarkand. Agents and subjects of the East India Company were appearing all along the southern rim of the Qing empire. The British empire, together with its Russian counterpart, had outstripped French, Dutch, Spanish, and Portuguese competition to match the Qing as a dominant Asian power.

Many Asian and European powers were alarmed by the Company's growing strength, and several made representations to Beijing about the danger posed by this voracious neighbor. At times, frontier incidents led Qing officials to launch their own inquiries into the activities of the Company. By the late 1830s, the Grand Council had filed away memorials and depositions from many points on the frontier describing relevant wars and incursions, interviews and applications. These show that the Qing court continued to apply a frontier policy. Intelligence was assiduously gathered, but not synthesized. Links between different frontiers were occasionally recognized, but not systematically pursued. Each remained a distinct field of strategic analysis; the empire's overall strategic position was not considered. This regionally fragmented worldview caused the Qing empire's strategic outlook increasingly to diverge from that of its neighbors. While Indian and European states sought allies and feared hostile coalitions, the Qing empire deliberately shunned international engagements and made ready to defend its territory, if necessary, on the frontier itself. To understand this policy it is necessary to reconstruct the Qing state's perspective in this turbulent period, seen from the coast, Tibet, and Xinjiang.

Views of British India from the Chinese Coast

INDIAN TRADE AND INDIAN MERCHANTS AT GUANGZHOU

When the East India Company took over the administration and defense of Bengal, it sought to increase tax revenues by bolstering agricultural production. Particularly attractive was the cultivation of crops for export to China, which both increased domestic income and realized cash at Guangzhou to finance the purchase of tea.[2] Maritime trade between India and China formed one side of a triangular Indian-Chinese-British traffic that was crucial to the finances of the East India Company.[3] As early as 1787 the country trade, as it was called, supplied over half the funds required for the purchase of tea.[4]

At first the role of opium in this trade grew slowly: in 1820 China imported 4,186 chests, fewer than the 4,570 of 1801. By 1830, however, the number had almost quadrupled to 16,257; by 1838, on the eve of the Opium War, it had doubled to 34,373. This led China into a persistent trade deficit with India amounting to millions of silver dollars annually, and helped upset the copper-silver balance crucial to China's bimetallic currency system. China's economic instability began to concern officials and private scholars.[5]

Maritime trade led to a permanent Indian resident population at Guangzhou.[6] The first Parsi merchant visited China in 1756, and the Indian population subsequently rose in parallel with private British traders.[7] W. C. Hunter, in Guangzhou between 1825 and 1844, recalled seeing "Parsees, Moormen, or other natives of India."[8] Another merchant claimed there were two hundred Parsi residents of Guangzhou in 1825, against forty "born Englishmen," and Parsis constituted a quarter of the major opium merchants singled out in 1839.[9] No standard term, Guo Deyan notes, was applied to all resident Indians. Aside from various Chinese transcriptions of the term "Parsi," descriptions included "white-headed" (*baitou*) foreigner, a term Chen Lunjiong had already applied to Indians and Central Asians almost a century before.[10]

Indian merchants at Guangzhou did not increase official knowledge of growing British power in India. No connection, etymological or otherwise, existed between the names used for India and Indians at Guangzhou and those on other frontiers. Generic names for India, such as Tianzhu or Yindu, were not applied to this community. The Parsis, the largest group of Indians at Guangzhou, had a long-standing and fundamentally symbiotic relationship with the British government and merchants, and no incentive to raise Qing alarm at Britain's Indian empire.[11]

Still, the growing presence of Indian subjects of the British did show Qing officials that "England" was not monolithic. Their appreciation of this fact was colored by local geographic lexicons. At Guangzhou the ports of British India (and by extension India itself) were termed "Gangjiao," a word of obscure origin and slippery usage. Today, China's premier dictionary defines it as "the various commercial ports of British India prior to the Opium War," and also to "British and Indian merchants trading at that time in Guangzhou who did not belong to the East India Company."[12] The English word of equivalent scope was "Country," which in Anglo-Indian vocabulary was "used colloquially, and in trade, as an adjective to distinguish articles produced in India . . . from such as are imported, and especially imported from Europe. Indeed Europe was . . . used as the contrary adjective . . . '*country* ships' are those which are owned in Indian ports."[13] Scholarly consensus regards Gangjiao as a Chinese transcription of the English word "Country," although several anomalies remain to be explained.[14]

Broadly speaking, Qing officials before the 1830s recognized Gangjiao as a distinct territory maintaining certain ill-defined connections to England proper. An 1816 memorial by Governor-General Jiang Youxian referred to "twenty-some Company (*zujia*) ships belonging to the king of this country [i.e., England] and Country (*Gangjiao*) ships belonging to people of this country."[15] Jiang elaborated on this distinction elsewhere: "Company (*zujia*) ships carry goods for royal trade, Gangjiao ships carry goods for the trade of commoners (*guoren*)."[16] Here "Gangjiao" was employed to distinguish private "Country" trade from royally charted Company trade, but it was not entirely without geographic connotations: *zujia*, literally "ancestral home[land]," referred to the imperial metropole. The private geographer Wang Dahai reported that the Dutch, when evicted from Java by the English, "fled back to their ancestral home" (*taohui zujia*).[17] Thus, *zujia*-Gangjiao also implied a homeland-colony distinction. In other instances, its ethnic or geographic overtones were more pronounced. As seen in Chapter Four, Gangjiao was selected by the Cantonese translator to render the English word "India" in George III's 1795 letter to Qianlong. Guangdong governor Li Shiyao (d. 1788) mentioned in a memorial of 1780 that a ship from "the English territory of Madras" had brought a petition from "a Gangjiao foreign devil" (*Gangjiao guizi*), presumably an Indian.[18] Ruan Yuan described newly arrived Arab merchants as "white-headed [i.e., white-turbaned] Muslims of the Small Western Ocean," and remarked that "the shape of their vessel, their visages and the sound of their language is similar to that of merchants from Gangjiao," presumably meaning Parsis or other Indians.[19] A Parsi was described by Governor-General Li Hongbin (1767–1845) in 1830 as "an English Gangjiao white-headed foreigner" (*Yingjili Gangjiao baitou yi*).[20] In these last three cases, Gangjiao was used to distinguish ethnically Indian merchants from Europeans; "white-headed" resembled the term "turbaned" (*chantou*), a common designation for overland Muslim traders.

Although often described as subject to the English, Gangjiao was regarded as a distinct political entity. Li Hongbin remarked to the emperor that "these foreigners speak different languages and practice different customs; for example, the various countries of America, Gangjiao, Luzon [Spanish vessels from Manila], and Holland, although not obedient, are still not very tricky; only the English foreign merchants are most disobedient."[21]

Implicitly, England and Gangjiao were considered separate, perhaps because the ties between the two remained poorly understood before the early 1830s.

Officials at Guangzhou had little incentive to investigate British India, despite its central importance for the trade and smuggling problems they confronted. Limited by the pressures of work and the instinct of self-preservation, they concentrated on problems within their jurisdiction, commenting on global politics only when they shed light on local events involving foreigners. Rough familiarity with international grudges was useful for interpreting the behavior of overseas merchants at Guangdong. Otherwise, official correspondence generally abstained from geopolitical commentary on trends and institutions beyond the frontier. In regard to the opium trade, the Jiaqing and Daoguang emperors generally endorsed a policy of "frontier prohibition" that tried to staunch its influx on the coast.[22] This prohibition was limited to coastal waters, and opium was not tracked to the land of its origin. As Li Hongbin and Lu Kun (1772–1835) commented in 1830, "The route of [opium] importation comes from [the lands of] foreigners (*waiyi*), separated by a great ocean, at a distance of several tens of thousands of *li*, so there is no way to prevent its arrival. This is not like countries such as Vietnam or Siam, where we can still strictly notify their king when they break the law, commanding them to stop."[23] For Li and Lu, opium originated beyond the reach of Qing political influence; it was infeasible to target the site of its production, and therefore there was no pressing need to pinpoint that exact location.[24] Alarm about opium importation did not at first lead to interest in India, or even the recognition that opium was almost entirely an Indian product.

BRITISH MILITARY OPERATIONS ON THE COAST

British India's influence on the Pearl River delta was not simply economic. During the Napoleonic Wars, in response to fears that French power over Portugal might end British access to Macao, essential for trade, two abortive missions were sent from India to occupy that city. In the first, Royal and Company forces reached the Pearl River delta in March 1802. Without instructions from Goa, the Portuguese governor refused to admit the troops ostensibly dispatched to support his own garrison. The prospect of British troops landing at Macao also alarmed the Select Committee, the permanent representatives of the East India Company's interests in China. They recalled Macartney's report of Qing suspicion, and added that the recent conquest of Mysore "more or less tended to produce in the minds of the Chinese a dread of the English Nation, and impressed them with an idea of their aiming at universal Conquest in the East."[25] Fearing a trade embargo, they opposed the disembarkation of troops without Qing consent. In late April news of the impending Peace of Amiens between Britain and France reached Macao, and the force returned toward India in early July.[26]

As a scholar of opium smuggling has justly observed, "officials at Canton distorted facts in their memorials in order to evade responsibility, and as a result it came to be that adequate and accurate intelligence was not transmitted to the central government in Beijing. In short, an extremely deep disparity emerged between the central and local [governments] in terms of the quantity and quality of intelligence."[27] This was the case with the Macao expedition. The governor-general of Liang-Guang had enormous power to sculpt the form of information reaching Beijing, and his primary interest lay in downplaying incidents in the area under his jurisdiction. The incumbent in that office, Giking (d. 1802), tried to conclude the 1802 affair as hastily as possible. He relayed to the throne Portuguese complaints about British behavior, and agreed that the dispatched troops should not be permitted to land in Macao, but in his memorial of May 17 reporting peace between France and England he seems to have considered the matter closed.[28] Tranquility was restored to the frontier, and the global military context behind the tension was no longer relevant.

The Portuguese, however, had other channels through which to complain. On August 29 Su-leng-e (d. 1827), grand minister of the Imperial Household Department and vice-president of the Board of Works, memorialized that he had received a communication from the Portuguese missionaries J. B. d'Almeida (d. 1805) and A. de Gouvêa (1751–1808), employed in Beijing, relating a private report from Macao. While acknowledging the information to come from a biased source, Su-leng-e considered it alarming enough to forward to the throne. Vituperatively anti-British, the letter accused the English of having for the past several decades "harbored intentions of engrossing themselves." British interest in Macao, d'Almeida explained, stemmed from Macartney's effort to secure an island off the Chinese coast. Having failed, the English had "specially dispatched six large warships from the territory they control in India (Xiao Xiyang)" to capture Macao. The priest portrayed himself as a devoted Qing servant offering strategic insight on the dangers of British imperialism:

> All Europeans know the ferocity of the English. Formerly, in India (Xiao Xiyang) they plotted under the pretext of trade to destroy a great country

called the Mughal empire (Menggao'er). At first they borrowed a small territory to live upon, but afterward they and their ships gradually grew more numerous. Finally, in 1798 they annexed (*tunshi*) this country.[29] This land is near Tibet, so China should be able to know about this.[30]

D'Almeida, like the English at Guangzhou, expected the Qing court to be familiar with Company expansion in India, but his warning had no appreciable effect. It is unlikely that the Qing court understood what was meant by Menggao'er: only Jesuits had used the name "Mughal" in any form, and they invariably transcribed it "Mowo'er." There is no suggestion that the Jiaqing court linked these two dissimilar names, or connected the terms in d'Almeida's report to comparable terms from other frontiers, such as "Hindustan" or "Delhi Padshah." A British conquest of "Menggao'er" therefore lacked strategic resonance. D'Almeida's failure to alarm the Qing illustrates the gulf separating the strategic world of Europeans and Indians, for whom British expansion in India was of epochal significance, from that of the Qing court, for which Indian affairs were perceived in fragments as basically insignificant. D'Almeida, despite serving in Beijing, knew only one of the many geographic idioms prevailing within the empire and could not convey the full import of his arguments. Jiaqing's response ignored the Jesuit's comments about the Mughal empire and addressed only the immediate situation at Macao. Giking, solicited for more news, reported that the British warships were only for convoy duty, adding that Portuguese officials in Macao were (in his view) unduly concerned because of enmity between the two countries.[31] This ended the matter, and d'Almeida's warnings about the British conquest of the Mughal empire went unheeded.

A second British attempt to occupy Macao, in 1808, had more serious consequences. The Select Committee, which in 1802 had dissuaded commanders from acting without Qing consent, now under a new president advocated forcing the local Qing authorities to accept a fait accompli. Troops were landed on September 19 and a three-month standoff followed, during which Governor-General Wu Xiongguang (1750–1833) halted trade until the British commander finally agreed to withdraw. Jiaqing then removed both Wu and the Guangzhou garrison general Yangcūn (d. 1818) for failing to evict the British more quickly and effectively.[32]

In dealing with this case, Qing officials did not neglect its international context. In addition to noting the rival claims of Portuguese and British officials, Wu gathered information from local sources about the Napoleonic War and the relationships prevailing between France, Spain, England, and Portugal. He deputed two agents whom he considered experts in foreign affairs to make secret inquiries in the vicinity of Macao. Cross-checking their reports with other testimony, Wu believed that the British were taking advantage of the weakness of the Portuguese to seize their coveted port. This judgment was tempered with the proviso that "with hearsay from overseas, it is difficult to get the truth" (*haiwai chuanwen, nan yu de shi*).[33]

Most of the troops landed in Macao were Company forces from Madras and Bengal, a fact not lost on the Qing government.[34] The Macao expedition was launched under the authority of British India's governor-general, Lord Minto. Its naval commander, Admiral Drury, according to the Chinese translation of his first letter to the Qing government, referred to the dispatch of forces from India by the "Bengal general" (*Mengliaola jiangjun*).[35] Wu was informed by the district magistrate of Xiangshan that only one or two hundred of the 760 troops landed were English (*Yingjili yi bing*), the remainder being "black foreigners" (*heiyi*), apparently the first reference in Qing records to sepoys. Unimpressed by their military worth, Wu described them as "ragged, emaciated, and weak." According to his information, they had been "seized by force in Bengal and brought here just to fill out the complement" (*zai Mengliaola difang yingzhuo, qianlai chongshu*). Supposedly inferior non-British troops seemed to favor the Qing, and the emperor noted that the British should be "even easier to drive off." Morally, he considered the use of foreign troops "extremely tricky and hateful."[36] Still, the presence of Indian soldiers did not spur research into the overall structure of British territorial holdings. Rather, the crisis at Macao was a local issue, to be addressed using intelligence resources on the coast. The deployment of Indian forces by the British was not connected to d'Almeida's warning, nor did it provoke a reappraisal of the empire's overall strategic position.

The British on the Tibetan Frontier

The Pearl River delta was not the only part of the Qing empire affected by growing British power in India. Along the Himalayas, Englishmen began to reach the frontiers of Tibet more frequently, leading to further encounters between the Qing state and the Pileng tribe, alias Calcutta. Although in 1793 Beijing had recognized that the Pileng were connected to the English, it continued to treat them (like Gangjiao at Guangzhou) as a separate group. This frontier-specific approach to the Pileng-Calcutta tribe persisted as British Indian activity in the Himalayas intensified.

THE CASE OF THOMAS MANNING

Thomas Manning (1772–1840), the first Briton to enter Tibet since Samuel Turner in 1783, was an unlikely candidate for that distinction. A talented scholar, he had studied at Cambridge and remained there to teach mathematics. Around 1800 he had conceived a wish to visit China, which he later expressed as a desire to gain a "moral view . . . [of] what there might be in China worthy to serve as a model for imitation, and what to serve as a beacon to avoid."[37] After studying Chinese in Paris he returned to England and gained permission in 1806 to live at the East India Company's Guangzhou factory, where he hoped to improve his Chinese and find a way of entering China itself. Trained in mathematics and medicine, he initially hoped to find work in Beijing as a sort of secular Jesuit. Rebuffed by local officials, he took passage to Cochin China (Vietnam) but found no route onward into the Qing empire, and returned to Guangzhou in time to help as a translator during the 1808 Macao expedition.[38]

Early in 1810 Manning departed for Calcutta, hoping to enter China via Tibet. He was accompanied by a Chinese companion invariably described in his journal as a "Munshi" (secretary or interpreter). This "Munshi," when he was later arrested by Qing authorities and sent to Sichuan for interrogation, testified that he had been born Meng Shengxiu in Taiyuan, Shanxi, but later moved with his uncle to Beijing to open a tea shop, where he was adopted into a family surnamed Zhao, taking the name Zhao Jinxiu. With the death of his uncle in 1807 he moved to Guangzhou and worked for the Jichang Hong. As Zhao told the story, he was offered employment late in 1809 by a Chinese tavern-keeper visiting from Calcutta, and sailed for that city via Macao.[39] Once there, Zhao came to know Manning as a frequent customer. It so happened, he continued, that the Englishman approached him to serve as interpreter for a proposed visit to the Dalai Lama just when the death of his employer rendered him homeless. With no other prospects, Zhao agreed.[40] Such was his version of events.

There is reason to suspect that Zhao's story, told under strict interrogation, was disingenuous in many details. He probably was indeed from northern China, because he spoke with a "Peking pronunciation."[41] Another of Zhao's attractive talents was Latin so fluent that, as the Englishman put it, "There was no sentiment or shade of sentiment we could not exchange."[42] Zhao could speak Latin because he was a devout Roman Catholic. This was a crucial detail, for in 1811 the Jiaqing emperor strengthened prohibitions against Catholic priests and converts. Zhao was well aware of the danger that Manning might be taken for a priest, and tried to repel such suspicions.[43] Furthermore, Zhao denied to Qing authorities that Manning had ever lived in Guangzhou.[44] Because Zhao's background, above all his Catholicism and service as Manning's Chinese teacher, would have displeased Qing officials, this autobiography presented under duress should be taken with more than one grain of salt.[45]

Authorities in Calcutta let Manning journey northward, but lent him no support. Evidently for that reason, he begrudged them a full account of his travels, and fragments of a terse journal are all that remain in English. This, combined with official reports from the Qing side, permit at least the basic details of his travels to be clarified. Manning and Zhao crossed into Bhutan and reached the Qing frontier at Phari in the Chumbi valley. It is often said that the Qing policies had "closed" Tibet after the second Gurkha War, but this was not in fact the case. Postwar regulations stipulated that members of "foreign tribes" (*waifan buluo*) might apply at the border to enter Tibet for audiences with the Dalai Lama, who was venerated by Buddhists living beyond the bounds of Qing control.[46] This left a loophole for Manning, because in the Tibetan context Calcutta Pilong had initially been regarded as a local tribe comparable to Bhutan or Sikkim, and evidently in 1811 was still technically eligible to send pilgrims to Tibet. The responsibility for inspecting visitors arriving via Bhutan fell to the new garrison at Gyantse, established during the augmentation of Chinese Green Standard forces in Tibet after the second Gurkha War. It happened that Manning reached Phari just before the commander of this garrison—whom the Englishman called "General" but held the rank of assistant brigade commander (*shoubei*)—came on a tour of inspection.

During their first audience the Green Standard officer "was very civil, and promised to write immediately to the Lhasa mandarin [i.e., Qing amban or Resident] for permission for me to proceed."[47] The content of this application can be inferred: Qing documents identify him as "a foreigner of the Calcutta tribe" whose stated purpose of visiting was to "pay obeisance to the Dalai Lama."[48] It is unclear if this guise was adopted by Manning or invented by Zhao, who referred to the Englishman as a "lama" in the presence of Qing officials. Strictly speaking, visitors were expected to wait at the frontier until permission to enter was secured from the amban. Manning, who presented himself as a doctor, treated Chinese soldiers in the "General's" retinue and won their assistance. Rather than forcing him to wait in Phari for a reply, it was agreed that he could accompany the contingent back to Gyantse. There, he learned that his application had succeeded and journeyed onward to Lhasa, under instructions to say nothing about his time among the garrison.[49]

How did the Qing state interpret Manning's visit politically and geographically? In Qing documents, he was invariably identified as a "foreigner of the tribe of Calcutta." In Lhasa, his first audience was with the Qing ambans. Manning had been chagrined to discover upon entering Tibet that one of them was Yangcūn, who had been dismissed from the command of the Guangzhou banner garrison for failing to repel the British more quickly in 1808. Not only was Yangcūn likely to be hostile, he might also remember Manning's role as a Company translator. Manning's fears were allayed during the audience when he discovered that "the old dog was purblind, and could not see many inches beyond his nose." The interview passed without incident. Shortly afterward, however, Chinese military officers in the city asked if Manning had ever been in Guangzhou, which his translator denied. Soon, men whom Manning took to be agents of the ambans began to ask him detailed questions about his background and travels. Zhao was several times called in for more formal interrogation. Manning also began to hear rumors of Yangcūn's antipathy. It was said that he "detested the Europeans" and feared they were plotting to invade Tibet, sometimes accusing Manning of being a missionary and other times a spy. Manning also believed he had been taken for an Englishman: "Though I passed for a Calcutta man, we could not conceal that Calcutta (in Bengal) was under the English. Ingelikus (English kingdom) [Yingjili-guo?] was a detestable sound in his ears." In response, Manning acquiesced in feeble countermeasures invented by Zhao. First, he agreed not to display knowledge of written Chinese, and to speak it as little as possible. To maintain his cover, Manning's "Munshi" pressured him to strengthen his lama credentials by worshipping at a Tibetan temple—Zhao, as a staunch Catholic, refused to do so.[50]

Around the end of December 1811, after his first audience with Manning and doubtless after the preliminary results of his other inquiries, Yangcūn reported to Beijing. Manning was correct in believing that Yangcūn had recognized neither his person nor his role in the recent Macao crisis. However, the amban did observe that Manning's face and appearance—he sported a large beard and dressed in Tibet entirely in the Chinese style—resembled that of a "man of the Western Ocean" (*Xiyang ren*). It seemed likely to Yangcūn that Manning was a Roman Catholic missionary who had entered Tibet on the pretext of venerating the Dalai Lama, hoping to propagate his faith. Manning (presumably via Zhao) claimed to come from Calcutta, known to be linked by sea to the Western Ocean. It was not a Buddhist country, making Manning's visit extremely suspicious. Jiaqing's edict, received back in Tibet on February 29, 1812, about two months after Yangcūn's initial report, commanded that Manning be expelled from Tibet as soon as the snows melted in the spring, by which time the incoming amban, Hūturi, should have arrived.[51] While the Englishman had optimistically hoped to exit at Guangzhou after an overland journey through China, he was ordered back as he had come, across the Himalayan frontier. He departed as soon as the weather allowed, on April 19.[52] Authorities in Sichuan, having interrogated Zhao, recommended that he be exiled to Xinjiang.[53]

Politically, Manning's remarkable journey had no lasting impact on Qing perspectives on British India, but it lends insight into the tenacity of a frontier policy. First, it shows the decentralization of intelligence gathering. Less than two decades earlier the Grand Council had accumulated archives indicating that "Calcutta" was an alias of the Pileng tribe, controlled by the English monarch. No reference was made to this at any point in the Qing response to Manning's visit, either in Lhasa or Beijing. Instead, he was identified only as a "foreigner of the Calcutta tribe." The archives kept in Lhasa seemingly did not record that the Pileng-Calcutta tribe was connected to the English, a fact only noted in Beijing on the basis of other information. Moreover, Yangcūn and other Qing officials in Tibet gathered most of their intelligence from oral inquiries and interrogations on the spot, and limited the scope of the case to bare essentials: whether Manning was to be expelled and whether Zhao was to be sanctioned. Further inquiries about Calcutta, its relationship to other countries in the Western Ocean, its Chinese community, or possible connections between Manning and the Chinese coast seem not to have been made. Yangcūn knew that such connections were likely, if we believe the rumors reaching Manning's ears, but presumably he wished to shut this open-and-shut case as quickly as possible. Once Manning had returned to Bhutan and it was decided that in the future no men of the Western Ocean claiming a wish to visit the Dalai Lama would be permitted into Tibet, Qing interest in the affair ended. In 1816 he achieved his goal of entering China, travelling (unrecognized) as a member of the Amherst embassy.

THE QING RESPONSE TO THE ANGLO-NEPAL WAR OF 1814–1816

Scarcely two years after Manning's departure, a more serious crisis forced the Qing government to reconsider the security of the Himalayan frontier. Nepal, almost from the moment it established tributary ties, had tried to persuade the Qing to support it in its military rivalries. Its pleading intensified when British India went to war with the Gurkhas in 1814, but Nepal failed to convince Jiaqing and his ministers that it was in their own interest to repel the Pileng from the Himalayas. This inability to persuade Beijing that the British conquest of India entailed risks for Qing security highlights the enormous gulf between the strategic worldviews of Nepal and British India on the one hand, and the Qing government on the other.

Soon after the Qing accepted Nepal as a tributary, the amban Sungyūn elaborated relevant Qing policy. Though now a tributary, he observed, the Gurkhas remained the single greatest threat to the Tibetan frontier. Their "greedy and violent nature," evident from their clashes with several other tribes, made it probable that the Gurkhas would soon provoke their own downfall. Once in difficulty, Sungyūn reasoned, they would turn to the Qing for assistance. In this case, he wrote, "it is most appropriate for [Qing ambans] to ignore it." Sungyūn emphasized this last point, observing that if pushed to "utmost desperation," the Gurkhas might claim that "since they are a Qing tributary we should immediately send troops to their rescue."[54] He explained that the Qing had no such duty, and that an amban's sole obligation was to counsel the Gurkhas to live at peace with neighboring states. By remaining avowedly neutral on its Himalayan frontier, the Qing government hoped to insulate the border from external turbulence.

Sungyūn recognized that the Gurkhas remained an expanding power. Barred from Tibet, they turned their attention in other directions. Gurkha expansion led to small disputes with the British over the ownership of fertile lands lying just below the Himalayan foothills, but behind this was a larger issue: whether Nepal would be brought into the orbit of British India or maintain its independence. Not only did the Gurkha court oppose the establishment of a permanent British Resident in Kathmandu, it also courted the remaining Indian powers to enter an anti-British alliance. Both sides expected a showdown in the near future.[55]

From the 1790s onward, the Gurkhas did everything in their power to transform their relationship with the Qing government into an anti-British strategic partnership, portraying themselves as a lynchpin in the security of

Tibet, and thus of the entire Qing realm. For this they expected material assistance. Powerless to compel such aid, their only option was to supply the ambans with information about Indian and Himalayan strategic conditions, hoping that the Qing court would adopt their outlook. British India was well aware of this strategy, and did its utmost to rebut the Gurkhas' interpretation of Indian conditions.

In the two decades between the end of its war with the Qing and the start of its war with the British, the Gurkha kingdom was in political turmoil. King Ran Bahadur Shah (1775–1805) assumed the reins of government in 1794, but strategically abdicated in 1799 to secure the throne for his chosen heir. Opposition to his choice was overwhelming, and in the ensuing crisis he fled to Varanasi, threatening to return under British protection.[56] Sikkim reported to the ambans in 1801 that Ran Bahadur Shah was "attacking the Gurkhas using borrowed Pileng troops," but Jiaqing judged that this was "their family matter, so we can fundamentally ignore it."[57] A year later the ambans reported rumors that the Pileng had seized Gurkha territory, leading him to fear that the Gurkhas might seek Qing military aid, but Jiaqing reminded him that the Qing had no need to interfere.[58] Non-engagement beyond the southern border of Tibet remained Qing policy.

In the spring of 1814 British India and Nepal went to war in a contest that both sides believed would decide Nepal's fate.[59] Anticipating a major British assault late in the year, the Gurkhas once again sought Qing aid. From the perspective of the Qing court, the ensuing conflict can be divided into two parts: the initial phase, in which repeated Gurkha requests for aid were set aside, and the closing phase, when it was decided that the crisis warranted moving forces from Sichuan into Tibet as a precaution.

The Gurkhas requested Qing aid against the British twice during a tribute mission in 1812, in Lhasa and in Beijing, and when war broke out in 1814 their requests for help became more persistent. Despite earlier rejections, the amban Hūturi memorialized in September 1814 that a third had been received. The impending war with the British, the Gurkhas maintained, was chiefly for the sake of the Qing. Pileng forces wished to push the Qing out of Tibet, occupy it, and then attack China proper (*neidi*). Because the Gurkhas had blocked these invaders, war would break out that winter. To prosecute it, they asked for money and materiel. Underscoring their altruism, Nepal added that the Pileng wanted only Tibet, and had even tried to buy passage to Qing territory with a bribe of six to seven million rupees ("silver coins"), which the Gurkhas had rejected. In short, the Gurkhas represented themselves as a buffer state fighting a proxy battle entirely on behalf of their overlord. Qing authorities, in keeping with established policy, rejected this view. First, the ambans found the strategic picture painted by the Gurkhas to be improbable. Hūturi observed that the Pileng tribe, southwest of the Gurkhas, "has never had contact with Tibet" (*su yu Tanggute butong wenwen*). Since there was no mutual enmity, and "people from this country have never come to Tibet," why would it attack? "Extremely untrustworthy" Gurkha claims were "fabricated" in the hope that by "scaremongering with overblown statements" the Gurkhas would be able to use Qing money to "accomplish their selfish wishes" (*sui qi siyuan*).

Jiaqing agreed with Hūturi's interpretation but tactfully replied to the Gurkhas that while a Pileng invasion was unlikely the Qing expected them to act as a "hedge" (*fanli*) if it did materialize. In that case, however, they must do so with their own resources because the Qing never gave material aid to "outer subject territories" (*waifan*). Hūturi reminded them to "live at peace with their neighbors, and watch over their own frontier." Jiaqing supplied the incoming amban Xi-ming with further arguments to use against "presumptuous petitions," and instructed him to place Qing frontier troops on alert and make further inquiries.[60]

Xi-ming shared Hūturi's skepticism of Gurkha claims.[61] However, about three weeks later, he relayed a report from a Tibetan agent in Kathmandu that war had broken out between the Gurkhas and Pileng and was going badly for Nepal. This was not unexpected, and Xi-ming commented that this "meaningless squabble" (*manchu xiangzheng*) emerged from long-standing Pileng-Gurkha enmity and should be ignored in accordance with imperial orders. The only danger was that the Gurkha state might collapse and send refugees flooding into Tibet, and he had ordered Qing frontier posts quietly to prepare to repulse them. Jiaqing foresaw that the Gurkha ruler himself might seek refuge in Qing territory, in which case Xi-ming should request further instructions.[62]

In a further petition, the Gurkha ruler reported victories but implored Qing aid to keep fighting his wealthy enemy. To loosen the imperial purse strings he pointed out that Kathmandu was a critical strategic pass "under the control of the Qing emperor," and that the Gurkhas were duty-bound to "protect the south[ern frontier]" (*bashou nanfang*). With Qing funds, the Gurkhas could destroy the Pileng. Xi-ming, like Hūturi before him, considered these requests (which had also been made to the Dalai and Panchen Lamas) a ruse to solicit Qing aid for a private Gurkha venture. Fully agreeing, Jiaqing armed his official with fresh rebuttals to deploy if these presumptuous requests continued. One was to emphasize Qing neutrality. The Gurkha ruler was to be informed that if the emperor granted aid to the Gurkhas, would he not then be obliged to grant (hypothetical) Pileng requests for aid as well? Xi-ming was ordered to maintain frontier troops in full readiness, but to fight only if the Pileng really did invade Tibet. Developments across the border were to be entirely ignored.[63]

One tactic adopted by the ambans to forestall Gurkha requests was to falsely reply that they were too outrageous to pass on to Beijing. Instead of chastening the Gurkha ruler, this response stimulated even more pressing requests to compel them to report the affair upward. Thus, the Nepali king petitioned once again, averring the truth of his earlier declarations. Now he also asked for an imperial edict ordering the Pileng to remain within their own frontier and for permission to send a tribute memorial (*biao*), clearly an attempt to circumvent communication by ordinary petitions (*bing*) that the ambans ostensibly refused to forward. Faced with these demands, Jiaqing reiterated the need to emphasize neutrality: the Gurkhas should be informed that the Qing had never given "inequitable aid to only one country" (*pianzhu yiguo*) and could not grant assistance to Nepal without also lending it to the Pileng.[64] This echoed Qianlong's argument that the Qing would not aid the Gurkhas just as it had not helped the Bal-po tribes whom the Gurkhas had conquered. Jiaqing now authorized a sterner reprimand. Gurkha claims that the Pileng aimed to conquer Beijing itself after taking Tibet were "preposterous in the extreme" (*jiwei beimiu*). The Gurkha ruler was to be reminded that Tibet was well guarded and had nothing to fear from a "puny tribe" like the Pileng; Beijing was still more secure. By making false claims, Jiaqing warned, it was the Gurkha ruler himself who would face the imperial wrath.[65]

One dimension of the Gurkha ruler's petition sheds light particularly on the Qing tribute system. For the Gurkhas, tribute was part of a strategic alliance.[66] For this reason, Beijing's tenacious neutrality was unfathomable: "I think the Gurkhas are people who have submitted (*toucheng*) to the Qing court; how can they be compared to the Pileng?" In his next petition the Gurkha ruler expanded on this line of reasoning, reporting that "[the Pileng] have also ordered us to submit (*toucheng*), and I am truly in a difficult situation. I have submitted to the Qing and should request instructions to carry out. If you command me that as a Qing subject I absolutely cannot submit to the Pileng, then I beg that you will quickly bestow on me a large sum of money and assist me." Xi-ming initially replied that surrendering (*toushun*) to the Pileng would be viewed as a betrayal, but Jiaqing's edict corrected this view. The emperor wanted the Gurkhas to be informed that, "in regard to the passage about the Pileng ordering you to submit, you two states are at war, and whether or not you submit, the Qing court will in no way interfere."[67]

Despite being rebuffed, the Gurkha government continued to depict the tributary relationship as a strategic agreement. Its next petition reported that the Pileng demanded a steep price for a peace treaty: the Gurkhas would have to cede passage to Tibet and become Pileng subjects. Having already submitted to the Qing, the Gurkha ruler wrote, he could "never again make a second submission to someone else." Moreover, if he became a Pileng tributary the Pileng would "not permit us to pay tribute to the Qing." In other words, unless assistance was forthcoming, a crucial buffer state would pass under Pileng control. Jiaqing found this claim "truly deceitful and grossly disrespectful" and criticized Xi-ming for his failure to stem Gurkha misbehavior. If tribute did not appear at the appointed time, they were to be told, this would be considered treason (*beipan*).[68] In short, for the Gurkhas tributary status meant in principle a quid pro quo military alliance in which they protected the Qing empire in return for material aid and, as last resort, a guarantee of their survival. For Jiaqing, tribute was exclusively bilateral: provided it was submitted on schedule, the Qing would neither constrain their agreements with other states nor support them in their quarrels. If they were defeated, tributary relations would be established with their successor.

For Nepal as for d'Almeida in Beijing, events had to be analyzed against the background of the British conquest of India. An 1815 letter from the Gurkha field commander Amar Singh Thapa to his superiors, a copy of which was intercepted by the British, included a draft petition to the Qing government. It proposed exciting Qing interest by referring to politics on the subcontinent. The English were described as "the people who have already subdued all India and usurped the Throne of Delhi." Chinese troops sent to the subcontinent would immediately find Indian allies to expel Europeans: "by such an event your name will be renowned throughout Jumboo Dweeh [i.e., Jambudvipa], and whenever you may command, the whole of its Inhabitants will be forwarded in your Service." Thapa added that the Qing could easily send a force of two or three hundred thousand troops into India via Burma.[69] He hoped both to alarm the Qing government and to tempt it with the possibility of hegemony in India. Some points from Thapa's draft made it into correspondence with the Qing ambans, for instance his request that a Qing edict be sent to the British, but his remarks about Indian politics seem to have been largely excluded or lost in translation. The most extensive comment about Indian conditions found in a Gurkha petition from this period reads: "The men of Pileng harbor ill intentions, and have occupied all the lands from the sea in the south to the mountains in the north; and the kings of each place have been subdued and incorporated"; another petition around that time accused the Pileng of having "completely occupied areas from Kumaon to the Sutlej River (Sadaluda'er he) and all the places of India (Jiaga'er)."[70] These references to the extent of British conquests in India attracted no attention from Lhasa or Beijing.

The Anglo-Nepal War proceeded fitfully. Apart from a small British victory in the far west of Nepal, the first round of fighting in 1814 and 1815 ended without a significant penetration of the Himalayan foothills. Abortive negotiations followed, and only in the winter of 1816 did another concerted British push get underway. By that time, the crisis had unsettled the Himalayas for almost two years, and Jiaqing saw the need for more active measures. In an edict of February 20, 1816, he appointed Saicungga, the commander of the Chengdu banner garrison, as an imperial commissioner with a brief to enter Tibet and "watch the situation."[71] The parameters of his mission were made extremely clear. Reports indicated that the Pileng were in the ascendant, and might even seize Nepal and exterminate its royal line. Provided they did not violate the Qing frontier, "then this is entirely a matter between foreigners, a meaningless squabble, and there is no need to interfere whatever the outcome" (*deshi ju bu ke wen*). Under no circumstances, Jiaqing told Saicungga, was he to threaten the Pileng for reasons to do only with the Gurkhas. He authorized force only if one of the sides—Gurkha or Pileng—violated the border, or if the Gurkha king fled into Tibet and the Pileng tried to compel his extradition.[72] It was also crucial, the emperor added in his next edict, that Saicungga keep his arrival quiet so that the Gurkhas would not falsely assume the Qing were preparing to save them.[73]

Disregarding his instructions, Saicungga struck out on a bold diplomatic course after he arrived in Lhasa in May 1816, bringing about the first direct Anglo-Qing contact across the Himalayas in over twenty years. He entirely concurred with Qing policy, but worried that the Gurkhas might resent China's neutrality to the point of abandoning their tribute payments or even inciting the Pileng against Tibet. To forestall this, he decided to bring matters to a head. Assuming that the Gurkhas' charges against the Pileng were fabricated, he informed both sides that a massive Qing force had been sent to Tibet to annihilate whichever party, Gurkha or Pileng, had invented the disrespectful claims about ceding a route to Tibet and halting tribute payments. Saicungga expected that the Pileng would confirm that the charges were false, and he could then use this evidence to force the Gurkhas to confess their misrepresentations and beg forgiveness. One bold stroke, he expected, would end the festering affair. To underscore Qing resolve he and Xi-ming would conspicuously inspect the border defenses.

Jiaqing was outraged that the commander of his secret reserve force had decided to make an aggressive bluff, "the very extreme of reckless bungling!" The emperor pointed out that the diplomatic results might be very different than those envisioned. Suppose the Pileng leader was angered by the false charges of the Gurkhas and asked the Qing to join with him in exterminating them? Worse, suppose the Pileng leader, safe at a distance, actually admitted to the Qing that he had uttered the words attributed to him by the Gurkhas as a bluff? Would not the Qing government then be forced to wage war over a "single phrase" (*yi yan*)? Moreover, might not the Gurkhas rejoice at his arrival and try to usher the Qing army down through Nepal to attack their foe? Worse still, Saicungga had decided to give his gambit extra bite by promising that if he should attack the Gurkhas he would make their destruction even more certain by acting in tandem with the Pileng. For Jiaqing, even the empty threat of such an alliance was abhorrent: "The Gurkhas have been our tributaries for many years, and for us not to pity them in their difficulties but to the contrary to lead foreigners to catch their territory in a pincer movement, how can this be reconciled to the high principles of our august dynasty?" (*tangtang tianchao, dati an zai hu*).[74]

By then it was too late; Saicungga's letters had been sent. That to the Pileng was translated into Persian and transmitted via the ruler of Sikkim to the British Indian government. The sense of the letter, addressed to the "King of the Pileng, Gewo'er Zhe'ernaili [governor-general]," is substantially the same in its Chinese and English versions. However, where Qing records use "Pileng" the translation invariably uses the word "English," presumably because Pileng was put back into Persian as "Farangi," which British translators habitually rendered as "English." Thus, certain passages in translation imply that Qing officials knew the Pileng to be the English, but give a very different impression in the Chinese. For instance, the English translation of Saicungga's letter, reads:

> Such absurd measures (as those alluded to) appear quite inconsistent with the usual wisdom of the English. It is probable that they never made the deputation imputed to them. If they did, it will not be well. On a former occasion when Thoon Than [*zhongtang*, grand secretary, i.e., Fuk'anggan] came here to make war against the Rajah of Goorkah a letter was received from the English addressed to Thoon Than asking assistance.[75]

By contrast, the Chinese text of the communication read:

> When we accurately ascertain from whom these preposterous words [attributed to the Pileng] derive, we will then send troops to exterminate them. We note that you Pileng in 1792 submitted a petition to the former Duke, Grand Secretary and Great General Fuk'anggan, most respectful in sentiment and wording, and have not caused trouble over the past decades.

This implies only that Saicungga and Xi-ming were familiar with the communication Fuk'anggan had held with the Pileng ruler during his tenure in Tibet, not with the findings compiled later in Beijing that showed the Pileng to be English. This impression is confirmed by a statement in Saicungga's next memorial that the Pileng "have never submitted tribute" (*xiangwei nagong*). Since Qianlong replied in 1796 to George III that "your king sent an emissary to Tibet," acknowledging the Pileng to be subjects of a Qing tributary, Saicungga's claim reveals ignorance of this connection.[76]

In reply to Saicungga, the governor-general, the Earl of Moira, tried to reassure him that British India was no cause for alarm: "The British Government has no views of aggrandizement and only seeks to remain at peace with other states, and no motives of ambition and interest prompt it to extend its influence and authority beyond those barriers which appear to have been placed by nature between the vast countries of India and China."[77] This was translated into Chinese (using transliterated Tibetan names) as: "We Pileng are not evil-doers who recklessly desire the lands of others, each [should] respect their own frontiers, and remain at peace with their neighbors. In the past the Gurkhas have resided in the mountains directly between China proper (*neidi*) and India (Jiaga'er), and we have no intention of going to their lands."

A sustained push toward Kathmandu early in 1816 brought the Gurkhas to terms, and a treaty was ratified on March 4, 1816. From the Qing perspective, this settlement contained only one sticking point. On the Indian subcontinent the British had used Residents, permanent British agents, to supervise and often undermine Indian states. Aware of this, the Gurkhas hoped to escape the British residency stipulated by the peace treaty. To this end they systematically attempted to convince the British deputation supervising postwar developments in Nepal that the Qing government resented the residency clause. Confused about why Saicungga was advancing toward the Nepali frontier, the British were also apprehensive about this issue. Their policy aimed at "the avoidance of any engagement with the Nepaulese or any other measure that might embroil us with, or even give umbrage to the Chinese," and they were even willing to relinquish the residency "for the greater objects involved in the maintenance of pacific and friendly relations with China."[78] However, they were prepared to do so only as a last resort, if Qing officials positively insisted on it.

Faced with these competing statements, Saicungga reluctantly found himself forced to arbitrate between the Pileng and the Gurkhas. In his first reply to the Qing imperial commissioner, the British governor-general pointed out that exchanging Residents allowed better communication and a more solid peace. For their part, a Gurkha agent informed Saicungga in early October 1816 that they feared the Resident would seize Kathmandu, and asked the Qing to force him out. Saicungga refused to help the Gurkhas renege on their agreement and cited the Pileng claim that Residents were a means to keep the peace. To the Pileng leader, however, Saicungga replied that an envoy would promote peace only if willingly received and that given Gurkha objections it might be better to show good faith and withdraw him.[79] In February 1817 the British agreed to withdraw their Resident if the Qing would send an agent to Kathmandu and mediate future disputes.[80] Ambans Xi-ming and Ke-shi-ke replied that the Qing had many subject tribes, but had never sent a permanent agent to any of them. They added that, "We expect that you Pileng, who often trade at Guangzhou and have long been acquainted with imperial prestige, must naturally be well acquainted with fundamental Qing policies."[81] This reply made no further mention of withdrawing the Resident, and the matter dropped.

Strategic calculations apparent in this episode will be considered below, but two brief conclusions can be made: first, there is no evidence that Qing officials in Tibet recognized the Pileng specifically as the English (Yingjili), or even learned more about them than Fuk'anggan had reported from Tibet in the 1790s. Jiaqing's edicts also demonstrated no awareness of such a link.

Second, there is no reason to think that the Qing court was bending its usual policies to dodge a showdown with British India. In his study of Qing policy toward the Anglo-Nepal War, Suzuki Chūsei emphasized the fiscal and military crises besetting Jiaqing: "The Qing court, which entered a period of decline during and after the Jiaqing period, utterly lacked the power to be able to help the Gurkhas. Therefore, the Qing argument of neutrality (*yishi tongren*) was only reasoning used to dress up noninterference due to powerlessness."[82] Suzuki's assessment of decreasing Qing military power is correct, but his view that the court's neutrality resulted from its weakness is based on a misapprehension. He characterizes the Qing relationship with the Gurkhas as that of a "suzerain state" (*sōshukoku*) and a "subject state" (*zokukoku*). He assumes that in the Qianlong and Jiaqing eras the suzerain state understood itself to be responsible, at least in principle, for safeguarding its subject. In fact, however, tributary status did not influence the Qing military posture toward the state in question. Sungyūn, the premier Qing strategist on the Himalayan frontier, continued to regard the tributary Gurkhas as the greatest potential enemy of Tibet, and Saicungga later doubted their loyalty.[83] Not surprisingly, the Qing government felt no moral or strategic need to defend the Gurkha regime by force. It was also consistent in its blanket refusal to assist the Gurkhas against a third party, even one that threatened to extinguish them. This policy can be seen in the 1792–1793 responses of Fuk'anggan and Qianlong when the Gurkhas asked for aid against the Delhi Padshah—that is, before rebellions hampered the dynasty's financial and military ability to wage war. In other words, when the late Jiaqing court disavowed any obligation to act as a military guarantor of its Gurkha tributary, it was simply following a line of policy settled by Qianlong in the immediate aftermath of the Gurkha campaigns on the basis of established strategic reasoning, not short-term expediency.

The Moorcroft Expedition on the Frontier of Xinjiang

In the early 1760s, when the Qing state was gathering intelligence about Hindustan—Lahore, Delhi, and as far as the Deccan—British expansion was eclipsed by the nearer and more dramatic struggle between the Afghans and the Marathas. Before 1800 the British exerted virtually no influence over northwest India, and their presence was not noted by Qing officials in Yarkand. This changed when the Company seized Delhi from the Marathas in 1803 and pushed its frontier to the edge of the Punjab in 1809. Henceforth, British Indian strategists became increasingly preoccupied with defending this new frontier, and directed diplomacy and espionage toward Afghanistan, Persia, and even Central Asia to counter the real or imagined schemes of the French and later the Russians. Via territory seized from Nepal in 1815, British India also gained access to the Niti Pass into Qing-held western Tibet.

As early as 1812, the superintendant of the Company stud in Bengal, William Moorcroft (ca. 1767–1825), penetrated the western rim of the Qing empire. Disguised as a Hindu gosain and accompanied by Hindu and Muslim associates, he managed to cross the Niti Pass, proceed onward to Gartok athwart the main Ladakh-Lhasa trade route, and then cut east to Lake Manasarowar before returning to India. The last outpost of centrally dispatched Qing forces was far to the east at Dingri, and local Tibetan administrators were persuaded to overlook rumors that the party contained "*Felings* (so the *Tatars* call *Europeans*)" and accept Moorcroft's disguise as a gosain.[84] On Moorcroft's return he was briefly detained by the Gurkhas, and one of the charges made three years later by Nepal to the Qing as evidence that the Pileng wished to invade Tibet was that "earlier one disguised himself as an Acharya (*Azanla*) to search out routes in Tibet." Qing ambans could not corroborate this with their border guards, and dismissed it as false.[85]

Just before setting off on this journey into Tibet, Moorcroft engaged Mir Izzat-ullah, a secretary on the Company's staff in Delhi, to travel in the guise of a merchant to Bukhara via Ladakh and Yarkand. Izzat-ullah, of Bukharan ancestry, was able to pass through Qing territory without attracting official notice, and this led Moorcroft to plan a similar journey.[86] In 1819 Moorcroft set out for Bukhara with another party, including Izzat-ullah.[87] After the group reached Ladakh, Moorcroft's Indian assistants, particularly Izzat-ullah, whose earlier travels had given him a wide circle of useful acquaintances, were indispensible in his negotiations. Among the contacts Moorcroft was able to tap were the influential holy man Shah Niyaz Khan, then in Ladakh, and his disciple Abdul Latif, who lent the party important diplomatic assistance.

In Ladakh, Moorcroft acted as one of the earliest players in the nascent Anglo-Russian "Great Game" for influence in Asia by investigating Russian influence in the area; he also persuaded Ladakh's ruler to make a commercial and strategic agreement with the East India Company against the growing power of Ranjit Singh (although this was later repudiated by Calcutta).[88] This has drawn attention away from Moorcroft's negotiations with

Qing officials in Yarkand and Kashgar, and the perception of these activities from Beijing, which are the focus of this section.

According to Moorcroft's records, Shah Niyaz Khan was a crucial ally, defending his party (and by extension, the British in India) to the Ladakhi government against objections by Tibetan authorities in Gartok, and above all by Kashmiri traders dominating the lucrative shawl wool (*pashm*) trade between western Tibet and Kashmir, who feared that Moorcroft was attempting to break their monopoly to draw trade southward into British territory. Although Moorcroft convinced the Ladakhi authorities of his peaceful intentions, members of Kashmiri trade networks were able to renew the argument in Yarkand and Kashgar. There they were aided, Moorcroft believed, by an enigmatic Russian agent named Agha Mehdi (Mehdi Rafailov) who was in Yarkand when the Englishman opened correspondence with Qing authorities.

The earliest phase of Moorcroft's contact with Yarkand remains obscure. Based on fragmentary evidence, it is clear that he hoped Izzat-ullah's connections would allow the party to enter Qing territory as ordinary merchants, without reference to local Manchu officials or Beijing. To this end, letters preparing the ground were sent by Izzat-ullah to Kissak Shah, the "principal judge at Yarkand," and others were solicited from Shah Niyaz Khan to his friends in that city. These letters must have been sent in the late autumn or early winter of 1820, soon after Moorcroft's position in Leh became settled. It was reported to Moorcroft that Agha Mehdi countered these requests with warnings of British espionage. In consequence, Izzat-ullah was invited to proceed to Yarkand, but was told that instructions about Moorcroft would be conveyed to Leh by Agha Mehdi. Unfortunately, the Russian agent died while crossing the Karakorams, leaving Moorcroft's position unclear. In March 1821 a party of Kashmiri merchants arrived from Yarkand and returned after interviewing the Englishman several times about his intentions.[89] Finally, in the summer of that year, Moorcroft dispatched Izzat-ullah to Yarkand to make the necessary arrangements for his entry into Xinjiang.[90]

Upon his arrival in Yarkand, Moorcroft recorded, Izzat-ullah was received by "the Governor," the city's hakim beg or principal native officer, who served under the supervision of a centrally dispatched Qing official. Izzat-ullah presented him with a letter in Persian from the governor-general in Calcutta authorizing Moorcroft's journey, as well as a Chinese version prepared by the missionary Joshua Marshman, who had studied the language at Calcutta. This letter in its Manchu translation was stated to be from "the Marquis of Hastings, the honorable governor-general, chief of Calcutta in Hindustan" (*Undustan i harangga Kalkata sere ba i dalaha Markuwais Eb esten kis guwer nar jen rel baturu*), and the name of his tribe the Kampeni Enggeris.[91] At first, Izzat-ullah was told that the hakim beg would admit Moorcroft on his own authority, but he later changed his mind and insisted on referring the matter to the Qing officials at Kashgar. The reason, Izzat-ullah was told, was that a Kashmiri merchant had warned the hakim beg's son that the Englishman had sinister motives. Manchu officials journeyed to Yarkand and interrogated Izzat-ullah and his principal accuser, a Kashmiri merchant named Nuckajoo. Moorcroft's emissary was asked to sketch a map showing the relative positions of Calcutta and Yarkand, at which point "Nuckajoo . . . called out that Calcutta was the place to which the English had come as Merchants and from which they had taken the whole of Hindoostan."[92] After consultations in Kashgar, Izzat-ullah was informed that his party could not pass through Qing territory.

A memorial rescripted in Beijing on December 8, 1821, and thus sent about a month earlier, reported that an Englishman had sent a letter to the hakim beg, requesting permission to come to Yarkand to buy horses, and this had been rejected, doubtless a reference to the first letter to Moorcroft lost with Agha Mehdi. Now, it continued, Izzat-ullah (Aizitula) came bearing another letter in a foreign script.[93] This said he had been indirectly commissioned by the "English leader Guonai'er [i.e., governor]" to buy horses and trade in the northwest, and thus requested permission of the hakim beg to go to Bukhara by way of Yarkand and Kashgar. Ulungga, Manchu councilor at Kashgar, had instructed the hakim beg, Mohamed Esen, to issue a rejection as if on his own authority.[94] In a deposition, Izzat-ullah explained that he was accompanying two Englishmen, Moorcroft (Mu'erqilapu; in Manchu, Murkirab) and George Trebeck (Tieliboke; in Manchu, Tiyelibek) on a horse-buying and trading expedition. He gave a detailed description of their itinerary, noting that at a large river (the Sutlej) they had crossed from English territory into the lands of Yindi, indicating the kingdom of Ranjit Singh in the Punjab, finally arriving at the territory of Ladakh. Because Izzat-ullah had earlier found the route to Bukhara via Yarkand particularly safe, he explained that he now came to ask permission for his companions to follow him.[95]

At this juncture an important misunderstanding occurred, arising from the use of a single term. Qing documents make clear that Moorcroft was being denied entry on the grounds that he was an Englishman (*Yingjili ren*), for whom only Guangzhou was open. Moorcroft and his advisors believed that he was being denied entry on the grounds that he was a Christian. This confusion arose from the process of translation. In Ladakh, Izzat-ullah translated Moorcroft's Hindustani into Persian, and in Yarkand and Kashgar Persian was also the written medium of communication between the two sides. In Persian, *injīlī* indicates a Christian, from the term *injīl* or Gospel. Neither Moorcroft nor his Persian-speaking intermediaries would have realized that Englishmen were called "Yingjili" in Chinese and "Inggili" in Manchu reports, and evidently the Manchu memorialists were also unaware that Yingjili was being construed as the Persian *injīlī*.

This confusion shunted subsequent negotiations onto a dead-end track. Moorcroft and Izzat-ullah knew that Christians had been allowed to trade between Ladakh and Yarkand. From their perspective, Qing arguments were a canard. As the Englishman recorded in his journal,

> On the part of the Chinese it was stated that they had examined the Dangze or Custom-House records of the Khan and could only find the names of Kashmeerees and Indejanees [Andijanis] as Traders to Yarkund, that the Sahibs who wished to come in that capacity were Injeelees [Original note: "Gospelists"] and as Injeelees had never come before they could not be allowed to come now[,] the business of China being conducted by the precedent of custom. The Meer [Izzat-ullah] replied that if the precedent of custom was alone required there would be no difficulty in the case as he could shew that Agha Rafael, Agha Sauleeman and Agha Mehdee were Injeelees, were known to be such and had long traded between Ladakh and Yarkund.⁹⁶

For their part, Qing officials did indeed consult the local archives and reliable witnesses, and could find no evidence that an Englishman had ever visited Yarkand before, as Moorcroft and his allies puzzlingly seemed to insist.⁹⁷ Only one man in Yarkand grasped the source of the confusion. Izzat-ullah reported to Moorcroft on the arguments by one Abdul Rahman Begh, "a Native of Peking to whose acuteness the Meer [Izzat-ullah] pays the tribute of praise." During the initial negotiations, when Izzat-ullah was citing Christian traders who had previously come to Yarkand, they had the following exchange: "Here Abdoul Ruhman Begh stated that though the individuals alluded to were Injeelees [i.e., Christians] and had traded to Yarkund yet they were not English Injeelees as the Sahibs were who desired to be admitted into a participation of the Commerce of this City."⁹⁸ If we assume that Abdul Rahman was familiar with not only Persian but, as a native of Beijing, also with Chinese, this may explain why he alone seemed to have apprehended the confusion between *Yingjili* and *injīlī*, but this insight was not shared by others involved in the affair.

In the fall of 1821 Ulungga sent Kashmiri traders from Yarkand to visit Ladakh and find out more about Moorcroft and his goals. Although the Englishman was temporarily out of town when they arrived, they took back letters about him from the khalon (high minister) of Ladakh and the Kashmiri merchant community. Izzat-ullah, then returning from Yarkand to Leh, met the investigators on the road and feared the Kashmiris were carrying back hostile reports. He convinced them to return with him to Leh, and favorable letters were secured and sent back to Yarkand in the custody of Shah Niyaz Khan's disciple Abdul Latif. Delayed by the winter, the Kashmiri investigators finally returned to Qing territory around the end of March 1822, in the company of Moorcroft's representative. Interrogated first by the hakim begs of Yarkand and Kashgar and then by Qing officials, the party's leader, Meng-han, reported that there were indeed two Englishmen in Ladakh, together with twenty or thirty servants from Hindustan and Kashmir. Moorcroft wished to proceed via Yarkand to Bukhara, and Izzat-ullah ominously told them that the Englishman would enter Qing territory whether he was permitted to or not.[99] To corroborate this report, the khalon of Ladakh sent the hakim beg of Yarkand a glowing testimonial on Moorcroft's character. He offered to guarantee Moorcroft's conduct in Yarkand, and enumerated several men, claimed in the Manchu and Chinese translations to be "English merchants" (*Inggili i hūdašara niyalma*), who had formerly traded between the two cities. In the Persian version this document must have cited "Christian" (*injīlī*) merchants, for these included the names of the Russian agent and Orthodox Christian Agha Mehdi [Maidi], Rapail, as well as the unknown Yusub and Sulaiman, perhaps Armenian traders.[100] A formal affidavit (*akdulara bithe*) was added.[101]

Moorcroft and Izzat-ullah were certain their case was ironclad. Moorcroft's letter to the hakim beg pointed out (in its Manchu translation) that "English people" had irrefutably been to Yarkand, proved by the list of names given. If the hakim beg did not correct himself and plead Moorcroft's case to the Qing officials in Kashgar, the Englishman would take the case all the way to Beijing, submitting a memorial by sea from Guangzhou, and the emperor would be upset to discover his official disregarding precedent and refusing to allow Englishmen into Xinjiang. Izzat-ullah added his own short letter reinforcing this, and a similar letter from Moorcroft was addressed to Kashgar's councilor, Ulungga, the highest-ranking official in the area. The latter complained that the hakim beg (acting, unbeknownst to Moorcroft, under instructions from the Kashgar councilor himself) putatively refused to forward Izzat-ullah's request to Ulungga. Now that Ulungga could see the evidence, Moorcroft continued, he must admit him to Qing territory, otherwise he would face a complaint sent by sea. Moorcroft added that he had no choice in the matter, since unrest in Afghanistan made Yarkand the only feasible way to Turkestan.[102]

Copies of all these materials were sent onward to Beijing. As Ulungga pointed out, the English had always traded with China via Guangdong. Neither the Kashgar archives nor various begs and elderly locals offered any suggestion that Englishman had ever entered Xinjiang. For this reason, the request could be rejected out of hand. In reply to Moorcroft, Ulungga explained that regulations allowed the English to trade only at one fixed place. No Englishmen had gone to Yarkand, and none could come now. This response was vetted and approved by Beijing in the middle of June 1822, and presumably passed on to Moorcroft's emissary in mid-July. By September Abdul Latif had returned to Ladakh with word that plans to proceed into Qing territory had failed. After almost two years, Moorcroft departed Leh for Kashmir, and reached Bukhara via Afghanistan, dying on his journey in 1825.

Moorcroft's exchange with officials in Yarkand and Kashgar illustrates, even more vividly than the case of Manning or the Anglo-Nepal War, how a frontier policy influenced the intelligence gathering and strategic thinking of the Qing state. Unlike in Tibet, it was clear from the beginning that Moorcroft belonged to the English (Yingjili). It was also clear that he was coming from Hindustan, as India was called at Yarkand and Kashgar. After the 1770s, Hindustan had ceased to be an object of official or unofficial inquiry in Xinjiang, and the British conquest of Delhi had passed unnoticed. In the first response to Moorcroft's request, it was noted that Hindustan "was not a harbor for ships of that country." Qing officials had reason to revisit this conclusion with the arrival of Izzat-ullah, who explained in his deposition that he was a native of Bilali (Bareilly), and currently a resident of Zha'nabate (Jahanabad, i.e., Delhi). These cities were part of Hindustan, which had first been conquered by the English fifty or sixty years earlier, with Delhi falling to them later. Now, Hindustan was ruled by a governor (*guonai'er*) sent from England.[103] The Daoguang emperor pointed out the intrinsic uncertainty of such intelligence: "foreign tribes are extremely distant and hard to investigate, and matters beyond the frontier can fundamentally be set aside and ignored."[104] Only the frontier was critical, and he ordered that all frontier posts in the area be put on high alert. In other words, the Qing state would act in a zone where it had full control and adequate information. This in turn influenced Qing intelligence gathering. In dealing with Moorcroft, Daoguang and his officials recognized the need to make extensive local inquires, and even sent agents abroad to Ladakh. Kashmiris and Ladakhis could undoubtedly have provided information about recent political developments in Hindustan, yet for the Qing state the parameters of inquiry were limited to the episode at hand. Major geopolitical upheavals, if not directly pertinent to the case, were allowed to pass without comment.

The Logic of Frontier Policy in Comparative Perspective

Seen in Eurasian perspective, the most striking feature of official Qing strategic thought between 1790 and the 1830s is that it remained unaltered by the rise of British power in Asia. By the time Napoleon met his Waterloo in 1815, virtually every other Asian capital had come to view British India and its growing network of buffer states and outposts as one of the continent's major powers. In not doing so, the Qing government was out of step with neighboring Indian states and European empires. So out of step that anti-British strategic advice of self-evident validity to Nepalis, Portuguese, or Kashmiris carried little weight in Beijing. This can easily be explained if we accept that the Qing court, blinded by its own grandiose rhetoric and Sinocentric assumptions, looked inward and cared little for the outside world. Unquestionably, Qing rulers rated their strength higher than did foreign observers, but such biased confidence was hardly unique. Unquestionably, they took seriously their own duty to promote peace and reason in a world of squabbling and immoral rulers—but moral complacency was hardly incompatible with imperial success, as the British could attest. Yet Qing official correspondence does not support the view that Jiaqing or Daoguang were blithely uninterested in the outside world. To the contrary, emperors were worried about threats to their frontier and sought intelligence from territorial officials. If the Qing empire made judgments about its own interests that differed from those of its Eurasian imperial peers, more specific causes must be sought.

The primary difference in the Qing government's worldview relative to Indian and European contemporaries was its policy of evaluating the empire's security in segmented frontier zones, rather than through an integrated outlook. Such a frontier policy, sustained by strategic assumptions, bureaucratic structures, and geographic scholarship, was difficult to adjust. At Guangzhou, Yarkand, and Lhasa, officials treated the arrival of Englishmen or their agents as a local problem, to be confronted in narrow terms. Within those parameters intelligence gathering was vigorous, but the emperor and his staff eschewed open-ended inquiries or complex diplomatic ventures with uncertain outcomes.

A comparison with British India brings the distinctiveness of this approach into clear relief. There, offensive strategies were often adopted to safeguard frontiers. Malcolm Yapp, in his study of British strategy in India in this period, observed that the Company rejected "static defence" as unsuitable for Bengal.[105] Rather, it tried to forestall attacks through a "ring-fence" of buffer states, in whose affairs it actively intervened, and repeatedly expanded this defensive umbrella. Once India itself seemed secure, the "forward school" of strategic thinking "argued that it was necessary to pre-empt the advance of Russian influence by extending British influence into the intervening areas. This could be accomplished by alliances. . . . In one way or another the external enemy should be kept at a distance so that his vexations would exhaust themselves in places remote from British territory."[106] Faced with the Junghar threat, Qing emperors too had recognized the value of control over neighboring polities like Tibet, Khalkha Mongolia, and elsewhere. However, perceiving no further threat of that magnitude, they had switched upon victory to a defensive posture. After 1759 the Qing court launched punitive expeditions in retaliation for actual incursions across the frontier, but never initiated an offensive action solely to forestall a threat gathering at a distance but not yet in the frontier zone itself.

Not subscribing to a "forward school" of strategic thought, the Qing government also rejected the utility of alliances on strategic and ideological grounds. By the seventeenth century, major European wars were almost always fought between alliances, and in India, too, both the Company and its opponents cultivated agreements with allies for defense against rival coalitions. Indeed, the Company went so far as to impose permanent agents, or Residents, on neighboring states, who endeavored to control the host country's foreign policy by supervising its diplomacy.[107] In short, the Company used surveillance to maximize influence over its neighbors. Resident agents were employed by the Qing in Inner Asian warfare against the Junghars, but thereafter the Qing tried to avoid involvement in the domestic politics or diplomacy of neighboring states even when requested to participate. Far from extending a defensive umbrella over these states, Qing authorities were prepared to see them collapse or be conquered provided their own frontier remained secure. Internal documents and diplomatic letters made clear that the Qing government wanted neither allies nor enemies: as long as a foreign state—tributary or non-tributary—respected the frontier, no action would be taken against it. At root, this strategy reflected a cost-benefit analysis. The enormous expense and constant vigilance needed to engineer a grand coalition made sense only if the Qing empire faced enemies larger than itself. As long as this seemed unlikely, neutrality offered better value than engagement.

Qing rulers were also skeptical of military alliances for practical reasons. In India, the Company enforced military cooperation with local states through the mechanism of "subsidiary alliances" whereby those states paid for the British garrisons that guarded them. Anti-British powers explored the possibility of their own alliances. The Gurkhas, for instance, sent envoys as far as Burma, Afghanistan, and China in the attempt to enhance their strategic position.[108] Qing emperors, though acknowledging the theoretical utility of foreign allies, remained wary. During the second Qing-Gurkha war, Qianlong had commanded Fuk'anggan to notify tribes around Nepal that they could earn Qing favor by joining the impending attack.[109] Yet the emperor soon criticized the implementation of this strategy. One major worry concerned the empire's long-term prestige. If foreign allies were so effective as to obviate the need for Qing military action, Qianlong worried that the result "would be the success of each tribe itself, and would have nothing to do with the Qing government." Such independent success would not "cause them to fear our power, embrace virtue, and forever act as a fence for our frontier."[110] Thus rebuked, Fuk'anggan minimized the importance of foreign tribes to his strategy. He reassured Qianlong that "last year, in issuing a call to arms to this chieftain [Lord Cornwallis] ordering him to send troops and aid in the extermination of the Gurkhas, I wished only to slightly divide the strength of the Gurkhas, and absolutely did not rely solely on the strength of foreign troops."[111] We have seen Qianlong's rebuttal when he thought George III was claiming to have used English troops to help the Qing. An aversion to coordinated military action was maintained in the Jiaqing period when, as noted, the emperor rebuked Saicungga for even the empty threat of arranging a coalition with the Pileng against the Gurkhas.

Skepticism of alliances was not limited to the Himalayan frontier. Qianlong's most intractable foe after 1760 was the rising Konbaung dynasty of Burma. Warfare was conducted overland, on and beyond the Yunnan frontier, but difficult terrain prevented the Qing from winning victories deep in Burmese territory. It had long been realized in China that Burma had a maritime frontier close to Siam, a state paying tribute by sea to Guangzhou. Faced with setbacks, the governor-general of Yunnan and Guizhou, Yang Yingju (d. 1767), proposed that the Qing send an agent by sea from Guangdong to Siam, to conclude an agreement coordinating attacks on Burma. Qianlong met this suggestion with sarcastic derision: "As for the point about making an agreement (*yuehui*) with Siam to attack on two fronts, this is even more absurd and laughable. To rely on the strength of foreigners during military operations is not only useless in the affair at hand; we would moreover, to no purpose, be looked upon slightingly by our tributaries. This is something that absolutely cannot be done."[112]

Yet Burma proved a tenacious opponent. Having little to show for his enormous casualties, Qianlong was more receptive to such ventures the following year. He ordered the governor-general at Guangzhou to send agents to learn more about Siam's geography and current politics. He was not yet considering sending a Qing naval force to the region, he stressed, but if the beleaguered king of Siam wished to revenge himself on Burmese invaders, "and should he wish the Qing to send forces to act in concert with him, this would be an opportunity that might be taken advantage of."[113] Reinforcing Siam was not dismissed out of hand, but careful inquiries would be needed before a decision was made.

Although the plan was never put into effect, and the Burma War ended without a decisive Qing victory, Qianlong remained interested in avenues of vengeance. By the 1770s, Qing authorities were receiving solicitations from Phraya Taksin (d. 1782; Ch., Zheng Zhao), who had emerged as Siam's most powerful figure after the fall of the Ayutthaya dynasty. Taksin was professedly willing to join an attack on Burma, but wanted material aid in return. The governor-general at Guangzhou proposed sending a mild response leaving the possibility open, but Qianlong rebuked him for his naiveté in managing foreigners. If the Qing relied on Siam to defeat Burma, "then [Taksin] would certainly grow arrogant on the strength of his success. With the passage of time he would increasingly imitate their wrongdoing, and become more difficult to control. This is a fixed principle." In its reply to Taksin, the Grand Council tried to steer a middle course, beginning with a long preamble about Qing strength—"why would we rely on your speck of overseas territory to collect troops for a joint attack?"—but welcoming independent action by Siam and hinting at possible rewards.[114] Somewhat later, the governor-general at Guangzhou proposed measures that might allow Taksin to raise a force to divide Burmese attention during a future Qing assault. Qianlong was willing to allow this in principle, provided there was no hint of his own personal involvement in any future negotiations. Subsequent edicts, however, stressed that Taksin must be told that Qing forces never acted in alliance with a foreign power, and no formal military collaboration would be permitted.[115] These diplomatic principles were hardly products of a distinctly Chinese culture, and Qianlong's position can be compared to his contemporary George Washington's advice to Americans to treat all countries with good faith while avoiding political connections: "Taking care always to keep ourselves . . . on a respectably defensive posture, we may safely trust to temporary alliances for extraordinary emergencies." Washington rejected entangling alliances because of the "detached and distant situation" of the United States; Qianlong because of what he considered the extraordinary size of his state, a lone superpower in a world of smaller powers.[116]

That the Qing frontier policy continued to appear viable in the 1820s and 1830s must be understood in the context of intelligence gathering. Qing authorities knew the critical value of information in managing foreign relations, and when necessary interviewed knowledgeable subjects and foreigners or even sent agents to make inquiries beyond the frontier. Compared to British India, however, this activity was decentralized. The task of collecting and analyzing intelligence fell principally to officials overseeing a given frontier, whose bureaucratic responsibility was limited to protecting the immediate border zone and not dealing with distant upheavals. Rarely did the emperor and Grand Council look beyond this information when weighing policy choices. And with so many apparently distinct frontiers to manage, attention to any one zone fluctuated. By contrast, as Michael Fisher has observed, the British network of Residents was designed precisely to triangulate individual reports into a coherent picture that superseding the vantage from any one spot: "As the number of Residencies grew, the amount of material thus made available to the Company about the important courts of India gave it an ability to coordinate its efforts in a way unmatched by any single Indian ruler. This growing network provided the Company with what Mountstuart Elphinstone called 'the immense advantage of a familiar knowledge of all the Durbars in India' that the Company held over any single Indian Ruler."[117] British military success in India, Christopher Bayly likewise observes, derived in large measure from an extensive intelligence network that allowed them "to anticipate the coalitions of the Indian powers and to plot their enemies' movements and alliances."[118] Only a systematic synthesis of all reports in the capital could achieve this.

A precondition of such centralized coordination, however, was awareness that various frontiers formed part of a single field of political activity. Given the methods used to study geography in the Qing period, tracing interconnections was difficult. The Qing collected intelligence on many dimensions of British expansion in Asia, but did not assemble it into one picture. In operational analysis, no standard term was in use for India, its sub-regions, or political entities. Instead, overlapping terms were found in various regions: officials in Lhasa learned of the Pileng conquest of Jiaga'er, in Yarkand of the English seizure of Hindustan, and in Guangzhou of vague English control over Gangjiao. The "Guonai'er" mentioned at Yarkand was not recognized as Gewo'er Zhe'ernaili, the "Pileng king" reported at Lhasa, or the "General of Mengliaola" reported at Guangzhou. William Moorcroft, known in Yarkand in 1821 as Mu'erqilapu was referred to in Lhasa in 1830 as Eliyamu Mo'ergere; Thomas Manning, known in Tibet in 1812 as Malin, reappeared in the Qing record as "Mr. Manning" (*Misi Wanning*) when he entered China four years later during the Amherst embassy.[119]

Philological difficulties in raw intelligence led foreign politics to be viewed as an inherently uncertain web of rumors and hypotheses, precluding certain knowledge. Qing rulers doubted the value of hearsay reports, and realized that inquiring into distant events would unearth conflicting and confusing claims, difficult to verify or evaluate, from informants of partisan allegiances. Territorial officials prudently disclaimed the possibility of sure knowledge about foreign affairs, and emperors agreed. Instead, the Qing state concentrated on the border zone itself, where intelligence was more certain. This meant the relatively uncritical use of local vocabularies taken on their own terms. Thus, the Qing official record shows a striking passivity in geographic matters, where the emergence of new names or the disappearance of older groups led to little comment, analysis, or interpretation within the confines of state correspondence.

The influence of bureaucratic incentives extended beyond intelligence gathering. For India, "experience and their monopoly of information gave the frontier agents a peculiar importance in the shaping of British policy on the north-west frontier."[120] Officials on the frontier were often strong advocates of aggressive action. In the Qing case, incentives were inverted. A crisis on the frontier was, to adopt Philip Kuhn's terminology, an "event" or "unit of accountability," and the duty of an official was to defuse the problem quickly, normally by restoring the status quo.[121] With its assumption of minimalism in foreign affairs, the Qing court was normally reluctant to devote resources or attention to frontier troubles if this could be avoided. For the throne, frontier trouble indicated bureaucratic mismanagement, a possibility routinely investigated and often discovered. Even if exonerated, officials were expected to solve the trouble quickly, giving them reason to ignore or downplay problems. Profound inquiry or bold action might only aggravate the situation. To harp on the significance of a foreign threat, or to unravel strands that stretched beyond the limits of their official responsibility threatened perilous responsibility out of proportion to any likely reward. Territorial officials—the Qing empire's eyes on the world—had good reason to take a very narrow view of bureaucratic "events" on the frontier. Nor was the Grand Council expected to digest and synthesize all incoming reports, as would have been done in British India (or, indeed, any European chancellery).

These strategic, bureaucratic, and geographic factors were at times challenged individually. The Qing government sometimes coordinated its inquiries into foreign conditions between different frontiers and fit together local geographic understandings; even alliances were sometimes contemplated. But major change in any one sphere was difficult precisely because these factors reinforced each other. A segmented administrative structure and strategic assumptions that all threats were local made synthesizing geographic knowledge seem less urgent. In turn, neither strategic nor geographic knowledge seemed to urge a modification of bureaucratic structures and procedures. These institutional and intellectual factors allowed a major shift in Asia's balance of power to pass without any perceived need for a major strategic reassessment. For a foreign policy to emerge as an alternative to frontier policy, change was required in all three spheres simultaneously.

The analysis presented in this chapter has considered only the *official* understanding of the outside world, the information, policies, and opinions shaping the Qing government's internal correspondence. At no time did the highly circumscribed stream of bureaucratic communication monopolize the empire's total understanding of the outside world and how best to handle it. This was particularly true after 1800, when the death of the Qianlong emperor gave the Han literati new freedom to enter fields of research off-limits or heavily restricted under his rule, including foreign geography, military planning, and policies toward the outside world. We can now turn to assessing the consequences of this trend.

SIX

The Discovery of British India on the Chinese Coast, 1800–1838

Between the 1790s and 1830s, as tentacles of the British octopus inched nearer to Yarkand in the east and the Zhoushan archipelago in the west, the Qing state made no major policy changes to adjust to the multi-armed reach of its neighbor. Britain's vault to predominance in Asia during the Napoleonic Wars passed without a sharp Qing reaction, this study has argued, because of the Qing empire's entrenched frontier policy. Individual dimensions of British expansion came to the attention of the Qing government, but in state documents there was no acknowledgment that fundamental geopolitical changes were occurring that threatened to engulf the empire and required coordinated countermeasures.

Outside of formal bureaucratic correspondence, however, there emerged in this same period a more integrated and flexible view of the outside world, one that in time would undermine the Qing frontier policy. In the eighteenth century, the state had virtually monopolized discussions of policy toward the outside world. Military and strategic commentary by men not charged with managing frontier affairs was unwelcome; private scholarship about non-Chinese territories also noticeably declined. With Qianlong's death in 1799, however, the empire's military history, military strategies (at first in regard to internal rebellion), and external geography all began to be discussed in print by Han literati outside of ordinary bureaucratic channels.

Statecraft (*jingshi*) scholarship, as this policy-oriented research and advocacy was known, could depart significantly from official modes of analysis. Private essayists normally lacked access to state intelligence resources, but could compensate by consulting private informants or peers within the administration. While memorials were limited to matters under the jurisdiction of their authors, essayists could speak as synthesizing generalists with a panorama as broad as their knowledge would sustain. Although bureaucrats hewed closely to relevant and indisputable facts, private authors could veer into speculation or abstraction. While bureaucrats had to consider their political careers, essayists could propose ambitious policy changes without incurring responsibility for risks inherent in their implementation. Although they lacked influence over state policy, except insofar as they could persuade officials to advocate their ideas, private statecraft writers could nonetheless radically reinterpret the Qing empire's place in the world. Still, differences in content and spirit between official and private commentary did not necessarily reveal a fundamental gap in outlook between serving bureaucrats and literati out of office. Many influential private commentators had degrees and bureaucratic experience, and were in close contact with provincial administrators, as friends, correspondents, or private secretaries. If eminent officials were less forthcoming on major geographic or geopolitical issues, this reflected the strictures of their position rather than ignorance or apathy.

For officials and statecraft scholars alike, opium was of growing interest. Its importance to China rose slowly in the late eighteenth century, and by around 1800 the Qing state began to step up prohibitions. The trade grew in the teeth of stringent new legislation. After a sharp rise in imports after 1820, even literati who neither lived along the southern coast nor had any official connection to the problem began to take notice. By 1830, opium came to be identified as the root of an even more pressing difficulty, the surging value of silver, which upset the empire's bimetallic monetary balance. At this point, China's relations with the maritime world received closer consideration by the empire's intellectual elite in Beijing and the prosperous cities of the Jiangnan region, along the lower reaches of the Yangzi River.

Analysis of the opium crisis ultimately drew attention to the site of its production, India, and the ties between that territory and the English homeland. By the mid-1830s, the foundations for a reappraisal of the Qing empire's geostrategic position were laid. Under the galvanizing influence of the Opium War, this intelligence base would ultimately support both a unified worldview transcending the kaleidoscope of regional outlooks, and a corresponding foreign policy that tried to coordinate all frontiers. In the process, the unique geographic lexicon for describing foreign territories in memorials from the Pearl River delta was synthesized with geographic names used widely throughout China. This standardization, when extended to other frontiers, allowed Qing scholars to succeed in their long-standing ambition to systematize the empire's geographic knowledge. With a clearer geographic outlook, the crisis on the coast was linked directly to the administrative and fiscal structure of the British empire.

The Emerging Private Study of India on the Maritime Frontier

In 1818 the high official and eminent scholar Ruan Yuan (1764–1849), recently transferred to Guangzhou as governor-general, took the first steps toward preparing a new provincial gazetteer, the *Guangdong tongzhi*. Precedents established by the previous version meant his editors would have to discuss foreign countries currently or historically in contact with Guangzhou's busy port. When the project began, virtually no descriptive or analytical accounts of the outside world were being produced in the Pearl River delta. Upon its conclusion in 1822, however, the region had become the primary site of Chinese research into the maritime sphere.

Before that time, despite Guangdong's unparalleled volume of foreign trade, Fujianese authors were the principal authorities on lands beyond the seas. Although an important study of Macao, the *Aomen jilüe*, had touched on foreign geography in the mid-eighteenth century, its influence paled beside that of Chen Lunjiong's *Haiguo wenjian lu*. First published in 1744, Chen's work had been copied into the prestigious *Siku quanshu* manuscript collection decades later, and maintained its popularity beyond the Qianlong period, being reprinted at least four times between 1793 and 1833.[1] A preface to the first of these reprints described it as "a book essential for frontier defense and commerce."[2] Large portions of Chen's work were copied into the *Yue haiguan zhi*, an 1838 account of the Guangdong maritime customs.[3] Yao Ying (1785–1853), a coastal administrator who will feature prominently in the next two chapters, took Chen's work with him after being transferred to a post in Taiwan in 1819, and found reprints available in the island's bookstores when he returned in 1838.[4] Later, he recalled that Jiaqing-era piracy had led to competition for copies among those charged with coastal defense. Despite Yao's claim that these users were mainly interested in its charts of the Chinese coast and "still had only vague conceptions" about the world map, it was also widely consulted in this period.[5]

In 1800, Chen Lunjiong's fellow provincials still dominated the slender corpus of writings by Qing subjects with direct experience overseas.

Aside from Chen's own work and Cheng Xunwo's short volume on Java, the most up-to-date account of overseas geography then available was the *Haidao yizhi* of Wang Dahai, who in 1783 had left his home in the Longxi district (modern Zhangzhou) to travel and teach in Java. His book (preface 1791, printed 1806) concentrated on that island, but made reference to other foreign countries. Of England (termed "Hongmao" or "Yingchili/Engkitlêy"), it said that it excelled all the other "nations to the northwest" in manufacturing.[6] As the phonetic rendering of "England" shows, Wang used a geographic vocabulary distinct from that employed in contemporary Guangdong, probably reflecting both his own dialect and that of his informants on Java (who in turn were probably influenced by Dutch place-names). Several Indian locations featured in his list of foreign countries, for instance Mangalore, Ceylon, and Cochin. Bengal was mentioned (as Mingjiaoliao/Bengkala), and some editions add that the Dutch, English, and Portuguese lived there at various sites, though Wang did not explicitly state that it was a European colony. Chinese did not go to these Indian regions, he added, except criminals in Java exiled to Ceylon.[7] Presumably this was the understanding of Fujianese merchants in Java, since Calcutta had a fledgling Chinese community by this time.

England's rising prominence in Asia is reflected in the textual history of Wang's work. In his first edition the English were only said to possess "newly opened lands" (*xinken zhi di*) at Penang; he added that "the laws they establish are cruel and ruthless, and all Chinese who lived there were not able to endure them and moved elsewhere."[8] Twenty years after returning to Zhangzhou (presumably around 1811–1812) Wang wrote an addendum describing how the English had finally conquered long-coveted Java in 1811. Now, however, he emphasized that "[the English] eliminated the cruel laws of the Dutch, summoned merchants back as before, and everyone happily submitted to them, and no merchant from near or far did not trade there; the circumstances of the English can be called flourishing!" Opium, strongly denounced by Wang, was depicted as a Dutch product, unconnected to the British Indian government.[9]

Ruan Yuan and the Guangdong tongzhi Project

Ruan Yuan's decision to replace the previous edition of the provincial gazetteer, then almost a century out of date, required great deliberation.[10] Listed as its chief editors would be the highest civil officials in the province. Upon completion it would be submitted to the throne and to the Office of State History, where its contents would become the raw material for subsequent editions of the empire's unified gazetteer. For scholars, it would represent the foremost available reference work on Guangdong, and a model of the gazetteer art produced by the realm's most capable editors. Given this close scrutiny, its content and format had to be pondered with care.

Particularly problematic were the records of maritime countries. Impeccable standard histories could be consulted for countries known prior to the Qing period, and indeed, most entries were culled from them, beginning with the *Nan shi* of the Tang scholar Li Yanshou and ending with the *Ming shi*, completed less than a century earlier. Material of this authority was not yet available for countries newly encountered during the Qing period, but many had entries in other officially published works, notably the previous Yongzheng edition of the gazetteer, and the *Da Qing yitong zhi* and *Huang Qing zhigong tu* issued by the court. It was also deemed appropriate to draw on Verbiest's *Kunyu tushuo* and Chen Lunjiong's *Haiguo wenjian lu*, both granted a place in the *Siku quanshu* collection.[11] Yet the newest of these written sources were almost forty years old, and by 1818 the situation at Guangzhou had changed dramatically from the mid-Qianlong period. England, not even meriting an entry in the edition of 1731, had now decisively eclipsed the Dutch and Portuguese as the dominant power in the maritime world. The United States had also emerged, along with a host of smaller countries listed in no obvious textual sources.

For part of its content, then, the gazetteer would have to depart from authoritative evidence. Guangzhou had many potential informants about England, its imperial possessions, and other countries. But simply recording oral interviews with foreigners would put the editors in the position of vouching for the validity of their testimony. To address this problem they divided the section on foreign countries in two. First came those that could confidently be described entirely on the basis of existing written sources. Then the editors broke in with a note, explaining that "when the maritime prohibitions were removed in the Kangxi period, among the foreigners arriving at Guangzhou were those who came only once, and those who came less than once a decade. The various islands conquer and annex each other, their names abruptly change, and their details cannot be examined. Details about those countries [whose ships] currently come are recorded hereafter."[12] Thus warned, the reader was presented with a series of descriptions, often terse, of countries in Europe, India, and elsewhere.

Where did these details come from? In October 1818, just a few months after the project was mooted, the East India Company Supercargoes reported to London that,

> Puankhequa sent to-day to Mr. Morrison a map of the world executed by a Chinese on a small scale, to enquire, for the information of the Viceroy, where it was that the English were fighting in India. The person who brought the map thought he wanted the situation of the Goorkas pointed out.
>
> There was on the same map the whole Eastern coast of China drawn out at great length with the names of places and islands, and the soundings in some parts. The map of the world was so small, and so ridiculously erroneous, that it was impossible to point out the relative situation of any two places.[13]

Although it is possible that Ruan was seeking information about the Anglo-Nepal War, which had ended two years earlier, I have found no documents to support this interpretation.[14] It seems more likely that this was a preliminary inquiry for the gazetteer project. Strengthening this hypothesis is the fact that Morrison himself described a very similar process less than six months later, in April 1819: "The Governor . . . is at present editing a new statistical account of the extensive districts over which he presides. . . . He has very judiciously thought of inserting some account of the foreign trade to the port of Canton, together with such notices as he can collect respecting foreign nations, particularly Europeans. He applied to the native merchants to make inquiries for him, which they have done in various quarters." He added that he himself had been applied to for information, including an account of Napoleon, and that his Chinese interviewer made a written abstract of his testimony.[15]

The *Guangdong tongzhi* shows circumstantial evidence of having used oral inquires. Because the editors took care to cite their written authorities by name, it can be inferred that many unattributed passages came from an oral informant. Certain entries, for instance those on Mexico and the United States, could not have come from written sources cited elsewhere in the book. Informants and state archives made it possible to give information about Indian ports and regions, specifically the Maratha empire (Matala), Bombay (Wangmei), Surat (Sula), and Pondicherry (Benzhili).[16] Geographically, the locations assigned to these places by the gazetteer are difficult to decipher. Thus, Bombay has the following entry: "north of Goa (Xiao Xiyang) is the country of Vengurla (Wangsuoluo), and further north is the country Malwan (Malunni); further north and slightly west is England (Yingjili-guo), and further north and slightly west is Bombay."[17] Bombay and Surat were stated to be subject to the Hongmao, indicating the English. In its own entry, England is acknowledged to possess extensive overseas territories: "it is not known when they occupied lands in North America, which are called Canada. England is called a country of Europe, this is the home country (*benguo*). . . . The series of subject lands in which they trade are called 'Gangjiao'; many of their ships come here."[18]

The terseness of the *Guangdong tongzhi*'s entries on foreign countries should be ascribed not to the indifference or intellectual limitations of its staff, but rather to the restrictions inherent to formal gazetteers, specifically the imperative to prefer written sources to unverified oral testimony as far as possible. Although constrained in their officially sponsored writings, several members of the editorial team undertook personal research into foreign geography. The highest-ranking editor to do so was Jiang Fan (1761–1831), Ruan Yuan's friend and fellow Yangzhou native. The longest citation in the gazetteer's section on England, which contained references to Gangjiao and Canada, was from his *Zhouche wenjian lu*.[19] Other aspects of Jiang's work, as we shall see below, also indicate that he was researching foreign geography in parallel with service on the *Guangdong tongzhi*.

Wu Lanxiu (d. 1839), a lower-ranking editor and prominent scholar in Guangzhou, also made parallel private research into foreign geography. His inquiries centered on the person of Xie Qinggao (d. 1821), a native of Jiaying in eastern Guangdong who had taken to sea at the age of eighteen. Traveling on foreign vessels, Xie had sailed for fourteen years before being forced by blindness to retire to Macao and go into business.[20] Like many other residents of the Pearl River delta, Xie's profession had made him familiar with the maritime world and its inhabitants; unlike others, he found an avenue for transmitting his experience in writing. There are two accounts of how this occurred. Yang Bingnan (granted the *juren* degree in 1839), like Xie and Wu a native of Jiaying, recorded that he met the sailor while visiting Macao in the spring of 1820, and had a full conversation about conditions in the southwestern ocean. Struck by the depth of Xie's knowledge and the simple way he expressed himself, Yang was receptive when "Mr. Xie exhorted me to record it, thinking that by this means his lifetime's experience could be passed on and endure after his death."[21] Perhaps moved by the urgency of the request—Xie would die the following year—Yang agreed and recorded Xie's testimony item by item, naming it the *Hailu*. For his part, the geographer Li Zhaoluo (1769–1841) records being told the following account by Wu Lanxiu:

> His home region [of Jiaying] had someone named Xie Qinggao, who when young had gone with foreign ships throughout the maritime countries, reaching everywhere. Wherever he went he invariably made careful inquiries, examining things with his eyes and verifying them with his reason. Having traveled for over a decade he went totally blind and now, no longer able to sail, makes a living as a merchant. He frequently said that he regretted that he could not find anyone to record what he had seen and pass it on to posterity, and Wu Lanxiu sympathized with him and took down his works, making the *Hailu*.[22]

Although scholars have not yet succeeded in reconciling these two accounts, it is clear that Xie's testimony was recorded via hometown connections with other scholars hailing from the predominantly Hakka area of Jiaying.[23]

One of the places visited by Xie was British India, and he offers the most detailed eyewitness description of its ports made by any Qing subject before the Opium War. His longest entry, on Bengal (Mingyala), explained that it was several thousand *li* in circumference and subject to the British, who maintained a garrison in a fort in the capital of Calcutta (Guligada). High officials in Bengal, Xie noted, were appointed directly by the British monarch. The English population he estimated at over ten thousand, while there were also "fifty to sixty thousand sepoy troops (xubo *bing*), that is, Bengali natives." He described other major Indian ports, including Madras (Mandalasa), Bombay (Mengmai), and Goa (Xiao Xiyang), as well as Indian states such as that of the Marathas (Malata-guo).[24]

Xie recounted navigational matters, ethnographic details, popular customs, and local products, but injected virtually no strategic or political commentary. He knew the English had incorporated enormous Indian territories into their empire, enrolling many native troops. In his entry on England he commented that, "their livelihood comes from maritime commerce, and they vie to obtain all profitable places within the seas," establishing "external administrations" (*waifu*) in Bengal, Madras, and Bombay.[25] Still, he had little to say about British expansion as a general phenomenon or the threat it might pose for China. Xie was also aware that opium came from India, describing the various types produced there, but made no editorial comment beyond remarking that "it is not known where this flowing poison will stop."[26] These relatively understated reports about British expansion may reflect the fact that Xie returned home in the mid-to-late 1790s, before British expansion in India intensified under Wellesley's governor-generalship. In the 1830s, Chinese commentators paid much closer attention to the British empire's political economy.

Part of the *Hailu*'s significance is that it was written at all. Previously in the Qing period no private scholar had systematically set down in writing the report of an illiterate sailor or merchant with wide experience outside China, nor had such a person ever found a willing amanuensis through his own efforts. Records of personal experience in the maritime world before the *Hailu*, such as those of Chen Lunjiong, Wang Dahai, and Cheng Xunwo, were composed by literate sojourners or their descendants. As a preface writer to Wang Dahai's work had complained, such accounts were exceptional: "those who maintain communication and trade with these [foreign] countries only think about making a profit, and do not know how to write, so they both lack any inclination to write accounts of them and are incapable of doing so."[27] Only with Xie do we begin to find a degree of cooperation between a mariner and local literati in studying the outside world.

Also significant was the speed with which the *Hailu* was drawn into other scholarly enterprises. Although accounts of its genesis acknowledge no link between the *Hailu* and the ongoing gazetteer project, a copy of the *Hailu* entered the hands of one of its editors, Wu Lanxiu, almost at once. Xie's testimony was drawn upon by the *Guangdong tongzhi* for countries without other written records. For instance, the entry for Bombay contains passages drawn verbatim from the *Hailu* and that for the Marathas shows close parallels.[28] Around the same time, Xie's record found a powerful backer in one of China's most influential geographers, Li Zhaoluo. Reaching Guangdong in 1820, Li was in close contact with the incoming provincial governor, as well as Ruan Yuan, both editors of the gazetteer. He also met Wu Lanxiu, and through him was able to read Xie's testimony and apparently make his own copy.

Although the history of the *Hailu* shows that literati were becoming more interested in intelligence from the maritime world, textual research techniques remained predominant. Xie Qinggao's testimony was treated not as a discovery making older accounts obsolete, but rather as a complementary piece of textual evidence advancing claims that had to be interpreted in relation to other writings. Li Zhaoluo's encounter with Xie's work highlights this approach. When he arrived in Guangzhou, Li tells us, he was struck by the foreign presence and wished to find a local who was well acquainted with the outside world, "so perhaps I could in that way critically examine older books and fathom current conditions." To his regret, however, inquiries among local translators produced only cursory or unreliable answers.

He was therefore delighted to encounter a manuscript of Xie's testimony, which supplied precisely the kind of information he sought. However, "it was written down in haste, and not perfectly scrutinized, so there might be mistakes or internal contradictions." Li asked Wu to summon the sailor for further questioning, but Xie died just as the letter was sent. Unable to find someone else with similar qualifications, Li was left to make what he could of Xie's testimony.[29]

The first stage of Li's editing, undertaken on a riverboat as he journeyed homeward, was to rearrange the original draft and add some short comments of his own. This he entitled the *Haiguo jiwen*. Later, however, he explained why Xie's oral account required more elaborate textual study. Unlike older works that relied on hearsay, the sailor's testimony had the merit of being based on direct experience. For Li, it was obvious that Xie's testimony "was sometimes in agreement with what was recorded in ancient works, sometimes not in agreement, and sometimes there appeared to be a vague similarity." Yet Xie himself, no scholar, "could not verify when he was in agreement with ancient sources, nor point out the distinctions when he differed from them." Li had thus set to work—evidently already in Guangdong—by poring through histories and other records of foreign countries, excerpting passages that seemed relevant to Xie's testimony. He had hoped to cross-examine the sailor with this textual evidence, but was prevented by Xie's untimely death. He therefore created a second work, the *Haiguo jilan*, in which he appended these citations to the pertinent passages of Xie's raw testimony, "so that if in the future there is someone who delights in such matters, and perchance encounters such a man as Qinggao, he can compare them by taking evidence from it." Li excluded as unreliable sources from the Tang period and earlier, and declined to excerpt material from the *Dong-Xiyang kao* of Zhang Xie (1574–1640), Aleni's *Zhifang wai ji*, and Chen Lunjiong's *Haiguo wenjian lu*, because all three were so detailed that they had to be consulted in the original.[30]

Seen narrowly, the finished *Guangdong tongzhi* itself shows little evidence of marking a radical break in the study of the maritime world. Although it did admit a limited amount of evidence drawn from direct testimony, this was not explicitly acknowledged or justified. Yet a much greater shift is evident if we step back from the gazetteer itself and consider the activities of its editors or their friends in the period between 1818 and 1822. From this vantage point, it is possible to discern not only an upsurge of interest in the maritime world among private scholars, but the emergence of tight connections, during Ruan Yuan's tenure in Guangzhou as governor-general, between the increasingly vibrant local academic milieu and scholars and scholarly trends from the empire's intellectual heartland in Jiangnan.[31] Much of the writing in this period on the maritime world beyond China was composed by eminent scholars visiting the Pearl River delta, notably Jiang Fan, Li Zhaoluo, and Ruan himself. These eminent scholars with an empire-wide profile collected local information and made it available to their peers elsewhere in the Qing domain. Although the gazetteer that ostensibly formed the focus of their labors remained relatively conservative in its use of evidence, its editors were much less cautious in composing their own private writings. In short, decades before the Opium War, the empire's intellectual elite—including, crucially, scholars unconnected to the southeast coast—was beginning to pay much closer attention to conditions in the maritime world. Over the next two decades the cross-fertilization of new evidence from Guangzhou with other sources produced results that would revolutionize the way Qing scholars viewed the outside world.

Enemies of Geographic Agnosticism

The grip of geographic agnosticism was not threatened merely by a surge in the volume of information entering across a single frontier, if this information continued to reflect only that region's particular linguistic and cultural milieu. Indeed, it was precisely the incommensurable elements contained in each emerging regional viewpoint that had led Qing scholars to consider many conflicting worldviews without opting decisively for one or another. On the coast in the 1820s and 1830s, however, two interrelated trends began to alter not only the amount of empirical evidence available to Qing geographers, but their research methods themselves. One was the decision by some scholars to use European world maps, albeit gingerly, as a tool in their geographic research. The other was the increasing credence paid to missionary publications about foreign affairs. Information of Western origin, known in China for centuries, was becoming a master system of geographic organization that would not replace, but rather subsume and reorganize, other geographic worldviews.

GLOBAL CARTOGRAPHY AND GEOGRAPHIC RESEARCH

In 1818, as at the start of the dynasty, no one visual schema of the world's shape commanded broad assent among Qing geographers. For lands within the empire, leading private scholars consulted the court's official survey maps. For lands beyond, however, those maps—indeed all maps—played a limited role in research. Arguments about foreign geography continued to be constructed primarily by citing written sources, and presented either without maps or (more rarely) with rough sketches summarizing claims expounded in detail in the text. Giving cartographic evidence a larger role had the potential to revolutionize geographic inquiry. Qing scholars knew that the corpus of written descriptions contained a superfluity of names. If any single map became accepted as a correct depiction of the world's shape, it could then serve as a template for organizing this surfeit of names, offering an avenue out of the morass of evidence and ultimately permitting definitive judgments about foreign geography. Absent in 1800 were not maps purporting to show the entire inhabited world, but confidence in their claims. European purveyors of maps supposedly based on empirical experience in all corners of the globe were suspected—reasonably—of offering them with the hidden political and intellectual agenda of self-aggrandizement. These doubts, and the prestige of older cosmologies, prevented Western world maps from rising above the status of untested hypotheses.

Such qualms did not imply a rejection of the technical underpinnings of European maps. By 1800, mathematical and astronomical knowledge was increasingly widespread among elite Chinese scholars outside of court, many of whom praised the imperial survey maps for their technical excellence. Skepticism prevailed only when these techniques were applied to foreign lands where their findings were unverifiable. Ruan Yuan himself was accomplished in mathematics and astronomy, acquainted with leading scholars in those fields, and in 1799 completed a series of biographies of eminent Chinese and Western practitioners in those disciplines. Around the same time, Qian Daxin (1728–1804) gave him a copy of Michel Benoist's Chinese treatise on the earth, the *Diqiu tushuo*, which Qian and He Guozong had polished earlier in the Qianlong period. Ruan supplemented the work and printed it with his own preface. It included a written summary of world geography using the vocabulary of the Jesuit tradition, and a small, sketchy woodblock version of Benoist's original map. Ruan, who believed that European astronomy ultimately derived from ancient Chinese scholarship, generally defended the validity of Jesuit theories, urging his peers not "to delight in their novelty and revere them, nor harbor doubts about their oddness and reject them."[32] However, he pointedly withheld his endorsement from Benoist's description of terrestrial geography, commenting that "this translated *Diqiu tushuo* talks extravagantly about foreign countries and their customs, which perhaps cannot be relied upon."[33] Like the *Siku quanshu* editors, Ruan considered Jesuit writings about the world worth preserving, but far from implicitly reliable.

Ruan's approach to compiling the *Guangdong tongzhi* showed equally his respect for the techniques of Western cartography and his reluctance to accept Jesuit empirical findings when these could not be verified. Like others in the kaozheng or evidential scholarship movement, Ruan tried to present information in a clear format for ready reference, particularly through the use of tables (*biao*) and illustrations (*tu*).[34] In keeping with classical precedents, he believed that local gazetteers should be carefully illustrated.[35] His gazetteer exceeded the standards of cartographic rigor set by court publications in the Yongzheng and Qianlong reigns.

The unlikely instrument of this achievement was a Daoist priest. Li Mingche (1751–1832), a native of Panyu, Guangdong, developed an early interest in Daoism and made a living as a European-style painter. In the 1780s he and his work were presented to Beijing by the provincial government, and while in the capital he had visited the Directorate of Astronomy, presumably meeting Jesuits as well as Chinese scholars. He also studied European astronomy and geography in Macao, possibly with the aid of an interpreter.[36] Li had at some point gained access to a copy of the court survey map, not unusual given his link to the directorate. This map (evidently a Kangxi edition) was included in his astronomical treatise, the *Yuantian tushuo*, together with a European map of the world.[37] Li evidently had few links to the Confucian scholarly community, and his expertise was discovered only by chance when a low-ranking member of the gazetteer editorial team happened to meet him while lodging at a Daoist temple and passed his work upward to Ruan, who composed a complimentary preface, arranged for it to be printed, and hired Li as the project's cartographer.[38]

Li's *Yuantian tushuo* reproduced a European-style world map in two hemispheres and outlined the principles of global mapping and the boundaries of continents as given in Western sources, but revealed no particular interest in foreign countries.[39] Li's world map was based closely on one prepared by the Suzhou scholar Zhuang Tingfu, completed in 1794.[40] A noteworthy feature of Zhuang's map, copied onto Li's, was its collection of geographic names from several styles of available European world maps, so that its depiction of India borrowed many typically Jesuit names, but supplemented them with terms such as "Geshita" and "Xiao Baitou fan" taken from Chen Lunjiong, as well as "Wendusitan," common in Qing official geography but not used by Chen or the Jesuits.[41]

Li's cartography for the *Guangdong tongzhi* was supervised by Ruan, who in turn was guided by court precedent on the use of maps. From the Yongzheng period, comprehensive reference works had included maps of Qing territory based on court surveys, but normally without a graticule of latitude and longitude. Ruan, by contrast, considered the graticule essential.[42] New maps drafted by Li Mingche for each county showed latitude and longitude. It is unclear whether Li's productions were based on new field surveys or adapted from existing survey maps, but nonetheless Ruan's project was the first Qing gazetteer to show county-level maps explicitly bearing the hallmarks of European cartographic techniques.

When maps were deemed appropriate, then, Ruan and his cartographer took great care to supply the best possible examples. Both men were familiar with Jesuit maps, and their decision to omit them and leave the section on foreign countries map-less was certainly a deliberate judgment on their inadequate evidentiary value. This judgment is not hard to understand. Ruan, at least, was avowedly skeptical of Jesuit descriptions of the globe. Moreover, the precedents for map usage in court productions indicated that they should be reserved only for the empire's own territory (and parts of non-Qing Central Asia in certain Qianlong-era works). The Qing state did not publically endorse any map of lands beyond its control. Even if Ruan had wished to include a Jesuit map, technical impediments stood in his way. Countries were noted in the *Guangdong tongzhi* according to the names used in the Pearl River delta. No map showed all the names in the gazetteer, so the project's staff would have had to figure out the location of those sites, an almost impossible task. Officially, the outside world remained unmapped.

Ruan's decision to exclude a Jesuit world map indicated doubt rather than hostility. Far from suppressing Jesuit arguments, his gazetteer briefly summarized them at the end of the section on foreign geography: "In the Ming the Westerner Matteo Ricci entered China and presented the Map of the World (*wanguo tu*) which divided the world into five continents. . . . The disciples of Aleni and Verbiest all propagate this theory as their tradition (*zushu qi shuo*). China is at the center of Asia. Thus, Korea, Japan, and the Liuqiu Islands in the east, India [or Goa] (Xiao Xiyang), the Philippines (Xiao Lusong), and Judea in the west; Siam in the south; and Russia, the Ottoman empire (Honghai'er), the Gurkhas, Hindustan, and various other countries in the north, these are all Asia."[43] Qianlong court scholarship had also cited Jesuit views of the world for reference in similar contexts, but this list was not just a mechanical copy, and had been updated (presumably by

Ruan and his editors) to reflect names like Gurkha first known in China only at the end of the Qianlong period. Even the gazetteer, then, showed some engagement with European geographic ideas.

As with its text, the maps included in the gazetteer did not reflect the limits of its editors' personal knowledge and curiosity. Unofficial research was already beginning to use European maps. Morrison reported that when Ruan's Hong merchant envoys came to question him in 1819 they brought along a map (based on his description, probably Chen Lunjiong's rendering of the eastern hemisphere).[44] Ruan himself was aware of Chen's map, and it was consulted by others working on the project.[45] Notes in Jiang Fan's *Zhouche wenjian lu* show that he employed cartography as an ancillary tool to solve the problem of multiple names for the same place. He stated: "[In regard to] 'Dingjiyi' in the *Ming shi*, 'An'eli' in the *Zhifang wai ji*, and 'Yingjili' in the *Haiguo wenjian lu*, I checked them using maps (*yi yutu he zhi*), and they refer to England (Yingjili)."[46] At the very least he compared two maps, from Aleni and Chen (the *Ming shi* had no world map). This technique dated back at least to the late Qianlong period, when another edition of Chen Lunjiong's world map commented that it used "modern designations" rather than earlier names, but "the reader can take ancient maps and ancient names, and examine them (*he zhi*) based on location, thus learning that a place today was anciently such-and-such country."[47] Zhuang Tingfu presumably used this technique to tentatively synthesize naming systems on his own map. Li Zhaoluo, in Guangzhou at the same time as Jiang, recorded that he added a map to the start of his now-lost edition of Xie Qinggao's maritime geography.[48] Once again this was probably a version of Chen Lunjiong's map, because Li later included that work at the start of a dictionary of geographic terms completed in 1837.[49]

Although none stated this explicitly, the very basis of their technique presumed that European renderings of the world were essentially correct. Reconciling place-names on the basis of location worked only if all the maps consulted roughly agreed about the shape of the world: European multicontinent maps could not fruitfully be superimposed over those from other traditions. Other evidence suggests that, at least on the edges of the maritime world, Chinese scholars were becoming more comfortable with European maps in the early nineteenth century. Ding Gongchen (1800–1875), a native of Fujian from a Muslim lineage who later gained fame during the Opium War as an expert in armaments and fortification, had interspersed exam study with coastal trading and farming. In 1831 he went abroad, spending time in the Philippines and sailing as far as Iran and Arabia, during which time his frequent astronomical observations attracted the notice of European navigators, who shared their materials with him.⁵⁰ In 1836 the scholar Cai Tinglan (1802–1859) met Ding in Guangdong. Cai recorded that,

> Gongchen was conversant with astronomy, as he had once sailed as a merchant to Luzon . . . and lived there for several years studying the astronomical methods of Europeans, acquiring a very fine command of the subject. He spoke with me daily about astronomy without tiring, and showed me [or, "bestowed upon me," 授] maps of the globe and astronomical instruments. For the most part they had an equator in the Western style, with curved lines [of longitude and latitude].⁵¹

Mariners and sojourners were particularly attuned to the importance of mapping for navigation. Wang Dahai had viewed maps used by the Dutch. The missionary Karl Gützlaff encountered a Chinese sea captain in the 1830s who "showed us a Chinese map; and, being aware of its geographical errors . . . was desirous of correcting and extending his information."⁵² The 1832 gazetteer of Xiamen quoted several works dealing with the navigational accomplishments of Europeans, touching upon the accuracy and utility of their maritime maps.⁵³

At first glance, the *Guangdong tongzhi* upheld the standards of eighteenth-century official scholarship on the outside world, denying maps to the section on foreign countries and (when possible) basing accounts of those countries on the most authoritative sources rather than the most current. Yet upon closer inspection, the wider milieu of the gazetteer project shows that a different approach to foreign geography was beginning to take hold even among elite scholars. Maps were being used as an auxiliary research tool to aid in textual inquiry: not simply to illustrate textual findings but as evidence in the process of reasoning itself. By the early 1840s, as we shall see, European world maps came to be acknowledged as correct by China's leading geographers, and their use became a crucial aid for unifying the diversity of place-names employed in textual scholarship.

PROTESTANT GEOGRAPHIES AND THE EMERGENCE OF "BRITISH INDIA"

Several years before Ruan Yuan completed the *Guangdong tongzhi* project, Protestant missionaries began to write in Chinese about geography. Centuries of precedent gave little reason to expect profound effects from these works. After all, in essence the Protestant geographic project was that of the Jesuits: to adjust Chinese understandings of their position in the world, especially vis-à-vis the West, and thereby ease China's conversion to Christianity. The Jesuits had the advantage of direct access to the emperor, high ministers, and some elite scholars, but despite making their claims well known, they were not accepted as more than an unproven hypothesis. Protestant missionaries lacked this access, and were forced to publish on the fringes of the empire and often beyond, in Malacca, Java, or Singapore, to an audience of sojourners, sailors, and merchants marginal to the empire's intellectual life. Their one advantage was topicality. With the opium trade swelling and British power rising, current information about the outside world—even from unorthodox sources—was increasingly in demand. Within a few decades, Protestant geographic accounts joined the mainstream of Qing scholarship.

Robert Morrison (1782–1834), the first Protestant missionary in China, arrived at Guangzhou in 1807. Hoping to preach the Gospel, he was perforce also a scholar of Chinese and, from 1809, interpreter and translator for the East India Company. By 1811, he began to produce religious tracts in Chinese. An unhappy encounter with the *Guangdong tongzhi* project seems to have turned his efforts toward geography. When asked for information, he found that what he had to say was not well received:

> The antiquity of the Greeks and Romans was very unpalatable to Chinese vanity; and when explaining the christian [sic] era, the epithet "Savior of the world" applied to Jesus, and the mention of some privileges of the peoples of England—such as NO TORTURE . . . excited the inquirer's FEARS: he DARED NOT, he said, mention such things to his Excellency the Governor; and he therefore sent for my approval, a distorted abstract of some parts of the statement given him, in which he falsified the matter of fact.

Morrison, clearly frustrated, fulminated against "men . . . UNWILLING to know the truth."[54] In that same year he wrote his first description of world geography, couched as the fictitious journal of a thoughtful scholar from Sichuan who sets out to see the wide world for himself.

As more laborers entered the mission field, geographic description formed a small but flourishing subset of their output. William Milne (1785–1822), the second Protestant missionary to arrive in China, studied Chinese at Guangzhou and then established himself at Malacca, where in 1815 he first issued the *Chinese Monthly Magazine* (*Chashisu meiyue tongjizhuan*).

Milne was soon assisted in his printing endeavor by Walter Medhurst, who in 1819 used the *Magazine* as a vehicle to publish a treatise on geography, including a map of the world and a map of Asia, the *Dili biantong lüezhuan* or *Geographical Catechism*.[55] In the same year Morrison published his own geography at Guangzhou.[56] As early as 1820 Milne regularly devoted a section of his *Magazine* to geography, and these were collected and published in 1822 as the *Quandi wanguo jilüe*. After Milne's death in 1822, Medhurst, now based in Batavia, became the primary missionary publisher of geographic and political material. In 1823 he started to issue the periodical *Texuan cuoyao meiyue jizhuan* (*Monthly Magazine*) to carry on Milne's monthly, the next year he wrote in Chinese a geography of Java, and later a Chinese-Western historical chronology. At Malacca, Samuel Kidd (1799–1843) began the short-lived *Tianxia xinwen* (*Universal Gazette*) in 1828.[57]

These early missionary geographies made clear the extent of British rule on the subcontinent. Morrison explained in 1819 that India was a "subject state" (*shuguo*) of the English. Likewise, Milne's magazine reported in 1820 that Hindustan (Xiyindushidan) or the Five Indias (*wu Yindu*), once formed by many independent countries, was now mostly ruled by England. Its capital, Calcutta (Jialeguda), directed three provinces (i.e., presidencies), Bengal, Madras, and Bombay, each with its own governor-general (*zongdu*, in imitation of Chinese usage).[58] Medhurst's Batavia-based *Texuan cuoyao* informed its reader that opium was grown in Bengal and also shipped out of Bombay and Madras, also remarking that the English had once sent the "king of Bengal" with a large military force to prevent a French invasion of Java.[59]

These earliest examples of Protestant geography did not have an immediate impact on Chinese scholarship, but even Southeast Asian publications were noticed by the elite. Distributed to overseas Chinese and vessels returning to China, their magazines were known to literati in coastal provinces, who in turn informed others. As early as 1826, the well-connected statecraft scholar Bao Shichen (1775–1855) knew that the English were publishing Chinese-language works in Singapore, and two years later he recorded that they had summoned poor Jiaying scholars and Cantonese craftsmen to educate their youth and publish Chinese books. He did not say whether he possessed copies of these works himself, but mentioned that many scholars in coastal cities knew about the British "widely printing" works in Chinese.[60]

Morrison, when he embarked on his ambitious attempt to reform Chinese worldviews, faced a difficulty that bedeviled all authors on Chinese geography: what terms to use. Like Ruan's team of scholars elsewhere in the city,

Morrison realized that geographic writing required a solid base in canonical sources and current Chinese works. In these readings he discovered at least seven distinct ways of expressing "India," each with different shades of significance. For English readers he translated an outline of Qianlong's views of Hindustan, as summarized in the *Da Qing yitong zhi*, mentioning the "wu Yindu" or "Five Yin-too, Indo, or Gentoo nations." The same work recorded the Chinese rendering of Bengal as "Pang-kŏ-la" (Banggela).[61] Morrison's Chinese dictionary defined Gangjiao as "a port or harbour; the ports of India are so called at Canton; and India itself," and gave the following Chinese definition of the English word: "INDIA in the religious books of Budh is called 天竺 tëen-chŭh. Central India, 中天竺 chung tëen-chŭh." He also stated that "Xiao Xiyang" (Small Western Ocean) could be translated as "India."[62] When his Sichuanese protagonist was made to reach India via Tibet, Morrison piled on the fruits of his studies, having him explain that "I wished to reach what the *Han shu* calls the Five Yindu. . . . Then [I] arrived at a large city called Calcutta; this city is now reckoned the capital, what the *Da Qing yitong zhi* calls the land of Banggela. Anciently it was also called Tianzhu, and further designated the country of Shendu."[63] In the same text he also provided "Yindiya" as a variant name, suggesting that he had also read Aleni's Ming-era *Zhifang wai ji*. Later, in translating a pamphlet about England and its empire, Morrison made reference to "the ancient country of Xindusitan" (*Xindusiyuan gu guo*), showing familiarity with the "ancient Xindu" (*gu Xindu*) mentioned in both the Yuan-era *Daoyi zhilüe* and the *Ming yitong zhi*.[64]

Ironically, what made Morrison's work so revolutionary was his wish to be scrupulously faithful to what he regarded as the high Chinese geographic tradition. Contemporary Chinese geographers at Guangzhou described the contemporary outside world using a regional patois with names like Gangjiao and Mengjiala that had no authoritative textual sanction. Morrison eschewed these terms as mere colloquialisms. He informed his Chinese readers that Gangjiao was the term used for India by the "common people of Guangdong" (*Guangdong suren*), ignoring its use in official memorials and by scholars. Morrison and his missionary colleagues instead discussed India using only words licensed in standard histories or court publications (although these were sometimes modified to make them more "correct," and neologisms were invented for regions of India they deemed not to have standard Chinese names).

This divergence is evident in the *Guangdong tongzhi*. The editors of that work were, of course, familiar with "Tianzhu" and "Yindu," as well as with the names for overseas territories under British control, such as Bengal and Gangjiao, but the gazetteer identified no link between the two sets of terms. Tianzhu was never used in reference to places in the maritime world. Indeed, the editors claimed that Tianzhu was no longer of any relevance to the coast because while it had once paid tribute via Guangzhou, "today it is a foreign country (*waifan*) in the Western Regions."[65] Still, Jesuit sources and Chen Lunjiong supported at least the inference that several ports named in the gazetteer were close to, it not actually part of, Tianzhu or Yindu. Ruan Yuan knew this, for in the early 1820s he questioned students in his Xuehaitang Academy in Guangzhou on the origins of the calendrical systems of the Great and Small Western Oceans, adding the gloss: "The Small Western Ocean (Xiao Xiyang), that is, today's Gangjiao and other countries; it is south of the present Muslim Frontier (*Huijiang* [i.e., southern Xinjiang]), the ancient Tianzhu and other places." However, Chinese authors in Guangzhou generally used the local lexicon for current affairs, referring to "Yindu" or "Tianzhu" only in a historical context, whereas Protestant authors jettisoned local terms like "Gangjiao" in order to describe a monolithic India under a single, standard, classically sanctioned name. By the early 1840s, prominent Qing geographers of the outside world would follow suit.

But what, in practice, was this single name for India to be? Although their geographies became more sophisticated, missionaries could not settle on one. Karl Gützlaff (1803–1851), by the 1830s the most active Protestant missionary author on geography, like Morrison was frustrated that his Chinese audience was not more receptive, and hoped that his secular writings would steer his readers from what he regarded as their self-conception as "first among the nations of the earth," with "high and exclusive notions," by trying to "convince the Chinese that they still have much to learn."[66] Like his colleagues, Gützlaff read widely in Chinese and saw the enormous vocabulary available for India. His own magazine, inaugurated in the summer of 1833 as the *Dong-Xiyang kao meiyue tongjizhuan*, drew upon various Chinese sources, selected according to Gützlaff's constantly shifting sensibilities. An edition from 1833 included a map of part of India, labeled in bold characters "a country subject to Great Britain" (*Da Yingguo fanshuguo*); smaller characters indicated "the province of Bengal" (*Banggala sheng*), Hindustan (*Yindusitan* rather than Qianlong's *Hendusitan*) and "the capital of Calcutta" (*Jialiquda jing*). That he erroneously placed Baltistan (Baleti) and Afghanistan (Aiwuhan) within the borders of Bhutan suggests that his borrowing outpaced his understanding. The next year Gützlaff dropped "Hindustan" for "India," explaining that the East India Company had now been abolished as a trading entity, and could only "manage its subject territories in various parts of India (Yindu) and other lands." In the same month he stated, however, that Tibet bordered not Yindu but Tianzhu-guo to its southwest. And, where on his 1833 map he had termed Nepal Gurkha (*Guo'erka*, not the standard Qing *Kuo'erka*), he now described it with the neologism "Niboli-guo."[67]

Gützlaff's most extensive description of contemporary India was in an issue for the fifth month of 1835. He entitled his entry "A General Account of Tianzhu or the Five Yindu" ("Tianzhu huo wu Yindu-guo zonglun"), but explained elsewhere that Hindustan (now the official Qing "Hendusitan") was an equivalent term. India was divided into four parts: "northern Hindustan" (including "Nepal or Gurkha"), "central Hindustan" (including Bengal, Awadh, Multan, Malwa), "southern Hindustan" (including the Karnatic and Malabar coasts), and the Deccan. Politically, India was split into the three "provinces" (*sheng*) or presidencies of Bengal (Banggela), Bombay (Gangmai), and Madras (Matalaxi), nine countries forming the "newly gained subject states of Great Britain" (*Da Yingguo xinjiang fanshuguo*), and a further group of "autonomous countries" (*zi cao qi quan zhi guo*). Collectively these vast and populous territories, Gützlaff told his readers, held a rank in Asia second only to China. Gützlaff did not explain how Britain had acquired these lands—due perhaps to his determination that the magazine "not treat of politics"—but the section concluded in a passage consonant with the mission of chastising "the apathy, the national pride, and the ignorance of the Chinese" undertaken by the Society for the Diffusion of Useful Knowledge in China, for which he was a Chinese secretary.[68] To justify his account, Gützlaff explained, "men of your country still are not paying attention or thinking about the affairs of this country [i.e., India]; few Chinese people go there and no Chinese record includes a treatise on Hindustan, and so everyone must ponder it rationally (*tuilun daoli*). Apart from this, subject states of China border on the English subject state of Hindustan, and Yunnan is not far separated from it; further, the heterodox religion of Buddhism emerged from India."[69]

By the early 1830s Protestant missionaries were gaining more Chinese readers. A watershed was crossed in 1832, when someone, probably Morrison, translated a short work by Charles Marjoribanks (1794–1833), president of the Company's Select Committee, entitled a *Brief Discourse on the People and Affairs of Great Britain* (*Da Yingguo renshi lüeshuo*). This introduction included a short discussion of the British empire, defending it against accusations of expansionism: "The intentions of the British court are often baselessly discussed by people in the East (*dongtu*), to the point that some falsely say that the English are always very greedy to open up broad new territories; no falsehood is greater than this. Indeed, the territories of England are at present too numerous, they cannot be expanded and it would be better that they were reduced!" British imperial holdings were then listed, with the statement "The places in what was anciently Hindustan have all become English territory."[70]

In February of that year, the East India Company sent the vessel *Lord Amherst* to convey its employee Hugh Hamilton Lindsay (1802–1881) and the missionary-interpreter Gützlaff the length of the Chinese coast to test the possibility of trade in other ports. During the trip Lindsay decided to distribute the *Da Yingguo renshi lüeshuo*, which "contains a plain account of the English nation, its power and magnitude."[71] It was given out at every port north of Xiamen, including Ningbo, Shanghai, and Tianjin, and Lindsay was pleased with "the effect produced by the distribution of our books, particularly the Ying-kwo, the fame of which has spread greatly, and almost the first request of our visitors is to be favoured with a copy."[72] Officials in particular were reported to have paid close attention to the work. At Ningbo, when the prefect sent messengers to the ship to ask about the pamphlet, Lindsay recalled that "explanation as to the subjects of grievances complained of at Canton, and regarding our Indian possessions, which we alluded to as nearly bordering on the Chinese empire, were the topics on which most questions were asked, and all the replies which appeared important were taken down in writing."[73] Gützlaff also recorded the great demand for the pamphlet.[74] In both Fujian and Zhejiang officials requested copies to send to Beijing for inspection. Elsewhere Gützlaff mentioned an encounter with a Taiwanese captain who "was slightly acquainted with our nation, from the perusal of the pamphlet before mentioned."[75]

During the voyage Lindsay emphasized his Company's possessions in India and the consequent proximity between the Qing and British empires, several times remarking that this particularly interested his Chinese audience. Here again Gützlaff corroborates Lindsay's account:

> Some of the inferior officers asked us what were the countries bordering on our territories in Asia, and how far our power extended. . . . The mandarins in general are exceedingly ignorant of all the concerns of foreign countries which are either not immediately under the sway of the Celestial Empire, or

bordering upon it. They were astonished to hear that our Indian possessions were separated only by forests and mountains from the Chinese province of Yunnan, and could scarcely believe that we were so near them.[76]

It was doubtless this astonishment that led Gützlaff, in his 1835 account of India, to mention that Yunnan was not far from Hindustan.[77]

Even over the course of this one voyage Gützlaff vacillated over how best to refer to India. He answered early Chinese inquiries by stating that "the ship is of the English nation, from Pang-ka-la (Bengal)."[78] The ship was identified as Bengali at least as far north as Xiamen. However, later in the voyage Gützlaff seems to have taken up the term Hindustan, probably because India was translated as "Hindustan" in the pamphlet about the English. For instance, the Chinese text of his correspondence with Korean officials read: "This vessel comes from Hindustan, a subject state of England, and this land borders the southwest of the Qing empire." The references to Da Yingguo and Xindusitan in this document are probably what Gützlaff was referring to when he commented that "we had to explain to them why England was called Great Britain, and why India was called Hindostan."[79] At some point Lindsay and Gützlaff switched back to "Bengal" in their self-description, informing the government of the Liuqiu (Ryūkyū) Islands that the captain "is from the country of Bengal (Banggela-guo)."[80]

Local officials dealing with the vessel focused their reports on matters directly relevant to the frontier, identifying the ship as English and ignoring its putative origins in India and English claims to dominate that region. Copies of the pamphlet on England reached the highest levels of the Qing government: the governor-general of Fujian and Zhejiang, Wei Yuanlang, commented on it, and Nergingge, governor of Shandong, transmitted the full text to the Grand Council.[81] Here again, bureaucratic analysis of the pamphlet focused on its denunciation of the treatment of the English at Guangzhou (seen as a guise adopted to justify the pursuit of trade elsewhere) and ignored statements about English power in India.

On his return to Guangzhou Gützlaff almost immediately embarked back up the Chinese coast aboard the opium ship *Sylph*, which he also claimed to have Indian origins. According to a memorial by the Liang-Jiang governor-general Tao Shu, the ship was flying a flag bearing the Chinese inscription "A Commercial Vessel of India" (*Tianzhu-guo shangchuan*) and Gützlaff had stated in response to inquiries that "India is a subject of England" (*Tianzhu xi Yingjili shuguo*).[82] A memorial of December 4, 1832, reported that a foreign vessel near Fengtian had identified itself as an English ship blown off course while on route from India (Tianzhu) to Singapore.[83] It is not clear why Gützlaff switched from "Bengal" and "Hindustan" to "Tianzhu."

By the 1830s, Protestant missionary writings enjoyed a considerable circulation on the coast of China, with some reaching the upper echelons of the bureaucracy. Simply being read did not demonstrate influence. Catholic claims had a toehold in official reference works, but were regarded as only one strand in a larger tapestry of geographic sources, totally convincing very few readers. Yet from a marginal position in the early 1830s, Protestant geographic materials in Chinese became widely used in early 1840s. Coastal crises gave Protestant geographies more immediate relevance than earlier Jesuit works had possessed, a fact that British missionaries exploited. Private Chinese scholars, increasingly writing without governmental restraint after 1800, were also much freer to make use of them. Yet rather than triumphing by displacing other sources and becoming an unmediated authority on the outside world, as their authors hoped, the role of Protestant geographies—and Western world maps—continued to depend on their reception, analysis, and evaluation by Chinese scholars.

British India Enters Qing Geostrategic Writing

As late as the 1820s, Qing geographic research into the maritime world was conducted largely in isolation from commentary on maritime policy. Editors of the *Guangdong tongzhi* were by no means indifferent to current affairs, but deemed that topic inappropriate for their work. Ruan Yuan struggled to suppress opium smuggling, but his gazetteer's entry for Bombay did not mention it as a source of the drug, though it listed every other product of that city given in the *Hailu*. Nor did those who tracked down Xie's testimony attempt to influence state policy. Li Zhaoluo singled out the fact that the *Hailu* touched on both opium production and the British annexation and fortification of coastal territories as one of its major virtues, but neither he nor the text's other editors commented on how this knowledge should guide Qing policy. Treating foreign geography as primarily an academic subject was in keeping with the commitment of Ruan, Li, and Jiang Fan to kaozheng or evidential scholarship research. It may also indicate, as has been argued, a common interest among serving officials and Guangzhou's intellectual elite to avoid presenting coastal affairs in a way that might generate pressure to stop or radically alter foreign trade.[84]

Conversely, private scholars who concentrated on trade policy and coastal security tended at first to talk generically about "foreigners" without mentioning specific groups or geopolitical trends. At the beginning of the Jiaqing period, when indigenous piracy was the main coastal threat, commentators studied late Ming and early Qing responses to the piracy epidemic in the sixteenth century. They devoted attention to measures on the coastal frontier itself, such as controlling maritime populations or fortifying the shoreline. Conditions among foreigners appeared irrelevant. Yan Ruyi (1759–1826), the first influential private scholar of naval defense in the nineteenth century, composed the *Yangfang jiyao*, based on experiences as private secretary to the governor-general at Guangzhou around 1805. His work, not published until 1835, drew on Ming-era sources for its maps and commentaries on the maritime world (including Southeast Asia and India), ignoring even the prominent writings of Chen Lunjiong.[85] The *Huangchao jingshi wenbian*, a large collection of statecraft writings completed in 1826, limited itself to coastal defense, without geopolitical commentary on the outside world. For early statecraft writers, as for official memorialists, the frontier alone was relevant.

Only in the early 1830s did coastal defense and foreign geopolitics come to be seen, at least for certain essayists, as two dimensions of the same security problem. In the 1830s opium imports more than doubled, and the trade was widely identified as a cause of serious economic and social problems.[86] From the early 1830s private vessels carrying opium were routinely anchoring off the coast of Fujian, and by the end of the decade they set their eyes on the Zhoushan archipelago off the coast of Zhejiang and nearer the large Jiangnan market. When the East India Company lost its monopoly on the tea trade to England and withdrew from Guangzhou, an influx of more ambitious and strident private traders followed. William Napier (1786–1834) was dispatched by the British government as superintendant of trade, to replace the Select Committee. When in 1834 he refused as an officer of the Crown to follow precedents worked out for the merchant Select Committee, trade was halted and armed clashes broke out before he backed down and retreated to Macao. Maritime affairs were becoming urgent.

Statecraft analysis fusing China's coastal problems to overseas geopolitics emerged from research initiated by Bao Shichen, a *juren* from Anhui who served as a private advisor to high officials. Bao's thinking on the opium question was first elaborated in an essay of 1820. This, Inoue Hiromasa has persuasively argued, should be read as an exchange with the Guangdong official Cheng Hanzhang (1762–1832), who around the same time wrote an essay arguing a contrary position. Bao believed that the total expulsion of foreign traders would end the opium scourge, and the silver thereby retained in China would amply compensate for lost customs revenue. Cheng, who had served in Guangdong for most of his career, criticized those who would peremptorily halt foreign trade. Abolishing legal trade, he pointed out, would cause coastal smuggling. Foreigners, aided by traitorous coastal residents, would likely respond by force, and it would take decades to end the resulting conflict. In his turn, Bao denied that an abrupt end to trade could lead to war. Foreigners, in his view, had negligible power: England had not one percent of China's size and population. Their arrogance was deliberately nurtured by Hong merchants (*yangshang*), whose interests, from their monopoly of foreign maritime trade, coincided with those of the Westerners. Bao accused local officials (Cheng was then prefect of Guangzhou) of protecting the lucrative status quo by amplifying false claims of a foreign military threat. Chinese ships might still be sent abroad with products desired by Westerners, Bao conceded, but only the abolition of the Hong system could sever troublesome foreigners from the Chinese masterminds guiding them.[87]

Bao's 1820 essay was geographically vague, referring to "foreigners" and only once mentioning the English as the strongest among them. Soon, however, he gained new sources of information. By 1826 he was corresponding with Xiao Lingyu, a native of Jiangsu, who shared Bao's interest in contemporary affairs and statecraft reform. Through acquaintance with Ruan Yuan, Xiao had been able to learn more about the British and the opium problem. In 1814, when Ruan was living in Huai'an as director-general of grain transport, Jiang Fan presented him with some of Xiao's writings.[88] Later, after Ruan moved down to Guangdong, Xiao followed him and remained there for several years as his private secretary, also working on customs affairs.[89] From Guangzhou, Xiao kept in correspondence with Bao, expressing to him the fear that within a decade the British might trouble the coast of Jiangnan and Zhejiang as the *wokou* pirates had done in the Ming. Bao praised this as farsighted. Xiao also reported to Bao the presence of the British in Singapore, where they recruited Fujianese and Cantonese "runaways."[90]

Xiao hoped to compose a "Collected Treatise on the Guangdong Maritime Customs" (*Yueque zhichu*), and Bao encouraged him to record "what you have truly seen and heard," advising him that a work based on the archives of the governor-general's office and the Guangzhou customs would prove a "timeless accomplishment."⁹¹ From the results of Xiao's research, outlined in an essay entitled *Ji Yingjili* (A Record of the English), composed around 1833, we can see that he attempted to use as many sources as possible.⁹² This piece was praised for its detail by Ruan Yuan, who composed a postface for Xiao's collected works.⁹³ Virtually the entire corpus of scholarship on the British is cited in his work, from official records to specialized studies of the maritime world such as the *Haiguo wenjian lu*, *Aomen jilüe*, *Hailu*, and even Jiang Fan's *Zhouche wenjian lu*. In addition, Xiao consulted "old records in the office of the governor-general of Liang-Guang" and frequently referred to "inquiries in Guangdong" (*Yuezhong caifang*), perhaps indicating oral interviews.⁹⁴ He was even open to Protestant newspapers, pointing out that despite their awkward phraseology, such works "cite old sayings, give records of neighboring areas, outline the news, or discuss astronomical measurement and the globe."⁹⁵ Xiao was not alone in this. Ye Zhongjin, a scholar from Huizhou (Anhui province) who spent time in Guangdong and penned a long essay about the British empire in the first half of the 1830s, also commented on the utility of this source material:

> What are called "newspapers" (*xinwen zhi*) in Macao first appeared in Italy. Afterward, whenever in each country something emerges from an event that is new and strange or relevant, it is permissible to publish and distribute it for sale without prohibition in any country. If at the time of an incident one takes care to seek and read it, one can also spy upon conditions in various countries, which cannot be overlooked for frontier defense.⁹⁶

This description drew on the missionary magazines it introduced.⁹⁷ Taken with a grain of salt, they were entering the corpus of acceptable source material.

The study of the outside world remained a literati enterprise. Apart from Xiao, Bao Shichen sought information from *juren* of Fujian and Guangdong whom he had questioned in Beijing. These informants were able to tell him about the founding of Singapore and the British printing of Chinese newspapers. Bao singled out Yi Kezhong (1796–1838), another alumnus of the *Guangdong tongzhi* project, as being particularly well informed about these matters.⁹⁸ By contrast, he did not systematically pursue the testimony of Qing subjects in Guangzhou familiar with foreign conditions: no second *Hailu* emerged after 1820. In an 1828 letter to the official Yao Zutong (1762–1842), Bao explained his doubts about such informants. In Bao's understanding, around the year 1775 impoverished people from Huizhou and

Chaozhou in Guangdong, and Zhangzhou and Quanzhou in Fujian, had gone illegally to open land in Penang (Xinpu). These Chinese settlements had then been conquered by the English, who not only received their submission but later enticed poor scholars from Jiaying to move there. As the opium trade had expanded, Hong merchants and "great households" along the coast had become deeply implicated. Englishmen were restricted to Guangzhou, but the "sojourning Qing subjects of Xinpu" (*Xinpu kemin*)—indistinguishable from other Chinese despite having submitted to the British—could unobtrusively visit ports along the coast, so that "although the British have not yet come to Jiangsu and Zhejiang, yet their factions are already in fact firmly intertwined" (*qi dangyu shi yi goupan laogu*). For Bao, then, not only Hong merchants but also overseas Chinese under British rule were presumptively traitors. For accurate intelligence, Bao suggested, "it seems we should choose an official outstanding in both courage and knowledge to go secretly to Penang and find out the truth." In this way it might be possible to pardon these outlaws, remove them back to China, and prohibit emigration as before.[99]

Bao was not the only one suspicious of Hong merchants. To curry favor with the British, according to Ye Zhongjin, they hampered official inquiries:

> Hong merchants are of varying ability, and strive each against the other. If one leaks a shortcoming of the foreigners, the foreign company will certainly learn of it, and when a problem arises will force them out. Therefore, when a local official asks a Hong merchant about foreign affairs they will all falsely profess themselves ignorant (*miuwei buzhi*), while conversely the foreigners hear everything about China's personnel matters, administration, and the activities of high officials.[100]

In 1835, the official Huang Juezi (1793–1853) argued that foreigners were made arrogant by their improperly close relations with Chinese merchants, which allowed them secretly to acquire detailed maps of China and follow its affairs.[101] Given the prevalence of such attitudes, it is not surprising that the participation of Hong merchants in Guangzhou's cultural and intellectual life did not generate an extensive dialogue about changes in the maritime world.

Statecraft essayists writing in Guangzhou in the 1830s made two seminal contributions to Qing geopolitical thought. Geographically, they were the first Chinese authors to note the existence of "British India," clarifying the relationships between England and Gangjiao, and between Gangjiao and India, that had been only vaguely recognized by earlier official and private authors. Xiao Lingyu commented, "The English at Guangzhou say that they control India (*Tianzhu-guo wu Yindu di*). The traders who come to Guangzhou from East India also call it the country of Gangjiao. People in Guangzhou know Gangjiao, but they do not know that it is East India. India neighbors Further Tibet and Burma. It is extremely far from the British homeland, but it attentively accepts orders from there."[102] In another essay he explained how geographic terminology had led people mistakenly to conflate Europe and India, obscuring the fact of European domination there:

> The arrival of Europeans (Da Xiyang) began in the Ming period. India (Tianzhu), also called Shendu, is in the Southwest Ocean (Xi'nan yang) and is not the Western Ocean (Xiyang). [But] in the late Ming and early Qing the various countries of the Western Ocean seized its ports, fortified them, and established marts of trade. The white-headed foreigners of Gangjiao who now come to Guangdong to trade, and fly the English flag, are [people from] the ancient country of India. From this point Europe (Da Xiyang) and the Southwest Ocean were conflated.[103]

Thus, not only did Xiao identify Parsis and other subcontinental merchants in Guangzhou as "Indians," he also specified their connection with the English. Ye Zhongjin echoed Xiao's conclusion that the British ruled part of India, known as Gangjiao:

> As for East India, all [the people there] are Muslims, and they each still have their own leaders. Although the English have captured their ports, they have not yet penetrated deep into the interior. The Muslims there trade with China, but are not familiar with the vessels they sail and need an Englishman to navigate in order to proceed, therefore they use the English flag. [This place] is named Gangjiao.[104]

Used in the geographic lexicon since at least 1780, it was only in the 1830s that new intelligence allowed Qing analysts to connect Gangjiao with India, dominated by the British.

Another important innovation of these essays was to parse the operations and structure of the British empire. Coastal geographers had known for centuries that Europeans had come from a distant homeland to conquer territories close to China, but the rationales and mechanics of this had received virtually no detailed consideration. Now, in the early 1830s, it was recognized that this network of conquests was more relevant than English home territories for explaining coastal troubles. One question above all captured the attention of Qing statecraft commentators: the relationship between private merchants and the British monarch in the process of imperial expansion, specifically the capture of foreign ports for commercial purposes. Even for those intimately familiar with the British state, the legal niceties of this issue were complex. The East India Company had originally received a royal charter as a commercial enterprise, not a territorial power. After the conquest of Bengal, the Regulating Act of 1773 stipulated that its Indian territories would be governed by a governor-general and council, supervised by the Company's Court of Directors but with loose parliamentary oversight. In 1784 the India Act created a "system of dual control," in which instructions to Company servants in India continued to flow from the Court of Directors, but now under the tighter control of a parliamentary Board of Control.[105] Although by 1800 the Crown had great influence, British India (outside the Crown Colony of Ceylon) nonetheless belonged to a consortium of private investors seeking profitable commerce.

For the Qing state, the dissolution of the Company brought the political complexity of the British empire to notice. After the crisis that ensued when the Crown appointee Lord Napier replaced the Company's Select Committee as the superintendant of British trade at Guangzhou, Governor-General Lu Kun submitted a detailed report. He explained that trade had hitherto been controlled by a company (*gongsi*) that dispatched four officers (i.e., the Select Committee) headed by a taipan. When it had been reported in 1831 that this company would expire, the previous governor-general, through the Hong merchants, instructed the English to ask their ruler to continue dispatching a supervisory taipan. Instead, Napier had arrived as a "foreign officer" (*yimu*), that is, putatively an agent of the British state. Lu was not sure whether Napier indeed held an official commission from his monarch, but his troublesome behavior distinguished him from the docile private merchants (*sanshang*). Lu saw Napier as a revenue collector: "Because the company is dissolved they wish to tax the various foreign ships."[106] Later, he blamed Napier alone for recent troubles, reporting that "this episode was absolutely not the intention of the English king, and it is unconnected with the private merchants."[107]

Lu's official memorial concerned the command structure of the British locally at Guangzhou, but private essays probed deeper. Xiao Lingyu dwelt at length on Britain's military and economic affairs, asserting that it fought to gain territories overseas in order to seize a share of the profit generated by these lands: "they divide up their troops and station them on guard [in conquered territories], every year collecting tribute and taxes."[108] Significantly, Xiao noted that the English "raised people of other countries as troops, of whom the most powerful were [from] India."[109] Because royal revenue derived from trade, the English paid close attention to the price and volume of imports and exports. What distinguished them from other nations, Xiao observed, was that their merchants did not act individually but rather all—even the king—invested in a single company and received a share of the profits annually. Ordinarily the company was renewed at the end of each thirty-year term, but now (due, Xiao thought, to the malfeasance of the taipan) there were rumors that it would be dissolved.[110] Although not entirely clear about how the British arrangements in Guangzhou related to their imperial holdings elsewhere, Xiao was certain that the English expansion was tied to commercial profit.

Ye Zhongjin gave an even more detailed description of the British empire's institutional structure. Profit came not from the products of the home country (*benguo tuchan*), he asserted, but from those of places like India that were exchanged in China for silk and tea, to be sold in European countries. By monopolizing this trade, the English had become extremely rich. Their ruler lived in London, and each major port had a taipan directing English trade. If, however, this taipan saw an opening he would call in forces to conquer the locale, at which point a "foreign officer" (*yimu*) would be established. Having taken political control, the English would then tax the import and export of goods, something that had already occurred in Bengal, Singapore, and elsewhere. Like Xiao, Ye pointed out the symbiotic link between commerce and expansion, because "military supplies are purchased out of the money collected by the company at each port." Ye went further, however, in stressing the decentralized structure of the empire. It was up to individual leaders to make their own ventures fiscally solvent, so that while the profits returned to the ruler in London every thirty years, in the interim the English overseas were all basically free agents.[111]

Another essayist of the 1830s, the Guangzhou native Yan Sizong, also presented the British as a loose consortium of freebooters, sailing around Asia opportunistically snatching territories. Rather than using land taxes, he explained, they extracted a tithe on their primary enterprise, commerce. Having a small population, they recruited soldiers from other countries, but placed them under their own officers. Although they seized lands from others, this was not necessarily directed by their ruler. Rather, warships were distributed among their overseas holdings. "Three to five wealthy men will dwell together in consultation [the Company's Court of Directors?], and if they wish to seize a certain territory belonging to a certain country, they will notify their monarch, who permits them to set forth. They assemble provisions and select warships from various places, commanding them to go and conquer. If they are victorious and take that land, then its profits are divided equally among the monarch and the investors (*chuzi zhi ren*)." Yan added that the British empire was effectively composed of two parts, the homeland (*zujia*) and Gangjiao, but people of the former guided expansion: "The white-headed *Gang* foreigners [i.e., Indians] have ambition for gain, and although they are under [English] control they do not like fighting, so that on their ships the captain is always English."[112]

For these Qing observers, the British empire was a clinic on how not to run a state. First, it was blatantly organized to make its rulers rich, without concern for the welfare of its subjects. Second, it appeared to be a loose consortium of individuals pursuing their personal interests, without a clear hierarchy of command or oversight. Third, its military power was supported not by a stable agricultural economy but rather by a vulnerable commercial revenue stream. Fourth, by dominating the maritime world and bullying other countries, it forfeited the goodwill of its neighbors and could not rely on them in a crisis. Morally, administratively, and economically, it was the worst possible structure.

In the early 1830s, these Qing commentators regarded the British empire as fundamentally unsustainable. Although all three essayists—Xiao, Ye, and Yan—realized that British power was expanding, they remained confident that it posed no grave threat to China. As Ye saw it, the English king was greedy, administration was slack, military expenditures were rising, commanders were aggrandizing themselves, and the Company was becoming insolvent and would probably soon dissolve. With the monopoly gone, the Qing could bring the English back under control by manipulating a host of small players.[113] Xiao made a similar judgment. Greed was the basis of the British conquests, he argued, and their administrative structure existed solely to extract revenue. They lacked the "regulations and systems" (*gangji zhidu*) required by good government, nor did they have a plan to cultivate their territories and hand them down to future generations. With the British blinded by short-term profit and without a "farsighted strategy" (*yuanlüe*), the Qing could contain them by economic incentives, a strategy used on other foreigners in the past.[114] Similarly, Yan pointed out that the Qing held a trump card by regulating access to China's markets. If trade was closed, the English could neither sell their produce nor buy tea, and would be unable to make a living. He too was confident that the English could be brought back under control.

Although these three essays did not agree in every detail, taken together they suggest that a relatively coherent appraisal of the British empire was emerging. England itself was small and poor in resources, but had expanded by capturing strategic seaports, monopolizing maritime trade, and using the profits to grow further. Its ruler was guided by no comprehensive strategic plan, and simply licensed the use of force by commanders or investors on the condition that a share of the spoils was sent back to London. China had the power to unplug this entire machine by closing its ports and depriving the British of their economic engine. Being able to strangle the British economy, Qing emperors had ample leverage to compel obedience.

The slender essays of Xiao, Ye, and Yan were dwarfed in the 1830s by larger projects of formal scholarship. In 1834 the governor-general Lu Kun founded an official editorial bureau in Guangdong, which by the end of the decade produced the *Guangdong haifang huilan*, a compendium on maritime defense, and the *Yue haiguan zhi*, a treatise on the maritime customs.[115] The former drew most of its scant commentary on foreign countries from standard histories and Ming-era works. Of England it commented only that it was hard to determine exactly how distant it was.[116] The latter borrowed heavily from the *Guangdong tongzhi* for its description of England and other countries, adding ample citations from official documents and Chen Lunjiong.[117] Based on their content, it might appear that official editors in Guangzhou were less interested in the maritime world than their predecessors in 1820.

As with the *Guangdong tongzhi*, however, the intrinsically restricted contents of formal compendia should not be mistaken for a reflection of the overall knowledge or interests of their editors, let alone the empire as a whole. While the *Haifang huilan* betrayed little interest in the outside world and used Ming sources, one of its editors, Wu Lanxiu, had helped produce Xie Qinggao's *Hailu*, and another, Yi Kezhong, was cited by Bao Shichen as an expert on current affairs in Southeast Asia. Likewise, the editors of the *Yue haiguan zhi*, Liang Tingnan (1796–1861) and Fang Dongshu (1772–1851), both cited Ye Zhongjin's essay on the British empire in their personal writings, though they excluded it from the official work.[118] As we shall see in the next chapter, these essays and the *Hailu* were circulating among influential officials and scholars, and played a significant role in shaping state policy during the Opium War.

Conclusion

Taken individually, few of the developments described above were completely new. Literati in earlier periods had studied foreign geography, eyewitness descriptions of the maritime world had appeared, Christian missionaries had written accounts of the globe, and European world maps had circulated. No specific event between 1800 and 1838 marked a revolutionary breakthrough. Seen in a broader context, however, the period was of critical significance. In the eighteenth century, especially after 1750, the central government had virtually monopolized the analysis of foreign geography and the empire's defense. Beginning tentatively in the late 1790s, Chinese literati gained more freedom to discuss both state policies and the world beyond China. By the 1830s, the volume of geographic research published by the court in Beijing had dropped to a trickle, and unofficial policy discussions were more vigorous than those in official channels.

This trend toward private scholarship began to corrode the three major pillars of the frontier policy. Local sources of intelligence, with their distinctive linguistic and cultural features, remained important. However, the *Guangdong tongzhi* project and subsequent growth in the field increasingly drew in scholars from Jiangnan and Beijing, trained not to accept local Cantonese or Fujianese lexicons without further analysis, but to search through textual evidence and systematically relate local information to other sources. Ultimately, they aspired to establish a universal geographic lexicon transcending any single frontier. Protestant authors also aimed (as yet with limited success) at a standard Chinese usage; they too had little patience for local dialect terms. Forces of geographic synthesis were thus beginning to wrestle with the empire's incommensurable geographic data even more vigorously than under Qianlong's reign. The first conspicuous success involved identifying Gangjiao as Tianzhu or Yindu. Translating a local geographic idiom into a comparatively general vocabulary, if applied to other regional names, could standardize all references to India and render other terms obsolete.

Private scholarship also tightened the link between geographic research and strategic policy proposals. Coastal crises led scholars to look increasingly at foreign geography in order to understand the forces threatening the empire. Analytical essays treated this subject in a way official memorials and formal compendia could not, using sources of uncertain authority to paint a sweeping picture of the British empire that went far beyond any one frontier incident. The Qing bureaucracy had no comparable mechanisms to produce such arguments or even permit them to be made, and as seen in Chapter Five official analysis remained geographically fragmented, limited to the frontier itself and concerned with individual cases or "units of accountability." Still, private investigation into the British empire before 1838 was largely restricted to sources on the coast, and while it identified a sprawling and far-flung network of territories, it had yet to ascertain its proximity to the Qing empire's inland frontiers. This would be crucial for reconceptualizing the relative size and strength of the two empires and in undermining the perceived value of a frontier-by-frontier approach.

While the Opium War is often viewed as an unexpected crisis that suddenly provoked sui generis changes in perceptions of the outside world, in fact most conceptual innovations attributed to the war and its immediate aftermath are evident in the 1820s and 1830s. At first the response to the war, especially beyond formal channels of memorials and responding edicts, quantitatively expanded the audience for new information, which before 1839 circulated relatively narrowly. Ultimately, by the close of the war, this allowed a qualitative shift to a unified conception of the outside world and a corresponding reconsideration of the empire's foreign relations. This is the subject of the final two chapters.

PART FOUR

Foreign Policy and Its Limits

SEVEN

The Opium War and the British Empire, 1839–1842

Conflict stimulated the Qing state's intelligence gathering. During the Opium War the volume and scope of collecting and analyzing information rose to match the gravity of the threat. When British ships entered the Bohai gulf in the summer of 1840, it was the closest hostile foreign armies had come to Beijing since Kangxi halted the Junghar leader Galdan 350 kilometers to the north in 1690. Now, however, the Qing found no effectual response to a sea-based attack on the empire's economically vital territories near the mouth of the Yangzi River. As fighting drew close to home for many of the empire's influential scholars and officials, it understandably attracted more immediate and sustained interest than any earlier war in the empire's history.

India held a significant place in the research agenda provoked by the war. In the opening months of the crisis Lin Zexu (1785–1850) and his advisors, influenced by interpretive trends evident in the early 1830s, pondered the ties binding the nearby Asian fountainheads of British wealth and power to the distant ruler in London. Like earlier commentators, Lin was inclined to believe that Gangjiao, controlled by a loose coalition of freebooters, would not offer formidable resistance to his policies. When the arrival of the British expeditionary force discredited this interpretation, scholars in and out of office pursued different concerns. What, they asked, lay behind the unexpected strength of the enemy? As John K. Fairbank perceptively remarked, "Both the motivation and the power of the British invaders of China derived from British India."[1] Contemporary Chinese observers soon grasped this reality. Whether they traced the money funding the war, the troops waging it, or the rationales guiding the British leadership, Qing officials and scholars returned to the central fact that they were fighting an empire, a political structure in which one country had harnessed the resources of many. India's role as the fiscal and military keystone of the British empire was appreciated, even exaggerated, by these observers. During the war, as in the 1830s, the vulnerabilities of British imperialism impressed themselves just as forcefully as the strengths. For many commentators, India was both the pillar of their enemy's might and its most glaring weakness.

New appreciation of the British as an empire gave a special quality to the increased quantity of research conducted during the Opium War. Like earlier struggles, the Opium War was essentially limited to one frontier, China's long coastline. But if the foe being fought in China also wrapped around the boundaries of Tibet and up toward Afghanistan on the western edge of the Qing empire, then attention had to move beyond the maritime world to consider other questions: What was the position of the British near Tibet and Xinjiang, and how ought this to influence Qing offensive and defensive calculations? Should the Qing still fight in splendid isolation, or seek to cooperate with allies? These questions provoked some to twist and refashion earlier patterns of strategic, bureaucratic, and geographic thought, while others hewed to older conclusions.

Lin Zexu's Evolving Understanding of British India

Lin Zexu's mission to extirpate the opium trade in Guangdong and the crisis this provoked have been studied in painstaking detail.[2] These studies have shown that, paradoxically, Lin was an innovative and enthusiastic student of foreign conditions who did more than previous officials to develop new channels of information about Britain and its empire, but also radically misconstrued the response his actions would provoke, leaving him and the Qing government ill-prepared for the onslaught of a British expeditionary force. Rather than retell the dramatic story of Lin's mission, this section will highlight an important factor largely neglected in previous accounts: the way Lin's policy choices and strategic assumptions drew upon lines of thinking about the British empire that had emerged in the early 1830s, and the fashion in which he bequeathed certain of these assumptions to a generation of influential statecraft thinkers in the closing days of the war.

By the late 1830s, Qing officialdom was preoccupied by the intractable opium problem. On June 2, 1838, the throne considered a memorial submitted by Huang Juezi, a remarkably pessimistic document that on its face was unlikely to provoke a war. As recently as 1835, Huang had believed that the solution to the problem lay in aggressive measures against foreign opium traders and their domestic accomplices. Now, however, he rejected two confrontational tactics: ending legal maritime trade would gain the Qing no leverage, because the illicit trade in opium was far larger; stricter customs inspections were now impossible, because opium profits had corrupted low-level functionaries. Instead, Huang argued, the state had to adopt the extreme measure of executing, after sufficient advance warning, addicts who persisted in consuming opium. Without customers, the trade would wither.

Canvassing senior officials about this proposal, the Daoguang emperor obtained only eight favorable responses, against twenty-one that found it unjust or infeasible. Among the minority was Lin Zexu, governor-general of Hunan and Hubei, who possessed a reputation as a vigorous and conscientious bureaucrat. Lin's speedy reply showed him to be well-informed about the opium trade, and within his jurisdiction he took effective action against opium dealing networks. On November 9, Daoguang summoned him to Beijing, signaling that he would be the official charged with implementing tough new opium regulations in Guangdong.[3]

Despite Huang Juezi's inward focus, the most obvious solution to the opium problem was to sever the nexus between foreign suppliers and domestic wholesalers on the frontier. But could this be done without war? Two positions had been staked out as early as 1820. Some, especially those with experience in Guangdong, feared that an abrupt move against foreign trade might spark a catastrophic conflict. Others contended that China held the upper hand, a fact obscured by foreign bluster and pusillanimous or traitorous domestic commentators. As Huang argued in 1835, only mismanagement and spinelessness allowed the English to intimidate the empire. New studies of the British empire in the 1830s seemed to agree that the Qing possessed decisive economic leverage. The authors of these essays were connected to high officials like Ruan Yuan and prominent statecraft scholars like Bao Shichen and Wei Yuan (who possessed these writings by 1842), and it seems likely that they had a significant readership.

Lin was keeping current with recent scholarship on England. In 1837, while in Hubei, he engaged Yu Zhengxie as a private secretary and set him to work editing the *Haiguo jiwen*, almost certainly Li Zhaoluo's now-lost work based on the *Hailu*.[4] From this he would have learned that opium came not from England itself, but overseas territories under its control. On February 1, 1838, Deng Tingzhen (1776–1846), governor-general of Liang-Guang, reported together with the governor and maritime customs commissioner that of the twenty-five opium hulks off the coast, "many are from Gangjiao, which is subject to the English."[5] In October of that year Deng listed not England but "Gangjiao, which is subject to the English" as one of the four places trading in opium.[6] He consistently referred to major opium broker William Jardine as "a foreigner from the English subject country of Gangjiao."[7] When Daoguang solicited Lin's opinion on the opium problem in 1838, this information had reached him in Wuchang. Zhang Yuesong, who resided elsewhere in that city as acting governor of Hubei, commented in his reply that "generally, foreign ships that carry opium are mostly from Gangjiao, English ships make up [only] 20 to 30 percent."[8] Lin's comments on Huang Juezi's proposals took this assessment further and stressed its policy implications: "Your servant has further made extensive inquiries about the source of opium. In truth, it is all brought by treacherous foreigners of Gangjiao, absolutely unconnected to those undertaking official duties of the English nation (*Yingjili-guo zhi xiu zhizezhe*). They are only crafty brokers seeking individual profit; there is no place where they collect together [their stock], nor is there anyone directing them (*zhushi zhi ren*)."[9] Thus, from the time he began to become officially involved in formulating opium policy, Lin believed that a crackdown would not necessarily entail a clash with the English state.

Lin reached Beijing on December 26 and the next day began a series of eight interviews with the Daoguang emperor. By appointing Lin imperial commissioner, with control over naval forces and the power to act independently of local officials, Daoguang was approving a decisive showdown with foreign states over the opium question, and was willing to countenance the use of force if necessary. As Lin later recalled in an 1840 letter, the emperor "emphatically commanded me to block the source [of opium] with vigor. Certainly no source was greater than the English. I feared that once I had taken measures, advisors would immediately block me on the grounds that I was provoking hostilities on the border. I repeatedly told the emperor about this, and received an edict that he would definitely not restrain me from afar."[10] Lin set off for Guangzhou relatively sanguine that he would win any clash. In Beijing, his friend Gong Zizhen (1792–1841) had sent him a letter containing retorts to naysayers. Some "unreasonable and exaggerating students," Gong warned, might claim that foreigners should be met with leniency rather than force. At Guangzhou, however, Lin would not face the conventional overland warfare his critics had in mind. His task would be to seal the coast and expel or exterminate foreigners and their traitorous accomplices. He did not have to completely destroy their distant homelands, or even fight on the high seas; thus any skirmishes could not be compared to "provoking border hostilities on land." Lin praised this point, judging it a "fixed principle."[11] His belief that he was facing the disorganized merchants of Gangjiao likely contributed to his willingness to risk a clash.

Lin made preparations to deal with foreigners. Among the entourage accompanying him to Guangzhou was Yuan Dehui, who had returned to Guangzhou in 1827 after having studied Latin at a Catholic school in Penang and English at Malacca's Anglo-Chinese College. In 1829, through Hong merchant mediation, he became a translator for the Lifan yuan's Latin correspondence with Russia. According to William Hunter, he had returned to Guangzhou twice in 1830 and 1838 to buy foreign books.[12] Presumably, Lin brought in Yuan as a trusted private secretary for communicating with Westerners in a way that bypassed suspect Hong merchants and their interpreters.

Lin's understanding of the England-Gangjiao relationship when he arrived at Guangzhou can serve as a benchmark for his developing views. He regarded opium traders as private merchants working for their own profit, only nominally under the control of the English state. This is clear from the first draft of his letter to Queen Victoria, which William Hunter received in an English version on March 18, 1839, scarcely a week after Lin reached Guangzhou, on March 10.[13] In 1830, Lu Kun and Li Hongbin had rejected as infeasible the idea of ordering foreign rulers not to trade in opium, but Huang Juezi in his 1835 memorial had proposed that the Qing government "officially notify (*xizhi*) the king of this country that foreign vessels will subsequently not be permitted to carry this item [opium], and violators will be punished according to the statute for treacherous Chinese."[14] Another official also urged this policy in 1836.[15] Lin agreed, recalling that he had "memorialized in audience requesting the issuance of an official notice (*xiyu*) to foreigners."[16]

Since Yuan gave Hunter an English translation of the letter shortly after arriving in Guangzhou, he may have been attached to Lin's suite for this exact purpose.[17] Lin's letter professed confidence that the opium traffic ran counter to the intentions of the British monarch in London: "These poisons are privately manufactured by vile traitors within tribes subject to your country (*guiguo suoshu ge buluo*), and naturally their production has not been ordered by you, the monarch."[18] To judge from earlier memorials of Lin and Deng, Gangjiao was the principal "subject tribe" intended. For Lin, the opium trade was the result of the lax oversight of the English monarch, not her active encouragement.

Once in Guangzhou, Lin continued to gather intelligence about the opium trade and its foreign backers, adding to what he had already gleaned in Hubei, Beijing, and his journey southward (when he met with the well-informed Bao Shichen in Nanchang). When Lin was governor of Jiangsu earlier in the 1830s, he had become impressed with a certain Guo Guichuan, who had later joined the private staff of customs commissioner Yu-kun in Guangdong. One of Guo's duties was to copy customs archives for Liang Tingnan, general editor of that agency's gazetteer. Learning of Lin's impending arrival, Guo asked Liang to compile from his materials a manuscript synopsis of maritime affairs. A "large bundle" of documents was presented to Lin when he arrived, and Liang lived in a neighboring lodging "in order to serve in his field headquarters" (*yi bei xingyuan*).[19] Lin also asked governor Iliyang (d. 1867) for a copy of Ruan Yuan's *Guangdong tongzhi*, and quoted the *Hailu* on England (part of Chen Lunjiong's *Haiguo wenjian lu* was included in Liang's *Yue haiguan zhi*).[20]

Lin's boldest effort to collect new sources was his decision to translate English books and newspapers using Yuan and other Chinese assistants. The most accomplished member of his staff was Liang Zhi (*zi* Jinde), the son of Protestant convert and missionary Liang Fa, who had studied English, Greek, and Hebrew from the early 1830s under the American missionary Elijah Bridgman in preparation for Bible translation and lived for a period in Malacca and Singapore. By 1835 he had a "tolerable knowledge of the English language."[21] Another translator, Aman, was half-Bengali and had studied under the British missionary Marshman at Serampore and assisted in translating the Bible into Chinese.[22] Aman may be the Wen Wenbo whose testimony, collected by Lin, recorded that he had once been to Bengal but had returned to China "almost thirty years ago."[23] A fourth interpreter, Lieaou Ah See, known in English as William Botelho, had studied in a Connecticut Christian school between 1822 and 1825 before returning to China.²⁴ Some translators doubled as informants, and testimony was collected from other former sojourners, including a certain Rong Lin, who had visited England.²⁵

Lin was understandably reticent about this translation project. All of his translators had lived abroad (three in English colonies) and owed to a missionary education their rare ability to read English. In other words, they fit the ideal-type of a Chinese traitor set out by Bao Shichen, Huang Juezi, and others. Liang and Aman could have been prosecuted for assisting missionaries, though this activity was not mentioned in Chinese documents. Moreover, Lin used this dubious staff to translate materials from foreign sources, hardly intelligence of unimpeachable credibility. For this reason he rarely alluded to these translations in official memorials and submitted very few of them to the throne. He himself was cautious about the value of the information produced by this means. In a letter to Iliyang written during his first month in Guangzhou he outlined his intention to organize existing translations into several volumes for his colleague's reference, but warned that "a great deal within it is nonsense (*wangyu*) and cannot be relied on as accurate; I am simply using it as a way to make inquiries about conditions among foreigners."²⁶ Later, he described newspapers to incoming imperial commissioner Kišan (d. 1854) as a means the British used to transmit information between England and Guangzhou, analogous to the use of *tangbao* to publicize government business in China. Again he cautioned that a critical attitude was needed: "Although in recent times things have been falsely reported (*weituo*) in them, the veracity [of an account] can be gauged by a comparison of references, and there is no harm in gathering information from a variety of sources (*bufang jianting-bingguan*)."²⁷

In Lin's eyes, a point in favor of newspapers was that he was able to translate them without missionary mediation. As he explained to Yi-shan, "[Foreigners] originally did not give [English-language newspapers] to Chinese to read, and Chinese people do not understand the foreign script, so they were not read; in recent years I hired translators, and therefore bought newspapers indirectly (*zhanzhuan goude*) and secretly had them translated."²⁸ Lin overstated the secrecy of his operation—he already possessed a translated article from the local English press praising his earlier translations—but his rhetorical aim was to distinguish his products from accounts prepared by foreigners for Chinese use, that is, genuine intelligence from propaganda.²⁹ Merchants and overseas Chinese had been a one-way mirror, allowing Westerners to inquire into Qing conditions without giving Chinese officials comparable intelligence about the outside world. Lin was now trying to use these potential traitors to look in the other direction. Still, he by no means wholly or implicitly relied on this method, and, as Mao Haijian has observed, he seems to have used it selectively to buttress his interpretation of events.[30]

A final source of intelligence Lin used was interviews (voluntary and involuntary) with foreign informants. Late in April 1839, he wrote to Iliyang about two Bengalis shipwrecked off Fujian. Aware that Bengal was a site of opium production, he wanted them questioned about how opium was manufactured, the capital costs per chest, and how much tax revenue it generated.[31] On June 10, Lin sent agents to question the American missionary Peter Parker about geography and other subjects.[32] On June 16 he asked the Americans Bridgman and Charles King for "maps, geographies, and other foreign books."[33] He questioned Mr. Stanton, a British prisoner taken on August 6, about "foreign countries and policy."[34] A Dr. Hill, briefly in Lin's custody, observed that by December he possessed partial translations of a general account of China (probably that of J. F. Davis) and an English clergyman's denunciation of opium trafficking. Lin had the translations prepared for him checked and counter-checked with care, having both Parker and a Chinese translator work independently on Vattel's *Law of Nations*.[35]

Lin's intelligence gathering led him to believe that firm measures were unlikely to provoke a major war with Britain itself. He acted on this belief, and at first events corroborated his view. On March 18, just over a week after his arrival in the city, Lin ordered foreign merchants to submit all the opium held in hulks around the Pearl River delta and sign a bond pledging that under penalty of death they would never again trade in the substance. On March 24, unhappy with the response, Lin blockaded the foreign community in its factories. Three days later, the British chief superintendant of trade, Charles Elliot (1801–1875), ordered his countrymen to submit their opium to him, to be conveyed to the Chinese authorities. On May 5 Lin was satisfied that he had indeed received the opium in full and ordered the release of all but a handful of foreigners, the remainder leaving with Elliot for Macao on May 24. The last of the opium was destroyed on June 25. Although the matter of the bonds was not yet settled, Lin appeared to have correctly anticipated that the foreigners and their Chinese allies, outwardly formidable, would cave in almost immediately in the face of stern action.

In fact, Lin's surmise was incorrect, but London's reaction took over a year to manifest itself. By commanding that opium be surrendered to Lin through his own superintendancy, Elliot had structured the transaction so that the Qing empire was arguably expropriating the property of the British government. On April 16, 1839, while still in detention, he wrote to the governor-general of India requesting that warships be sent to China. This message reached Shimla in the Himalayan foothills on May 25. By the end of August, the HMS *Volage* arrived from India. Around that time, Elliot's April letter to the foreign secretary Lord Palmerston requesting a military response arrived in London. At the start of November Palmerston began to assemble an expeditionary force, and by February 1840 Elliot was informed of this by a confidential dispatch. Five months later, in July, this British expeditionary force initiated the first major round of fighting in the Opium War when it seized Dinghai in the Zhoushan archipelago.[36]

During this long interval, Lin continued to believe that his strategy was well founded and that he faced a response from outport merchants, not the British state itself. As Lin knew, opium was not a product of England, its traders held no public office, and it was grown and sold privately. The company producing it had, in the apt words of Michael Greenberg, "perfected the technique of growing opium in India and disowning it in China."[37] To Qing authorities, Elliot had distanced himself from the opium trade as a representative of the British crown, maintaining that London had no cognizance of it, and in 1837 denying that he or his superiors had "formal knowledge" of it.[38] Lin was also aware of moral opposition to the trade among missionaries in Guangzhou and England. In mid-June 1839, following the interview with Peter Parker, he supplied a detailed memorial based on "inquiries into foreign conditions." He specified that Gangjiao, the primary source of opium traffic, consisted of three ports subject to the English called Bengal, Bombay, and Madras, located two months by sea from the English homeland. According to Lin's intelligence, opium smugglers were violating not only Qing but also foreign laws that enjoined them to avoid causing problems in China, and were therefore liable to severe penalties from their homeland.[39] Research had strengthened his presumption, predating his audience with Daoguang, that only rogue merchants lay behind the opium problem.

Gangjiao, as noted in previous chapters, was a general term for British India commonly used in official documents written in Guangzhou, sometimes found together (as here) with names of individual regions or ports such as Bengal and Bombay. In the 1820s, Protestant missionaries had made clear that the English ruled these territories. By the 1830s, Chinese essayists had pointed out that Gangjiao indicated a region of Yindu or Tianzhu. The Chinese-language correspondence of English functionaries also referred to Yindu: Frederick Maitland, commander of the Royal Navy's East India Station, was described on his 1838 visit to the Pearl River delta as having charge of naval affairs in "the entire Indian Ocean and such places" (*Yindu quanhai deng chu*).[40] Lin, however, was the first to introduce the Gangjiao-India link in official correspondence, submitting a translation of a letter from Elliot that mentioned "the subject territories of Gangjiao in India" (*Yindu zhi Gangjiao shudi*).[41] By around August 1839, Lin ceased referring to Gangjiao, mentioning only "India" (Yindu) and specific locales within it.

A wedge, Lin continued to believe, could be driven between Indian opium traders and the English homeland. In a memorial of August 3, 1839, he submitted for the emperor's approval a second Chinese version of a letter to Queen Victoria, an elaborate production put into English by Parker, Dr. Hill, and one of Lin's interpreters.[42] In this letter Lin continued to give the British monarch the benefit of the doubt, noting that English vessels were obliged to submit an undertaking to their own government not to deal in opium, which the authorities in London did not know was being ignored. Furthermore, Lin pointed out that Britain itself produced no opium, which came from "Indian lands you control, such as Bengal, Madras, Bombay, Patna, Varanasi, Malwa, and such places."[43] Despite his diplomatic willingness to offer Victoria a way to deny culpability, Lin's real assessment was more hard-headed. From the mid-1830s, observers in Guangzhou had recognized the English monarch as the relatively passive recipient of profits submitted by aggressive merchants operating with little formal oversight. Lin concurred. According to Liang Tingnan, a close advisor,

> [Lin] Zexu learned from his investigations that the tax on opium at the foreign ports [i.e., in India] was extremely high, and was retained each year to pay the administrative costs of Bengal, the surplus returning in its entirety to the national treasury, so the ruler had long enjoyed substantial profits. Although China now prohibits opium smoking, the source has not been cut off, and this should be blamed on the ruler. If the ruler respectfully submits to the Qing court, it is appropriate that she first ban its sowing, so that afterward private production will not proceed, and hopefully she can forever enjoy happiness and profit.[44]

Not the prime mover in opium production, England's queen nonetheless acquiesced in it for a share of the profit. To preserve legal trade with China, Lin hoped, she might give it up.

Until their forces reached Dinghai, Lin did not recognize the gravity of the British response. Even available British newspapers did not make clear that war was certain before the forces arrived.[45] Only rumors warned him about the arrival of a retaliatory strike, and many observers (including Lin) discounted such rumors as a tactic to bully Qing officials. Moreover, these rumors contradicted the findings of his research. In the summer of 1839 he reported to the Daoguang emperor,

> Those who come to trade are only a group of peddlers (*fanhu*) from this country, and not nobles (*guiqi*) or high ministers. Furthermore, they all smuggle opium privately (*sidai*) and have not received orders from their ruler [to do so]. Moreover, since the dissolution of the Company in 1834, all of their commerce has had no connection to the ruler.[46]

In a September 1 memorial he explained that the East India Company had originated in the Qianlong period as a device for the British government to raise revenue for its wars, and that it had finally been abolished in 1834 because of merchant opposition. More significantly, he pointed out that the current British ruler was a twenty-year-old woman with only four years experience on the throne, and also (according to his sources) worried about her ambitious uncle.[47] As such, she had no leisure to manage imperial affairs, leaving the British without centralized control. His assessment was almost identical to that made earlier by Ye Zhongjin and Yan Sizong:

> Foreign traders have often in the past fought to occupy ports in other countries. Although without commissions from their monarch, they can privately make an agreement with a warship to go seize [a port] by force and gain new territory. Then, the individual who made the outlay is permitted to take its profits for thirty years, at which time it reverts to the monarch. Therefore, they always hope to annex land wherever they trade. . . . When they occupy a place they guard it with a foreign official (*yimu*).[48]

In sum, Lin was on the cutting edge of Qing geographic thought in believing the British network of ports was run by merchants and freebooting military officers with enormous latitude to operate, while the ruler passively collected some of the profits.

This interpretation allowed the arrival of naval vessels from India to be explained away. The coming of the HMS *Volage* need not indicate that the entire English state was committed to a war with China. Rather, it was an informal transaction between imperial outposts: "Even if they have made a private agreement with one or two warships from an external port . . . these have not been dispatched by their national ruler."[49] Lin maintained this perspective in December 1839, when he remarked that the British central government "is not necessarily fully aware of the situation" and would repudiate Elliot's policies when it learned that its overall trade with China had become imperiled.[50] Even in June 1840, on the eve of the expeditionary force's appearance in Chinese waters, Lin continued to believe that only a small Indian force was on its way:

> According to my investigations, the foreign ports of this country, such as Bengal, have learned of the strictness of Chinese measures against opium. The sales are daily dwindling, and new and old opium is piling up at these foreign ports. Unwilling to lightly abandon [opium], they have precipitously dropped the price, and are employing fully loaded three-masted ships to come here. Treacherous foreigners are taking advantage of this to spread exaggerated rumors and make bullying threats (*jie yi yangyan donghe*).[51]

Nothing he had learned in Guangzhou fundamentally altered Lin's view in 1838 that the Qing was opposing a loose coalition of ambitious merchants.

This interpretative framework had major strategic consequences. Mao Haijian, who has studied Qing policy during the Opium War in great detail, suggests that Lin's single greatest mistake was his enduring belief that reports of British military preparations were "empty bluster," "bullying," and "rumors." Lin believed that Elliot, with only a small force, was relying on the terror of being blamed for border conflicts normally felt by Qing officials. As Mao persuasively argues, Lin had to select among many conflicting reports, even within the materials he had translated from English, and it was only natural that he interpreted his intelligence based on his own preconceptions about the British political situation and on the news he wished to hear.[52]

This interpretation was not limited to Lin, nor did it die with the arrival of the British forces. In late July 1840, another official reported rumors that the arriving warships were coming from foreign ports under British control.[53] On September 13, 1840, the acting governor-general of Liang-Jiang, Yu-qian (1793–1841), reported that the British were circulating a document composed in London on March 3, 1839, before Lin's arrival in Guangzhou. Yu-qian inferred that the British expeditionary force did not represent the response of the British monarch to Lin's measures. He memorialized that "warships of this country [England] had moored at places like Bengal and Madras, over twenty thousand *li* from Guangdong, that were established solely for the purposes of selling opium. All [of these warships] are dispatched on Elliot's orders. The ruler of this country is only familiar with collecting taxes and does not manage military affairs . . . and so we can see in broad outline that the current rebellious conspiracy . . . is entirely the work of Elliot, and not done on the orders of the ruler of this country."[54] When Kišan, who replaced Lin in 1840 as the official in charge of dealing with the British, created his own intelligence operation he too discovered that the English held numerous subject states from which they could dispatch ships and emphasized, like Lin, the lax oversight and weak central control of the British government. According to his agent's research, England was ruled by a young girl uninterested in foreign affairs, allowing over twenty great clans to provide over-mighty ministers (*quanchen*) and set national policy. He surmised that some of the captured opium had belonged to these men, sparking the British invasion.[55]

Empire, Finance, Ethnicity, and Qing Strategy

Wartime events ultimately overturned the assumption that the invasion was not fully supported by the British state. This did not shift attention from India, but did shift its significance: instead of representing a weak and loosely organized coalition of outports, India came to be seen as a rich territory that supplied Britain with both troops and vital tax revenues. Indeed, India came to be regarded as the lynchpin of British power. After fighting began in earnest in 1840, British India became increasingly salient for Qing officials and private commentators. To many, it seemed that a thin stratum of English officers was directing a far larger cohort of sepoys. As they pondered their foe, Qing observers were quick to note the potential financial and military vulnerabilities of the multiethnic British empire.

British reliance on sepoys was known in China before the war: as early as 1808 Bengali soldiers had been observed during the British occupation of Macao, and their recruitment was also mentioned in Xie Qinggao's 1820 *Hailu*. These references, however, said little about the ties binding the sepoys to the English. When war broke out, the composition of the enemy's ranks became of greater interest, and new conduits of intelligence opened. One was translation. A geographic work by Hugh Murray, put into Chinese under Lin's direction, clarified the basis of British India's military strength. The original text read,

> The sepoys (Indian troops commanded by British officers, and trained after the European manner) are found nearly as efficient as troops entirely British; and, so long as nothing is done to shock their religion and prejudices, they are equally faithful. Their number amounts to 181,517 men. The purely European troops maintained by the Company do not exceed 8000, but a large body of the king's troops are always employed in India; these at present are about 20,000.[56]

Lin's translators boiled this down to the following synopsis: "Overall, they have established 181,517 sepoy troops (*xupo bing*), 800 [*sic*] English troops (*Yingjili bing*) and 20,000 London royal troops (*Landun wangjia bing*)."[57] Although references to modes of training and the relative effectiveness and loyalty of sepoys were lost in translation, readers learned at least of the diversity of English forces.

Captives also proved informative. Indians figured prominently among the prisoners who entered Qing hands as the war unfolded. As early as June 12, 1840, Min-Zhe governor-general Deng Tingzhen reported that his forces had taken two Indian sailors.[58] Other prisoners from the first few months of fighting included Captain Peter Anstruther of the Madras Artillery and eight lascars (Indian sailors) captured on separate occasions.[59] At Guangzhou in August 1840, Stanton was captured along with two Indians.[60] The survivors of the September 15, 1840, wreck of the brig *Kite* included ten lascars and an Indian cook. Although English accounts are vague about the identity of the Indian captives, Yi-li-bu (1772–1843) memorialized a detailed list. Of the twenty-nine prisoners in Qing custody in Zhejiang on September 28, 1840, fourteen were Indian (ten from Bengal and four from Madras). Five of these were sailors, two were cooks, one a laborer, and six were soldiers, the youngest fifteen or sixteen and the oldest forty.[61] After two vessels were wrecked in Taiwan later in the war (see below), the vast majority of prisoners were Indian.

Qing officials were struck by the costs of operating a mercenary sepoy army. As early as 1840, Lin Zexu was arguing that the burden of hiring troops and purchasing supplies was putting an intolerable strain on the enemy's finances.[62] A more emphatic estimate was made by the statecraft scholar Wei Yuan, who was able through the mediation of a friend to "personally question" Anstruther during his captivity in Ningbo, probably via his interpreter and fellow prisoner Bu Dingbang.[63] Combining Anstruther's testimony with other materials, he wrote the *Yingjili xiaoji*, a brief description of the British empire. Perhaps because the prisoner served in the Company's army, Wei came away with an enormously inflated sense of India's strategic significance. According to his findings, Britain, before augmenting its resources through trade, had been merely a small country comparable to Taiwan. Weaker countries encountered in the course of trading would be defeated and either forced to surrender as a "subject territory" (*shufan*) like Bombay and Bengal, or seized outright as a "national outpost" (*fenguo*). These territories, often larger than the home country and up to six months away by sea, were then garrisoned and officials stationed there to collect tax. Although England itself generated an annual revenue of only around two and a half million dollars, Wei recorded, its imperial territories produced around twelve million dollars, nearly five times as much. These funds were disbursed on the spot rather than remitted to the home country. Opium financed the British empire: Bengal earned six million dollars and Bombay three to four million each year by growing it and selling it to China, so that Indian opium provided about two-thirds of all English income. Using these revenues he calculated that the British were able to hire 190,000 troops at 72 dollars a year in rations.[64]

Even those without access to Anstruther did not need to be reminded of the prominent role of Indians within the British ranks and the tactical and strategic questions this raised. It was evident Indian troops occupied low-ranking positions, and that their European commanders did not treat them well. Yu-qian, in a memorial reporting on the high death toll among British forces, referred to "their black foreigners whom they do not greatly cherish, do not treat when they are ill, and who are thrown away when dead."[65] Awareness of this hierarchy influenced Qing officials. In the summer of 1840, soon after the arrival of the English fleet, Lin Zexu offered a bounty of one hundred dollars for the killing of a "white devil," but only fifty dollars for a "black devil" (*heigui*).[66] In Zhejiang, Yu-qian also offered twice as much for a "white devil" as for a "black devil."[67] Acting governor of Zhejiang Song Qiyuan (1780–1840) complained of a subordinate who had found Indians so easy to capture that he eliminated the bounty for them altogether.[68] Similar distinctions continued after capture. John Scott, who was imprisoned at Ningbo along with a number of lascars, observed that the Chinese officials "always made a marked difference between the white men and the men of colour," and noted that the Chinese would "treat them [i.e., lascars] with more severity" than the white prisoners, for instance requiring them to wear shackles until shortly before their release, long after the British prisoners had had theirs removed.[69]

Aware that leadership positions were monopolized by Britons, Qing officials questioned them more closely than Indian captives. When necessary, however, it was found possible to communicate with Indian prisoners. Scott recorded that his captors in Ningbo had procured a Chinese interpreter who could speak Bengali, presumably in a pidgin form, and similar interpreters for lascar prisoners may have been available elsewhere.[70] Another official interrogated Indian captives using two Chinese Muslim military officers familiar with the "Muslim language" (*Huiyu*, here perhaps indicating Persian).[71] William Hunter described an 1837 pseudo-interrogation of a lascar in Guangzhou by a comprador for Country ships who could speak only a few Bengali phrases, indicating that the sophistication of such discussions could be quite low.[72] Yet, language barriers aside, most Indian prisoners could not provide the detailed survey of British motives and war plans demanded by Qing officials. The six Indian sailors in Yi-li-bu's custody before the wreck of the *Kite* stated only that they were Bengalis who had been hired to work on English ships, not soldiers, "and also did not know the reasons for the English coming to Zhejiang."[73]

British reliance on sepoys raised the question of whether ties between officers and soldiers could be severed. Early in the conflict, Song Qiyuan urged his superior Yi-li-bu to isolate the "white" English by targeting their "black" troops, arguing that "black foreigners are the instruments of predation [*zhaoya*, "talons and teeth"] of the white foreigners, and should these be lost for a single day the white foreigners would find their forces diminished and lose courage."[74] As Qing officials grew more desperate, ways of exploiting presumed ethnic tensions drew more attention. The first step was to discern the ties connecting non-English troops to their officers. On April 24, 1842 Yi-jing (d. 1853) interrogated English and Indian prisoners and reported that the force of seventeen to eighteen thousand men attacking Zhejiang were "not from a single country," but "collected and hired in various places."[75] Daoguang demanded clarification on this point, observing that apart from English and Kashmiris the British force consisted of people from Bengal, Greater and Lesser Luzon (i.e., Spain and the Philippines), and Shuangying (Austria?). The emperor wished two points to be settled. First, were these soldiers hired directly by a royal commission, or did commanders privately assemble their own forces? Second, were these troops coerced into service, or lured by the prospect of gain?[76] His English prisoner, Yi-jing reported, informed him that the troops coming to Zhejiang were all Englishmen sent by the English monarch, while people from other countries were workers on commercial ships or servants and sailors hired privately by the military officers.[77] The Manchu commander issued proclamations that promised clemency to Indians who did not fire on Qing forces.[78]

Attempts to induce sepoys to abandon the British also occurred elsewhere. Late in 1841, after recapturing Dinghai, British observers found Chinese placards (which they attributed to Yu-qian) that laid out a scheme to induce Indians to turn against them. According to the plan,

> the black men will have no interest in risking their lives for the others, as their commanding officers appropriate to themselves all the spoils. In every engagement they have to bear the brunt of the battle, so that many of them are wounded or killed; and they complain frequently of this with tears, showing their unwillingness to engage in that which does not concern them in the least degree. Therefore, to effect a mutiny in the ranks of the enemy, we shall treat these men with leniency . . . with the secret understanding that they shall surrender to us their commanding officers.[79]

At the end of July 1842, Shengjing General Xi-en reported hearing that the British force was an amalgam of troops from different places, including India (Tianzhu), Luzon, and Fo-nan, some coerced by threats of force, some enticed by profit, and some solicited by trickery (*zhayao*). He therefore proposed that a document be circulated among these non-English troops outlining their wrongdoings and promising clemency. If that message was reiterated in person by Chinese merchants experienced in dealing with Indians and others, non-British foreigners could realize their folly and withdraw. Coupled with a strict blockade to starve the British, he hoped that when their foreign associates had no food, "they will then know that their assistance was an ill-conceived plan and [they] will naturally become angry and return; thus, even though these rebels [i.e., the English] seek help from their neighbors, we can make their neighbors not be used by them."[80] Daoguang agreed with this strategy, observing that as the British ranks were coerced or induced to "band together" (*jiuhe*) rather than "sincerely" assisting their masters, it was crucial to "cause them not to be duped by the rebellious foreigners," thereby "isolating" the English force.[81]

Confusion and consternation over Indian willingness to fight for the British led to a contemptuous assessment of sepoys and camp followers. Their inexplicable loyalty to a political order that exploited them was attributed to a lack of intelligence. Bu Dingbang, taken prisoner for having aided the English, was given the task of deposing a Bengali camp follower. By way of a preface Bu explained to Qing officials that three sorts of people lived in Bengal, "upper whites," "middle whites," and "black foreigners":

> Upper white people and middle white people have white flesh and are clever, black people are extremely stupid (*heiren ji yuchun*). When English (*Hongmao*) ships pass through Bengal they purchase black foreigners to go to their ships and do their bidding . . . and some are [simply] taken as prisoners. All are trained as soldiers, and those incapable of being soldiers act as sweepers and servants on their ships.[82]

Shortly after the war, Qi-ying (d. 1858) submitted the results of his detailed study of the fighting prowess of the English. He explained that their soldiers could be divided into two kinds, the "white" soldiers of England proper and the "black" soldiers from places like Bengal and Bombay subject to the English. Both men and officers did not marry before the age of forty, and therefore they entered battle focused solely on glory rather than their families. The "black" troops, however, had distinguishing characteristics: "The black troops are very strong but with a stupid nature and do not know how to respond to the circumstances (*qubi*). The foreign leaders make them work like slaves or servants and rear them (*chu*) as one would a dog or a horse—and yet they willingly devote their lives to serve [their leaders]. This is also something that cannot be reasonably explained."[83] As we shall see, similar assessments were made elsewhere during the war.

Caution is required when applying current analytical categories to the behavior of Qing officials. It is hard to gauge whether Qing assessments of the roles of Indians in the British empire were purely empirical, based on how sepoys were treated by the British, or whether they reflected preexisting ethnic prejudices. Frank Dikötter has argued that in imperial China "the elite developed a white-black polarity at a very early stage," and that the "equation of 'black' with 'slave'" had developed in China before the arrival of Westerners.[84] Don Wyatt accepts this view as valid for the late imperial period.[85] Frederic Wakeman, writing in 1966, assumed the Cantonese to have "racial antagonism toward 'black' Indian troops."[86] Certainly, "black slaves" (*heinu*) in Macao had long been familiar in the Pearl River delta, and were mentioned in the recent local gazetteer and imperially authored works.[87] Since Indian sepoys were described simply as "black," a blanket term also applied to Africans and some Southeast Asians, earlier white-black relations in Macao may have influenced their perception.⁸⁸ Still, in more peaceful times there is little evidence that Qing officials treated Indians in China worse than Europeans. It should also be noted that the rhetoric of "stupidity" was also widely applied in Qing official discourse to foreigners and Han Chinese peasants forming the rank-and-file supporters of a rebel leader.

Nor should Qing attempts to split the British ranks be seen as evidence of solidarity with India. Not yet having internalized the geographic concept of "Asia" or a sense that China's position in the face of Western imperialism was analogous to that of other lands, Qing officials in the early 1840s had no conceptual basis for the pan-Asianism or anticolonialism that would influence views of India by Chinese intellectuals later in the century. Captured Indians seem to have been treated as low-level accomplices of the British, in practice receiving no more leniency than their masters. Attempting to lure Indians away was simply a pragmatic response to obvious inequality in the British ranks.

It was in Taiwan that the greatest number of Indian prisoners fell into Qing hands, and their treatment by the ranking civil and military administrators, Yao Ying and Dahūngga, respectively, offers a case study of the complex strands of Qing policy.⁸⁹ In late September 1841, according to British records, the transport ship *Nerbudda* ran aground off the north coast of the island. After the 21 Englishmen on board abandoned ship, 240 Indians were left behind, 70 of them lascars and 170 litter-bearers.⁹⁰ According to the account submitted by Yao and Dahūngga, this vessel had been sunk by Taiwanese defenses after a battle in which 5 "white," 5 "red," and 22 "black" foreigners were killed, and a total of 133 black foreigners taken prisoner. Maps, books, and other writings were also seized.⁹¹ Because of a local rebellion in Taiwan, it was not until early in 1842 that these prisoners could be interrogated in the prefectural capital.

Two interpreters were found in Taiwan to deal with this entirely Indian batch of captives, a Cantonese physician named Song Tinggui and a certain He Jin. In what language the interrogations were conducted is unclear. Robert Gully, who was later taken captive in Taiwan, reported that his party was interrogated by one Ayum "who had been some time at Singapore and picked up a little smattering of Hindostanee and English."⁹² This interpreter he criticized for making up answers when his linguistic competence ran out. Gully's fellow prisoner Captain Denham likewise complained that Ayum was "humbugging and telling lies (his knowledge of the language being confined to a few words)."⁹³ It seems likely that all questioning on Taiwan was carried out in pidgin English and Hindustani.

Without English prisoners, Qing interrogators on this occasion paid unusual attention to their Indian captives. According to the highest-ranking prisoner, Mu-li-kong, the "islands" controlled by the English (*suoxia gedao*) presented their rulers annually with a "tribute-tax" (*gongshui*) of opium. When Qing measures halted the sale of opium, the British tried to demand cash from their subjects, but these "island foreigners" were unable to realize the sums demanded, forcing the British to continue collecting opium. In response, the English had "hired and dispatched" (*gudiao*) warships, collected them all in Bengal, and sailed to China to force the reopening of trade. The captives summarized British operations and personnel shifts on the coast, and (supposedly) corroborated the story of their capture during battle. Upon cross-examination, the Indians asserted that Bengal and Shili were "islands subject to the English," while Penang, Singapore, and elsewhere were "major ports" (*da matou*) in the vicinity of Java.⁹⁴ Asked about a volume of maps and other books, they explained that these belonged to the "white captain," and that "they, black foreigners, cannot read the script and are unable to explain them."⁹⁵

The intelligence value of the Indian prisoners became a point of dispute within the Qing bureaucracy. In their initial report Yao and Dahūngga had requested permission to execute the prisoners at the prefectural seat in Taiwan because of their large numbers and the distance and uncertainty involved in conveying them to the mainland. This plan was opposed by the censor Fu-zhu-long-a, who urged that they be temporarily reprieved and sent to the provincial capital of Fuzhou for detailed questioning about Western technology, Qing subjects in English employ, and the sources of British military supplies.⁹⁶ Presumably these prisoners would also have been questioned about the battle that led to their capture, an uncomfortable subject for Yao. Not surprisingly, Yao opposed this plan. His 119 Indian prisoners (14 having died in captivity) were described as "rebellious foreigners" (*niyi*) who had obeyed British orders to attack China and were therefore no less culpable than their masters in this "most evil crime." Yet they were not intelligence assets, but rather "a rabble of fools from the various islands" (*gedao wuhe yuchun zhi ren*) who were unable to yield information about "secret and important foreign affairs" (*miyao yiqing*).⁹⁷

As the interrogation of the *Nerbudda* survivors wrapped up, the crew of a second ship entered Qing hands. On the night of March 10, 1842, the brig

Ann, a transport serving the British expedition, ran aground off Taiwan with a crew of 57. This time the captives included "red" (British), "white" (Portuguese), and "black" (Indian) foreigners, along with five Chinese collaborators. Surmising that some among the captives were "fully conversant with foreign affairs," the court provided a list of questions it wanted answered.[98] Yao Ying and Dahūngga supervised intensive interrogations about England and its empire, relying chiefly on the testimony of Captain Denham, supplemented by other English and Indian informants. Denham's English was translated by Zheng A'er, a Cantonese who had once worked as a merchant in Bombay and collaborated with the British.[99] Yao summarized his findings in a long memorial of July 6, 1842 and an accompanying "Explanation of a Map of England" (*Yingjili ditu shuo*).

Geographically, Yao explained that the English possessed 26 "islands" (including Indian lands) that served as ports, most seized from other countries. His description of these conquests resembled those submitted by other officials: England had once been small but had used its skill in arms manufacture to "coerce through force and craftiness" (*qiangxia xiezhi*) several small independent nations into becoming its subject territories, and had then linked these territories into a network (*lianluo*) connected by long sea voyages. At each node in this network the British had established civilian and military officials of various ranks. Around these territories were other islands, independent or the colonies of Holland and other powers. British overseas possessions supplied troops: Yao asserted in his report that "their troops are all black foreigners hired from the various islands." Bombay and Bengal were two of the three main sources of opium (the other being Turkey) sold by private English traders and taxed by the English state.[100]

Like other Qing observers, Yao became convinced of the fundamental vulnerability of the British empire. A thin layer of white English officers was attempting to maintain control over a scattered collection of large colonies that supplied their wealth and power. In war they relied (he believed) almost completely on "hired" (*gu*) black troops, who presumably fought only for pay. Yao estimated the British employed forty to fifty thousand such troops, each commanding a salary of from two to ten dollars a month. On top of these salaries, millions more would be needed to hire, outfit and provision the fleet, buy weapons and gunpowder, and pay high officials. The total cost of the two-year-old British campaign he estimated at over twenty million dollars. Ultimately, the British relied on trade, and that with China Yao assumed to be the largest and most lucrative. Since war had halted legal trade, and smuggling (he thought) was greatly diminished, opium prices had fallen steeply and it seemed reasonable to expect a financial collapse—"Although the foreigners are rich, how can they long support such an outlay!" Based on his interrogations, Yao concluded that a resolute Qing defense would soon force the British into retreat.[101]

In Taiwan, Yao emphasized the advantages to the Qing flowing from the heterogeneity of the British empire. In a letter of July 1, 1842, to Iliyang describing the interrogation of his English and Indian prisoners, he added,

> Although the foreigners are strong, yet fundamentally it is the red and white foreigners who have gathered a rabble (*wuhe*) of black foreigners from the various ports to come and vie with us for profit. These people are few, only some tens to each vessel. The rest are black foreigners, foolish and ignorant (*yuchun wuzhi*), who only look to the red and white foreigners for sustenance. They require an extremely large amount for salaries and provisions.

Yao outlined his view that the British were heading for bankruptcy. Qing officials should therefore not be fooled by rumors that yet more forces were proceeding toward China, because it was in the tricky nature of the British to make more outlandish threats as their actual situation became more precarious.[102] As in the early 1830s, the more Qing officials and scholars learned of the structures behind the British empire, the more they doubted that it would endure.

The Inner Asian Opium War

Wartime intelligence made clear that the Qing empire was fighting not a single country but a diffuse constellation of ports and territories, yet the logic of a frontier policy meant that the location of these lands was not an urgent question: if the English chose to fight on the coast, the Qing would resist them there. However, maritime warfare posed particular strategic problems. With overland foes, such as the Junghars, Burma, or Nepal, an expeditionary force could put direct pressure on the enemy's homeland. No navy could reach distant England, but might it not be possible to hit a more proximate—and perhaps more vital—piece of the British military machine? Contrapuntally, did the British threaten any other part of the Qing frontier? Even without the specter of a British invasion, Qing Inner Asia was far from secure. In Tibet, the Gurkhas had never been fully trusted by Beijing. In Xinjiang, Khoqand was a constant threat. In between, Ladakh had come under the sway of the ambitious raja of Jammu, Gulab Singh. The Qing state could not ignore its inland frontier during the coastal struggle.

Trying to coordinate intelligence from China and Inner Asia was difficult. Information about the British empire was pouring in from the coast, where new maps, translations, and interrogation transcripts joined an already substantial body of description and analysis by Chinese scholars and sailors. Yet coastal informants were often silent about Inner Asia, and the connections they did draw were sketchy. Contemporary Britons had a poor understanding of the mountainous terrain between India and Qing territory. Missionaries like Gützlaff, though familiar with Chinese accounts of Xinjiang and Tibet, had not fully mastered them. Officials in Lhasa and Yarkand had difficulty relating local intelligence to coastal events. The emperor and Grand Council treated incoming information with understandable caution.

Newspapers translated under Lin's orders alluded to the overland proximity of British India to the Qing empire, but gave different assessments of its military significance. One translated letter, first printed in the *Canton Press* of October 12, 1839, detailed four conceivable routes by which a force from India could invade China: through Kabul or Kashmir to Ili or Yarkand, then across Mongolia to Beijing; through Nepal and Tibet to Beijing; through Assam into Sichuan; and through Burma.[103] Although its author judged these routes impractical, others disagreed. An article from December 17, 1839, pointed out that the British had many troops and possible allies in India, so that (to quote the Chinese translation) "If we went to the western frontier of China via Nepal, Tibet, Assam or Burma it would also not be difficult."[104] Just over three months later, a second long article translated from the *Canton Press* raised similar issues. It was rendered into Chinese thus:

> I will now cite the instance that in 1837–1838 the Indian territories subject to us [i.e., the British] prepared arms in great numbers, and we dispatched an army from the northwest of India, which is subject to us [into Afghanistan].... People in England have also already seen our forces approach the western border of Chinese Tibet (Zhongguo Xizang), not far from Yarkand and Kashgar.... In 1837–1838 we fought with Nepal (Nibu'er), and Beijing also feared this. The capability and courage of we English in attacking has long been known in the East. China sees that formerly in India we only traded, but later we completely conquered India.[105]

Whether he found these translations baffling, unreliable, or untrustworthy, Lin seems never to have referred to these passages in his memorials or personal writings.

A communication from Nepal rather than Guangzhou established a clear link between the Tibetan frontier and the fighting on the coast. Despite the steadfast refusal of the Qing court, Nepal's rulers had persisted in attempts to win assistance against the British. Although this tangent in Gurkha policy had been moderated in the 1820s under Bhim Sen Thapa (d. 1839), who tried to mend relations with the British, it resumed after 1837 as a new administration began once again to seek Qing aid. One request was rebuffed in 1837, but the outbreak of hostilities between the Qing and British empires made a fresh overture appear timely.[106]

The Gurkhas' first attempt to turn the Opium War to their strategic advantage was reported in a memorial of October 27, 1840, from the ambans Mengboo (d. 1873) and Haipu (1796–1860). The Gurkha king Rajendra Bikram Shah (1813–1881) had reported hearing of six clashes between "that place subject to the capital" (*jingshu nabian*) and the Pileng tribe. Later, his agent in Delhi informed him that a counterattack had been launched against the Pileng, who had in turn gathered 25,000 troops, horses, and weapons at a place called Niegajinna (*nagar cīna*, "city of China"?) to prepare a new offensive. A Pileng fleet carrying 55,000 troops had also been burnt at a place called Macao (Maguaye), frightening the Pileng into recalling all their forces. More recently, the Gurkha king had heard that another Pileng fleet had been surrounded. Ostensibly, the Nepali raja wrote to congratulate the Qing emperor, but he also reminded the ambans that the Gurkhas stood pledged to protect the southern border of Tibet. Accordingly, they had prepared a force and awaited only Qing authorization to pour down and crush the Pileng.

Following Qing policy since the 1790s of not aiding or fomenting Gurkha attacks on the Pileng, the ambans continued to interpret Gurkha requests as part of their long-running private feud with the Pileng. The proposal was rejected, but the claims in the petition still required interpretation. The ambans realized that the phrase "subject to the capital" referred to China proper, glossing it in their memorial as "Chinese (*Hanren*) in that place subject to the capital." Inquiries discovered that Niegajinna was in the "outer seas" (*waiyang*), and so Pileng preparations there "had implications for the coast of China proper." But where exactly it was, and whether the Pileng were indeed preparing a force there, they could not say. Replying to the Gurkha king, they explained that the Pileng had behaved improperly and provoked the burning of their own vessels. Now that Qing forces had won, there was no need to trouble the Gurkha army. Even as they implicitly linked the Gurkha report to the Opium War, they did not overtly identify the Pileng with the English. In an edict of November 30 the court approved of their response, but ordered clarification of what precisely was meant by Niegajinna and "subject to the capital."[107]

Within a week of receiving orders to investigate further, the ambans offered a more detailed explanation. "Subject to the capital," they explained, was a standard phrase of the Gurkhas for "lands controlled by China proper" (*neidi suoguan difang*). Niegajinna was a coastal territory of the Pileng, far from China. To clarify regional geography they cited annotations to the *Xizang fu*, He-ning's 1797 descriptive poem of Tibet, which basically reproduced intelligence generated at the time of the Qing-Gurkha wars. Dili Bacha, the poem's notes explained, was a large country southwest of Tibet, which ruled the three subordinate tribes of Pileng, Calcutta, and Acharya (i.e., Bengal). He-ning took Fuk'anggan's correspondent, the Guoerna'er, to be the ruler of Dili Bacha, and recorded that he traded at Guangzhou.[108] To tie this explanation more tightly to the situation at hand, Mengboo and Haipu added that Calcutta, subject to Dili Bacha, was located east of Pileng and "extends directly to the frontier of Guangdong" (*zhida Guangdong bianjie*). Moreover, their inquiries had also uncovered the news that *Dili* was the Gurkha term for the English. For the first time in almost half a century the Qing state directly connected the English to the polities below Tibet.

Fearing that their information was probably "not entirely correct," they had secretly consulted Tibet's most senior official, the Dalai Lama's regent Ngag-dbang-'jam-dpal-tshul-khrims.[109] According to him, Niegajinna was on the coast, though he could not specify its precise location and had never heard of its being a distinct tribe. However, he too claimed that Calcutta shared a frontier with Guangdong (*yu Guangdong bianjie pilian*).[110] The root of this claim may lie in the well-known trade between Calcutta and Guangdong. The court allowed this statement to pass without comment, an extreme illustration of the Qing emphasis in military operations on field reports over academic reference works (which clearly identified Vietnam as the only foreign state bordering Guangdong).

To further clarify these reports, the Qing court turned to Guangdong itself, and on March 30, 1841 ordered Governor-General Qi Gong (1777–1844) to investigate whether the Pileng were subject to the English, and how far they were from Guangdong.[111] Qi and Guangdong governor Iliyang forwarded the order to the Guangzhou prefect, who in turn passed it on to linguists serving the Hong merchants. The linguists found Calcutta easy to identify: it was clearly the "inner city" (*neicheng*) of the English territory of Bengal. Foreigners, they claimed, pronounced *jia* as *ga* and *er* as *li*, so Tibet's "Galigada" was equivalent to the place known on the coast as "Jia'ergeda." Pileng they identified as another place subject to the English, located west of Calcutta in a country called Malabar (Malaba), which was said to border Bengal on the west, Madras on the south, Bombay on the north, and the sea to the east. As for *Dili* being a Gurkha term for the English, the prefect reported that this doubtless had some basis but was not a name known to the Hong merchants or translators.

With the linguists stumped, Qi Gong made further inquires about Dili and Niegajinna. He learned that Englishmen called a high official a "mandarin" (*mandili*) and that the English ruled a place called Dilimali (Trincomalee?), although neither quite matched "Dili." For "Niegajinna" he turned to translators (*fanyi sheng*), presumably with a better foundation in English grammar. In English, they reported, *nie* meant "in" and *ga*, "coast." If one assumed that *Jinna* was an error for *Chaina*, and translated the term in the reverse order, it would then mean "on the coast of China." This, however, raised the difficulty that Tibetan informants considered Niegajinna to be far from China. All of these conclusions were prefaced with a disclaimer stressing the difficulties posed by foreign place-names:

> Foreign languages have sounds for which no [Chinese] character exists to represent them, and in each instance of this we take the nearest corresponding character and add a *kou* ["mouth"] radical to its left side, and in punctuating it one must also reverse the order. Foreign sounds do not match the sound of Chinese characters, and the Cantonese dialect differs from those in other provinces, and still more is it distinct from Tibetan.

Under these conditions, Qi continued, his findings should be considered no more than guesses (*yiduo*). He could, however, state definitely that neither England, nor Pileng, nor Calcutta shared a land frontier with Guangdong.[112] Assiduous research using experts from various regional and linguistic backgrounds was often not sufficient to reach firm conclusions about geographic problems, and could even add new wrinkles of complexity.

Recognizing the Opium War as a peerless opportunity for securing a Qing alliance against the British, the Gurkhas kept up their solicitations. In August 1841 they reported further rumors that the Pileng had seized six areas in Guangdong before suffering a defeat at the hands of Qing troops. The ambans replied that the Qing court would soon exterminate the Pileng invaders. Undaunted, the Gurkhas requested material aid to thwart an anticipated attack. The ambans pointed out to Daoguang that such requests were unavoidable given the greediness and indecorousness of the Gurkhas, and that a simple rejection rather than a strong rebuke would be appropriate. They reiterated to the Gurkhas that the Qing would not provide material aid to foreign states, and that the Pileng were unlikely to attack them, interpreting the issue as a private Gurkha-Pileng quarrel rather than a strategic matter involving the Qing state.[113]

By the time they responded to this second Gurkha petition, the ambans were confronting an unexpected border crisis, the invasion of western Tibet by Gulab Singh. Ladakh, conquered in 1834, gave him a strategic foothold between Yarkand to the north, Tibet to the east, and Kashmir to the west. Now he took advantage of China's preoccupation with affairs on the coast. According to British sources, he had first intended to invade Yarkand, taking as his pretext the seizure of Punjabi opium in that city, and had reportedly sent a letter commanding Qing officials there to dispatch an envoy to Lahore to submit to the Sikh state. In the event, however, Gulab Singh's forces moved west across much easier terrain into Tibet, occupying territory up to the Mayum Pass. His forces reached almost to the northwest border of Nepal before Tibetan soldiers succeeded in destroying them at the end of the year. The following summer, the Tibetans launched a counterattack to capture Ladakh.[114]

In 1842 the Gurkha court made a particularly forceful overture for Qing assistance. Because it was due to send a mission to Beijing, it was able to submit a tributary memorial directly to the emperor rather than the normal petition to the ambans. Taking advantage of this direct access, the Gurkha ruler claimed that in September 1794 his grandfather Bahadur Shah had received imperial assurances that if a foreign power occupied Nepali territory the Qing court would send troops or money. This seems spurious, because the Qianlong court at that time had explicitly disclaimed having any such obligation, and the Nepali government itself had never before cited these supposed assurances even when urgently seeking assistance. Ignoring the Anglo-Nepal War of 1814–1816, the king added that thanks to Qing protection his country had been at peace even though the Pileng lived to its south and the Sikhs (Senba) to its west. However, he continued, the kingdom's affairs had for a time been handled by Bhim Sen Thapa, who had good personal relations with the Pileng and had made them a number of concessions before being forced from office. Now, the Pileng had written to the raja that they had taken Guangdong; Nepal must either surrender and allow them to take Tibet, or be attacked. In light of this purported demand, Qing aid was requested.[115]

This tributary memorial also raised a novel proposal, asking that the Qing court swap its territory of Daba near the Nepali border in western Tibet for the Gurkha territory of Mustang (Mosidang). In return, the Gurkhas would help fend off Gulab Singh. More boldly, it also proposed that the Qing cede them the right to govern Ladakh (at that time occupied by Gulab Singh), which under their control would send tribute to Beijing. Finally, it drew attention to the fact that the Pileng were building a road into Sikkim. To counter this, it suggested that the Qing court cede Nepal a strip of land ten *li* wide adjacent to the Bhutanese border, in exchange for which Nepal would guarantee Tibetan security. With these requests the Nepalis, who had stayed neutral as Tibet and Gulab Singh had fought near their border, were clearly attempting to take advantage of the stresses besetting the Qing empire.[116]

The ambans mistrusted the Gurkhas' motives, and criticized this memorial to Beijing. First, they pointed out that the Nepali ruler had improperly "intruded his private affairs" (*sishi*) into the document, "presumptuously seeking imperial generosity." In other words, the plan sketched by the Gurkha ruler had nothing to do with Qing interests and was beyond the legitimate concerns of tributary correspondence. The ambans also discounted reports of Pileng bullying, attributing them to the "insatiable" greed of Nepal. Although phrased mildly, the ambans' reply to Nepal again rejected the possibility of giving aid or exchanging territory, and asked why previous statements to this effect had been ignored.[117]

The Qing government had no interest in extending the Opium War into Inner Asia offensively or defensively. Daoguang had dealt in the first years of his reign with Moorcroft's arrival in Ladakh, and had learned of Izzat-ullah's claims that Hindustan was now ruled by the English. Neither the emperor nor his officials, however, alluded at the outbreak of the war to the possibility that Xinjiang might be accessible to their enemy. In 1839 the Qing court addressed the issue of opium in Xinjiang, but as part of its broader opium suppression policies unconnected to the British at Guangzhou.[118] On September 4, 1839, a memorialist urged the strict enforcement of opium regulations in Xinjiang when managing that territory's foreign trade.[119] On January 26, 1840, Yarkand Grand Minister Consultant En-te-heng-e reported that all opium in Xinjiang came from abroad, mostly from Kashmir, Badakhshan, and Yindi (i.e., the Sikh empire in the Punjab). He also listed Bukhara and Andijan, but not Hindustan. On February 18 Ili general Yi-shan submitted his own memorial regarding opium imports, but without naming individual foreign states.[120] Only in August 1840 was a link proposed between Xinjiang and the maritime theater of the Opium War. Having in the previous month warned against the sale of saltpeter overseas, a censor now informed the court that he had heard of another way the commodity might slip abroad, an overland route (*hanlu*) connecting Yarkand to "a place where the English traded" (*Yingjili yiren jiaoyi zhi chu*). In response, the court on August 30 ordered En-te-heng-e to investigate whether such an overland route existed.[121] On December 28 he reported that he had learned of no route connecting the cities of Xinjiang to the country of England (Yingjili-guo), but had nonetheless strengthened frontier defenses.[122]

Thus, officially the Qing state acknowledged no connection between Xinjiang and the British, but private sources paint a different picture. On September 9, 1840, soon after the censor's memorial, Li Xingyuan (1797–1851) met in Beijing with Yi-shan, recently returned from Ili. The general informed him that Hindustan, which grew opium, bordered the "maritime foreigners" (*yangyi*) and that news passed between the two areas (*shengxi xiangtong*). This perhaps indicates that Yi-shan learned something about the troubles at Guangzhou via Hindustani traders.[123] By implication, Yi-shan knew a route connected Xinjiang to English-held territory, but chose not to formally raise this point with the emperor. It is also odd that En-te-heng-e, stationed at the terminus of that route in Yarkand, chose to omit Hindustan from his list of opium-producing states, while Yi-shan (farther away at Ili) was aware that it grew the drug. Moreover, when responding to the censor's query about whether Yarkand was linked to a "place where the English traded," En-te-heng-e made no reference to the obviously germane Moorcroft episode recorded in his archives. This is especially peculiar because Izzat-ullah had named Kashmir and Yindi—which En-te-heng-e noted to be sources of opium—as places that "obeyed" (*tingcong*) the English. Perhaps it is significant that when asked if Yarkand was connected to "a place where the English traded," En-te-heng-e replied that it had no route to "the country of England"—not necessarily the same thing. Presumably officials in Xinjiang, already in a precarious position, wished to avoid becoming involved in the disaster on the coast.[124]

Still, connections between the far west and the coast were not lost on Beijing, and concerns remained about a possible overland link between Xinjiang and England. In April 1842 Yi-jing informed the court that four Indians captured in Zhejiang were "Kashmiri Muslims" (*Keshimi'er Huimin*). Upon receiving this news, the court ordered the questioning of an English prisoner about how far Kashmir was from England, if it was accessible by water, and whether the English traveled there. He replied that Kashmir was subject to the control of Bengal (Mengkala), which was itself subject to the English. From Calcutta (Jialajida), he continued, it was possible to reach Kashmir by both land and river routes.[125] Around the same time Yao Ying was ordered to inquire about whether there was a land route between England and Muslim Central Asia (*Huijiang gebu*), and if so whether it was frequently used. Denham, his captive, knew little about this area and described it as "extremely far" from England.[126] These inquiries seem to have been defensive, ensuring that the British could not suddenly attack by land, rather than exploring the possibility of opening a second front.

In the closing days of the war, events just west of the Qing empire attracted interest in the highest circles of government. By then, observers on the coast were aware the British relied heavily on Indian revenues and sepoys. It stood to reason that Bengalis must be greatly dissatisfied with British rule and that a colonial revolt would cripple the English capacity to wage war—expectations of such an event dated back to the tenure of Lin Zexu at Guangzhou.[127] Such hopes were fanned by the catastrophic reverse suffered by British forces in Afghanistan. In the late 1830s, British Indian strategists began to worry that Russia might be able to gain influence in Central Asia or Afghanistan and threaten their territories from the northwest. In 1839, a large British force had invaded Afghanistan, expelled Dost Mohammad, the incumbent ruler suspected of pro-Russian sympathies, and enthroned their client Shah Shuja. This expedition was closely watched in British India, and reports about it filled English-language newspapers printed in the Pearl River delta. Articles on the subject were translated under Lin's direction, although these do not seem to have been widely circulated. After initial British successes, an uprising broke out in Kabul in November 1841. By January a force of 16,000 British and Indian troops and civilians had been almost totally destroyed. News of this disaster spread quickly, and in Afghanistan fighting continued for months as British forces in Jalalabad and Kandahar, joined by fresh forces from India, marched to retake lost territory.[128]

News of the British defeat trickled into the English press in China through several contradictory reports, and it was not until March and April 1842 that the scale of the disaster became clear. Soon, word of a major British defeat in India began to circulate in Qing bureaucratic channels. On May 22, 1842, the censor Su Tingkui (1800–1878) memorialized about rumors circulating at Guangzhou (*Yuezhong chuanwen*). According to his understanding, Bengal had attacked and defeated the English homeland. The English, he explained, had occupied that important commercial center and collected the entirety of its tax payments. Bengalis hated the English, and when the China campaign had hollowed out the imperial garrison, they had taken the opportunity to revolt. Faced with this attack, English vessels were beginning clandestinely to leave China and shore up the forces guarding their empire. Su cautioned that these rumors were unverified, but considered them plausible.[129]

Su's report was noted by the Daoguang emperor, who agreed that the British were vulnerable. High officials campaigning on the coast were ordered to investigate, and the most detailed response was provided by Yi-shan and Qi Gong in Guangdong. They discounted these claims, pointing out that ships were arriving from, rather than returning to, Bengal. On the other hand, they had heard news in a similar vein. Three months east of England was a country called Entian ("Indian," but indicating Afghanistan). The English had invaded it, only to fall victim to a reverse in which over ten thousand of their troops had been killed in the first month of the year (January by the Western calendar, though Qing officials seem to have meant the first lunar month, February 10–March 11). The British were still fighting foes in Kabul (Kabu'er), while those of Jalalabad (Zhilalaba) had recovered from the British a place called Ghazni (Gusini). Kabul and Bengal, Qi and Yi-shan added, belonged to the region generally designated India (Yindu). Like Su, Yi-shan and Qi observed that foreign hatred of British treachery made this uprising plausible, but investigating it was extremely difficult. Some foreigners admitted hearing rumors of this military reverse, but others denied there was an uprising. "Regarding the place-names [the foreigners] mention," they informed the court, "we fear there are some mistakes in the pronunciation." They promised further inquiries.[130]

Around the same time, Yi-shan and Qi related further evidence that British imperial policies were leading to disaster. In the second month of the year (March 12–April 10), British merchants at Macao had been heard to talk about a recent debacle in Bengal. Normally, a British officer was stationed in Bengal to guard it with several hundred "white" and "black" troops. However, the "black" troops had been sent abroad to serve and many had been wounded, and the white troops were too few to maintain order. Therefore, in the past winter the officer had begun forcing "black" merchants and citizens into military service. Furious, the people of Bengal had risen up and killed the officer and almost all the white soldiers. This report, Yi-shan and Qi again cautioned, was simply hearsay and should not be rashly believed. Another unverified report claimed that "Muslim devils" (*Molao guizi*) had recaptured Bengal. Without its opium profits to purchase rations, the English would soon run out of supplies.[131]

On Taiwan, too, Yao Ying heard rumors of impending British collapse. As he wrote to Iliyang, "I have heard that the foreigners' territory of Bengal had repeatedly been defeated by the country of East India, which has imprisoned over a thousand of their officers and wives, and the foreigners must return their forces to the rescue; if we can hold firm for another three months, the foreigners will face internal collapse (*neikui*)." In a second letter to Iliyang, on September 12, Yao similarly suggested that England had become "hollowed out" (*kongxu*), that the "mass of foreigners" (*qunyi*) were becoming angry with it, and that it was facing imminent collapse.[132] Around this time he suggested to Fang Dongshu that "the various island foreigners are about to rebel against them and scatter; they cannot long maintain themselves."[133] At the end of the Opium War, as in the early 1830s, Qing officials confronting the manifest power of the British remained unpersuaded that it rested on sound foundations.

Conclusion

During the Opium War Qing scholars and officials were forced for the first time to grapple with the task of fighting a geographically noncontiguous, institutionally complex, ethnically diverse empire. No attempt will be made here to tally a scorecard balancing their perspicacious strategic insights against prevalent exaggerations and misapprehensions. From one perspective, Qing officials and scholars were acute in identifying the inefficiencies and vulnerabilities of British rule in India. It is not difficult to find British critics of the oddities and weaknesses evident to observers in China: the hybrid Crown-Company imperial structure, the risks of relying heavily on the China trade, and the "powerful, but most dangerous instrument" of a sepoy army.[134] On the other hand, the tendency of Qing officials to overestimate the weakness of the British derived perhaps from worries about the Qing empire's own vulnerability on many of the same fronts. After all, the Qing state in the first decades of the nineteenth century faced a fiscal crisis, ethnic uprisings, internal rebellion, and an overtaxed military. From the Qing perspective it was only natural that the British, morally and institutionally underdeveloped, would face even greater problems. Unfortunately, since comparisons of this sort were ideologically precluded even in unofficial discourse, we cannot know if Qing officials acknowledged to themselves any such analogies.

For the purposes of this study, the importance of the Opium War lay in its impact on the empire's geostrategic worldview. By 1842, lines of intelligence gathering using multiple sources in different places had underscored India's key role in British power: underpinning Britain's finances as the source of opium and military might as the source of sepoys. Tiny England could challenge Qing power, Chinese observers believed, only when imperial resources multiplied its strength. As the principal pillar of that strength, and potentially the main factor in its collapse, British India was arguably more relevant to China's security than any other single foreign site, even the home island itself.

Within the bureaucracy, the Qing empire's position was still interpreted through the lens of the frontier policy. The Qing state structure was not designed for synthesizing the cyclone of new geographic and geopolitical information churned up by the war. Although Gangjiao was pushed out of the official lexicon and largely replaced by Yindu, and British rule over that territory ascertained beyond doubt, the court did not use a standard lexicon but instead recorded with little comment new words like "Entian" and "Kabu'er." It reached no decisive conclusions about how lands like Pileng and Kashmir fit in to the dynamics of the conflict. When a baffling place like Niegajinna appeared, its interpretation was not tackled centrally in the Grand Council, but outsourced to frontier experts in Tibet and Guangzhou, and then shelved when no explanation seemed satisfactory. In short, the state persisted in its frontier-specific operational geography even though this was ill-suited to illuminating the overall strategic situation of the Qing empire in relation to its multipronged British foe.

In the aftermath of the war, what was to be done? For the Qing state, the coast of China was the center of attention. Its shattered defenses had to be rebuilt and improved, the military command structure reorganized, and the technological superiority of British gunnery and navigation offset. Defensive measures could make a second invasion more difficult, even impossible, and perhaps one day bar the British from Chinese markets and destroy their war-making capacity. But could the Qing also take the offensive and turn the tables on the British? Distant England was not susceptible to attack, but was this true of British India, arguably of more strategic importance? By 1842, debate over these questions was beginning to take shape.

EIGHT

The Emergence of a Foreign Policy
*Wei Yuan and the Reinterpretation of India
in Qing Strategic Thought, 1842–1860*

When the Opium War ended on August 29, 1842, it was clear that in certain contexts the British empire could defeat Qing forces, but the wider lessons of the war remained open to debate. That debate required a broad view of the Qing empire's global position. The earliest and most systematic postwar exploration of its geographic and strategic predicament was written by Wei Yuan (1794–1856). He painstakingly assembled virtually all of the empire's geographic sources, synthesized individual lexicons and various regional and cultural perspectives, and presented an integrated picture of the world. His studies looked backward over Qing military history and forward toward possible methods of eliminating the British threat. His findings were set forth in two companion works completed around the same time, one an analytical study of his empire's military accomplishments and the other a politically engaged description of the outside world. Having coordinated his sources into a comprehensive picture that tallied the collective advantages and demerits of each frontier, Wei was able to devise an overarching "foreign policy," a program of action connecting all corners of the Qing realm from the Pacific to Central Asia.

To his peers, the validity of Wei's strategic program became controversial, and scholars have continued to debate the significance of his insights. For some, he was a pioneer who broke away from damaging ignorance and struggled to adapt to a new reality; for others, he was primarily interpreting and resurrecting earlier traditions of Chinese strategic thought; for still others, he was little more than a polemicist whose scholarship was merely a contribution to the partisan politics of his time.[1] Although all of these interpretations have a measure of truth, Wei's most important claim to our attention as a geographer and geostrategist is the unprecedented scale on which he thought. For the first time in Qing history, a scholar offered his reader a more or less total and coherent explanation of how every known source on foreign geography fit together. On that basis Wei built, again for the first time, a strategic analysis that transcended regional segmentation and showed that each part of the realm touched different corners of the same, connected world. In other words, Wei was able to formulate a foreign policy that broke decisively with the geographic and geopolitical assumptions of a frontier policy.

As a geographer Wei paid careful attention to place-names, and the skill with which he took up and solved yan'ge problems—reconciling nomenclature across time and space—was his most original and important contribution. By the start of 1843 he had achieved a goal that had tantalized and eluded his peers for centuries: demonstrating that beneath the confusing linguistic, cultural, and political costumes that made sources on foreign geography appear incommensurable, each could be shown to be a partial description of the same outside world. By proving that it was possible to reduce to order almost all sources of foreign geography, he overcame geographic agnosticism arising from the seeming impossibility of decisive knowledge about the world's physical and political layout. To be sure, debate on questions of global geography continued long after Wei's work. Indeed many of his findings were challenged as early as Xu Jiyu's 1848 *Yinghuan zhilüe*. By that point, however, research and debate on foreign geography would be conducted as modifications to a single, integrated global picture, with growing confidence and within a consensus on agreed facts.

In parallel with his integrated geographic vision, Wei advanced radical proposals about how the Qing state could crush the British empire by targeting India. He buttressed his arguments with evidence from contemporary geopolitics and the empire's military history. For Wei, it was axiomatic that the Qing state required an aggressive foreign policy that harnessed all its potential strategic advantages toward a single end. Earlier analysis of the empire's position had failed to appreciate the unparalleled reach and scale of European empires. Earlier policy-makers, he argued, had seen only disjointed phenomena, not fully intelligible in a local context, which revealed a coherent pattern only when viewed in their entirety. In regard to British India, Wei took as his foil the frontier officials who had turned down the Gurkha offer to attack the Pileng, failing to grasp its full significance. Very few of Wei's peers believed he had found a solution to the empire's strategic problems. Even sympathetic readers found his proposals potentially dangerous. For its part, before 1860 the Qing state tried as far as possible to preserve existing practices and policies. Yet a true frontier policy, even if it seemed desirable, was no longer possible. After the mid-1840s, considerations of the Qing empire's strategic position in Inner Asia could not ignore the forces of British and Russian imperialism drawing close to every imperial frontier. Wei's activist program was repudiated, but defensive geostrategic thought became increasingly integrated and centralized. The era of viewing frontiers in mutual isolation had passed.

Tracing British India in Post–Opium War Private Geography

Although Wei Yuan had demonstrated no special interest in the geography of the maritime world before the Opium War, his background suited him to the subject. Already in his late forties when the war broke out, he had spent decades considering the details of policy reform while living in Beijing or working in the provinces as a private staff assistant to a series of high officials. In the process he had helped to edit a large compendium of statecraft writings, and become expert in the geography of Inner Asia. By 1840, he enjoyed a high reputation and a large network of contacts.[2] In that year, as noted earlier, official connections allowed him to interview Captain Anstruther, prisoner in Ningbo, and on that basis he wrote a *Short Record on England* (*Yingjili xiaoji*), his first rumination on the British empire. Wei's engagement with the subject soon deepened. In the summer of 1841 he was briefly reunited with his old acquaintance Lin Zexu, then under sentence of exile to Ili. Lin presented him with the translations he had prepared at Guangzhou, of which the centerpiece was a Chinese rendering of Hugh Murray's *The Encyclopædia of Geography*, entitled the *Sizhou zhi*. Working at a furious pace, by the end of the following year Wei had drafted his two celebrated works. One, the *Shengwu ji*, a history of Qing military campaigns and tactics, had its preface dated the seventh month of Daoguang 22 (August 6–September 4, 1842), precisely when the Treaty of Nanjing was being signed. Although the campaigns of the Opium War were not discussed, the book's content was deeply influenced by the crisis in which it was written, and Wei's historical judgments were explicitly formulated to support his policy ideas. Some months later, by January 1843, he completed the manuscript draft of the *Haiguo tuzhi*, which was printed at the beginning of 1844.[3] This work dealt more directly with the geopolitics of the contemporary world and the implications of the Opium War for Qing policy.

Wei's *Haiguo tuzhi* was pioneering not simply because it responded to the Opium War by engaging in detail with the geography of the British empire. After 1840 there had been a rush of scholars in this direction, virtually all of whom had composed textual studies based on collecting and juxtaposing various sources. The 1842 study of the English and their empire by Wang Wentai (1796–1844), though brief, drew on well over ten sources.[4] In late 1843 Zheng Guangzu (1776–1866) issued a collection of eighteen works on foreign countries and frontier regions entitled *Places Reached by Boat and Cart* (*Zhouju suozhi*), attaching to each work his own critical notes and comments.[5] In 1844, Wang Chaozong published a collection of existing works on the maritime world.[6] Nor was Wei unique in consulting writings by Westerners or based on Western informants. Setting aside the centuries-old use of Jesuit materials, and the circulation of Protestant missionary newspapers in the 1830s, the Opium War had stimulated contact with new sources. Like Wei, Chen Fengheng (1778–1855) had interviewed Anstruther and written a short essay on England.[7] On Taiwan, Yao Ying interviewed Denham and similarly produced a sketch of Britain and its empire. At that time, Yao had envisioned the grander project of combining this testimony with other materials into a *Collectanea of Works on Foreign Regions* (*Yiyu congshu*).[8] By 1843, Xu Jiyu was at work collecting European geographic sources and soon completed the first draft of what would become his celebrated *Yinghuan zhilüe*. This was a compilation of written explanations (*tushuo*) to accompany his Western maps, using materials culled from Chen Lunjiong, Cišii, Wang Dahai, and the *Gaohou mengqiu* (which dealt with Jesuit geography) by Xu Chaojun (fl. 1796–1815), along with oral testimony from Protestant missionaries. In time, it would surpass Wei Yuan's work as a geographic reference of choice for Qing officials.[9] In 1846, Liang Tingnan completed a study of the United States and Britain using Western sources.[10] The following year Pan Shicheng, a Cantonese scholar-official expert in foreign affairs, published in his collectanea several works on the maritime world, including the *Waiguo dili beikao* of the Macanese translator José Martinho Marques (1810–1867).

Wei's methodology was no more unique than his topic and sources. In its structure, his book was essentially an annotation of Lin's translation of Murray's geographic encyclopedia. At the end of each translated section, Wei appended relevant passages on the same region excerpted from other Western or Chinese sources. This he openly acknowledged by modestly giving himself third billing in these chapters as "recompiler" (*chongji*), after the "European original author" (*Ouluoba ren yuanzhuan*) and the "translator," Lin Zexu.[11] In other words, his approach was precisely that adopted two decades earlier by his friend Li Zhaoluo when he was working on an annotated edition of the *Hailu*.[12] Wei supplemented the juxtaposition of sources with chapters detailing his own yan'ge research, relating new knowledge to the historical geography of earlier periods, but here too his methods and goals had precedents in Qing scholarship.

It is precisely because he was taking up a familiar task that the greatness of Wei's achievement as a scholar of foreign geography can be appreciated. To incorporate the translated *Sizhou zhi* within the geographic tradition, Wei had to grapple with the tasking but essential yan'ge problem of relating different systems of nomenclature. Murray's book claimed to describe the geography of the entire world. To annotate it, Wei had to read through the gigantic corpus of sources available to literati of his time and carefully group their contents according to the regional divisions used in the *Sizhou zhi*. In other words, he would have to do what no previous scholar had been able to accomplish: comprehensively reconcile all the major sources of geographic knowledge available in Chinese. This demanded mastery of a host of geographic lexicons, for only by deciphering place-names used in each source and aligning them with those found in Murray's book could he place each extract in its proper context. As an intellectual labor this was far more difficult than simple translation, but upon completion it vindicated the "commentarial assumption" that sources were only apparently incommensurable and could be reconciled by a sufficiently learned geographer. Wei's commitment to treating the entire corpus of available materials, not just new translations like Murray's encyclopedia, is demonstrated by his devoting two chapters to earlier Chinese sources on India, twice the space he gave to analyzing translated works and Protestant missionary writings.[13]

Wei followed yan'ge logic to order his information, selecting a set of master names and subordinating to them all other terms as variants. Hitherto, no scholar, not even court researchers, had been able to reconcile terms from all frontiers. Using his treatment of India as a case study, we can trace how Wei largely succeeded in this task. By the eve of the Opium War, scholars and officials on the coast increasingly used "Yindu" as a general name for contemporary India. Wei selected as his master names the concept of "five Indias" (*wu Yindu*), treating all other terms for India and its regions as equivalent to North, South, West, East, or Central India. On this basis, he culled materials about India from standard histories, Qing court reference works, Jesuit and Protestant writings, various books from the coast such as those of Chen Lunjiong and Wang Dahai, the *Hailu* of Xie Qinggao, and Lin's translations. Into these excerpted texts he inserted notes to demonstrate how the vocabulary in a particular source corresponded to his master lexicon.[14]

This method was critical to digesting the significance of newly translated European writings and making intelligible for Chinese readers content that would otherwise be completely baffling. For instance, the original translation of Hugh Murray's *Encyclopædia of Geography* described the territories of India belonging to the British as follows: "Subsequently [after 1765] thirteen parts of India were subject to the British: Bengal, Madras, Bombay, the Nizam [?], Awadh, Nagpur, Mysore, Satara, Gwickwar, Travancore, Cochin, the Rajputs, and Ceylon. Only a few tribes remained independent: Scindia, the Sikhs, Nepal, and Sindh, i.e., Multan (Xinni, ji Maoer'dan)." Wei then glossed the implications of this passage using his standardized terminology: "These tribes are on the edge of Central and South India, and are not fully taken over by the English. West and North India are also not included among these tribes."[15] In principle, with the *Haiguo tuzhi* as a guide, one could pick up almost any writing in Chinese dealing with India (or any other place), regardless of its age, academic background, or regional origin, and immediately convert its particular lexicon into that used in any other work. Its notes made it a geographical dictionary or thesaurus.

Although no previous work had been nearly as comprehensive or versatile, Wei's first draft was neither perfect nor exhaustive, and he continued to gather new information from emerging sources. For interpreting information about India from the Tibetan frontier, his most important correspondent was his friend and fellow researcher Yao Ying. The two had first met in Beijing in the 1820s and in the following decade participated in the same loosely affiliated social and political group, the Spring Purification circle.[16] Independent research during the war had convinced both of the crucial role of India in the British empire. Using the small library available to him on

Taiwan, Yao studied the world map drawn by Denham and printed a modest work of maps and explanatory texts.[17] To satisfy an interest in foreign affairs that dated back to his early reading on the Western Regions around 1811, and deepened during his earlier service in Taiwan, he initially planned to write something similar to the *Haiguo tuzhi*.[18] Only when he learned of Wei's scholarly achievement and discovered that he had "anticipated my thoughts" (*xian de wo xin*) did Yao relinquish this ambition.[19]

One reason Wei made faster progress was a disaster in Yao's professional life. During the war, as we have seen, he had reported defeating two British ships in battle. Ultimately, he and Dahūngga had executed virtually all their captives. The British lodged vigorous protests, and a Qing investigation found that Yao had falsely claimed victories over ships that had actually foundered by accident. Early in April 1843 he was sent to stand trial at the Board of Punishment in Beijing, a journey that interrupted his geographic studies.[20] After a brief imprisonment, Yao was demoted and sent to Sichuan to serve as a vice prefect, reaching that province in autumn 1844. Like many of his peers, he was already interested in the geography of Qing Inner Asia, and the war alerted him to the connection between inland and coastal affairs. On Taiwan he had been ordered to question Denham about overland routes between the Qing empire and England (a congenial assignment, since decades earlier he had learned about Russia from the experienced frontier official Sungyūn), and consequently Yao was "deeply exasperated" (*shen yi wei hen*) at Denham's vagueness about the geography of Inner Asia.[21]

Soon, however, Yao had a better opportunity to clarify the significance of Inner Asia to the British threat. Shortly after he arrived in Sichuan he accepted a mission to Litang near the province's western border with Tibet to mediate a dispute between incarnate lamas. Yao returned on January 29, 1845, and departed for a second mission to Zhaya, actually inside the boundaries of Tibet, on April 1. In this short interval, he received a copy of the *Haiguo tuzhi* sent to him by his friend Wei Yuan. This work seems to have been Yao's first encounter with Wei's theories about Inner Asia's strategic importance for coastal warfare. As he later recalled, upon receiving the book he set off on his second mission, delighted by the chance it gave him to "inquire of Tibetans about 'Western affairs' (*xi shi*)."[22] Specifically, Tibet seemed to be an ideal place to research Wei's theory that Gurkha and Russian hostility toward British India might play a crucial role in any future conflict (see below). By the time he returned to Chengdu the following year, Yao was armed with a stack of notes, which he edited and published as the *Kangyou jixing*, a work combining the form of a travel journal with short essays on historical and contemporary geography, political intelligence, and strategy.[23]

In short, in place of a comprehensive description of the world like the *Haiguo tuzhi*, Yao produced a more specialized work on Tibet's significance for contemporary geopolitics. Wei's treatment of Tibet's frontier was a weak spot in his *Haiguo tuzhi*. Wei Yuan was aware that India (Yindu), and specifically Bengal, lay below Tibet and the Gurkhas, and was privy to the memorials passing between Lhasa and the throne during the Opium War, but aside from commenting that Dili (misspelled "Lidi") was a term for the English, he had little to say about the complex relationship between the Pileng, Dili, Jiaga'er, and other terms of Tibetan origin.[24] Yao shed light on how this regional terminology fit into Wei's comprehensive worldview. Much of his new information derived from sources evidently more readily available in Sichuan than on the coast, such as the provincial gazetteer (which included details of the Qianlong Gurkha campaigns), as well as works mentioning the Pileng by Sungyūn and He-ning, all omitted from Wei's first foray. Wei was impressed by Yao's results, and incorporated passages from his *Kangyou jixing* (completed in an early draft by 1846) into the third edition of the *Shengwu ji*, finished in the same year. In discussing Tibet's place in the rivalry between the Qing and British India, both books were fruits of a loose collaboration.

Bengal was a major object of Yao's interest. In a long essay he pointed out that south of Further Tibet lay Nepal. Going westward one crossed a "small harbor" and reached a place called Pileng, which he identified as East India. South of Pileng lay a coastal land called Bengal (Mengjiala). The British had first conquered Bengal, and then induced the Pileng to submit to them. Chinese observers, Yao remarked, had never learned that it was the British who had conquered Bengal, and knew only that it belonged to a power called Dili Bacha. From this Bengali base, the British had absorbed all the surrounding territories. Having now linked the local Tibetan geographic lexicon to maritime sources, Yao was in a position to reinterpret the meaning of older passages concerning Pileng and Dili Bacha first recorded by Fuk'anggan and preserved in the Sichuan gazetteer. When the writings in question had been included in the Jiaqing-period gazetteer, Yao noted, scholars could not have known from the documents that Dili Bacha referred to the English. With this knowledge in hand it became clear, for instance, that the reason the Pileng "governor" was described as neither Muslim nor Buddhist was because he was Christian.[25]

Yao also directed his attention to other terms. According to Wei Yuan, citing both the *Sizhou zhi* and the *Xin Tang shu*, Hindustan indicated Central India, Kashmir indicated North India, and Jiaga'er indicated East India. Yao Ying agreed. Jiaga'er had to be the same as Bengal, he reasoned, because information from Tibet stated that it was south of Nepal and contained the Pileng within its boundaries.[26] Interestingly, Yao later cited a passage in He-ning's *Xizang fu* that "Jiaga'er" was simply the Tibetan translation of "Enetkek" (identified by Wei with Central India), but he made no comment on the implication that Jiaga'er might also encompass Central India as well.[27] Other complexities were raised by Jesuit sources. Verbiest's famous world map had marked a place called Yindusitan, clearly equivalent to the more familiar Hendusitan. Verbiest's Hindustan was surrounded by Bengal to its east, the Mughal empire (Mowo'er) to its northwest, and the Indus River to its west, thus in a position that corresponded to Central India, again corroborating Wei Yuan's equation of the two places.[28] But Verbiest had asserted in his text that Mowo'er contained within it all of the five Indias except South India. Strictly speaking, then, Mowo'er should encompass Hindustan. Yao rejected this, pointing out that Verbiest himself placed Mowo'er on his map to the north of the place named Hindustan. Thus, Mowo'er should really be North India, equivalent to Kashmir.[29]

Although Yao tended to agree with Wei's opinions and supply supporting evidence, he was not remiss in pointing out Wei's errors. For instance, Wei had asserted in the first edition of the *Shengwu ji* that the Gurkhas paid tribute to both China and Russia.[30] Yao Ying rejected this claim, observing that the Russians had only penetrated into the northwestern portion of India, so that Central and East India still stood between them and the Gurkhas. Since those two portions were under English rule, "it is false to say that they are near the Russians."[31] Wei Yuan deferred to Yao's expertise: in the third and final edition of the *Shengwu ji* he amended his claim, now placing the Gurkhas correctly between Tibet and India.[32] He also appended several long extracts from the *Kangyou jixing* to his essay on Qing-Nepali relations, another indication that he held Yao's insights into Indian geography in high esteem.

The Role of Cartography in Post–Opium War Geographic Research

A cause and consequence of Wei's geographic achievement was a growing rapprochement between text and map. Previous chapters have commented on the difficulty of reconciling the conflicting claims of textual sources into a single visual form, a fact that had kept cartography marginal to research and argument about foreign geography in the Qing period. In part, cosmological issues were at stake: different geographic systems posited a varying number of continents and seas arranged in incommensurable patterns, and to adopt one of these was tantamount to endorsing the ideological or political claims associated with it. On a more granular level, even if a single outline of the world's shape was accepted, it remained almost impossible to populate such a map with the many locations named in textual geographic sources. Only after 1842 were these problems overcome. The shape of the world presented in Western world maps was openly accepted as valid, and maps constructed on this basis were used for the first time to show the location of most places mentioned in textual sources. Yet despite the growing role of cartography after 1842, textual problems remained the foremost concern of Qing scholars, and the creation and use of maps by Wei and Yao reflected that priority.

The principle that maps and yan'ge textual arguments could complement each other had been recognized well before the Opium War. Superimposing maps on top of each other could reveal the various names assigned by different geographic systems to the same physical location. Zhuang Tingfu had made limited use of this technique by the end of the eighteenth century, as had Jiang Fan around 1820. Conversely, using textual research to identify overlapping place-names reduced the number of points that had to be plotted on a map, making the task more manageable. In practice, however, a precondition for granting maps an extensive role in the study of foreign geography was accepting one outline of the world's shape as a complete and authoritative basis for future research. Before the Opium War there was simply no consensus on the world's shape. European-style world maps circulated widely, but few scholars were willing to endorse them fully. By the 1830s the hesitation to use Western world maps was wavering, at least among private researchers on the coast, and by 1842 it had largely evaporated.

Part of the impetus behind this shift was political. In the face of foreign geography's manifest strategic importance it became necessary to select one cosmological system as the basis for further research: deferring the choice and maintaining a posture of dispassionate agnosticism had become an unaffordable luxury. Intellectually, too, Western maps had vindicated themselves. Yao Ying believed that maps in the European style were plausible because of their consistency: when he compared the independently composed maps of Chen, Verbiest, and his prisoner Denham, "their shapes truly corresponded to each other."³³ Although Wei's basic source, the translated *Sizhou zhi*, does not seem to have had a companion map, his decision to accept its multi-continent description as the organizing framework for his own book was tantamount to endorsing the validity of European worldviews. Wei likewise suggested that extensive examination had proved the accuracy of Western maps: "[people] having cross-examined them (*zhi*) among foreign trading ships at Guangdong and Fujian and tribute envoys coming from afar to present their treasures, these matters are mostly true and the words are not farfetched."³⁴ Both Wei and Yao ignored maps that presented the world as a single continent, implying that they no longer found them to have reference value. Xu Jiyu was by 1843 still more persuaded of the accuracy of Western world maps, explaining that since their authors had traveled the world and mapped what they saw, "their maps are therefore of singular authority" (*gu qi tu du wei ke ju*).³⁵ Neither the maps nor the claims were new, but attitudes had changed.

Although they conceded to European geographers a monopoly in representing the physical shape of the world, Wei Yuan and Yao Ying did not break with the existing methods or concerns of Chinese scholarship, which centered on textual research. Neither took particular care to obtain the most recent Western maps (Wei's newest exemplar was borrowed from Zhuang Tingfu; Yao included a very clumsy sketch map based on Denham's 1842 testimony). When they did construct original maps for their own works they included no graticule, and played fast and loose with the physical contours of continents, stretching or trimming them at will. Certain more localized maps created by Wei and Yao virtually ignored features prominent on European maps.³⁶ Neither scholar seems to have regarded cartography as a mathematical representation of space that might stand independent of text as a means of geographic expression. Place-names remained their chief geographical concern, and maps were simply a convenient tool to solve textual puzzles and succinctly display those solutions.

One indication of the continuing dominance of nomenclature-related problems within geographic research is the manner Wei and Yao prepared their general maps of the world in the 1840s. Wei used two maps to display the contemporary globe, a "round map" and a "horizontal map." In his preface to these, he explained that he borrowed the degrees of latitude and longitude from the original maps of Verbiest and other Jesuits, but had "completely changed the place-names to those in the present treatise."³⁷ Thus, the first "round" European world map was simply Zhuang's global map in two hemispheres (itself adapted from a Jesuit original), to which Wei made only a few spatial adjustments but undertook a major overhaul of its terminology.[38] On the second, "horizontal" European map, a copy of Aleni's world map in the *Zhifang wai ji*, Wei likewise made very sparing changes to the physical outline but an almost complete renovation of its nomenclature.[39] Yao Ying similarly created a map with "contemporary revisions" (*jin ding*) in which he depicted the world roughly according to European conventions but inserted the place-names he judged to be current.[40] In other words, for both scholars preparing up-to-date maps meant primarily adjusting terminology. This was hardly a technical breakthrough: Chen Lunjiong had used this technique as early as 1730, and Zhuang had followed his lead. Far more original and important was the comprehensive manner in which Wei (and to a lesser extent Yao) used maps as a tool to reconcile competing geographic systems, assigning locations not to only a small number of select names but to a vast array of them drawn systematically from all major sources. In order to make room for his names, Wei significantly distorted the contours of his cartographic model from map to map.[41] Yao too was far from fastidious when ostensibly copying Verbiest's world map, and was equally willing to shift continental boundaries to fit more names.[42] Sacrificing mathematical spatial precision to make the comparison of lexical systems more convenient is a striking indication of their priorities.

Placing toponyms on their maps was not a simple, mechanical process, but rather a challenging intellectual enterprise. No existing map treated the problem adequately. As Wei lamented,

> Although the maps of Ricci, Aleni, Verbiest, and the recent English map in Chinese [probably Captain Denham's] are accurate and regular in assigning positions and degrees, yet when they detail ports or explain inland areas they follow local usage and do away with ancient names, so if they reach a foreign country they hear a cacophony (*qunxiu*) of sound but not [intelligible] words, and they do not know which [name] to take as correct. Chen Lunjiong and Zhuang Tingfu used their maps as models, but all of these maps were inconsistent.... One must observe the nonsense in the *Yuan shi* and *Ming tu* [of Zheng He], the uneven clarity of the various dynastic histories, and the disagreements (*fencuo*) among the maps of Ricci, Aleni, and Verbiest, and then one will know that this book [of mine] and this map are indispensable.[43]

Yao entirely agreed, observing of Jesuit maps that "their local pronunciation of names" (*fangyin chengming*) differed from the various Chinese textual accounts of foreign geography, so that one had to "expend great investigative effort to ascertain that any given [name] corresponded to any given place."[44] For names already used on Western maps, as Yao noted, one could simply collate them and "point by point make a detailed judgment about [each case] where they assigned a different name to the same place."[45] But most place-names were not already located on maps, making research more arduous.

Yan'ge methodology meant that maps that showed only one standard name for each place were inadequate. For this reason, Wei made a second series of maps entitled "yan'ge maps of the maritime countries," on which he gave the "modern name," below which was a box of "variant names." Although the concept of yan'ge had been devised to handle name changes over time, Wei was applying it (wittingly or not) to deal chiefly with variety emerging from regional and linguistic diversity. For instance, his map showed that the standard "modern" name Central India (*zhong Yindu*) corresponded to the older terms "Tianzhu," "Yindu," "Hendu," "Wendu," "Xindu," the Manchu "Enatekeke-guo," the Jesuit "Mowo'er-guo," and other names in Buddhist scripture.[46]

Even Wei's innovative yan'ge maps, with twelve equivalents for "Central India," could not fully grapple with the complexity of his textual evidence. For instance, Chen Lunjiong made reference to a country called Xiao Baitou, unique to his own geographic lexicon. In copying Chen's remarks, Wei added the gloss, "this country is called Mowo'er, that is, Hindustan."[47] It would follow that Xiao Baitou was yet another equivalent for Central India, but it did not appear on Wei's map. Nor could the map discuss the important issue of false equivalents, and Wei thus relied on his text to steer readers away from the danger of specious identifications, noting for instance after the mention of the Marathas (Malata) in the *Hailu*, "the sound of this resembles 'Bengal' (Mengjiala), but they are different places, this being South India and that being East India—don't conflate them."[48]

Wei was far from a passive recipient of Western geographic data. Although boasting of the utility of his new sources, he nonetheless continued to believe Chinese scholars had a duty to corroborate them and the authority to correct even new European evidence. For Wei, each source was in some way imperfect, and needed an editor to gloss, explain, alter, or reject it according to critical judgment born of wide reading. There was no contradiction between boasting of "using Westerners to discuss the West" and sometimes modifying those sources according to his own conclusions.[49] Such critical arbitration was useful not only on the level of place-names, but even in regard to the most basic Western geographic conceptions. In his essay "Explaining the Five Continents" (*Shi wu dazhou*), Wei first summarized the European division of the world into two hemispheres, one containing Africa, Asia, and Europe, the other North and South America. European maps, he accepted, rendered the shape of the world correctly, but he rejected Jesuit interpretations of this shape. Beginning with the premise that continents (*zhou*ᵇ) had to be separated from each other by bodies of water (a proposition shared by Zou Yan's theory of "small seas" separating nine continents and the Buddhist view of a salt sea dividing four continents), he found the European system of continental division arbitrary and untenable. Even a major physical feature like the Pamir range could not justly divide Europe from Asia, because that system of mountains extended (so Wei thought) from Asia into Europe and Africa. Wei likewise rejected Aleni's claim in the *Zhifang wai ji* that the Tanais (Don) River was the boundary of Europe and the Amu Darya the boundary of Asia even though a vast distance lay between them. This he compared to taking the Yellow River as the boundary of northern China and the Huai and Yangzi Rivers as the boundary of southern China, leaving thousands of *li* in the uncategorized middle. Nor was the slender Mediterranean adequate to divide Europe from Africa. North and South America were likewise conjoined and properly a single continent. Since Europeans knew almost nothing about the southern continent of Magellanica, Wei concluded that their maps could only describe two, not five, continents.[50]

Wei proceeded to analyze European descriptions of the world through the lens of Buddhist scripture, specifically the claim of four continents surrounding a central Mt. Sumeru. He argued that Asia, Europe, and Africa were subdivisions of the single continent of Jambudvipa, and America was the single continent of Godaniya. As evidence, he adduced the venerable Buddhist view that Jambudvipa was split between an eastern Ruler of Men (China), a southern Ruler of Elephants (India), a northern Ruler of Horses (Mongols and Kazakhs), and a western Ruler of Treasure (Europe and Africa), a template that entirely fit the interpretation of Africa, Asia, and Europe as a single continent. Where were the other two continents? Wei argued that they were cut off by ice in the Arctic and Antarctic Oceans, which had never been circumnavigated. Verbiest had explicitly rejected this Buddhist theory of four continents, arguing that the "southern" continent of Jambudvipa would have to be below the southern temperate zone, but to Wei the Jesuit's critique was based on a misunderstanding of Buddhist geography.[51] A similar phenomenon is found in Yao Ying's *Kangyou jixing*. Yao complained that

Aleni on one hand postulated two types of seas, "inland seas" (*dizhong hai*) and "surrounding seas" (*huanhai*), but on the other hand summarily rejected Zou Yan's similar theory that there was a "vast sea" (*yinghai*) surrounding several "small seas." In Yao's view, Aleni judged this Chinese theory "unverified" and "almost nonsense" simply because of the unfortunate tendency of Europeans to regard their own views too highly and denigrate the ideas of others.[52] In both cases, the widely read and objective Chinese geographer knew better than the widely traveled but biased European missionaries.

An exception to the approach taken by Wei and Yao, which nonetheless proves the rule that place-names were central to post–Opium War scholarship, is found in the work of Xu Jiyu. Undertaking his project in close consultation with missionary helpers, Xu made maps the focus of his research. His cartography showed a painstaking fidelity to the mathematical precision of its Western models, and paid little attention to illuminating nomenclature. Yet Xu was nonetheless deeply concerned with yan'ge issues. He read as widely in Chinese sources as Wei and Yao did, and wrote long essays about how historical and regional lexicons could be reconciled to a single, standard usage.[53] In the 1840s, as in the 1740s or 1640s, no Chinese geographer could satisfactorily study foreign geography purely on the basis of materials from a single intellectual tradition. Now, however, the resulting synthesis was comprehensive.

Wei Yuan's *Haiguo tuzhi* marks a watershed in the history of Qing geographic research into the outside world not because it made extensive use of translated Western data, nor because it endorsed (with reservations) the validity of the European multi-continent theory of the world, but because it succeeded in bringing into dialogue elements from virtually all geographic traditions within the Qing empire. It vindicated the yan'ge assumption that with enough care and learning it should be possible to arrange data from seemingly incommensurable accounts into one finite picture of the world. Wei did not solve every geographic puzzle or satisfy every reader, and an uncharitable partisan of the rival geographer Xu Jiyu termed his work "mostly unverified opinionating."[54] Far from being the last word in foreign geography, Wei's *Haiguo tuzhi* was the first in a torrent of accounts about the outside world that became available after the 1840s, and these brought with them many new and sometimes confusing place-names. However, the *Haiguo tuzhi* marks the end of geographic agnosticism, the attitude that foreign geography was a topic simply too complex to permit certain knowledge. Thereafter, the "latitude of expectation" within which Qing geographers operated was vastly constricted. To adapt the ideas of Thomas Kuhn, Qing geographers had individually been scientists before the 1840s—Wei was not a more industrious or rational researcher than Ji Yun—but now they had collectively agreed on the basic methods and authoritative data of their science (see Chapter One). The age of competing worldviews, at least for elite Han Chinese scholars, was ending.

Geographic Knowledge as a Strategic Tool: The Development of Wei Yuan's Foreign Policy

Wei's ambitious attempt to stitch together disparate threads of geographic sources into a single fabric was intended to offer a clearer picture of the world and of the relative positions of the Qing and British empires within it. With an integrated vision of the world, policy-makers could subordinate the management of each individual frontier zone within the Qing empire to a centralized program of action that coordinated the resources and advantages of each border zone. To convince contemporaries that his strategy was practical and justified, Wei had to go beyond geography into commentary on historical precedent and contemporary geopolitics. Arguments on both topics were elaborated in his *Haiguo tuzhi* and *Shengwu ji*. Here we will consider in depth only one strand in Wei's rich and complex strategic thinking, his belief that it was both feasible and necessary to "use foreigners to fight foreigners." Based on new information and older sources, he argued that it was possible to build a coalition of allies sufficiently powerful to topple British India and end the threat it posed to China. To put this into operation meant a fundamental departure from two aspects of Qing strategic practice: it would be necessary to fight far beyond the Qing frontier, and primarily to use foreign troops. Aware that his plan would seem unorthodox, Wei marshaled evidence that history, geography, and the latest translated intelligence all supported his proposals.

The premise of Wei's foreign policy was that the Qing response to the British empire had to be informed by a global geopolitical awareness, transcending parochial regional outlooks. One reason Qing strategy had failed during the Opium War was that a lack of interest in distant geography and politics blinded high officials to opportunities:

> If one had [earlier] translated books or searched into foreign affairs one would invariably have been called "meddlesome" (*duoshi*), but once trouble arose some asked about the distance between the English and Russian capi-

tals, or the route by which the English could reach the Muslim Regions. It even reached the point that when the Gurkhas obediently requested to attack India, this was rejected, and when the French and Americans were willing to aid us with their warships and discuss terms on our behalf they were doubted. Can not knowing the direction (*fangxiang*) or mutual relationships (*lihe*) of countries that had traded with us for two centuries still be called paying attention to frontier affairs?[55]

Wei was explicit that Qing commentators had to take the widest possible perspective: "all around the earth the English have ports, so those who wish to manage them must be fully conversant with the complete form of the globe (*bi xi diqiu quanxing*)." Once that was familiar, it became clear that England itself was not the strategic key to the situation facing the Qing: "Those who view maps and only look at the one showing the home country of the English do not know how to examine maps; those who read geographies and only read the chapters concerning the home country of the English are not skilled in reading geographies."[56]

Rather, Wei had learned from his interview with Anstruther that India was the territory most crucial for British power. It therefore served Wei as an axiomatic case to demonstrate that the Qing had paid a high price for lacking the global vision he was now elaborating. He connected the dots:

> If we do not know the situation in East India then we would not know that we could use the Gurkhas, and even if we formulated the strategy of a two-pronged attack we would not dare to trust them; if we do not know the situation in South India then we would not know that we could use France and America, and even if we formulated a strategy of desiring to buy or make warships we would have no way to finalize it (*wei you jue*); if we do not know the situation in Central and North India then we would not know of the strategy of associating with Russia, and if we [only] inquired about the distance between the English and Russian capitals we would not be aware that [England and Russia] are near each other in India, and not in their capitals.[57]

The position of the Qing empire was ripe with latent advantages, visible only to those with a comprehensive grasp of foreign geopolitics. In short, Wei was trying to recalibrate the empire's notions of strategic relevance: it was not only events near the frontier that determined China's security, but also imperial rivalries throughout the world.

British India was the vulnerable keystone of the enemy's empire. Wei believed that the greed and jealousy of foreign powers could be manipulated to exploit this weakness. If the Qing were able to coordinate policy across all imperial frontiers, Russia, America, and France, as well as the subject states of Nepal, Burma, Siam, and Annam could be used as proxies to attack India by land and sea. These states would be motivated not principally by any loyalty to the Qing ruler, but by their self-interest. As he observed in his preface to the chapter on Indian conditions in the *Haiguo tuzhi*,

> The British station heavy defensive forces in East India, and when they employ troops against various countries they are all dispatched from Bengal. . . . [East India] also neighbors our subject states Burma and Gurkha, which have age-old enmity toward it, therefore it is the crucial point for England pressuring China and for China restraining England. South India juts out into the Southern Sea and is ringed by French, American, Portuguese, Dutch, and Luzonian [i.e., Spanish] ports, but the English ports of Madras and Bombay both produce as much opium as Bengal, and since the various countries cannot share the profits there is always suspicion beneath apparent friendship. Therefore South India and Macao are the crucial points for joining together with (*lianluo*) France and America and for buying ships and cannons. Central India is where England and Russia oppose each other, divided only by the large mountains of the Hindu Kush. Should the Russians cross them, they could seize Hindustan, so the British maintain crack troops there to resist them. Therefore, Central India is the crucial point for joining together with Russia.[58]

In other words, the Qing empire could use India as a fulcrum to raise a grand coalition against the British. It should be stressed that Wei did not emphasize tributary relationships. For both "subject states" (in which category he did not include Russia) and others, he was careful to show that all of his potential allies would fight the British from greed or revenge, not loyalty to the Qing. Indeed, he used the neutral term "joining together" (*lianluo*) to describe his proposed connections with Russia and other powers, a term not only devoid of tributary overtones but precisely that adopted by Yao Ying to describe the nodal linkages connecting different parts of the British empire.

Wei took pains to marshal historical precedent putatively demonstrating the feasibility of his plan. Impeccable evidence showed that India could be attacked by the routes he outlined:

> In the past, in the Zhenguan [627–649] reign era of Tang Taizong, Wang Yuance used Tufan [Tibetan] troops to attack India, which is [now] the route for the Gurkhas to attack Bengal. Troops of Yuan Taizu [Chinggis] reached North and Central India and returned, and Xianzong [Möngke, 1209–1259] commanded Prince Xulie [Hülegü, 1217–1265] to go in advance

and seize West India [i.e., the Middle East, in Wei's schema], and later to return and take the five Indias, which is the route by which the Russians are now impinging upon Hindustan. In the Ming the *sanbao* eunuch Zheng He used a naval force to destroy Ceylon . . . which [illustrates] the route by which today the warships of foreigners at Guangzhou go to South India.[59]

British India was indisputably within the reach of Wei's proposed coalition.

The most controversial dimension of his strategy was that it relied so heavily on the fighting power of other countries, with little or no commitment by regular Qing forces. This was bound to arouse opposition on both practical and ideological grounds. During earlier frontier crises, Qing officials had studied local geopolitics and sometimes tried to exploit dissension between foreign groups. When Fuk'anggan had identified states that had reason to loathe the Gurkhas and ordered them to help the Qing, Qianlong was quick to criticize his general for relying too heavily on foreign assistance. Although the emperor was not categorically opposed to collaboration with foreign groups, he wished to ensure that the vast preponderance of force came from the Qing side and to avoid any kind of explicit agreement or alliance. When Wei turned to historical precedent for support, then, he had to sculpt the facts in his narrative fit his policy arguments.

Wei's military history was deeply colored by his concern for the present. For instance, writing about operations in Tibet led him into a long digression about routes linking the Yunnan frontier to Bengal. Given the relative proximity of the two regions, Wei observed that if the "savages" (*yeyi*) living between them became Qing subjects, "then [our territory] would reach the frontier of India." He went on to point out that the Nu people paid an annual tribute of furs at the frontier at Tengyue, so that if the Qing were to "develop" their territory it would push the empire's boundary up to that of India. Until this point Wei drew primarily from Qing official records, but he then turned to more recent foreign intelligence to show that this aboriginal force would be close to the major source of British opium production. Threading together these two strands of foreign and domestic geopolitical argument, he identified a strategic opportunity: "It is indeed possible to gather 10,000 native troops at Tengyue, who will cross the Salween River and thrust toward the southwest, striking [Bengal] from behind. Pushing through to a far-distant area and making it a neighboring region (*tong jueyu wei linrang*) is truly an excellent method for controlling the Westerners."[60]

The intersection between geographic knowledge, Qing military history, and Opium War–era intelligence was even clearer in Wei's chapter "Record of the Qianlong-era Conquest of the Gurkhas" in his *Shengwu ji*. In official Qing histories of the 1792 Gurkha campaign, English-Pileng actions were of no significance to the final peace agreement, but Wei's narrative gave them a significant role. While Fuk'anggan was descending on Nepal from Tibet, Wei claimed, the British had taken the opportunity to attack from the south. It was from fear of a war on two fronts, rather than simply China's overwhelming victories, that had induced the Gurkhas to sue for peace. There was a kernel of truth in this claim, for the Gurkhas were diplomatically active in both directions during the war even if they did not then fear a British attack, but no Qing source gave Wei the documentary evidence he needed. Instead, he made surprisingly tendentious and selective use of other materials. The main basis of his claim was nothing other than the "tributary memorial" received from George III in 1796, in which the English king was interpreted to state that British forces had lent military aid to the Qing army against the Gurkhas. This claim, it will be recalled, had been explicitly repudiated by Qianlong in his edict, a fact Wei ignored. Wei also passed over in silence the rocky Qing-Gurkha relationship between 1792 and 1840, stating only that "the presentation of tribute has continued to the present without interruption."[61]

Wei ended his history of the Qianlong Gurkha war with a synopsis of Nepal's request for military aid against the British in 1840. Here again, Wei misled his reader. According to him, the ambans had been unaware that Lidi (an error for Dili) and Jingshu ("subject to the capital") referred respectively to the British and Guangdong and therefore dismissed the request for aid as a meaningless squabble.[62] This was a central rhetorical plank for Wei, because it vividly contrasted the narrow outlook of frontier officials with his own global vision. This claim resonated with several of his contemporaries. It was reproduced in Yu Hao's 1848 *Xiyu kaogu lu*, a study of the Western Regions.[63] Both Yao Ying and Liang Tingnan presented more elaborate versions of the story, in which the Gurkhas had actually invaded Bengal in 1842, requiring the British to rush back and ransom their territories (this confused the Gurkha offer with rumors of the Afghan debacle). In this version, the British had saved their Bengali possessions only because the Gurkhas had been rebuffed by the ignorant ambans and therefore felt no loyalty to the Qing.[64] In Wei's hands, then, the history of the Qing-Gurkha war was made to show that foreign powers (in this case the British in 1792) had played a major role in past Qing military victories and that the Qing themselves could have profited from loyal allies (the Gurkhas in 1840) if they had a fuller understanding of world affairs. To place this lesson in relief, Wei muted all references to mistrust between the Qing and Nepal evident in decades of frontier memorials and studiously ignored the refusal of Qianlong, Jiaqing, and Daoguang to aid the Gurkhas.

If Wei molded history to fit his policies, and not vice versa, then what was the genesis of his strategy? As early as his 1840 interview with Anstruther, Wei had recognized that Bengal and Bombay were of overwhelming financial and military importance for the British empire, but he was far from being the only Chinese observer to realize this. Nor was he alone in realizing that the Gurkha-Pileng rivalry was relevant to coastal affairs. In 1840 the ambans in Lhasa knew (*pace* Wei) that the Gurkhas were accusing the Pileng of attacking the coast of China, meaning that the Pileng were either the English themselves or an ally. Once Wei gained access to the memorials sent from Tibet during the Opium War he would likewise have appreciated the link. What made Wei's perspective unique, however, was that he tied together these two strands of information and pointed out that the Gurkhas were offering to attack the region known on the coast as Bengal, the single richest British imperial holding. This put their proposal in a very different light, because it meant that the core of British power in Asia was now within reach, and that Qing strategists could contemplate offensive as well as defensive measures. Such connections made Wei's outlook more than the sum of its parts.

Wei first advocated arranging a direct assault on Bengal in a historical essay, the "Record of the Qianlong-era Conquest of the Gurkhas" ("Qianlong zheng Guo'erka ji"), in the *Shengwu ji*. As Wei later realized that other states could be used to a similar purpose, this kernel sprouted into the idea of a grand multilateral alliance against the British. Translated sources given him by Lin Zexu revealed that the Anglo-Russian rivalry over Afghanistan (a major topic in the English-language press of the time) was analogous to the Anglo-Gurkha rivalry in the Himalayas. A close analysis of Wei's writings in the *Shengwu ji* confirms that his strategic interest in Russia was an offshoot of interest in the Gurkhas, and his interest in an alliance with European maritime powers was closely related to his proposed alliance with Russia. In his earliest formulation, Wei had argued that the British were on the verge of collapse. Nepal paid tribute (so he then understood) to Russia and the Qing, both states fighting British India. Because the British had overreached themselves by taking on two enemies at once, the Gurkhas wished to take advantage of their vulnerability by striking at the very core of British revenue and power, the territory Wei viewed as the primary source of the men and ships invading China. Thus, a Qing-sponsored Gurkha invasion would "trouble their fertile frontiers, strike while their forces are elsewhere, involve them in internal difficulties, and cause the Westerners to lose the basis of their wealth and power and become helpless." Russia's participation could be cemented by allowing it to trade at Guangzhou, which would naturally lead it to ally with France and America as a maritime bloc hostile to Britain's trading dominance. In that way, foreign support would also block British vessels from reaching China.[65]

In short, Wei's initial strategic plan was Gurkha-centric, giving only cursory attention to Russia's strategic position in a short commentary appended to the text. Kanda Nobuo has shown that these early proposals were included in the undated preliminary printing of the *Shengwu ji*. A few months later, Wei issued an additional, related essay in the 1842 (DG22/7) edition of the work.[66] This piece, "Supplemental Record on the Gurkhas" ("Kuo'erka fuji"), revealed an elaboration of Wei's thinking with new evidence to defend it. Wei was concerned that "the reader might consider that my discussion of using foreigners to attack foreigners in my previous essay was too impractical, and not examine its details."[67] Despite its title, Wei's focus in this second essay was not the Gurkhas but essentially how Anglo-Russian tension in Afghanistan could be turned to the Qing's advantage. At the end of it, he reproduced one of the newspaper articles translated under Lin's direction that explained recent events in that rivalry. Entitling this piece "Supplementary Record on the Gurkhas" shows that his proposed alliance with Russia was simply an extension of the Gurkha archetype. Only in later editions did Wei change the title to the more appropriate "Supplementary Record on Russia" ("Eluosi fuji") and move it to the section on Qing-Russian relations.[68] As the contemporary reader Chen Li (1810–1882) acutely observed of Wei's argument for alliances, "Mr. Wei's advancing this theory derives directly from a single petition by the Gurkhas."[69]

Qing participation in the Great Game as a Russian ally had already been mooted in British newspapers on the Chinese coast between 1839 and 1840, during their extensive coverage of the invasion of Afghanistan. Lin Zexu himself does not seem to have been influenced by these articles, leaving Wei to elucidate their implications. As the English had expanded northwest from Hindustan along the Indus, Wei explained, the Russians had simultaneously pushed southward from the Caspian. Consequently, the two empires were vying for control over the independent Islamic states between them. Tensions had escalated when Shah Shuja (Sha Suye) sought British aid against the Afghans (Afuyanni), leading the British to mobilize troops from their

Indian possessions. Russia was willing to aid Britain's foes to get nearer the rich British territories in India. The result was a proxy war in which the two sides were separated only by the Hindu Kush (Xingdu geshi). As proof that Russia would ally with the Qing against British India, Wei quoted a passage from an English newspaper that claimed the Russians wanted China to support their attack on India and arrange for Burma to participate.[70]

There was nothing new, Wei contended, in the Qing empire basing its foreign relations on close coordination with other countries. Qianlong, he elaborated, had conquered the Junghars because he was open to lending military support to Amursana (although his policy ended in conflict between the two men). Earlier, Kangxi had used the Dutch as intermediaries to contact Russia and forestall the possibility that it might ally with the Junghars. Kangxi and Qianlong boldly engaged in long-distance campaigns and diplomacy because a detailed knowledge of foreign conditions made them familiar with the circumstances of their enemies. Their successes, in turn, built up prestige for the dynasty that could now make Russia and Nepal willing allies of the Qing who "await our orders, and share in our hatred of the enemy. This is what is meant by saying 'When the empire possesses the Way, defense lies with foreign peoples': when we attack they will answer the call; when our might is established then our orders will be carried out, and when the opportunity comes they will be joined to us utterly."[71]

Wei's own suggestions were therefore putatively adaptations of strategies used with great success by past Qing rulers. Qianlong's war with Burma was adduced as evidence:

> It is the nature of savages to fear might more than they embrace virtue, to fear local recruits (*tuyong*) along the frontier more than they fear official troops, *and also to fear the strength of their neighbors more than they fear China*. . . . Once [the Burmese] heard that both Jinchuan peoples had been conquered they were terrified and requested to pay tribute; when they again heard that Siam had been enfeoffed and paid us due respect they asked to serve us; when they heard further that Siam had close relations with China they curried favor and paid tribute even when it was not due.[72]

Burma's supposed change of behavior in the face of Qing-Siamese relations had a historical precedent:

> In the Wanli period of the former Ming the governor of Yunnan, Chen Yongbin, made an agreement with Siam to attack Burma from two sides, and the country was almost overthrown; Li Dingguo also made an agree-

ment with Siam and the Gula general to attack Burma from two sides. This [Burmese reaction in the Qing period] is caution based on past occurrences, and a fear of acute disasters coming from their neighbor—from this the great utility of Siam can be known.[73]

For Wei, alliances with foreign powers were necessary because Qing forces were in certain contexts inherently weak. In Burma, "China (Zhongguo) dispatched its army in the tenth month and had to call it back in the second month to avoid disease, and it was difficult under these conditions to destroy a state of several thousand *li* in the span of five months. For this reason they were arrogant and stubborn, and gathered their forces to vigorously undertake their futile resistance."[74] Burma was brought under control only in the face of Siamese pressure from the opposite direction. In his frank acknowledgment that Qing forces could sometimes be outperformed by foreign troops, Wei was stating what the court would not publicly admit.

In short, Wei presented Qing policy toward Burma as a model for that toward British India, placing Russia and Nepal in the role once played (in his view) by Siam:

> In regard to the effectiveness of having foreigners attack other foreigners, a shortsighted person might view it as an impractical plan. Yet when Siam was enfeoffed in the Qianlong and Jiaqing periods, that was enough to control Burma to its west and Annam to its east. A master *go* player can save a game from being lost with one sudden move; how much the more so can we use our central position controlling outside affairs in order to restrain foreigners with their numerous feuding entanglements?[75]

Wei's interpretation of Qianlong's policy in Siam was not entirely wide of the mark. The emperor had been well aware that foreign polities had their interests, and that these could coincide with his own. However, Qianlong had also recognized the pitfalls of trying to exploit this harmony of interests, above all the possibility that an explicit agreement to take concerted action might lead foreign states to become impertinent and unmanageable. In the case of Siam, as noted in Chapter Five, he had been willing to give Phraya Taksin free rein to pursue his own goals but unequivocally repudiated the idea of making an arrangement to attack Burma from two sides (*jiagong*), arguing that any short-term benefit would be negated by a long-term loss in prestige. In an even more specific break with Wei's assessment, Qianlong had observed that foreign partners could safely campaign on the empire's behalf only if the Qing state could control them with troops on the ground:

"Although using barbarians (*manyi*) to attack barbarians in a strategy for controlling the frontier, it is necessary for Chinese forces to be able to reach the area [in question] and control things appropriately—only then are conditions sufficient for it to be effective."[76] On the Himalayan frontier as well, the Qing court had routinely declined involvement in "private" Gurkha quarrels. Only by ignoring these policy statements was Wei able to claim his seemingly novel grand alliance was in keeping with imperial precedent. As we shall see, most of Wei's critics retained Qianlong's skepticism about the military utility of foreign states.

The benefits and drawbacks of Wei Yuan's strategic ideas will not be debated here, although the judgment of contemporaries will be considered below. As with his geographic scholarship, Wei's importance as a geostrategist derived not from the extent to which his judgments were correct, but the unprecedented scale on which he drew together materials. For the first time in Qing history, a truly global strategy was being outlined. Having shown the full reach of Britain's empire, Wei attempted to respond in proportion. No longer could Qing policy-makers consider individual parts of the empire in isolation, solely on the basis of intelligence flowing from each region. Instead, it was necessary to see each of the empire's far-flung frontiers as one component in an integrated worldwide struggle, and formulate military plans at this level. In other words (although he shunned any hint of this) Wei argued that the ideal of splendid isolation pursued by Qianlong— the judgment that in balance disengagement from foreign political rivalries would better ensure the empire's security—no longer applied.

Three factors allowed Wei to break the frontier policy's monopoly on Qing strategic thought. Geographically, he blended almost all local outlooks into a total picture of the Qing empire's position, a prerequisite, as he himself boasted, for formulating his policy. Strategically, he recognized that the scale of foreign empires overmatched the reach and resources of his own state. Allies were thus needed to augment the empire's power, although the Qing state was to be the senior partner and prime mover. Finally, and just as important, Wei was able to express his ideas in private writings. Although he was intimately acquainted with high officials and had access to state documents and even prisoners of war, he nonetheless put forth his proposals outside the bureaucratic hierarchy and was therefore free to make radical suggestions without standing surety for their consequences with his life and career. At the very least, then, the Qing empire had one proponent of a foreign policy. How was this idea received?

Frontier Policy, Foreign Policy, and the Qing Empire, 1842–1860

Despite his contemporary and historical evidence, Wei's foreign policy failed to persuade most contemporaries. Even readers sympathetic to his aims drew back at his proposals to plunge the Qing empire into the vortex of global power politics. Significantly, almost all of the objections to this line of Wei's geopolitical thinking were based on pragmatic rather than ideological considerations. Of particular interest are those advanced by Chen Li. As a native of Guangzhou, he had witnessed the gravity of the foreign threat firsthand; as a scholar, he took an interest in geography and cartography, and may have personally edited Marques's world geography in the mid-1840s.[77] Chen had quickly gained access to a copy of the *Haiguo tuzhi* after its first publication in 1844 and was impressed by the systematic way it described foreign geography. He praised it as a "marvelous book," and even endorsed several of Wei's policy suggestions. Still, he detected errors so grave that if an official mistakenly adopted them, calamity would follow. These he first outlined in a letter to his patron Zhang Weiping, to whom Wei had sent a copy of his book, before sharing his views to the author in person.[78]

Chen's principal objection was to the idea of making alliances with foreign powers. Here he refuted Wei on two levels. First, Wei had misread current geopolitics. The Gurkhas had only offered to attack the British because they thought the Qing were powerful enough to defeat them; once they learned that China had sued for peace their attitude would surely change to scorn and they could hardly be expected to accept imperial orders. As for Russia, it had defied even Qianlong over his demands for Amursana's extradition, and would not be amenable to Chinese direction now. France and America had appeared to take a diplomatic interest in the Opium War only because of their own trade interests. Moreover, if they were capable of wresting India from British control they would already have done so, without waiting for China to suggest it. Ultimately it was of little consequence which European power ruled India, for they would all assuredly grow opium as the British had done, not ameliorating the Qing position.

Even if Wei was conceded his interpretations of current geopolitics, Chen continued, the whole idea of relying on foreign allies was flawed. Here his arguments mirrored those of Qianlong and Jiaqing. Foreigners might simply ignore China's bidding, shaming the Qing state. If they accepted but failed in battle, this would further harm the Qing position. If they won, they would pretend to have done China an enormous favor—despite having fought for selfish motives—and trouble would arise when their grasping demands could not be met. Finally, Wei's plan would fundamentally change the Qing state's approach to warfare beyond its frontiers. In the past, China had taken a neutral stance toward the quarrels between an aggressive Britain and its neighbors. If it now began to solicit attacks on the British without being willing to participate, it would justly earn the derision of its prospective allies. Wei, Chen wrote, was quite right to reject the view that the use of allies was intrinsically a sign of weakness. In fact, the opposite was true: only when China was strong could it safely try to give commands to foreign countries. Wei's own example of Siam being used to restrain Burma proved this. On this principle, Chen argued that the Qing government needed to recoup its strength by improving internal governance, not squander it on elaborate strategic plans, just as an exhausted man should take rest and medicine instead of going off to fight.[79]

Xu Jiyu, who shared many of Wei's geostrategic insights, also opposed an alliance with the Gurkhas. Although his 1848 *Yinghuan zhilüe* studiously avoided taking up matters of policy, his unpublished 1844 first draft was less reticent. There he recounted the history of imperialism in India, explaining that the British and other Europeans had first bought coastal territories and built ports, while "India was foolish and did not resist them." Eventually the English captured most coastal territories and coerced other Indian states into serving them.[80] England, Xu informed his readers, gained most of its soldiers and the majority of its revenue from India, resources raised by the sale of India's produce to China. Like Wei, Xu realized the Gurkhas coveted rich and fertile India, and had recently been fighting the Pileng, a reference to a part of British-controlled Bengal. Despite this, Xu endorsed the wisdom of the court and ambans in rejecting the Gurkhas' requests for aid. As he put it, "under the pretext of being helpful and obedient, [the Gurkhas] repeatedly asked to borrow materiel, but if one estimates their strength and resourcefulness they are no match for the English; moreover, they are by nature savage and treacherous, so if they became rich and strong they would be even more difficult to keep under control." He praised the court's refusal to help them.[81] Xu was at this time the third highest official in Fujian province and according to some accounts had been commissioned by the emperor himself to study foreign geography; this passage should be read as a defense of official policy against those who saw the Gurkha offer to attack the Pileng as a lost opportunity.[82] Although Xu equaled Wei in his familiarity with world geopolitics, he remained for pragmatic reasons deeply skeptical of alliances.

Other high coastal officials around this time also denied the wisdom of seeking alliances with foreign powers. Asked to respond to the proposal that the Qing rely on foreign countries to "discipline" the English, Liang-Guang governor-general Qi-ying cautioned against the idea on the grounds that foreign conditions were inherently unpredictable and the Qing state was currently weak. In the past, he memorialized, China had attempted to use foreigners only when it had the strength to keep them under control. Without such capacity, this strategy was dangerous. France was the most powerful potential rival of the English in the West, but it was distant and could never be controlled effectively (a worry Qianlong had harbored about Siam). If the French, doing the Qing's bidding, were defeated in battle, this would make future war with the British more likely; if they won, they would assuredly presume upon their victory to make insatiable demands on China, and become even harder to manage than they were at present.[83]

By the time the *Arrow* or Second Opium War with Britain and France broke out several years later, Qing officials were wary about planning strategy based on incoming intelligence about foreign events. In 1857, the second year of the war, parts of India revolted against British rule. This seemed to fulfill predictions made during the first Opium War about British vulnerability, and indeed the expeditionary force sent to assault China was diverted to shore up defenses on the subcontinent, precisely the event anticipated in 1842. Yet by this time the governor-general at Guangzhou, Ye Mingchen, had little faith that Indian affairs would greatly influence the ultimate outcome of any Anglo-Chinese conflict. Of rumors that the British were fighting in Bengal and had no spare troops to reinforce their contingent in China, he commented that even if true the British would certainly resume the attack when the Indian troubles were over. Lin Zexu erred precisely because he heeded rumors that the British were incapable of waging war, and Ye had no intention of falling into the same trap.[84]

Not every high Qing official was dismissive of the principles Wei outlined, and ultimately his strategic plan was formally considered by the Grand Council. It reached there by a somewhat surprising route. In February 1860, with the Taiping Rebellion blazing in the south, the Xianfeng emperor deliberated on a report forwarded by the Ili general Jalafuntai. His subordinate, the Qing official supervising Russian trade in Ili, had met with

Russia's consul, and current affairs had come up in conversation. The Russian, having told him that the French and British were preparing an expeditionary force to avenge their 1859 defeat off Dagu Fort near Tianjin, proffered some unsolicited advice. In addition to strengthening its coastal defenses, the Qing should launch a preemptive strike on India. Certainly the British had forces defending that rich and crucial (*yaohai*) territory, but its inhabitants hated them and had long wished to rebel. It would be in China's interest to send forces into India via Yunnan and Tibet, while simultaneously dispatching a capable agent to travel ahead and coordinate with Indian rebels. On the remote chance that the Qing empire actually did capture India, it could grow rich, but even if it failed the mere attempt would petrify the British and force them to attend to affairs on the subcontinent, probably halting the impending hostilities. In short, this Russian officer was suggesting to China precisely the same strategy—using the threat of external invasion to trigger an internal uprising—that worried British strategists in the era of the Great Game.[85]

Evidently this Russian diplomat, the eminent scholar of Manchu and Chinese Ivan Il'ich Zakharov (1817–1885), was persuasive. In a twist of fate, he had arrived in China in 1840 as a junior member of the ecclesiastical mission accused in a British newspaper of attempting to incite China against British India. That article, translated by Lin, was later cited by Wei Yuan as evidence of Russia's hostility to England. In a first memorial responding to Zakharov's suggestions, Jalafuntai simply passed along his statements with the bland comment that a renewed Anglo-French assault could plausibly be expected. In a second, however, Jalafuntai made a more elaborate response. He began by explaining that he had considered the consul's remarks in view of "recorded Qing precedent, other writings on foreign affairs I chanced to see here and there, and coastal monthly magazines from years past." Wei Yuan's *Haiguo tuzhi* was probably one of the items indicated here, a possibility that becomes clear as Jalafuntai proceeded cautiously to endorse the Russian's ideas and elaborate on them. To the Ili general it seemed clear that Russia was a beneficiary of great generosity on the part of the Qing; America had recently exchanged treaties with China; and France, England's historical enemy, was not fundamentally hostile to China. The key to bringing these countries into an anti-British alliance, however, was India. England had recently seized that land, "the most fertile in the West," and collected tens of millions in annual revenue. From this point, Jalafuntai's analysis followed Wei very closely, pointing out that Russia had been greedily moving toward India from Central Asia, the Gurkhas would have invaded during the Opium War had not the ignorant ambans dissuaded them ("which commentators deeply regret"), and America, Burma, and other countries could also be allied to a Chinese force invading India via Yunnan and Tibet. Even without using Qing troops, multipronged attacks by these allies coupled with an embargo could neutralize the British. Such arrangements had precedents in the Qing period, and moreover the Qing would only have to guide the existing inclinations of their partners, which could not be construed as "asking for help" (*qiuzhu*).

Faced with a formal proposal to put Wei's plan into operation, the emperor displayed little enthusiasm. Although he conceded that Jalafuntai's memorial was detailed, it betrayed fundamental misapprehensions of the actual position of the empire. The Russians, far from showing loyalty or gratitude, had in fact sent Nikolai Ignat'ev to demand parts of Jilin. It was clear that Russia, England, and France were colluding. Even if it was possible for Russia to seize India from the British, China would not benefit; and it was quite possible that if Beijing suggested such a plan, Russia would leak it to the English. As for the Gurkhas, they were not only few and poor, but served the English and would never dare turn on them. Seeking their aid would simply open China up to extortion. If the Russian consul raised the issue again, he was to be told that China emphasized sincerity in its treatment of foreign countries, and would never provoke conflict by deceptive schemes. This virtuous response, it is clear, came from an appreciation of the limits of Qing power.[86]

The Qianlong- and Jiaqing-era policies reiterated by the court to justify standing aloof from foreign geopolitics were also endorsed by the reformist Feng Guifen (1809–1874). Feng was a careful reader of Wei's work and, like Chen, sympathetic to some of Wei's ideas. However, he strongly opposed the idea of using foreigners to attack foreigners. Because the Qing state was simply not accustomed to close interaction with Westerners, and linguistic barriers intruded between the two sides, a sudden shift toward intimacy with foreign powers was infeasible. Wei's mistake, according to Feng, was his belief that contemporary foreign conditions were basically analogous to the free-wheeling diplomacy of China before its imperial unification by the Qin (221–207 BC). Although Wei was closely acquainted with translated sources, he had failed to note the great differences between the two eras because he extravagantly fancied himself a successor to the "strategists" (*zonghengjia*) of the Warring States period. If China was to indulge in his complex schemes without internal strengthening, it would suffer defeat. Still, Feng's own foreign policy, based in large part on his understanding of the recent Crimean War, emphasized the desire of foreign empires to maintain a global balance of power. He believed the Qing empire could profit defensively from the same rivalries Wei hoped to exploit through warfare.[87]

Wei Yuan in Perspective

Assessments of Wei Yuan's ideas about the place of the Qing empire in the contemporary world have varied strikingly. For many, Wei's attention to global geography and advocacy of a vigorous response to the foreign threat made him a progenitor of the Self-strengthening Movement, which gathered pace after 1860, and thus a pioneer in a new and important stage of Chinese political and intellectual history.[88] Certainly, Wei's worldview was in unprecedented alignment with the assumptions and practices of contemporary European empires. His fear of the British as the dominant power in Eurasia was precisely the attitude many non-Qing observers had been trying to impress upon Beijing since the 1790s; his advocacy of engagement with allies who shared the same strategic goals, and his belief in the effectiveness of a direct strike on India from the north, put him on common ground with at least some Russian, Nepali, and British geo-strategists. More than any other Qing thinker of the 1840s, Wei saw his empire's geopolitical predicament in terms that Western observers could endorse. Yet there is reason to pause before labeling Wei "modern." The individual elements informing his worldview—the maps he consulted, many of his written sources, the idea of an alliance with Nepal, his awareness that India supplied Britain with troops and revenue—were available decades before Wei wrote, and some much earlier. What radically new element suddenly reassembled this mass of material into something "modern"?

Other scholars have stressed the "traditional" elements of Wei Yuan's geopolitical worldview, particularly aspects of his strategic thinking that can be traced back to the Ming period or earlier. Wei certainly made use of existing scholarly techniques, pursued long-standing research agendas, and sought precedent in history. As a geographer, his concerns remained rooted in yan'ge methodology, and it was in this context that he used his translated material to greatest effect; as a strategist, he took care to argue that his ideas were fully compatible with earlier imperial policies, at least as he interpreted them. Yet it is equally necessary to pause before labeling him "traditional." Wei believed that his outlook superseded even those of his immediate predecessors. Although some today glibly claim that "using foreigners [or, if one prefers, barbarians] to fight foreigners" is an "old Chinese strategy," most Qing commentators found Wei's suggestions unnerving and misguided. Ideological ties binding tributary states to the Qing emperor, supposedly the cornerstone of China's "traditional" foreign relations, are virtually ignored in Wei's strategic arguments in favor of open calculations of pragmatic interest. Wei expected no one to fight without tangible reward, whether in revenge, money, or security. In this respect Wei was partially inheriting the strategic thinking of the eighteenth century—after all, the Qing court also ignored tributary ideology in its military planning, instead concentrating on a hard-headed calculus of self-interest—but his input to policy debates underway since at least the Qianlong period was nonetheless innovative, and taken as such.

Wei made several major contributions as a geographer and geostrategist. He drew connections across time and space on an unprecedented scale. By integrating systems of geographic nomenclature he was able to reconcile into a clearer picture worldviews that had once seemed incommensurable. With this, he could rewrite the equally fragmentary recent strategic history of the empire into a coherent narrative. Readers could see Britain rising through trade and conquest, above all in India, and track its outward expansion from that "Bengal bridgehead." From what had seemed a jumble of squabbles and petty rivalries, Wei drew out the broader logic of imperial expansion and showed how the British empire was a single geopolitical problem impinging simultaneously on multiple Qing frontiers, demanding a response of equivalent geographic reach. These contributions repudiated major principles guiding Qing foreign relations during the preceding century (disengagement from foreign geopolitics, neutrality, and bilateralism), but his intervention is only "modern" if currents of strategic thinking before 1840 were "traditional." If we take "traditional" to mean decisively influenced by ideological and cultural conceptions, this label does not fit. Far from being self-satisfied within a Sino-centric cocoon, Qing emperors were as nervous and paranoid as those ruling any other Eurasian empire. Far from seeking refuge in illusion and introspection, they were watchful and inquiring, and assumed in their policies and calculations that their neighbors would be guided by pragmatic self-interest. They placed virtually no weight on intangibles like loyalty arising from tributary status when predicting external developments.

Qing perspectives on the world before the 1840s differed from those prevailing in rival empires, and appeared obtuse to foreign observers, not because they were "traditionally" ideological but because they were predicated on a frontier policy that analyzed external developments in a segmented rather than integrated fashion. Synthesizing local outlooks took evidence that had been available to Qing officials and scholars before 1839 and revealed in it new connections and patterns. The significance of the Opium War was not that it forced the empire's leaders and literati to face a reality they had been willfully avoiding, but rather that it accelerated a process of discovery about British imperialism in Asia underway since the first decades of the nineteenth century. It would be wrong, then, to place Wei, his admirers, and his critics, along a teleological spectrum leading from the outmoded past to the "realistic" future. Wei's significance was to offer an alternative, but not inevitable, worldview.

The emergence of a foreign policy as an alternative perspective on the world was impelled by two factors. Global imperialism was a precondition for seeing the world as a single field of political rivalry. Before 1757 Qing activity in Inner Asia, from Tibet to Outer and Inner Mongolia, had been coordinated in response to the Junghar threat. When that danger evaporated, so too did the need to consider the realm's far-flung borders, or even long stretches of it, as forming a strategic unity. As new and larger empires began to operate on multiple Qing frontiers, to the point that by 1850 virtually the entire Qing frontier was encircled by territory under British or Russia influence, the need for a more integrated perspective became clear.

A second factor was a community of observers in the Qing empire whose worldview was comprehensive enough to track these external changes and free enough to debate their implications. The Qing state's formal modes of scholarship and bureaucratic procedures made official channels an unpropitious environment for fostering such a community. Ironically, by the 1840s authors like Wei Yuan became more centralized and synthesizing in their geographic and geopolitical outlook than the central state itself. To see this, we can compare Wei Yuan to Sungyūn. When Wei wrote the *Haiguo tuzhi* he held only a purchased clerkship and had never visited any Inner Asian frontier (or even Guangzhou). Sungyūn, by contrast, had negotiated with the Russians as the ranking official in Urga, escorted Macartney, administered Tibet, Guangdong, and Xinjiang, and had helped guide the empire's affairs as a Grand Councilor. He was also a prolific writer about frontier affairs. Yet it was Wei Yuan, far less familiar with actual frontier conditions, who was able to establish how each frontier was simply one part of a global game board of competition. This should give us pause. However much we may admire Wei's acumen, something was lost as well as gained in moving from a frontier to a foreign policy. Excessive centralization might not necessarily appear desirable to those with intimate experience of actual frontier conditions. In adapting to one reality, there was the danger of losing sight of another.

Conclusion
Between Frontier Policy and Foreign Policy

By the 1840s developments in geographic and geostrategic thought allowed a foreign policy to emerge as an alternative to the previously dominant frontier policy. In its earliest form, this foreign policy was not necessarily more realistic or effective than frontier policy, nor did it replace it in the worldviews of most officials or private observers. Tracing the evolving relationship between these two approaches after 1860 falls beyond the boundaries of this study, nor can the brief space available do justice to the political upheavals, administrative innovations, technological advances, ideological shifts, and greater intimacy with the political, economic, and cultural forces of Western imperialism characterizing the decades after 1860. Rather, it concludes by raising questions about the subsequent relationship between frontier and foreign policy, suggested by the trajectory it has described.

An enduring advantage of frontier policy was the attention it gave to local conditions on specific sectors of the empire's borderlands: weighing the resources of the central state against obstacles of terrain and climate, and precedents implicit in the history of Beijing's relationship to local elites and neighboring foreign peoples. A frontier policy favored the cautious maintenance of equilibrium, and this became especially attractive after the Taiping Rebellion, erupting in 1851, threatened to shatter the court's control over Xinjiang and Tibet. With its military and financial resources diverted elsewhere, neighboring states like Nepal and Khoqand menacing the border, and grave difficulties of communication, even maintaining something like the status quo would have been a great accomplishment. Bold moves to counter the less immediate threat of Russian or British imperialism were beyond contemplation. Moreover, especially before 1860 the pillars of a frontier policy, though wobbly, remained upright. Geographically, local informants remained crucial for intelligence gathering. Strategically, there was good reason to doubt the wisdom of trusting foreign allies. Bureaucrats, facing a surfeit of individual problems, had little appetite for the sweeping, abstract commentary now common among private authors.

Even so, a pure frontier policy was no longer possible after 1842. Given the reach of the British and Russian empires across multiple frontiers, maritime and Inner Asian affairs could no longer be considered in mutual isolation. Even cautious defensive measures required attention to a web of geopolitics reaching from Ili to Shanghai. The stirrings of this new approach, evident during the Opium War when the court tried to gauge the proximity of Tibet and Xinjiang to the British, grew stronger thereafter. A comparatively minor crisis that unfolded in 1846 illustrates this shift.

By the early 1840s, the only genuinely independent, militarily formidable state beyond British rule on the Indian subcontinent was that built in the Punjab by the Sikh ruler Ranjit Singh. With his death in 1839, and that of his son and grandson the following year, this state became unstable, and by 1845 it was at war with British India. A settlement the following year effectively curtailed its independence. One of its nominal vassals, Gulab Singh, had earlier conquered Ladakh and attempted to annex western Tibet. Having courted the British during the war, his reward was to have his territories, ceded by the defeated Sikh government to the Company, returned (minus certain strategic corridors) to his control. In the process, British India gained the right to determine the boundary between this new Dogra kingdom and Qing Tibet.[1]

British victory in the Punjab, like previous upheavals on the Indian subcontinent, reverberated on several Qing frontiers. In Xinjiang, it became pertinent to the court's deliberations over Russian requests to trade at Kashgar. As officials there pointed out, the English, "termed in Muslim speech the Pailang [i.e., Farangi]," had formerly neighbored Yindi (as the Punjab had been called in Altishahr since at least 1820), and had now conquered it. Kashgar was therefore accessible to them from the south, and if Russians were granted trade rights the English would surely seek the same privileges.[2] This fear was prescient, for with Ladakh under their protection the British indeed wished to expand India-Xinjiang trade.[3]

More direct consequences were felt in Tibet. The Gurkhas realized that the conquest of the state built by Ranjit Singh boded ill for their ability to stay autonomous of Calcutta. As early as January 1846, while the war was ongoing, the Gurkha ruler wrote to the ambans in Lhasa that his agents had informed him of a recent British victory over the Senba (i.e., Sikhs). If they fell, he warned, the British would look onward to Qing territory; already they had (he claimed) offered him British troops to help invade Tibet. The Nepali ruler had naturally declined this offer, and requested Qing aid to fend off their mutual enemy. Adhering to fixed policy, the ambans offered none.[4]

Geographically, this letter marked a watershed in Qing official correspondence. No memorial submitted from Tibet, even those during and immediately after the Opium War, had ever explicitly identified the Pileng with the English (Yingjili). Now, the Chinese translation of the Nepali raja's letter referred only to the Yingjili (although the ambans, in their reply, continued to refer to the Pileng). This shift was helped by the arrival of new informants. Around the start of 1846, two French missionaries had arrived in Lhasa from Mongolia, the celebrated Joseph Gabet and Régis-Evariste Huc, who had studied Mongolian, Manchu, and a smattering of Tibetan in addition to Chinese. Already in Gansu they had met a Tibetan reincarnate lama who asked if they were "Péling" of "Galgata," and many in Lhasa ascribed to them the same identity.[5] Having these missionaries at hand when he received the Gurkha ruler's letter, the amban Kišan deposed them on the subject. Gabet gave the fullest explanation, explaining: "Pileng is Yingjili; these are the same place. This is because in Tibetan foreign countries are called *qileng* [Tib., *phyi-gling*]; *qi* [*phyi*] means 'outer,' and it is corruptly written *pileng*; this is not the name of a country.[6] The place is called the country of Yingjili, and the people are called Anggele [*anglais*]." Kišan accepted this identification, adding that Senba (Tib., Seng-pa) was said by Muslim merchants in Tibet to be "a place subject to the western route of Hindustan."[7]

Around the same time it reached Tibet, news from the Punjabi battlefront also arrived in the Pearl River delta. In 1846, Qi-ying, governor-general of Liang-Guang and the official managing the empire's relations with Britain, memorialized that English newspapers reported a victory over a part of India called the country of Saige, although the import of this news was not immediately apparent.[8] More information was demanded, and Qi-ying was able to corroborate this report by a letter from J. F. Davis, the governor of Hong Kong and principal diplomatic representative to China, and inquiries among Portuguese and Americans.[9]

Soon, the links between the Tibetan and maritime frontiers became apparent. In the summer of 1846, British India deputed commissioners to survey the border between Dogra Ladakh and Qing Tibet. The governor-general of British India sent two letters to Qing authorities, one to Lhasa and the other to Qi-ying at Guangzhou. Almost simultaneously, the Qing court received memorials on the topic from its officials in these two widely separated cities. Early in 1847, Qi-ying reported Davis's claims that the English had conquered the Xike, seized the territory of Kashmir (Jiazhimi'er), next to Tibet, and wished to define the border. Qi-ying parried this demand, replying that the English could not trade with Tibet because they had the right to visit only the five ports outlined in the Treaty of Nanjing.[10] Sending his subordinates to inquire among Westerners, Qi-ying was further able to ascertain that Xike was the same as Saige, a place in northwest India about 2,000 *li* from Tibet, and gained a somewhat garbled account of affairs in the region. Negotiations with Davis dragged on in Guangzhou.[11]

Less than a week after learning of Davis's letter via Guangzhou, the Qing court confronted the same issue via a memorial from Kišan in Lhasa. Tibetan officials in Gartok, he reported, had received an incomprehensible letter from the Pileng, whom he recognized to be the English. The messenger explained orally that the Pileng had conquered the Senba and seized Ladakh and Kashmir (Keshimi'er). They therefore wanted the Tibetan authorities to send a delegation to negotiate a trade treaty.[12] Tibetan agents sent to the border with Ladakh reported that the Pileng indeed now ruled much former Senba territory, including Kashmir.

The Daoguang emperor faced this situation by trying to change policy as little as possible, hoping to insulate Tibet from British India and channel relations to the coast. Unlike Wei Yuan, he saw no strategic advantage in the overland proximity of the two empires. Yet by the mid-1840s crucial changes had occurred. It was clear that the Qing court needed to coordinate the lexicons in use in various regions, and this was no longer difficult. As the emperor and Grand Council commented on the Tibetan border question, "There are many kinds of foreigners. The Pileng are the English. The Senba are what Davis calls the Xike. Keshimi'er is Jiazhimi'er."[13] To be sure, local lexicons persisted: the Xike, Saige, Xiguo, Yindi, and Senba all appeared in Chinese documents after 1840 as references to the Sikh state in the Punjab. "Pileng" continued to be used in Tibet. But whereas in the past such terminological discrepancies had proved almost impossible to overcome, the Qing state was now able to determine in broad outline, with reference to standard terms like Yingjili and Yindu, how regional worldviews fit into an integrated picture of foreign politics. Multiple sources of intelligence, once virtually incommensurable, were now coordinated and interpreted with relative ease even if certain details remained problematic. Even if the late Qing state remained largely defensive in its policy outlook, it could not ignore the need to coordinate policy across multiple frontiers.

From one perspective, it is possible to see the history of Qing foreign relations in later decades as the inexorable intensification of a coordinated foreign policy, buttressed by new institutions. The founding of the Zongli Yamen in 1861 and its increasingly sophisticated diplomatic apparatus drew an unprecedented wealth of perspectives to central observers and underscored the need to view policy through the widest possible lens. Indeed, one of the arguments justifying the establishment of the Zongli Yamen was that foreign empires were active on so many sites along the coast that it was no longer tenable for individual territorial officials to manage them in the zone under their jurisdiction under loose Grand Council oversight. As early as 1856, the court had at its disposal the *Chouban yiwu shimo*, a digest of cases concerning Western imperialism from maritime and Inner Asian frontiers. After 1861, the Zongli Yamen improved lateral communication among imperial officials as they dealt with the same foreign states in different regions.[14] Coordination became more complex as diplomats began to be stationed abroad in the 1870s and the Yamen became a central node in China's domestic and international telegraph network in the 1880s.[15] Compared to the frontier official–Grand Council dialogues of the period before 1840, the policy-making of the Qing central state drew upon more sources. Further entrenching the dominance of this centralized perspective was the presence in Beijing of Western legations, which complemented internal information sources by drawing the court's attention to incidents and problems on all corners of the frontier. Episodes like the famous 1874–1875 debate over the priority of maritime or Inner Asian defense, in which the two protagonists, Li Hongzhang (1823–1901) and Zuo Zongtang (1812–1885), showed they were aware these two spheres were intimately linked, and the Ili Crisis (1879–1881), in which diplomats reporting to Beijing from abroad settled the fate of an Inner Asian frontier, demonstrated that localized frontier policies were obsolete by the 1870s.[16] In an age of large-scale imperialism, the defense of the realm was a single problem with many interconnected facets, not a plethora of unconnected episodes.

From another perspective, however, the period after 1860 saw a diminution of central control over the empire's borderlands. The stresses of rebellion between the 1850s and 1870s had undermined the power of the Qing state over its Inner Asian frontiers. If this power was substantially restored in Xinjiang by the 1880s, it remained weak in Tibet and Mongolia until the radical state-building program of the post-1900 "New Policies" provoked open conflict between the court and indigenous elites.

More research needs to be done on the way information circulation had a differential impact on various groups within the Qing empire between 1860 and 1911 as they interpreted how external trends impinged upon the continued viability of its internal political order. As this study has shown, members of the Han Chinese literati elite were the first to form a global picture of European imperialism and to argue that the Qing empire could best counter this threat by coordinated activities on each frontier. After 1860, they increasingly dominated the military and diplomatic councils of the Qing state. To what extent did the newly integral worldview of Han Chinese officials discredit policies that had diffused power and thereby sustained local political compromises in earlier periods? To what extent did this shift in outlook drive a wedge between the priorities of Han Chinese elites and indigenous aristocratic and clerical groups holding power in Inner Asia? This raises several questions about which we know little: Through what sources of information did Mongol, Tibetan, and eastern Turkestani elites come to understand European imperialism near the Qing frontier? When interpreting this information, for the interests of what political community were they concerned, and how far did this community overlap with that which Han Chinese elites believed themselves to represent?

It is premature to associate non-Han elites in the late Qing with the continuation of a frontier policy centered on the interests of a sub-imperial unit, diverging more and more from the empire-wide foreign policy outlook of the elite in Beijing. Still, it can be hypothesized that a diminished sensitivity to local perspectives in pursuit of a foreign policy designed to counter Western imperialism played some part in the upheavals within the Qing realm in its last decades. At least by the end of the Qing, the acuity of the foreign threat seemed for some to justify the attempt to raise a more homogenous administrative structure firmly under central control, and indeed inaction in this sphere could imply that the dynasty was no longer effective. Yet those not persuaded that shifting global geopolitics warranted such a fundamental reconfiguration could also regard Beijing's assertion of greater control over the periphery as a breach of precedent, undermining the dynasty's right to rule. In both cases, recalibrating the influence of one centralized versus many localized perspectives in Qing policy-making touched upon dynastic legitimacy.

After the 1860s, then, new questions emerged. Did the Qing empire, in its foreign relations, have basic interests that were the same for all subjects, everywhere in the empire? If so, who legitimately determined them? Was this community of interest predicated on the continuation of the ruling Aisin Gioro house, or did it exist independently? If the latter, could common interests be used to enforce the unity of the Qing realm in a post-imperial age? Would those hoping to enforce this unity claim power partly on the basis of more perfect knowledge about global trends? These are questions central to the modern history of lands and peoples once subject to the Qing empire. The discovery of British India had profound implications.

Reference Matter

Character List

Adan 阿丹
A'erbi 阿爾璧
Afuyanni 阿付顏尼
Aiwuhan 愛烏罕
Aizitula 愛孜圖拉
Alusi 阿魯斯
An'eli 諳厄利
Anggele 昂格勒
Aza'er lama 阿雜爾喇嘛
Azanla 阿咱拉
Ba'erji 巴爾機
baitou 白頭
Balebu 巴勒布
Baleti 巴勒提
Ban'gala 班噶拉
Banggala 榜噶剌
Banggela 榜葛剌
Bao Shichen 包世臣
Baoshe 包社
bashou nanfang 把守南方
bei 備
beipan 背叛
beixiang 備詳
benguo 本國
benguo tuchan 本國土產

Benzhili 咘芝唎
bi xi diqiu quanxing 必悉地球全形
biao 表
Bilali 比喇里
bing 稟
bu gan huncheng Xiyang, suoyi bie zhi ye 不敢混稱西洋, 所以別之也
budui zhi chu 不對之處
bufang jianting-bingguan 不妨兼聽並觀
bushi 布施
buzhang 部長
Cai Xin 蔡新
Cangji 藏基
canzan dachen 參贊大臣
Chaina 釵那
chantou 纏頭
chantou Huihui Kaqi Bacha 纏頭徊徊卡契八㗳
Chen Shangyi 陳尚義
Cheng Xunwo 程遜我
Cheng-de 成德
Chini 赤泥
chongji 重輯
chu 畜
chuanwen 傳聞
chuzi zhi ren 出資之人
cun[a] 存
cun[b] 寸
cun guang yiwen 存廣異聞
cun guang yiwen, yi wu buke ye 存廣異聞, 亦無不可也
cun zhi yi si kaozheng 存之以俟考證
Da Baitou 大白頭
da guo 大國
da matou 大馬頭
Da Xitian 大西天
Da Yingguo fanshuguo 大英國藩屬國
Da Yingguo xinjiang fanshuguo 大英國新疆蕃[sic]屬國

daduan 大段
daoyi fanqing 島夷番情
dayue Galigada ji xi Yingjili 大約噶哩噶達即係嘆咭唎
deshi ju bu ke wen 得失俱不可問
di 地
Dibo Suwo'erdang 第博蘇渥爾噹
Dilimali 咄哩嗎哩
Dimi 啲嘧
Dingjiyi 丁機宜
dizhong hai 地中海
dong Jiaga'er ji Azanla 東甲噶爾即阿咱喇
dongtu 東土
du 都
duoshi 多事
Eliyamu Mo'ergere 俄哩牙木莫爾格熱
Eluo'elesu 鄂羅厄勒素
Enatehe-guo 厄納特赫國
Enatekeke-guo 額納特珂克國
Eneitehei buluo 厄內忒黑部落
Enetehei 厄訥特黑
Eneteke-guo 厄訥特克國
Enong'ake 額農阿克
Entian 恩田
er guowang qian shi qianfu Wei-Zang 爾國王遣使前赴衛藏
E're'nang 誐惹曩
fabing xiangzhu 發兵相助
Fa'erxi 法而西
faliu 發流
Fang Wei 方煒
Fangdizheli 房低者里
fangge 方格
fangxiang 方向
fangyan Yindu yin ge shu 方言印度音各殊
fangyin chengming 方音稱名
fanhu 販戶

fanli 藩籬
Fanwen 梵文
fanyi jianghe guxi 番夷講和故習
fanyi sheng 繙譯生
fencuo 紛錯
fenguo 分國
fentu 分圖
Fo yiji 佛遺跡
Foguo 佛國
fu 附
gai yinlei er yan zhi 蓋引類而言之
gaibei 賅備
Gang-ga-le-ta-ze-xi 崗噶勒塔則西
gangji zhidu 綱紀制度
Gangjiao deng chu difang guanyuan 港腳等處地方官員
Gangjiao guizi 港腳鬼子
Gangmai 綱買
gedao wuhe yuchun zhi ren 各島烏合愚蠢之人
Geshita 戈什喀
Gewo'er Zhe'ernaili 格卧爾遮爾奈哩
gongshui 貢稅
gongsi 公司
gu 雇
gu lu cun zhi, bei cankao yan 姑錄存之，備參考焉
gu qi tu du wei ke ju 故其圖獨為可據
gu Xindu 古忻都
Guangdong suren 廣東俗人
gudiao 雇調
guiguo suoshu ge buluo 貴國所屬各部落
guiqi 貴戚
Guli 古里
Guligada 咕哩噶噠
Guo'erka 郭爾咯
guo'erna'er 果爾那爾
Guonai'er 果迺爾

guoren 國人
Gusini 古斯尼
hai 海
hailanda'er 海蘭達爾
haiwai chuanwen, nan yu de shi 海外傳聞, 難于得實
hang hai zhi Yue 航海至粵
hanlu 旱路
Hanren 漢人
Hanwen zhengyin 漢文正音
he 呵
He Guozong 何國宗
he zhi 核之
heinu 黑奴
heiren ji yuchun 黑人極愚蠢
heiyi 黑夷
hen 痕
Hendu 痕都
Hendu ji Yindu zhi zhuanyin 痕都即印度之轉音
Hendusitan yu 痕都斯坦玉
Honghai'er 紅孩兒
Honghuo'er 洪豁爾
Hongmao 紅毛
Hongmao linguo de ren 紅毛鄰國的人
huangmiao mokao 荒渺莫考
huanhai 寰海
Huihui 回回
Huijiang 回疆
Huijiang gebu 回疆各部
huitu juzou 繪圖具奏
Huiyu 回語
Hulumo 忽露摩
Hulumosi 忽魯謨斯
Huo-ji-si 霍集斯
ji xi Hongmao-guo 即係紅毛國
Jia'ergeda 加爾格打

Jiaga'er 甲噶兒
jiagong 夾攻
Jialajida 架喇咭叭
Jialeguda 加勒古大
Jialiquda jing 甲利屈搭京
Jiang Fan 江藩
Jiang Youxian 蔣攸銛
jianglun shiwu 講論事務
Jianrui ying 健銳營
jiaoduan 角端
Jiazhimi'er 加治彌耳
Jibin 罽賓
jie yi yangyan donghe 借以揚言恫喝
Jilibadi 幾哩巴底
jin ding 今訂
jingshu nabian 京屬那邊
jiuhe 糾合
jiwei beimiu 極為悖謬
jixi Da Xitian 極西大西天
Kabu'er 喀布爾
Kala Tubote 喀喇土伯特
kaozheng 考證
Keshimi'er Huimin 克什米爾回民
Kezhi 柯枝
kongxu 空虛
kou 口
Lakanawo 拉卡納窩
Langyaxiu 狼牙修
Langyaxu 狼牙須
li 里
Li Hongbin 李鴻賓
Liang Zhi 梁秩, zi Jinde 進德
lianluo 聯絡
lihe 離合
Liu Zhi 劉智

Lu Kun 盧坤
Ma Laichi 馬來遲
Ma'erta han Nabalachi 瑪爾塔汗納巴拉池
Maguaye 馬瓜野
Malaba 嗎辣吧
Malata-guo 嗎喇他國
Malunni 麻倫你
manchu xiangzheng 蠻觸相爭
Mandalasa 曼噠喇薩
mandili 滿第哩
Matala 馬塔拉
Matalaxi 瑪塔拉西
Menggao'er 蒙告爾
Mengjiala 孟加臘
Mengkala 孟咖喇
Mengliaola jiangjun 蒙了喇將軍
Mengmai 孟買
Mingjiaoliao 明絞簝
Mingyala 明呀喇
Minya 民呀
Misi Wanning 米斯萬寧
miuwei buzhi 謬為不知
miyao yiqing 秘要夷情
Molao guizi 嚹咾鬼子
Mosidang 莫斯黨
Mowo'er 莫臥爾
Mu'erqilapu 木爾齊喇普
Mu-li-kong 目莉唉
nan Jiaga'er 南甲噶爾
nan Jiaga'er zhi Dili bacha buluo 南甲噶爾之第里巴察部落
Nanhai 南海
Nanman 南蠻
Nanyang 南洋
Nanyizhi 南夷志
neicheng 內城

neidi 內地
neidi suoguan difang 內地所管地方
neikui 內潰
Neiting 內庭
Nibao'er 尼保爾
Niboli-guo 尼波利國
Nibu'er 尼布爾
Niegajinna 聶噶金那
Niyanbada 呢顏八達
niyi 逆夷
Nu 怒
Ouluoba 歐邏巴
Ouluoba ren yuanzhuan 歐羅巴人原譔
Ouriba 偶日巴
paitu 排圖
Panipate cheng 帕尼帕特城
Pengbai-guo 澎拜國
pianzhu yiguo 偏助一國
pihai 裨海
Pileng 披楞
Piluo-guo 毘羅國
qi dangyu shi yi goupan laogu 其黨羽實已鉤盤牢固
qiangxia xiezhi 強點脅制
Qianzhu 乾竺
Qiao Renjie 喬人傑
qileng 奇楞
qinli 親歷
qiuzhu 求助
quanchen 權臣
qubi 趨避
qunxiu 群咻
qunyi 羣夷
Sadaluda'er he 撒達魯達爾河
Saige 噻嘚
sanhe 三合

sanshang 散商
Senba 森巴
Sengqieluo 僧伽羅
Sha Suye 沙蘇野
shen 身
shen yi wei hen 深以為恨
Shendu 身毒
sheng 省
shengxi xiangtong 聲息相通
Shibanya 是班呀
Shili 嚩叻
Shizi-guo 獅/師 子國
shoubei 守備
Shuangying 雙英
shufan 屬藩
shuguo 屬國
shui 水
sidai 私帶
sishi 私事
sōshukoku 宗主國
su yu Tanggute butong wenwen 素與唐古忒不通聞問
sui qi siyuan 遂其私願
Sula 蘇剌/喇
Sula huizi 蘇喇犭回子
Suodang 鎖當
Suoli 瑣里
suoxia gedao 所轄各島
ta zuole haoshi yu Zhongguo junzhen 他做了好事與中國軍陣
tangbao 塘報
tangtang tianchao, dati an zai hu 堂堂天朝，大體安在乎
taohui zujia 逃回祖家
tiandi zhi da, he suo bu you; lu er cun zhi, yi zu yi guang wenyi ye 天地之大，何所不有；錄而存之，亦足以廣異聞也
Tianfang 天方
tianhua xinpi tuyu 添畫新闢土宇
Tianshun 天順

Tianzhu 天竺
Tianzhu-guo jie 天竺國界
Tianzhu-guo shangchuan 天竺國商船
Tianzhu jiao 天主教
Tianzhu xi Yingjili shuguo 天竺係噯咭唎屬國
Tianzhu zimu 天竺字母
Tiaozhi 條枝
Tieliboke 鐵里伯克
tingcong 聽從
tong jueyu wei linrang 通絕域為鄰壤
toucheng 投誠
toushun 投順
tu 圖
tuilun daoli 推論道理
Tumote 土默特
tunshi 吞噬
waifan 外藩
waifan buluo 外番部落
waifu 外府
waiyang 外洋
waiyi 外夷
Walanaxi 瓦拉那西
Wang Wenxiong 王文雄
Wangjiaola[a] 望絞喇
Wangjiaola[b] 網礁臘
Wangmai 網買
Wangmei 望嗊
Wangsuoluo 望娑羅
wanguo tu 萬國圖
wangyu 妄語
wei you jue 未由決
weituo 偽托
wen 溫
Wendusitan 溫都斯坦
Woqi'ertu suolin 斡齊爾圖瑣林

Woya 我呀
wu Yindu 五印度
wuke zhengyan 無可徵驗
xi cao Xiyang tuyin 悉操西洋土音
xi shi 西事
xi Tianzhu 西天竺
xian de wo xin 先得我心
xiangwei nagong 向未納貢
xiangzhu 相助
Xiao Lusong 小呂宋
Xiao Xiyang 小西洋
Xiao Xiyang Bengala dengchu shuguo difang 小西洋本噶拉等處屬國地方
Xiao Xiyang Hongmao linguo de ren 小西洋紅毛鄰國的人
xiege 斜格
Xi'eryang 細爾洋
Xifan-guo 西梵國
Xike 西刻
Xilan (shan) 錫蘭(山)
Xilinaga 西里納噶
Xilong 西壟
Xilun 西崙
Xilun dao 西倫島
Xi'nanhai 西南海
Xindi 新低
Xindu 忻/欣都
Xindusi 欣都思
Xindusitang 欣都斯塘
Xingdu geshi 興都哥士
xinken zhi di 新墾之地
Xinni, ji Maoer'dan 新尼, 即茅爾旦
Xinpu kemin 新埔客民
xinwen zhi 新聞紙
Xirong 西戎
Xiyang 西洋
Xiyang ren 西洋人

Xiyanghai 西洋海
Xiyindushidan 希印都士但
Xiyizhi 西夷志
xiyu 檄諭
Xiyu 西域
xizhi 檄知
Xundusi 遜都思
Yalin-guo 啞啉國
Yan Tingliang 嚴廷良
Yandushidan 咽嘟士丹
yang 洋
yan'ge 沿革
yangshang 洋商
yangyi 洋夷
yanhai-waiguo quantu 沿海外國全圖
yeyi 野夷
yi bei xingyuan 以備行轅
yi yan 一言
yi yutu he zhi 以輿圖核之
Yidaliya 意大里亞
yiduo 臆度
yijiao 異教
Yili jiu tu 伊犁舊圖
yimu 夷目
yin 印
Yindi 音底
Yindiya 印第亞
Yindu 印度
Yindu lianggong huo 印度良工夥
Yindu quanhai deng chu 印度全海等處
Yindu zhi Gangjiao shudi 印度之港腳屬地
Yindusitan 印都斯坦
Yingchili 膺吃黎
Yingdiya 應帝亞
yinghai 瀛海

Yingjili 英吉利/嘆咭唎
Yingjili Gangjiao baitou yi 嘆咭唎港脚白頭夷
Yingjili yi bing 嘆咭唎夷兵
Yingjili yiren jiaoyi zhi chu 嘆咭唎夷人交易之處
Yingjili-guo Mengjiala difang 嘆咭唎國嗑嗲唎地方
Yingjili-guo zhi xiu zhizezhe 嘆咭唎國之修職責者
yishi tongren 一視同仁
yiwen 異聞
Yixibaniya 以西把尼亞
you yan e'ren 猶言惡人
yu Guangdong bianjie pilian 與廣東邊界毗連
yuanlüe 遠略
yudi 輿地
yuehui 約會
Yuezhong caifang 粵中採訪
Yuezhong chuanwen 粵中傳聞
zai Mengliaola difang yingzhuo, qianlai chongshu 在嚎叮唎地方硬捉,前來充數
zai Zhonghua xibei difang, yu benguo haidao pilian 在中華西北地方,與本國海道毗連
Zawang A'erbutan tu 雜旺阿爾布灘圖
zenggai 增改
zewen 責問
Zeyilan 則意蘭
Zhaga'nata 扎噶納塔
Zhang Chao 張潮
Zhang Zongying 章宗瀛
zhanzhuan goude 展轉購得
zhaoya 爪牙
zhayao 詐邀
Zhebusa 哲布薩
zhida Guangdong bianjie 直達廣東邊界
Zhilalaba 治拉拉拔
Zhong hai 中海
Zhongguo Xizang 中國西藏
zhongtang 中堂

zhongtu daguo 中土大國
zhou[a] 州
zhou[b] 洲
Zhoushan 舟山
Zhu Gui 朱珪
zhushi zhi ren 主使之人
zi cao qi quan zhi guo 自操其權之國
zokukoku 屬國
zongdu 總督
zonghengjia 縱橫家
Zongle 宗泐
zujia 祖家
zushu qi shuo 祖述其說

Notes

Abbreviations

BL APAC	British Library, Asia, Pacific & Africa Collections
CBYWSM	*Chouban yiwu shimo*
CR	*The Chinese Repository*
FHA JJC LFZZ	First Historical Archives (Beijing), *Junjichu, Lufu zouzhe*
FHA JJC MWLF	First Historical Archives (Beijing), *Junjichu, Manwen lufu zouzhe*
GDTZ	*Guangdong tongzhi*
HGTZ1	Wei Yuan, *Haiguo tuzhi*, 1st ed.
HGTZ2	Wei Yuan, *Haiguo tuzhi*, 2nd ed.
KYJX	Yao Ying, *Kangyou jixing*
PDZGFL	*Pingding Zhunga'er fanglüe*
QDZSZD	*Qingdai Zangshi zoudu*
QDWJSL	*Qingdai waijiao shiliao*
QSL	*Qing shi lu* (Zhonghua shuju edition, *1985*)
RZH	*Jindai Zhongguo dui Xifang ji lieqiang renshi ziliao huibian*
SKQS	*(Yingyin Wenyuange) Siku quanshu*
SKZM	*Qinding Siku quanshu zongmu (zhengliben)*
XXSKQS	*Xuxiu Siku quanshu*
YZDS	*Yapian zhanzheng dang'an shiliao*

Introduction

1. *QSL* Taizong, 1:552 (42.6b).

2. The concept of an imperial "information order" is borrowed from Bayly, *Empire and Information*; for its application to the Qing empire, see Mosca, "Empire and the Circulation of Frontier Intelligence."

3. Fairbank's views were first set forth in the detailed 1941 study "On the Ch'ing Tribute System" (co-written with S. Y. Teng), and later outlined in a 1968 introductory essay, "A Preliminary Framework."

4. Fairbank, "Preliminary Framework," 11.
5. Fairbank, *Trade and Diplomacy*, 10–22.
6. Wills, *Embassies and Illusions*, 171.
7. Ibid., 179.
8. Polachek, *Inner Opium War*, 3.
9. Ibid., 203.
10. Needham, "Geography and Cartography"; Yee, "Traditional Chinese Cartography"; Smith, "Mapping China's World."
11. Smith, "Mapping China's World," 92.
12. Leonard (*Wei Yuan*, 96) argues that before the Opium War Qing geographic writings, especially the few works on the maritime world, were "largely ignored."
13. Fairbank's view of Qing rule over Inner Asia as basically Sino-centric ("Preliminary Framework," 3–4) was challenged in the 1960s by Farquhar ("The Origins of the Manchus' Mongolian Policy") and by Fletcher, who saw early Qing rulers as not yet "Chinese," and later ones as pragmatic ("China and Central Asia"). Wills later contrasted the "defensiveness" of Chinese officials on the coast with the "aggressiveness" of Mongol and Manchu officials governing Inner Asia ("Tribute, Defensiveness," 227). Only in the late 1990s, however, did Inner Asia come to have equal footing with the coast in the study of Qing foreign relations.
14. Historians who fall under the loose banner of "New Qing History" including Peter C. Perdue, Laura Hostetler, Joanna Waley-Cohen, and Evelyn S. Rawski, have drawn parallels between the Qing and other contemporary empires in Europe and Asia. Citations below.
15. Bartlett, *Monarchs and Ministers*, 120–21.
16. Perdue, *China Marches West*, 74.
17. Perdue, "Boundaries, Maps, and Movement," 264.
18. Mann Jones and Kuhn, "Dynastic Decline and the Roots of Rebellion."
19. Pomeranz, *Great Divergence*.
20. Newby, *Empire and the Khanate*, 9–10.
21. In *Qing Colonial Enterprise*, Hostetler argues that while in the eighteenth century the Qing state "was in a position to choose to be involved in the forefront of empire building using early modern technologies . . . this was no longer possible in the nineteenth century" (210–11); Rawski sees the "early-modern paradigm" as relevant specifically to the "Qing formation," that is to say primarily the seventeenth and eighteenth centuries ("The Qing Formation and the Early-Modern Period," 207). Waley-Cohen has remarked in regard to this development that Qing rulers were once "worthy competitors for the title of imperialists with the Western powers" but came later to be "all but overwhelmed" by them (*Sextants of Beijing*, 94).
22. Perdue, *China Marches West*, 547–51.
23. As Dai observes, the Burma war, unlike the Junghar campaigns, was not "on the overall empire building agenda" of the court, but rather a local conflict that got out of hand ("Disguised Defeat," 155).
24. Bayly, "First Age of Global Imperialism."

25. This struggle for alliances was not limited to Europe: evidence for it can also be found throughout the Muslim and Indic worlds, in the Ottoman empire, Persia, Mysore, the Sikh empire of Ranjit Singh, and Nepal, to name only a few examples.
26. Burke, *Social History of Knowledge*, 119.
27. Newby, *Empire and the Khanate*, ix.
28. See, for instance, Yapp, *Strategies of British India*.
29. Agoston, "Information, Ideology, and Limits of Imperial Policy," 76–77; Parker, *The Grand Strategy of Philip II*; and LeDonne, *The Grand Strategy of the Russian Empire, 1650–1831*.
30. Wills, "Contingent Connections," 177–79.
31. Morgan, "Persian Perceptions of Mongols and Europeans," 215.
32. McDermott, *Social History of the Chinese Book*, 163.
33. Elman, *Cultural History of Civil Examinations*, 276–77.
34. Rudolph, *Negotiated Power*, 88–90.
35. For approaches to this question, see Athar Ali, "The Evolution of the Perception of India"; Subrahmanyam, "On the Window That Was India."

Chapter One

1. This book deals with the way Qing scholars and officials studied territories not directly ruled by the Qing imperial government. The distinction between foreign and domestic territory was clear in Chinese historiography as early as the *Shi ji*, which discussed foreign peoples in its *liezhuan* ("biographies") section, and its successor, the *Han shu*, which described China's own administrative geography in a separate *zhi* ("treatise") section. Later standard histories and other historical genres generally observed a similar distinction.
2. Legge, *Shoo King*, 150.
3. Fracasso, "Shan hai ching," 357.
4. Lewis, *Construction of Space*, 249–52.
5. Ibid., 252–58.
6. On gazetteers, see Wilkinson, *Chinese History*, 152–58.
7. Zhu, *Yugong changjian*, 67:208 (12.25a–b).
8. Ibid., 67:208 (12.36a).
9. Ibid., 67:208–9 (12.26a–27a).
10. Hu, *Yugong zhuizhi*, 67:805–6 (18.24b–26a).
11. Schwartzberg, "Cosmographical Mapping," 335–36.
12. Sadakata, *Buddhist Cosmology*, 30–38.
13. Lü, "Fojiao shijieguan," 76–77.
14. Zürcher, *Buddhist Conquest*, 266.
15. Rao, *Rao Zongyi*, 7:258–59.
16. Dorofeeva-Lichtmann, "Yellow River Source."
17. Rao, *Rao Zongyi*, 7:259–60.
18. Muroga and Unno, "Buddhist World Map," 50–57.
19. Qian, "Shijia fangzhi bian," 422 (43.6a–7b).
20. Fuchs, *"Mongol Atlas" of China*, 3–11; Allsen, *Culture and Conquest*, 107–14.

21. Leslie and Wassel, "Arabic and Persian Sources," 92–93.
22. Ma, *Qingzhen zhinan*, 34 (2).
23. On Song, Yuan, and Ming maritime geography, see Park, "Delineation of a Coastline."
24. "Eastern" and "Western Ocean" seem to have been first used by Chen Dazhen in 1304 (Park, "Delineation of a Coastline," 148).
25. Miyazaki, "Nanyō o Tō-Seiyō ni wakatsu konkyo ni tsuite."
26. Yee, "Traditional Chinese Cartography," 171–75.
27. Luk, "Giulio Aleni's *Chih-fang wai chi*," 61.
28. Chu, "Trust, Instruments," 387. On the novelty of Jesuit cartography, see Ch'en, "Matteo Ricci's Contribution," 337–41.
29. Ch'en, "A Possible Source"; Aleni, *Zhifang wai ji*, 33; Mungello, *Curious Land*, 119–21.
30. D'Elia, "Recent Discoveries," 89–92.
31. Ch'en, "Matteo Ricci's Contribution," 347–49.
32. Zürcher, "Xu Guangqi and Buddhism," 165–66.
33. Yee, "Taking the World's Measure," 127; Smith, "Mapping China's World," 60.
34. Elman, *On Their Own Terms*, 57.
35. Elman, *From Philosophy to Philology*, 4.
36. Henderson, *Scripture, Canon*, 115.
37. Ibid., 77.
38. Hua, *Zhongguo dimingxue*, 292–95.
39. Ibid., 250.
40. Xu, *Yinghuan zhilüe, fanli*, 8.
41. Yu, *Yu Zhengxie quanji*, 2:227.
42. (*Qinding*) *Da Qing yitong zhi*, 2nd ed., 483:731 (424.1a).
43. *Gudai Nanhai diming*, 978–79; Miyazaki, "Rōgashū koku."
44. You, *Ming shi Waiguo zhuan*, 141 (5.4a).
45. Hummel, *Eminent Chinese*, 2:935–36.
46. You, *Waiguo zhuzhi ci*, "preface," 1.
47. Mao, *Huang Ming xiangxu lu*, 291 (5); Yan, *Shuyu zhouzi lu*, 312 (9).
48. Yan's source for a Xilan-Langyaxu link is not evident.
49. Yan, *Shuyu zhouzi lu*, 312 (9).
50. *Da Ming yitong zhi*, 2:1387 (90.21a).
51. *Ming shi*, 302:745 (326.1a).
52. *Gujin tushu jicheng Fangyu huibian*, 15:286.
53. Aleni, *Zhifang wai ji*, 58–59.
54. Lu, *Bahong yishi*, 1, 31–32, 34 (2).
55. *Da Ming yitong zhi*, 2: 1386 (90.19a).
56. Yan, *Shuyu zhouzi lu*, 385 (11).
57. Ibid., 2.
58. Luo, *Xianbin lu*, 1–2.
59. *Gujin tushu jicheng Fangyu huibian*, 15:13, 160, 290.
60. Zhu and Luo, *Guang yutu*, 388–89; 400–401 (2).

61. Smith, "Mapping China's World," 77–83; Ma, *Yugong tushuo*, 726. This fourth map copies one by Hu Wei (cf. *Yugong zhuizhi*, 67.251).
62. Smith, "Mapping China's World," 83.
63. Kuhn, *Structure of Scientific Revolutions*, 13.
64. Ibid., 17.
65. *SKZM*, 2:494 (69.18a).
66. *SKZM*, 2:474 (68.49a–b).
67. Teng, *Taiwan's Imagined Geography*, 22.
68. Shapin, *Social History of Truth*, 122–25.
69. Lu, *Bahong yishi*, preface, 1.
70. Ibid., *liyan*, 1.
71. *SKZM*, 2:534 (71.10b).
72. *SKZM*, 2:536 (71.15a–b).
73. *SKZM*, 2:534 (71.11b).
74. *SKZM*, 2:542 (71.27b).
75. *SKZM*, 2:531 (71.5b).
76. *SKZM*, 2:532 (71.7b).
77. *SKZM*, 2:538 (71.18b), 2:541 (71.24a).
78. Elman, *From Philosophy to Philology*, 101.
79. *Gu Hanyu changyongzi zidian*, 11.
80. Henderson has noted that for Qing astronomers "a certain indeterminacy is woven into the fabric of the cosmos, and a corresponding imprecision into man's knowledge of the world" (*Development and Decline*, 246). Qing geographers, however, rarely questioned the theoretical possibility of perfect knowledge.
81. Another reason for this tolerance, as Chu notes in regard to debates over the sphericity of the earth, was that geographic views were for scholars "nothing more than an intellectual opinion; one that would not critically influence their careers." Moreover, "no immediate decisions had to be made and no direct interests were involved" ("Trust, Instruments," 399).
82. Randles, "Classical Models."
83. Broc, *La Géographie de la Renaissance*, 18; Randles, "Classical Models," 38.
84. Edson, *The World Map*, 1–10.
85. Broc, *La Géographie de la Renaissance*, 19.
86. Flint, *Imaginative Landscape*, 116.
87. Parker, *Grand Strategy of Philip II*, 63–65.
88. Crane, *Mercator*, 119–20; Broc, *La Géographie de la Renaissance*, 51.
89. Jacob, "Mapping in the Mind," 41.
90. Kuhn, *Structure of Scientific Revolutions*, 35.
91. Jacob, "Mapping in the Mind," 35–39.
92. Ji, *Yueweicaotang*, 1150–51 (20).
93. Yule and Burnell, *Hobson-Jobson*, 433; Feng, *Xiyu diming*, 35; Bagchi, "Ancient Chinese Names of India," 371.
94. On expanding significance of Shendu and Tianzhu, see Mukherjee, "Shen-tu."

95. Xuanzang, *Da Tang Xiyu ji*, 63.
96. Bagchi is incorrect to assert that Yindu came to be considered the sole "correct" name for India after its introduction ("Ancient Chinese Names of India," 367).
97. For other names, see *Gudai Nanhai diming*, and Bagchi, "Ancient Chinese Names of India."
98. Bagchi, "Ancient Chinese Names of India," 375.
99. Sen, *Buddhism, Diplomacy*, 214.
100. For terms used in the Song and Yuan, see *Gudai Nanhai diming*, 951–52.
101. Enoki, "Tsung-lê's Mission."
102. Ray, *Trade and Diplomacy*, 78.
103. Ptak, "Yuan and Early Ming Notices," 148.
104. Aleni, *Zhifang wai ji*, 39; Unno, "Tō Jakubo oyobi Shō Yūjin," 102–4.
105. Foltz, "Uzbek Central Asia," 29–31; Yule and Burnell, *Hobson Jobson*, 570–71; Thackston, *Baburnama*, xlvi.
106. 110 Aleni, *Zhifang wai ji*, 44.
107. Ricci, *Qiankun tiyi*, 787:757 (1.3b); Harris, "Mission of Matteo Ricci," 92–99.
108. Ricci, *Il Mappamondo cinese*, plates 15, 19.
109. Harris, "Mission of Matteo Ricci," 65–66, 85–90.
110. Mish, "Creating an Image of Europe for China."
111. Luk, "Giulio Aleni's *Chih-fang wai chi*," 65–67.
112. Buglio, *Xifang yao ji*, "preface," 1.
113. Chu, "Trust, Instruments," 396–98.
114. Cited in Mish, "Creating an Image of Europe for China," original text, 5, translation, 31.
115. Brook, "Early Jesuits and the Late Ming Border," 28.
116. Ricci, *Il Mappamondo cinese*, plate 19.
117. Certain late Yuan and Ming sources did use the terms "Great Western Ocean" and "Small Western Ocean," perhaps influencing Ricci, but these earlier distinctions bore no connection to his usage. "Great Western Ocean" in pre-Jesuit sources referred to part of the Arabian Peninsula, lands that bordered the Jesuit "Small Western Ocean" (*Gudai Nanhai diming*, 140–41, 160–61).
118. *Ming shi*, 332 juan, 302:742–43 (326.22b–23a).
119. Ruggieri and Ricci, *Dicionário Português-Chinês*, 109b.
120. *Ming shi*, 332 juan, 302:742 (326.22a).
121. Zhang, *Waiguo ji*, 875.
122. *Ming shi*, 332 juan, 302:742 (326.22b).
123. *Da Qing yitong zhi*, 1st ed. (*ce* 120).
124. *GDTZYZ*, 564:658–59 (58.18a–20b).
125. *Qing shi lu* in the *Hanji dianzi wenxian ziliaoku* database (hanji.sinica.edu.tw; accessed Feb. 18, 2008).
126. Mei, "Lun Huihui li yu Xiyang li tongyi"; Hu, "Cosmopolitan Confucianism," paraphrases this passage (93–94).
127. Smith and Van Dyke, "Muslims in the Pearl River Delta," 7–9; Das Gupta, "India and the Indian Ocean in the Eighteenth Century," 192.

128. Gaubil, *Correspondance de Pékin*, 70.
129. *Kangxi chao Hanwen zhupi zouzhe huibian*, 7: 1148, 8:905–6.
130. Walravens, "Father Verbiest's Chinese World Map," 31–47.
131. *Aomen lishi ditu jingxuan*, 26–27, 30–31, 32–33, 42–43.
132. Fan Shouyi's *Shenjian lu* discussed only European geography. Fang, *Zhong-Xi jiaotong shi*, 2:856–62; *Handbook of Christianity*, 1:450–51.
133. *QSL KX*, 6:505 (253.8a).
134. Lombard-Salmon, "Un Chinois a Java (1729–1736)."
135. On Chen's life, see Ng, *Trade and Society*, 205–7.
136. Wang, *Lenglu wensou*, 212–14.
137. It seems possible that Chen Mao was one of the three Chinese agents sent from Xiamen to Madras by Shi Lang in 1688 (see Wills, *1688*, 286–87).
138. For Chen Mao's geographic reports, see *Huangchao wenxian tongkao*, 632:701 (33.28a–29a).
139. *Fujian tongzhi*, 8:4166–67 (229.4b–5a), and Chen, *Haiguo wenjian lu*, "preface."
140. *Guochao qixian*, 167:494–95 (284.41a–42b).
141. Chen's world map resembles a 1694 world map of Nicolas de Fer presented to Kangxi and later put into Chinese and Manchu: *Aomen lishi ditu jingxuan*, 26–27, 32–33.
142. Funakoshi emphasizes the Jesuit influence on Chen's work. His map indeed follows a European outline, but avoids Jesuit geographic conventions ("Zai Ka Iezusu kaishi no chizu sakusei to sono eikyō ni tsuite," 154, 162n57).
143. *Handbook of Christianity*, 1:518.
144. Chen, *Haiguo wenjian lu*, 23.
145. Yin and Zhang, *Aomen jilüe jiaozhu*, 142; a Fujianese sojourner in Java later in the century called the same part of India "coast" (*Gaoshe*) (Salmon, "Wang Dahai," 41).
146. Cf. Wangjiaola[a] used by Fujianese migrants to Java.
147. Yin and Zhang, *Aomen jilüe jiaozhu*, 142.
148. Ibid., 189.
149. Lipman, *Familiar Strangers*, 46–57.
150. Fletcher, "Naqshbandiyya in Northwest China," 15–16.
151. Ma, *Chaojin tuji*, 21.
152. Lipman, *Familiar Strangers*, 49.
153. Ben-Dor Benite, *Dao of Muhammad*, 63.
154. *Zhongguo Yisilan baike*, 556–57.
155. Ibid.
156. Lu, *Bahong yishi*, 16 (2); Liu, *Tianfang zhisheng shilu*, 1160 (19).
157. Liu, *Tianfang zhisheng shilu*, 1159 (19).
158. Ma, *Qingzhen zhinan*, 44.
159. Verbiest, *Kunyu tushuo*, 594:748.
160. For the map, see Ben-Dor Benite, *Dao of Muhammad*, plate I, 210; Leslie and Wassel, "Arabic and Persian Sources," 92–93.

161. Ma, *Qingzhen zhinan*, 44 (2).
162. Morrison, *Memoir of the Principal Occurrences*, 92.
163. Heissig, *Religions of Mongolia*, 24–35.
164. Huber, *Holy Land Reborn*, 118.
165. Bawden, *Mongol Chronicle Altan Tobči*, 109. For the dating, see 13.
166. Elverskog, *Our Great Qing*, 90–99; Lomi, *Menggu Bo'erjijite shi zupu*, 337.
167. Rozycki, *Mongol Elements*, 69; Norman, *Manchu-English Lexicon*, 76. Some Mongol sources call India "Hindkeg."
168. Tulišen, *Kōchū Iikiroku*, 48, 50.
169. The earliest Manchu translation of the *benji* of the *Yuan shi*, describing Chinggis's encounter with India, was completed in 1639 (Chase, "Status of the Manchu Language," 90–91). *Yuan shi*, 1:23 (1): "In this year [1224] the emperor reached the country of East India; a *jiaoduan* appeared and he returned victorious." Chinggis himself never campaigned in India, although in his lifetime Mongol forces reached as far as Multan, in modern Pakistan. The *Secret History* mistakenly stated that Chinggis entered India and pursued foes "as far as the middle of the country of the Hindus" (Rachewiltz, *Secret History*, 1:145, 2:964–65).
170. Elliott, "Whose Empire Shall It Be?" 46.
171. Zhang, *Waiguo ji*, 873.
172. Kowalewski in his *Dictionnaire mongol-russe-français* identifies Balaša as Maghada (2:1075). Adaramamad may perhaps refer to Haydar Muhammad (ca. 1500–1551), Chaghataid ruler of Kashmir.
173. *Kangxi jixia gewu*, 95.
174. Petech, *China and Tibet*, 66–90.
175. *Fuyuan dajiangjun Yun-ti zougao*, 250.
176. Jiao, *Xizang zhi*, 148–49.
177. *Da Qing yitong zhi*, 1st ed. (131, *Xizang* 7b).
178. Zhang, *Xizang jishu*, 65.
179. Xiao, *Xizang jianwen lu*, 784–85.
180. *Gujin tushu jicheng*, 22:193.
181. *Xining fu xinzhi*, 548–49 (21).
182. Chen, *Xiyu yiwen*, 95:130 (31b).
183. *QSL KX*, 6:820–21 (290.4b–5a). Dr. Hoong Teik Toh kindly supplied me the Tibetan. Cf. a similar passage in *Kangxi jixia gewu*, 111–12.
184. Mosca, "Qing China's Perspectives," 505–20.

Chapter Two

Portions of this chapter were previously published in "Hindustan as a Geographic and Political Concept in Qing Sources, 1700–1800," *China Report* (November 2011).
1. Guy, *Emperor's Four Treasuries*, and Enoki, "Researches in Chinese Turkestan."
2. Mou, "Lun Qingdai shixue," 71–76; cf. Huang, *Price of Having a Sage-Emperor*, 8–19.
3. Ho, "Qingdai qianqi junzhu," 171; Struve, *Ming-Qing Conflict*, 60.
4. Chase, "Status of the Manchu Language."

5. *Yuzhi Manzhu Menggu Hanzi sanhe qieyin Qingwenjian*, 234:6–7 (preface, 8b–10a).
6. Van Gulik, *Siddham*, 52–53.
7. Wang, "Tibetan Buddhism," 150–51.
8. *Yuding yinyun chanwei*, 240:9 (*fanli*, 1b).
9. *Qinding tongwen yuntong*.
10. Stary, "Unknown Chapter"; Zhuang, "'Dazangjing' Manwen yiben yanjiu," 47–54.
11. Huber, *Holy Land Reborn*, 174.
12. Rizvi, "Trans-Karakoram Trade," 27.
13. Levi, *Indian Diaspora*, 37.
14. Ibid., 177.
15. Athar Ali, *Mughal India*, 327–33; Fisher et al., *Himalayan Battleground*, 34–41.
16. QSL QL 14:289 (12a); Holzwarth, "Change in Pre-Colonial Times," 315–16.
17. Grevemeyer, *Herrschaft, Raub und Gegenseitigkeit*, 64–65.
18. Bamzai, *Culture and Political History of Kashmir*, 2:428.
19. Petech, "Notes on Ladakhi History," 222–24.
20. Qing activity in western Tibet and contact with Ladakh can be seen in *Zhongguo diyi lishi dang'an guan suocun Xizang he Zangshi dang'an mulu*, 32–37. For Ladakhi surveillance of Xinjiang before the Qing conquest, see Petech, "Notes on Ladakhi History," 222–27.
21. *QSL QL*, 16:244–45 (571, 7b–8a).
22. *QSL QL*, 16:297 (574: 11a).
23. *QSL QL*, 16:314 (575:11a).
24. *QSL QL*, 16:449 (582: 37b)
25. Saguchi, *Higashi Torukisutan*, 69.
26. *PDZGFL*, zhengbian, 359:348 (75:14a).
27. *QSL QL*, 16:581 (592:2b).
28. Saguchi, *Higashi Torukisutan*, 70.
29. Ibid., 72.
30. *Huangchao wenxian tongkao*, 638:734 (299:20b).
31. *Qing shi gao*, 48:14722 (529). The modern historian Zhuang Jifa also records that while Khwaja-i Jahan was besieged in Badakhshan, Hindustan had "sent someone to claim him by compulsion" (*Qing Gaozong shiquan*, 97).
32. Wei, *Shengwu ji*, 402:244 (4:26b).
33. Since the weakened Mughal empire was in no position to aid the khwajas, either these references were unfounded rumors (perhaps confusing Hindustan with Qunduz, "Hundusi" in Qing sources) or another power is indicated. If the latter, Ahmad Shah was the most likely candidate. Given that he was frequently in India in this period, and that references to "Afghans" and Ahmad Shah do not seem to occur in Qing sources until 1760, it seems at least possible that these early reports of an aggressive "Hindustan" actually indicate Ahmed Shah. If the khwajas were ultimately fleeing toward the Afghans, as is stated in one official source, but

hoping to meet Ahmad Shah in India, this may have confused Qing commentators (*Huangchao tongdian*, 643:946 [99:12a]).

34. *QSL* QL, 16:792 (605:6a).
35. (*Qinding*) *Da Qing yitong zhi*, 2nd ed., 483:666 (420:1a).
36. *PDZGFL*, zhengbian, 359:489 (85:1b–2a), xubian, 359:526 (2.12a–b).
37. Sarkar, *Study of Eighteenth Century India*, 1:100–105, 127–41.
38. Bamzai, *Culture and Political History of Kashmir*, 2:427–39.
39. FHA JJC MWLF, 54-0082 (QL24/IC6/22).
40. FHA JJC MWLF, 59-1368 (received QL25/2).
41. This seems to refer to the decision of Imad al-Mulk (grandson of Nizam al-Mulk) in 1757 to turn from Afghan to Maratha support (Sarkar, *Fall of the Mughal Empire*, 101). The informant seems to conflate the forces of the Marathas and the Nizam's descendants.
42. FHA JJC MWLF, 57-1961 (QL25/7/27).
43. FHA JJC MWLF, 57-1961 (QL25/7/27).
44. *PDZGFL*, xubian, juan 8, QL25/12/dingyou.
45. Stein identifies Bolor as the area around Mastuj (in the upper Yarkhun valley) and also Yasin (*Serindia*, 33).
46. *PDZGFL*, xubian, 359:618–19 (8:25b–27b).
47. Bogle, *Bhutan and Tibet*, 247. In 1762, when selecting personnel to escort an embassy sent by the Afghan ruler Ahmad Shah, Qianlong chose Sultan Khwaja, an Andijani in Qing service who had formed part of Ming Žen's mission, because he had "formerly gone to such places as Hindustan" (*PDZGFL*, xubian, 359:758 [18:30a]). This should perhaps be taken to mean that Sultan Khwaja had visited Hindustan earlier in his life.
48. *Yuzhi wenji*, 1301:411 (21:3b).
49. FHA JJC MWLF, 59-1368 (QL25/2); 57-1961 (QL25/7/27).
50. *Baxun wanshou shengdian*, 661:459 (94:28b), 513 (98:8b); *Yuzhi shiji*, 1311:274–75 (part 5, 85:19b–20a).
51. Davies, "Aḥmad S̲H̲āh Durrānī."
52. Fletcher, "China and Central Asia," 220. Courant likewise suggests an Afghan confederation with the Kazaks against the Qing in 1764, perhaps lasting as late as 1768 (*L'Asie Centrale*, 128). Kim notes the evidence for such an alliance, but suggests the possibility that Ahmad Shah was using it as a front to attack Bukhara (*Holy War in China*, 20–21); see also the observations of Yuri Bregel in Munis, *Firdaws al-Iqbāl*, 591–93n406.
53. FHA JJC MWLF, 62-1866 (QL27/3/6); *PDZGFL*, xubian, 359:723 (16:16b–17a). In reality, Alamgir II was murdered in 1759 by his vizier, Imad al-Mulk, who installed not Alamgir's grandson but the grandson of Kam Bakhsh, son of the last powerful Mughal ruler, Awrangzib.
54. FHA JJC MWLF, 64-1353 (QL27/8/10); *PDZGFL*, xubian, 359:753 (18:21a–b).
55. FHA JJC MWLF, 65-1759 (QL27/11/6), 65-1126 (QL27/11).
56. *QSL* QL, 17:561 (676:13a–b).
57. *QSL* QL, 17:516 (672:20a–b).

58. FHA JJC MWLF, 66-0247(QL27/11/15).
59. *QSL QL*, 17:563 (676:18a–b).
60. *QSL QL*, 17:588–89 (678: 15a–17a).
61. Newby, *Empire and the Khanate*, 36.
62. *Xiyu dili tushuo zhu*, 135, 160–61.
63. Yunggui and Suldei, *Xinjiang Huibu zhi*, 812.
64. On *qalandar*, see Wang, *Glossary of Chinese Islamic Terms*, 41.
65. Cišii, *Xiyu zongzhi*, 235–41 (4:13a–16a).
66. Ibid., 241–43 (4:16a–17a).
67. Ibid., 240 (4:15b).
68. Saguchi, *Higashi Torukisutan*, 75–77.
69. *QSL QL*, 17:955–56 (713:7a–9b).
70. *QSL QL*, 17:957 (713:10a–b).
71. *QSL QL*, 17:658 (684:15a–b).
72. Newby, *Empire and the Khanate*, 30–34.
73. *QSL QL*, 19:147–48 (835:10a–11b); Saguchi, *Higashi Torukisutan*, 80.
74. Onuma, "1770 nendai ni okeru Shin-Kazafu kankei," 19.
75. Newby, *Empire and the Khanate*, 43.
76. Yule and Burnell, *Hobson-Jobson*, 416; Mukherjee, *Foreign Names*, 120–40.
77. Chandra, *Sanskrit Texts*, 1:4–8.
78. "Tianzhu wu Yindu kao'e," *Yuzhi wenji*, part 2, 1301:411–2 (21:2b–5a).
79. Honghuo'er is a Chinese rendering of the Mongol word *küngyar/qungyar*, referring to the Ottoman ruler (Mosca, "Empire and the Circulation of Frontier Intelligence").
80. The contention that "Enetkek" was Tibetan seems to have been current in the empire before Qianlong's time, for d'Anville's 1733 map of Tibet, composed on the basis of Jesuit information that itself certainly derived from a source at the Kangxi or Yongzheng court, stated that "Anonkek or Anongen" were the Tibetan names for "*Mogol ou du Sultan des Indes.*" Jean-Baptiste d'Anville, "Carte Generale du Tibet," in J. B. du Halde, *Description géographique, historique . . . de l'empire de la Chine et de la Tartarie chinoise . . .* , v. 4.
81. Name of ruler taken from the Manchu version of Qianlong's essay (National Palace Museum, *Junjichu dang*, item 418000078).
82. (*Qinding*) *Da Qing yitong zhi*, 2nd ed., 726 (424.5b).
83. *Gugong suocang Hendusitan*, 12–13.
84. Ibid., 47 (poem 66).
85. Ibid., 43–44 (poems 47, 54).
86. Huber, *Holy Land Reborn*, 164.
87. *Gugong suocang Hendusitan*, 38, 44 (poems 27, 54).
88. Guy, *Emperor's Four Treasuries*, 67.
89. Ibid., 164; Struve, *The Ming-Qing Conflict*, 62.
90. (*Qinding*) *Da Qing yitong zhi*, 2nd ed., 483:666 (420:1a–b).
91. *Qinding Liao Jin Yuan sanshi guoyujie*, *Yuanshi yujie*, 296:281 (3:23a).
92. *Yuan shi*, *kaozheng* supplement, SKQS, 292:34 (3:2a).

93. *Ming shi, kaozheng* supplement, 302:277–78 (304:2a–b).
94. Jibin referred at different times to Kashmir, Gandhara, and Kapiśa (Sen, *Buddhism, Diplomacy*, 246n6).
95. *Qinding Huangyu Xiyu tuzhi*, 500:197 (5:38a), 882 (46:29a).
96. *(Qinding) Da Qing yitong zhi*, 2nd ed., 483:666 (420:1b).
97. *Ming shi*, 302:842 (332:2a).
98. Huang, *Siku quanshu*, 162.
99. *Zhongguo difangzhi zongmu tiyao*, 3:section 29:6–7.
100. *Liangchao yulan tushu*, 149.

Chapter Three

1. For recent studies of the Qing survey maps, see Perdue, "Boundaries, Maps, and Movement" and *China Marches West*, 447–57; Elliott, "Limits of Tartary"; Elman, *On Their Own Terms*, 144–48; Yee, "Traditional Chinese Cartography"; Hostetler, *Qing Colonial Enterprise*, 51–80. Classic studies are Bernard, "Éstapes"; Fuchs, "Materialien zur Kartographie"; and Foss, "A Western Interpretation of China."
2. Jami, "Imperial Control," 31–33; *Donghua lu*, cited in Li, *Yangyizhai wenji*, 76 (5:6a–b).
3. Foss, "A Western Interpretation of China," 225–26.
4. Jami, "Imperial Control," 38–39; *Qing shi gao*, 7:1668 (45); Elman, *On Their Own Terms*, 178–79.
5. Jami, *Méthodes rapides*, 38.
6. Foss, "A Western Interpretation of China," 219–20.
7. *Aomen lishi ditu jingxuan*, 26–27, 30–31, 32–33, 42–43.
8. Citation of J.-B. du Halde in Foss, "A Western Interpretation of China," 230.
9. Foss, "A Western Interpretation of China," 231; Petech, *China and Tibet*, 19, 25; Yee, "Traditional Chinese Cartography," 181; Ledyard, "Cartography in Korea," 298–305. Funakoshi, relying on Fuchs, suggests that the map of the territories of Tsewang Araptan was prepared by Fr. Fridelli in 1716, but it seems unlikely that he surveyed the entire area (*Sakoku Nihon*, 27).
10. Baddeley, *Russia, Mongolia, China*, 1:clxxxvii; Foss, "A Western Interpretation of China," 228–30.
11. Foss, "A Western Interpretation of China," 224, 226, 233–35. Funakoshi, relying on Fuchs, gives the following summary: 1717 woodblock, all Chinese script, 28 sheets, segmented format (*fentu*); 1717 copperplate test map, strip format (*paitu*), Chinese and Manchu; late 1718 draft map, segmented format, all Chinese, 32 sheets; late 1718 copperplate map, strip format, 41 sheets, in Chinese and Manchu; 1721 woodblock edition, 32 sheets, segmented format, all Chinese with emended placenames; 1726 version of preceding map for *Gujin tushu jicheng* project (*Sakoku Nihon*, 22).
12. Fuchs, *Der Jesuiten Atlas*, map 11, "Dsungarei-Tienschan-Kaschgar."
13. A member of this embassy, Tulišen, included a map of Central Asia in his travel account (printed 1723), but this was possibly based on a Russian map

(Bagrow, "The First Russian Maps of Siberia," 91). Already by around 1690 the court possessed a Russian-influenced map of Siberia and Northeast Asia (Elliott, "Limits of Tartary," 619).

14. Fu-ning-an, an official, composed a map in Manchu covering Ili and the Muslim Regions, probably during his frontier service between 1717 and 1726 (*Qing Neiwufu Zaobanchu Yutufang tumu chubian*, 24). If this dating is correct, it might be the source of the map of "Jungaria-Tianshan-Kashgar," which appeared in the 1718 printing of the Kangxi survey. Poppe observes that sometime before 1734 Johan Gustav Renat was presented with two maps of Central Asia while living in the lands of the Junghar ruler Galdan Tsering, both said to have been based on Chinese originals ("Renat's Kalmuck Maps," 157). According Baddeley (*Russia, Mongolia, China*, 1:clxxxviii), quoting Gaubil, by 1718 the Qing possessed multiple written accounts of the route to Ili.

15. Bernard, "Éstapes," 466.

16. Gaubil, *Correspondance de Pékin*, 171–75.

17. Yu, "Yongzheng shipai"; Qin and Liu ("Qingchao yutu," 72–73) give an earlier dating, to YZ4 (1726); Wang ("Sanchao quanguo zongtu," 4) dates it to autumn, YZ5 (1727).

18. Gaubil, *Correspondance de Pékin*, 174–75.

19. Yu, "Yongzheng shipai," 75; Wang, "Sanchao quanguo zongtu," 4. The *Zhonghua guditu zhenpin xuanji* (178) reports editions of 1725 (YZ3), 1727 (YZ5), 1729 (YZ7), and 1730 (YZ8). Other sources do not mention a 1725 edition.

20. A low-resolution image of the 1729 manuscript edition can be found in the *Aomen lishi ditu jingxuan*, 46. Editions in the First Historical Archives are not currently available to researchers.

21. Postnikov, "Russian Navy," 81.

22. Bernard, "Éstapes," 466. If this was the newest, 1725 edition of Homann's work (Vladislavich left St. Petersburg in late 1725) it would have incorporated data from the Caspian surveys (Postnikov, "Russian Navy," 81).

23. Fuchs, "Materialien zur Kartographie," 413

24. Gaubil, *Correspondance de Pékin*, 117.

25. A preface to the *Da Qing yitong yutu* states that the Yongzheng-period map included "South Asia" (Nan-Ya), but the two images of the map available to me, which should represent both Yongzheng editions, do not seem to depict any part of it. Moreover, Yu Fushun, who has viewed both editions in the original, states that only in the Qianlong period did Qing survey maps begin to include India ("Qing Yongzheng shipai," 75).

26. On Yin-xiang's interest, see Mosca, "Empire and the Circulation of Frontier Intelligence," 161–65.

27. Gaubil, *Correspondance de Pékin*, 237.

28. This map is most commonly available in the format known as the "Qianlong Map in Thirteen Rows" (*Qianlong shisanpai tu*), divided into thirteen horizontal segments and printed in copperplate, likely between 1769 and 1770. It was augmented and reprinted by Hu Linyi in 1863 (TZ2) under the title *Huangchao*

Zhongwai yitong yutu, and further reprinted in 1931 by the Beijing Palace Museum under the title *Qianlong shisanpai tongban ditu*. More recently it has been reprinted in Taiwan (1966) under the title *Qingdai yitong ditu*, and in China as the *Da Qing yitong yutu* (2003), and as part of the *Qingting san da shice quantu ji* (2007). The British Library holds a second version of this map, conventionally titled the *Da Qing yitong yutu* (India Office Maps X/3265). This has a different projection, is on a smaller scale in ten strips, and gives place-names outside of China in Manchu.

29. Wang, "Sanchao quanguo zongtu," 6.
30. Enoki, "Researches in Chinese Turkestan," 448.
31. Ibid., 447–48.
32. *QSL* QL, 16:58–59 (557:25b–26a).
33. *QSL* QL, 16:417–18 (581: 13b–14b).
34. The biography of Hošik, in the *Hesei toktobuha tulergi monggo hoise aiman i wang gung-sai iletun ulabun*, is reproduced in Li, *Manchu*, 50–59, translated 322–24.
35. *QSL* QL, 16:530 (juan 588, 5a). I am indebted to Dr. Onuma Takahiro for the identification of Khosh Kopek Beg and Khwaja Sir Beg. Some maps remain in the First Historical Archives in Beijing, but currently are unavailable to scholars (See Millward, "Coming on to the Map," 66n10).
36. FHA JJC MWLF, reel 054-312 (rescripted QL24/7).
37. For instance, a map submitted earlier by Jaohūi was given to the Oirat informant Belek for his comments (FHA JJC MWLF, 049-3262).
38. Postface to the *Luotu huicui*, cited in Qin and Liu, "Qingchao yutu," 76.
39. *QSL* QL, 16:517 (587:13b).
40. FHA JJC MWLF, reel 052-2396 (QL24/4/1, rescripted QL24/4/23).
41. *QSL* QL, 16:555 (590:2a–b).
42. *QSL* QL, 15:79 (485:23a).
43. Li, *Ouzhou shoucang bufen*, 175.
44. For instance, the 1761 catalog *Luotu huicui* lists as a *Kunyu quantu* a map from France dating to 1694 submitted by French Jesuits (see Qin and Liu, "Qingchao yutu," 75).
45. Enoki, "Researches in Chinese Turkestan," 448.
46. FHA JJC MWLF, reel 055:1012. Lateral communication of Deboo (QL24/10/25). The Manchu reads: "ba na i hanci goro be sara niyalma de fonjime bodome bolor badakšan wahan serekul jergi babe gemu dosimbume nirufi."
47. FHA JJC MWLF, reel 055-2348 (QL24/12/9, rescripted 25/1/4).
48. Hummel, *Eminent Chinese*, 1:285–86, 2:925–26.
49. Pfister, *Notices Biographiques*, 756.
50. *QSL* QL, 20:1047 (962:16a).
51. Wang, "Sanchao quanguo zongtu," 6.
52. *Qing zhong-qianqi*, 4:249.
53. Qin and Liu, "Qingchao yutu," 74.
54. *Qinggong Neiwufu*, 21:650.
55. No Kangxi edition had so many plates. The first, 1727, edition of the Yongzheng map had 98 plates, if its reprint is complete; the second edition presumably

had more, as it added the southern littoral of the Caspian Sea, missing from the first map. However this may be, the Yongzheng map was the basis for the expanded Qianlong edition (Wang, "Sanchao quanguo zongtu," 5).

56. *QSL* QL, 15:638 (527:14b).

57. *Qing zhong-qianqi*, 4:248–49.

58. FHA JJC MWLF, 055-2348. Wang Qianjin gives this date; see "Qianlong shisanpai tu," 113. Enoki, "Researches in Chinese Turkestan" (448), citing Xu Song, similarly suggests they returned in QL25/4 (May 15–June 12, 1760).

59. Qin and Liu, "Qingchao yutu," 73.

60. *Qing zhong qianqi*, 1:249–50.

61. Qin and Liu, "Qingchao yutu," 73; *Qinding Huangyu Xiyu tuzhi*, 500:3 (*yuzhi*:2b).

62. Scholars disagree over the date on which the 13-strip copperplate map was first printed. Here I follow the views of Pfister (*Notices Biographiques*, 820–21) and Enoki ("Researches in Chinese Turkestan," 449); it should be noted, however, that Yee ("Traditional Chinese Cartography," 186), Fuchs ("Materialen zur Kartographie," 236), and Simon and Nelson (*Manchu Books in London*, 98) favor 1775.

63. *Qinggong Neiwufu Zaobanchu dang'an zonghui*, 34:611; Enoki, "Researches in Chinese Turkestan," 452.

64. *QSL* QL, 21:570–71 (2b–4b).

65. Wang, "Qianlong shisanpai tu," 113–19.

66. See Jami, *Méthodes rapides*, 36.

67. By 1755 Gaubil had received some of d'Anville's most recent maps of Asia, and expected more to arrive the following year (*Correspondance de Pékin*, 826).

68. Measurements of longitude are taken from the 13-strip copperplate edition *Qingdai yitong ditu* version, and "Prémiere partie de la carte d'Asie . . . ," J.-B. Bourguignon d'Anville, 1751 (digital version, David Rumsey Map Collection). Measurements are approximate and rounded to the nearest half degree. The 10-strip map in the British Library gives slightly different degrees of latitude and longitude for these locations, but keeps roughly the same proportions. 1) The Persian Gulf: measured by the distance between Basra and the eastern tip of the Crimean Peninsula. Distance on Qianlong map: 1 degree; d'Anville map: 10 degrees. 2) Multan: measured by the distance between Multan and the center of the southern shore of the Caspian. Qianlong map: zero degrees; d'Anville map: 18.5 degrees. 3) The Indian Ocean: measured by the distance between the narrowest point of the mouth of the Persian Gulf to the western tip of the Kathiawar Peninsula. Qianlong map: 4 degrees; d'Anville map: 13 degrees. 4) Dhaka: measured by the distance from Dhaka to the center of Lake Manasarowar. Qianlong map: 1 degree; d'Anville map: 9.5 degrees. The position of Dhaka, not shown on the "Prémiere partie de la carte d'Asie . . . ," is taken from another of d'Anville's maps, the 1752 "Carte de l'Inde."

69. If the map was drafted by Portuguese rather than French Jesuits, its authors may not have had access to d'Anville's latest map. They might then have used de Fer's 1696 map of Asia. This map was weak on the Himalayas and Central Asia, because it predated the surveys of Kangxi and Peter the Great, but had long been

in the imperial collection and bore heavy Chinese notation. It is also possible that its companion world map (called the *Kunyu quantu* in Chinese) was taken on the survey trip. If de Fer's map was used, the finished survey map deviated somewhat less from its contributing European world map, because de Fer believed that Lake Manasarowar was north of the Gangetic delta. Even in this case, however, there are great differences between de Fer's European map and the completed Qianlong survey (de Fer's Ganges does not originate in Manasarowar; his Jamuna is a tributary of the Ganges, etc.), and we must reach the same basic conclusion: material from earlier survey maps was inviolable, and European world maps were used as supplementary material to be distorted as necessary to fit it (N. de Fer, *L'Asie*, 1696, http://gallica.bnf.fr/ark:/12148/btv1b59001460).

70. *Aomen lishi ditu jingxuan*, 46.

71. *Tenggis* means "large lake" in Mongolian (here a proper name), *omo* means "lake" in Manchu (Tulišen, *Kōchū Iikiroku*, 48).

72. In regions far from Qing territory, the makers of the court survey map seem to have mechanically translated names from European maps into Chinese and Manchu. Taking the region near the Kathiawar Peninsula in western India as an example, of the Manchu names used, many seem to be simple transcriptions of equivalent terms on French maps (given in parentheses): As mer (Azmer), Dada (Tatta), and G'angbaya (Cambaye). In other cases, however, the names on the survey map deviate significantly those on d'Anville's and other French maps: Sen (Sindi) and Baidari Surat (Surate). In the Indus region, however, only a minority of names on the Qing court survey map have obvious equivalents in contemporary European maps. The implication, which awaits further research, is that local informants displaced European maps for regions where they could offer firsthand testimony.

73. Enoki, "Researches in Chinese Turkestan," 450.

74. *Handbook of Christianity*, 1:314–15; Sivin, "Copernicus in China," 94–95.

75. Baddeley, *Russia, Mongolia, China*, 1:cxci.

76. *Lettres édifiantes*, 4:222.

77. *QSL* QL, 20:1047 (962.16.a–b).

78. Cordier, "Correspondants de Bertin," 338.

79. Ibid., 314.

80. *Lettres édifiantes*, 4:231–32.

81. Macartney presented Qianlong with a globe, but there is no evidence that it was annotated in Chinese or Manchu, or consulted by the Qing court (*Yingshi Majia'erni*, 122).

82. *Lettres édifiantes*, 4:232, 122.

83. Benoist, *Diqiu tushuo*, 1035:4 (1:3b–4a); *Lettres édifiantes*, 4:121–22; Ju, "Jiang Youren," 122.

84. *Lettres édifiantes*, 4:232.

85. Ibid., 4:122.

86. Ibid., 4:232.

87. *Qing zhong-qianqi*, 1:251.

88. Pfister, *Notices Biographiques*, 814.
89. Isnard, "Joseph-Nicolas Delisle," 40–49.
90. Gaubil, *Correspondance de Pékin*, passim.
91. Benoit explained to Qianlong that he used data from de l'Isle for Russian geography on his 1760 map (*Lettres édifiantes*, 4:211–12). For de l'Isle and Bering, see Isnard, "Joseph-Nicolas Delisle," 46–52.
92. Qin and Liu, "Qingchao yutu," 73.
93. Benoist, *Diqiu tushuo*, 1035:5 (1:5b).
94. Cordier, "Correspondants de Bertin," 314.
95. *Lettres édifiantes*, 4:210–13.
96. Ibid., 4:213.
97. Mosca, "Qing China's Perspectives," 180–89.

Chapter Four

1. Petech, *China and Tibet*, 161–64.
2. Balebu, from Tibetan *Bal-po*, referred collectively to the Newari kingdoms of the Kathmandu valley; see Bla-ma bTsan-po, *Tibetan Religious Geography of Nepal*, 13n9.
3. For narratives of this diplomacy, see Lamb, *British India and Tibet*, 3–7; Rose, *Nepal*, 23–35; and Cammann, *Trade Through the Himalayas*, passim.
4. Petech, "Missions of Bogle and Turner," 332.
5. For Tibetan views of India in this period, including the activities of the Panchen Lama, see Huber, *Holy Land Reborn*, 166–231.
6. Bogle, *Bhutan and Tibet*, 153; Petech, "Missions of Bogle and Turner," 334.
7. Petech, "Missions of Bogle and Turner," 335–38; Huber, *Holy Land Reborn*, 197–201.
8. Bogle, *Bhutan and Tibet*, 219–20, 233–34.
9. Huber, *Holy Land Reborn*, 215–22.
10. Bogle, *Bhutan and Tibet*, 80–83.
11. Ibid., 275.
12. Li, "Tibetan Aristocratic Family," 176.
13. *Kuo'erka dang*, 4:2177–78.
14. Bogle, *Bhutan and Tibet*, 230, 233, 262–63.
15. On Purangir, see Bysack, "Notes on a Buddhist Monastery."
16. Huber, *Holy Land Reborn*, 220–22.
17. Turner, *Account of an Embassy*, 464, 468–69.
18. Bogle, *Bhutan and Tibet*, 439.
19. Turner, *Account of an Embassy*, 239.
20. Wang, "Tibetan Buddhism," and Ishihama, "Panchen Rama," make no suggestion of references to Hindustan or British India in Tibetan accounts of the 1780 visit to Beijing.
21. Ishihama, "Panchen Rama," 321–61.
22. Turner, *Account of an Embassy*, 468.
23. Cammann, "Panchen Lama's Visit to China," 12–14.

24. For a comparison of dates, see Ishihama, "Panchen Rama," 328–32; Turner, *Account of an Embassy*, 457–58.
25. Dpal-ldan ye-shes, *Der Weg nach Śambhala*, 44–45. Cf. Bogle's explanation to the Panchen Lama: Bogle, *Bhutan and Tibet*, 212–13.
26. Suzuki, *Chū-In kankeishi*, 88, 98–99n40.
27. Huber, *Holy Land Reborn*, 217–18.
28. Uspensky, "Previous Incarnations," 219.
29. *Kuo'erka dang*, 4:2174–75.
30. Yule and Burnell, *Hobson-Jobson*, 352–54.
31. Bogle, *Bhutan and Tibet*, 212.
32. Petech, "Missions of Bogle and Turner," 334–35n5. Several Tibetan dictionaries support this reading: Jaeschke, *Tibetan-English Dictionary* (344), defines *phe-rang* or *pha-rang* as "Feringhi, Europeans," and Das, *Tibetan-English Dictionary*, defines *phe-rang* and *pha-rang* as "from Feringhi a man of European race" (817). Aris, in his translation of the *Discourse on India* (see below) likewise equates *Phe-reng-ba* with Farangi. Aris observes that the author of this text elsewhere used the variant *Phi-ling* in the same sense, and he suggests that this latter term was related to *Phyi-gling-pa*, meaning Europeans or "people of the outer islands" (68n32). Jaeschke also suggests that the expression *rgya-phi-ling*, an eighteenth-century term for British India, may either derive from Feringhi or represent a vulgarized form of the term *phyi-gling*, a much older term for "an out-country, a distant foreign country" (106). Berthold Laufer disputes this view. He notes the variants *Phe-rang*, *Pha-rang*, *Phi-ling* (or *rgya phi-ling*) and *Pho-rang*, and suggests that all derive from the Persian, observing that "the opinion that '*p'i-liṇ*' [*phi-ling*] represents only the more vulgar pronunciation of the genuine Tibetan word '*p'yi gliṇ*' [*phyi gling*], a foreign country and especially Europe, is untenable" (Laufer, "Loan-words in Tibetan," 562–63).
33. Dpal-ldan ye-shes, *Der Weg nach Śambhala*, 12, 44.
34. Petech, "Missions of Bogle and Turner," 340–43.
35. Bogle, *Bhutan and Tibet*, 222, 213, 221.
36. Ibid., 193–202.
37. Ibid., 211.
38. Dpal-ldan ye-shes, *Der Weg nach Śambhala*, 44.
39. Bogle, *Bhutan and Tibet*, 223.
40. Aris, *Discourse on India*, 5–9.
41. Ibid., especially 23–29, 34–47, 54–69.
42. For narratives of the war based on Qing official records, see Zhuang, *Qing Gaozong shiquan wugong yanjiu*, 417–92; and Satō, *Chūsei Chibetto*, 521–740. For the Nepali side, see Regmi, *Modern Nepal*, and Rose, *Nepal*. For Tibetan materials, see Shakabpa, *Tibet*, and Li, "Tibetan Aristocratic Family." For the British perspective, see Lamb, *British India and Tibet*.
43. Zhwa dmar was the elder half-brother of the Panchen Lama, who had died in Beijing in 1780. See Li, "Tibetan Aristocratic Family," 142–43.
44. Diskalkar, "Tibeto-Nepalese War," 368.

NOTES TO CHAPTER FOUR 347

45. On Tibetan-Gurkha negotiations, see Satō, *Chūsei Chibetto*, 564–65.
46. Diskalkar, "Tibeto-Nepalese War," 367–69.
47. Ibid., 371–74.
48. Satō, *Chūsei Chibetto*, 576–88; Li, "Tibetan Aristocratic Family," 144–50.
49. Satō, *Chūsei Chibetto*, 601–2.
50. *Kuo'erka dang*, 2:591–95.
51. Ibid., 2:734–35.
52. FHA JJC LFZZ, reel 572:1960 (Memorial, Fuk'anggan, QL57/1/26, rescripted 2/27).
53. Rao mistakenly lists Pileng as a reference to Penang (sometimes called Bileng) (*Rao Zongyi*, 10:384).
54. FHA JJC LFZZ, reel 572:1905 (Memorial, Fuk'anggan, QL57/2/13, rescripted 3/15). *Nan Jiaga'er* is a translation of *Lho-phyogs Rgya-gar*, which Aris glosses as "India" or "India to the South" [of Tibet], not southern India (*Discourse on India*, 14–15).
55. FHA JJC LFZZ, reel 573:1093 (Memorial, Fuk'anggan and Hui-ling, QL57/2/22, rescripted 3/23).
56. Diskalkar, "Tibeto-Nepalese War," 362–63n15; Regmi, *King and Political Leaders*, 7.
57. FHA JJC LFZZ, reel 572:2001–12 (Memorial and attachments, Fuk'anggan et al., rescripted QL57/5/4).
58. For the Gurkha perspective on these negotiations, see Regmi, *Modern Nepal*, 409–17.
59. Diskalkar, "Tibeto-Nepalese War," 375–76.
60. Ibid., 377–83
61. Ibid., 389–91.
62. Ibid., 387–89.
63. Lamb, *British India and Tibet*, 20; Rose, *Nepal*, 67n53.
64. FHA JJC LFZZ, reel 573:493 (Deposition enclosed in memorial rescripted QL57/8/21, sent 57/7).
65. FHA JJC LFZZ, reel 572:2042 (Memorial, Fuk'anggan et al., QL57/7/19, rescripted 57/9/3).
66. Cammann (citing Petech) identifies the "Acharya lama" Su-na-ge-li mentioned here as Suryagiri, an alias of Purangir. He identifies Da-qi-ge-li with Daljit Gir (*Trade Through the Himalayas*, 140n72).
67. Bysack, "Notes on a Buddhist Monastery," 91.
68. Diskalkar, "Tibeto-Nepalese War," 387–89.
69. FHA JJC MWLF, reel 155:3048–51.
70. FHA JJC MWLF, reel 155:3048–51.
71. *Qinding Kuo'erka jilüe*, 762–63 (51.3a–9b).
72. Ibid., 762–63 (51.3a–9b).
73. FHA JJC LFZZ, reel 572:2549 (undated enclosure).
74. FHA JJC LFZZ, reel 572:2042 (Memorial, Fuk'anggan et al., QL57/7/19, rescripted 9/13).

75. This refers to the mission of Sher Bahadur Shah, half-brother of Bahadur Shah, to Patna. FHA JJC LFZZ, reel 573:1093 (Memorial, Fuk'anggan et al., QL57/2/22, rescripted 3/23).

76. Suzuki Chūsei has argued that Fuk'anggan was ill-disposed toward the Pileng from the time of his arrival in Tibet, but his evidence is not persuasive. For an outline of his position and my interpretation, see Mosca, "Qing China's Perspectives," 225n76.

77. Rose, *Nepal*, 74.

78. *Baxun wanshou shengdian*, 660:251 (21.21b).

79. Satō believes that Zhwa dmar was behind this request (*Chūsei Chibetto*, 611–12).

80. Hindustan may here refer to the Delhi Padshah; Xiyang probably refers to Europeans; Borgi indicated Maratha soldiers raiding into Bengal (Aris, *Discourse on India*, 74n99). In prior Qing usage, as noted in Chapter Two, Hindustan referred to the Mughal empire; the Gurkhas had recently been warning the Qing about the "Delhi Padshah," also a reference to the Mughal emperor. This suggests that the Qing court was now able to associate Dili Bacha, which Fuk'anggan considered to be the largest state in Jiaga'er, with the vast country of Hindustan located southwest of Yarkand.

81. Zhuang, *Qing Gaozong shiquan wugong yanjiu*, 472.

82. For instance, the entry on Bhutan in the *Huang Qing zhigong tu* states that it originally belonged to "India" (Xifan-guo), 594:446 (2.7a).

83. *Yuzhi shi, wu ji*, 1310:440 (51.8a).

84. *Yuzhi wenji, san ji*, 1301:595 (4.8b).

85. Hindustan-India equivalence was recognized in an 1808 inscription in which the Tibetan "Rgya-gar or Hen-du-si-than" was given in Chinese as "Enetkek, that is, India" (*Enatekeke, ji Yindu*). See Richardson, *Ch'ing Dynasty Inscriptions*, 72; Huang, *Xizang tukao*, 44. In 1826 Wei Yuan defined Hindustan as "Central India" (*Zhong* Yindu): *Qing* [= *Huangchao*] *jingshi wenbian*, 3:1962 (80.2a).

86. Kirkpatrick, *Account of the Kingdom of Nepaul*, 355–70.

87. FHA JJC LFZZ, reel 572:1016–30 (Memorial, He-lin et al., with attachments, QL58/4/12, rescripted 5/26).

88. In India the Arabic *wilāyat*, originally meaning a province or kingdom, came to refer to foreign countries, especially Europe; "Blighty" as a name for Britain derives from the Anglo-Indian form of this word, *Bilayut* (Yule and Burnell, *Hobson-Jobson*, 93–94; Aris, *Discourse on India*, 55).

89. FHA JJC LFZZ, reel 572:1016–30 (Memorial, He-lin et al., with attachments, QL58/4/12, rescripted 5/26).

90. *Yingshi Majia'erni*, 91.

91. *Fort William–India House Correspondence*, 17:293.

92. BL APAC, IOR/G/12 (Diary of Select Committee at Canton), September 11, 1793.

93. Morse, *Chronicles*, 2:232–33, 237–38.

94. Macartney, *Journal*, 325–31.

95. Ibid., 86–87.
96. Ibid., 127–28, 181.
97. BL APAC, IOR/G/12/92: Macartney to Dundas, November 9, 1793.
98. BL APAC, IOR/G/12/92: Macartney to Dundas, November 9, 1793.
99. BL APAC, IOR/G/12/92: Macartney to Dundas, November 9, 1793.
100. BL APAC, IOR/G/12/92: Macartney to Dundas, November 9, 1793.
101. BL APAC, IOR/G/12/20: Macartney to Dundas, December 23, 1793.
102. Morse, *Chronicles*, 2:244–47; *Yingshi Majia'erni*, 162–64.
103. *Yingshi Majia'erni*, 91.
104. FHA JJC LFZZ, reel 572:2589 (Memorial, Fuk'anggan et al., QL57/11/21, rescripted QL57/12/17.
105. *Yingshi Majia'erni*, 185.
106. *Kuo'erka dang*, 4:2299–2300.
107. Pritchard, "Instructions," 499: Macartney to Shore, February 3, 1794.
108. BL APAC, IOR/G/12/93: George III to Emperor of China, June 20, 1795.
109. On "Gangjiao," a term used in Guangzhou for British territories in India, see Chapter Six.
110. *Yingshi Majia'erni*, 230–34, 493.
111. Ibid., 231, 233, 493.
112. *Wenxian congbian*, 1:158–59.
113. Hummel, *Eminent Chinese*, 1:255, 2:681, 1:286, 1:249.
114. For overview of these gazetteers, see *Zhongguo difangzhi zongmu tiyao*, 3:pt. 24, 8–12.
115. Ma and Sheng, *Wei-Zang tuzhi*.
116. He-lin, *Wei-Zang tongzhi*, 259–60 (15.14a–16b).
117. Sungyūn, *Xizhao tulüe*, 168–69 (*tushuo* 18a).
118. *Sichuan tongzhi*, 5613 (94.35a–b).
119. This refers to the East India Company's de facto authority as holder of the *diwani*, under the nominal suzerainty of the Mughal emperor.
120. Zhou, *Xizang jiyou*, 40–41.
121. Aris, *Discourse on India*, 23, 35. Fuk'anggan likely did not have access to 'Jigs-med-gling-pa's text; rather, both seem to have used terminology already in circulation.

Chapter Five

1. Cooper, *Anglo-Maratha Campaigns*, 303.
2. Greenberg, *British Trade*, 105–6.
3. India's trade surplus with China between 1814 and 1856 totaled over $514,000,000 (Lin, *China Upside Down*, 76–78).
4. Greenberg, *British Trade*, 26.
5. Lin, *China Upside Down*, 89.
6. Smith and Van Dyke, "Muslims in the Pearl River Delta," 6–15; Thampi, *Indians in China*, 73–77.
7. Guo, *Qingdai Guangzhou*, 32.

8. Hunter, *"Fan Kwae" at Canton*, 63.
9. Greenberg, *British Trade*, 33; Guo, *Qingdai Guangzhou*, 1–2.
10. Guo, *Qingdai Guangzhou*, 40–42; cf. Hunter, *"Fan Kwae" at Canton*, 63.
11. Guo, *Qingdai Guangzhou*, 29–32.
12. *Hanyu da cidian*, 5:1444. See also, for instance, Rowe, *Index*, 328, which defines the term as "India, by ref. to East India Co."
13. Yule and Burnell, *Hobson-Jobson*, 266
14. Guo supports the "Country" interpretation and cites the opinion that the Cantonese would have pronounced the term *Gangtui* (港腿), but written it *Gangjiao* (Guo, *Qingdai Guangzhou*, 42, 70n41). However, the term may have originally meant "port," and later become a proper noun. Thus, an 1819 Chinese-English dictionary defines *Gangjiao* as "Keang keŏ 港脚 the foot of a stream or passage of water; a port or harbour; the ports of India are so called at Canton; and India itself. Keang keŏ chuen 港脚船 English ships from India, are so called at Canton; country ships" (Morrison, *Dictionary*, II.1:396). Medhurst and Williams, who likewise lived in China before the Opium War, defined *Gangjiao* respectively as "harbour" and "the embouchure; a port" (Medhurst, *English and Chinese Dictionary* [1847], 1:658; Williams, *Syllabic Dictionary* [1874], 364). Significantly, *Gangjiao* seems never to have been written with the "mouth" (*kou*) radical, a component normally added at Guangzhou to phonetic transcriptions of foreign names. An article in the *Nanyang xuebao* (5.2) observes of Johore, "It may be seen that it was a large port in the Ming period, and today the locals still refer to it as Kang-kar, a transcription of '*Gangjiao*' in the Min-nan dialect pronunciation" (35). Finally, references to "outer seas *jiao chuan* (外洋脚船)" carrying cotton can be found in the Qianlong period *Qing shi lu* around 1777, before the first attested appearance of *Gangjiao*; there may be some connection between *jiao chuan* and *Gangjiao chuan*.
15. *QDWJSL* JQ, 533 (5.37a).
16. *QDWJSL* JQ, 618 (6.12b).
17. Wang, *Haidao yizhi*, in Zheng, *Zhouju suozhi*, 839. Medhurst also used *zujia* in this way (see his *Texuan cuoyao meiyue jizhuan*, *Jiaoliuba zonglun*, ch. 10). J. F. Davis used *zujia* for "Europe" in his 1824 *Vocabulary* (24).
18. Liang, *Guangdong shisanhang kao*, 151.
19. *QDWJSL* DG, 122–24 (2.3b–4b). Morse notes two Arab ships arriving at Canton in 1824 (*Chronicles*, 4:95–96); Qing documents attributed their origins to Yalin-guo.
20. *QDWJSL* DG, 313 (3.40a).
21. *QDWJSL* DG, 263 (3.15a).
22. Inoue, *Shindai ahen*, 290–91.
23. *QDWJSL* DG, 280–81 (3.23b–24a); cf. Inoue, *Shindai ahen*, 114.
24. By 1815, some Qing officials at Guangzhou identified "English Bengal" (*Yingjili-guo Mengjiala difang*) as the source of opium, but this view was not widely reiterated in official or private writings before the Opium War, where "Gangjiao" remained more common (*Putaoya Dongbota dang'anguan*, 1:133).

25. Morse, *Chronicles*, 2:373.
26. Wood, "England, China," 141–43.
27. Inoue, *Shindai ahen*, 70.
28. The first report of the incident by Giking (Ji-qing 吉慶): *QSL* JQ, 29:286–87 (96.25a–26b); the report on the conclusion of peace: *QDWJSL* JQ, 32 (1.10b).
29. Probably a reference to the defeat of Tipu Sultan in 1799.
30. *QDWJSL* JQ, 35 (1.12a).
31. *QDWJSL* JQ, 37 (1.13a).
32. Wood, "England, China," 145–54; Wakeman, "Drury's Occupation," 27–34.
33. *QDWJSL* JQ, 165 (2.23a–24b), 170–71 (2.25b–26a).
34. Rear-Admiral W. Drury arrived on September 11 with 300 troops from Madras, and troops from Bengal under Maj. T. M. Weguelin arrived on October 22 (Morse, *Chronicles*, 3:87–88).
35. *QDWJSL* JQ, 168–69 (2.24b–25a); another reference to the "Bengal commander" is in 246 (3.4b).
36. *QDWJSL* JQ, 173 (2.27a), 180 (2.30b).
37. Markham, *Narratives*, 280.
38. "Thomas Manning," *Oxford Dictionary of National Biography*, 36:509–10. For the failed attempt to go to Beijing as an astronomer and physician, see BL APAC, IOR/R/10/25, November 2, 1807.
39. By this time Calcutta had a substantial Chinese community. Father Matteo Ripa reports being fed in that city by a "pious Chinese Christian woman" around 1709 (Nair, *Calcutta in the 18th Century*, 39). At some point in the 1770s or early 1780s a sugarcane factory was established near Calcutta using Chinese workers (*Encyclopedia of the Chinese Overseas*, 344). In 1798 there were reportedly ten houses belonging to Chinese in the city, and by 1822, a decade or so after Manning's visit, the city's estimated Chinese population was 414 (Nair, *Calcutta in the 18th Century*, 228, 241n9).
40. FHA JJC LFZZ, Minzu, reel 591:2695–97 (Memorial, Cangming, JQ 17/5/18, rescripted 6/14).
41. Marshman mentioned that Zhao, "Manning's Chinese teacher," could speak Mandarin (*Elements of Chinese Grammar*, iii).
42. Markham, *Narratives*, 266.
43. *Handbook of Christianity*, 2:218–19.
44. Markham, *Narratives*, 262.
45. Manning's friend G. T. Staunton also secured as Robert Morrison's Mandarin teacher a Roman Catholic from Shanxi named Abel Yun, who had moved to Beijing and studied Latin under missionaries, before moving south to Guangzhou. See Morrison, *Memoirs*, 1:167.
46. *Qinding Kuo'erka jilüe*, 735 (49.4a–b).
47. Markham, *Narratives*, 217.
48. *Qing zhong-qianqi*, 3:974.
49. Markham, *Narratives*, 215–38.
50. Ibid., 259–62, 275–77, 289.

51. *Qing zhong-qianqi*, 3:974–75.
52. Markham, *Narratives*, 276–78, 294.
53. FHA JJC LFZZ, reel 591:2695–97 (Memorial of Cangming, JQ17/5/18, rescripted 6/14).
54. Sungyūn, "Suifu jilüe," 92–95 (44b–46a).
55. Rose, *Nepal*, 79–82.
56. Ibid., 76–77.
57. *QSL* JQ, 29:178 (89.15a).
58. *QSL* JQ, 29:399 (104.17a).
59. For the background to this war, see Rose, *Nepal*, 79–85.
60. *QDZSZD*, 1:12–14.
61. *QDZSZD*, 1:18.
62. *QDZSZD*, 1:19–20.
63. *QDZSZD*, 1:20–23.
64. *QDZSZD*, 1:23–26.
65. *QDZSZD*, 1:27.
66. Suzuki, *Chū-In kankeishi*, 168.
67. *QDZSZD*, 1:26–29.
68. *QDZSZD*, 1:29–33.
69. BL APAC, IOR/F/4/551/13382: Extract of Bengal Secret Consultations, May 16, 1815, letter of Amar Singh Thapa to Nepal Raja, March 2, 1815.
70. *QDZSZD*, 1:28–29.
71. *QDZSZD*, 1:31.
72. *QDZSZD*, 1:37–38.
73. *QDZSZD*, 1:39.
74. *QDZSZD*, 1:43–45.
75. BL APAC IOR/F/551/13382: Extract, Bengal Secret Consultations, July 13, 1816, item No. 17, enclosure in Latter to Adam, June 10, 1816.
76. *QDZSZD*, 1:46–47.
77. Cited in Rose, *Nepal*, 90.
78. BL APAC, IOR/F/4/551/13382: Extract, Political Letter from Bengal, November 16, 1816.
79. *QDZSZD*, 1:61–67.
80. National Palace Museum, *Junjichu dang*, document 052706: undated petition of Pileng chief.
81. Ibid., document 052707: undated response to Pileng chief.
82. Suzuki, *Chū-In kankeishi*, 173.
83. *QDZSZD*, 1:58.
84. Moorcroft, "Journey to Lake Mánasaróvara," 446.
85. *QDZSZD*, 1:24–25.
86. Alder, *Beyond Bokhara*, 123–24.
87. For Moorcroft's life and travels, see ibid. On Chinese records, see Suzuki, *Chū-In kankeishi*, 195–217.

88. Alder, *Beyond Bokhara*, 209–73.
89. Moorcroft and Trebeck, *Travels*, 168–69; Alder, *Beyond Bokhara*, 268; BL APAC, Mss. Eur. D.245 (Moorcroft to Swinton, October 29, 1821).
90. Moorcroft's letter to the hakim beg on this occasion, which survives in both Persian and in Manchu translation, is dated August 3, 1821.
91. FHA JJC MWLF, reel 192:2469.
92. BL APAC, Mss. Eur. D/245 (Moorcroft to Swinton, October 29, 1821).
93. Evidently, Marshman's Chinese letter was found indecipherable, a fact noted by Moorcroft; BL APAC, Mss. Eur. D/245 (Moorcroft to Swinton, October 29, 1821).
94. *QSL* DG, 33:463–64 (26.20a–21b).
95. FHA JJC LFZZ, reel 572:333–36 (Deposition of Izzat-ullah); *Shiliao xunkan*, 91–92 (5.169b–170b).
96. BL APAC, IOR/Eur. Mss. D/245 (Moorcroft to Swinton, October 29, 1821).
97. *Shiliao xunkan*, 114–15 (6.212b–214a).
98. BL APAC, IOR/Eur. Mss. D/245 (Moorcroft to Swinton, October 29, 1821).
99. FHA JJC LFZZ, reel 572:314–15 (Deposition of Meng-han et al.)
100. Rapail was distinct from Maidi, and may be Rafail Danibegov, a Georgian Christian who journeyed from Leh to Yarkand in 1812 or 1813.
101. FHA JJC LFZZ, reel 572:317 (letter), 325 (affidavit).
102. FHA JJC LFZZ, reel 572: 323–4 (Moorcroft to Yarkand Hakim Beg), 326–27 (Izzat-ullah to same), 329 (Moorcroft to Ulungga).
103. *Shiliao xunkan*, 91 (5.169b).
104. *QSL* DG, 33:463 (26. 20b).
105. Yapp, *Strategies of British India*, 153.
106. Ibid., 16.
107. Fisher, *Indirect Rule in India*, 229.
108. Rose, *Nepal*, 98–99.
109. *Kuo'erka dang*, 2:605; FHA JJC LFZZ, reel 572:1960 (Court letter, Agūi and Hešen to Fuk'anggan, QL57/1/20).
110. *Kuo'erka dang*, 2:861–63, 2:881.
111. *Qinding Kuo'erka jilüe*, 762 (51.7b).
112. *Mian dang*, 1:169–70.
113. *Shiliao xunkan*, 591 (30.105a).
114. *QSL* QL, 21:222–24 (990.19a–22a).
115. *QSL* QL, 21:819–22 (1031.11b–17b), 21:883–84 (1036.16b–18a).
116. Washington, "Farewell Address," *Writings of George Washington*, 35:231–35.
117. Fisher, *Indirect Rule in India*, 174.
118. Bayly, *Empire and Information*, 97.
119. FHA JJC LFZZ, Minzu, reel 592:13 (Deposition of Ahmed Ali, undated); *QDWJSL* JQ, 566 (5.53b).
120. Yapp, *Strategies of British India*, 182–83.
121. Kuhn, *Soulstealers*, 220.

Chapter Six

1. The Harvard-Yenching Library holds the 1793 and Jiaqing-era (*Yihai zhuchen*) editions; there is also an 1833 *Zhaodai congshu* printing. Wang Gungwu notes an 1823 edition ("'Haiguo wenjian lu' zhong de 'Wulaiyou,'" 106n2).
2. Chen, *Haiguo wenjian lu*, 1793 printing, "preface."
3. *Yue haiguan zhi jiaozhu ben*, 573–87 (30).
4. Chen, "Lüelun Yao Ying," 343; *KYJX*, 2:309–10 (10.5a–b).
5. *KYJX*, 2:531–32 (16.1a–b).
6. Engkitlêy is a dialect pronunciation given in Medhurst's translation (Ong-Tae-Hae, *Chinaman Abroad*, 30).
7. Wang, *Haidao yizhi*, 53–60, 86–89.
8. Ibid., 54.
9. Zheng, *Zhouju suozhi*, 837–39; Wang, *Haidao yizhi*, 34–36.
10. Wang, *Ruan Yuan nianpu*, 644.
11. *GDTZ DG*, 675:720–35 (330).
12. *GDTZ DG*, 675:734 (330).
13. BL APAC, IOR/R/10/Misc./2, entry of October 8, 1818.
14. The Qing government knew that fighting had ceased in Nepal in 1816, over two years earlier. Nothing in the Tibet correspondence linked the fighting specifically to the English in this period. It therefore seems unlikely that Ruan had been ordered to investigate this event in 1818.
15. *Indo-Chinese Gleaner*, 2.X (October 1819), 186.
16. The characters for "Matala" are inverted and should read "Malata"; Madras is here rendered as "Mandalasa."
17. *GDTZ DG*, 675:735 (330). On the identity of Goa and Vengurla, see Xie, *Hailu jiaoshi*, 90–91.
18. *GDTZ DG*, 675:733 (330).
19. *GDTZ DG*, 675:733 (330). Extant versions of the *Zhouche wenjian lu* lack this section.
20. Two short biographies of Xie Qinggao exist. That by Li Zhaoluo states he was born in Qianlong *yiyou* (QL30, 1765) at Jinpan bao in Jiaying department, and that at the age of 18 *sui* he took to sea on a foreign boat, sailing for fourteen years and returning at the age of 31 *sui*. By this calculation he would have set to sea in 1782 and ended his travels in 1795 or 1796. He died at the age of 57 in 1821 (*Haiguo jiwen xu*, in *Yangyizhai wenji*, 2.23b–24b); that by Yang Bingnan generally agrees, but states he was rescued by a foreign ship when his own vessel capsized, and sailed as a small merchant (*Hailu jiaoshi*, 329). However, legal records concerning a tenancy dispute suggest that he was in Macao in QL58 (1793) and had been paying rent for over twenty years as of 1808, which would put him back in the city by 1787 at the latest (ibid., 344). Perhaps Xie came and went from Macao, leaving his shop in the hands of others. Feng, based on Xie's reference to the highest British official in Bengal as *La* 辣 ("Lord"), speculates that he visited during the tenure (1786–1793) of Lord Cornwallis (*Hailu jiaoshi*, 67).
21. Xie, *Hailu jiaoshi*, 329.

22. Li, *Haiguo jiwen*, in *Yangyizhai wenji*, 2.23b–24a.
23. Different interpretations have been advanced by Rao Zongyi, Zhou Heng, and An Jing, but none explains all available evidence. Some cooperation between Wu and Yang, both Jiaying men and members of the same poetry association in 1821 (Inoue, *Shindai ahen*, 94–97), seems likely. It also seems likely that there is some tie between the collection of the *Hailu* and the *Guangdong tongzhi* project.
24. Xie, *Hailu jiaoshi*, 62–95.
25. Ibid., 250.
26. Ibid., 64.
27. Wang, *Haidao yizhi jiaozhu*, Liu Xicheng preface, *xiii*.
28. Cf. Xie, *Hailu jiaoshi*, 94, *GDTZ* DG, 675:735 (330).
29. Li, *Haiguo jiwen xu*, in *Yangyizhai wenji*, 2.23b–24b.
30. Ibid., 2.24b.
31. Miles, *Sea of Learning*, 9.
32. Benoist, *Diqiu tushuo*, 2 (preface 3b).
33. Ibid.
34. Elman, *On Their Own Terms*, 198.
35. Wang, *Ruan Yuan nianpu*, 652.
36. Chen, "Zhu 'Yuantian tushuo,'" 73–76.
37. Li, *Yuantian tushuo*, 315–28 (21a–46b).
38. Wang, *Ruan Yuan nianpu*, 652; Li, *Yuantian tushuo*, 226–28.
39. Li, *Yuantian tushuo*, 315–17 (21a–24b).
40. Zhuang, *Da Qing tongshu*.
41. Li, *Yuantian tushuo*, 315 (21a).
42. *GDTZ* DG, 670:603 (83).
43. *GDTZ* DG, 675:735 (330).
44. BL APAC, IOR/R/10/Misc./2, entry of October 8, 1818. The format described by Morrison, of a world map and coastal map on the same scroll, matches the version of Chen's map called the *Bianhai quanjiang tu*. Morrison's "soundings" could be the sandbanks on Chen's map.
45. *Ling Tingkan quanji*, 3:200.
46. *GDTZ* DG, 675:733 (330).
47. Chen, *Bianhai quanjiangtu*.
48. Li, *Yangyizhai wenji*, 2. 24a.
49. Li, *Lidai dilizhi yunbian jinshi*, 467–68.
50. Dai, *Yapian zhanzheng renwu zhuan*, 241–42.
51. Cai, *Hainan zazhu*, 27–28.
52. Gutzlaff, *Journal of Three Voyages*, 239.
53. Zhou, *Xiamen zhi*, 276.
54. *Indo-Chinese Gleaner*, 2.X (October 1819), 186–87.
55. Ismail, "Missionary Printing in Malacca," 182, 188, 197.
56. Wylie, *Memorials*, 5.
57. Ibid., 4–30, 48–49.
58. Milne, *Chashisu meiyue tongjizhuan*, 1820 issue, unpaginated.

59. *Texuan cuoyao meiyue tongjizhuan,* "Yaoliuba zonglun," pt. 10.
60. *Yapian zhanzheng shiqi sixiangshi,* 2–5.
61. Morrison, *View of China for Philological Purposes,* 78–79, 83.
62. Morrison, *Dictionary,* II.1:396, 699, III, 226–27.
63. Morrison, *Xiyou diqiu wenjian lüezhuan,* 3a–3b.
64. *Da Yingguo renshi lüeshuo,* 3. Yuan 垣 is an error for *tan* 坦.
65. *GDTZ* DG, 675:721 (330).
66. Quoted in Lazich, "Diffusion of Useful Knowledge," 312.
67. Gützlaff, *Dong-Xiyang kao meiyue tongjizhuan,* 40, 101, 104.
68. Quoted in Lazich, "Diffusion of Useful Knowledge," 312, 315–16; see also Chen, "Information War."
69. Gützlaff, *Dong-Xiyang kao meiyue tongjizhuan,* 174–75 (DG15/5 issue).
70. *Da Yingguo renshi lüeshuo,* 2–3.
71. Lindsay, *Report of Proceedings,* 32.
72. Ibid., 62.
73. Ibid., 103.
74. Gutzlaff, *Journal of Three Voyages,* 217.
75. Ibid., 239.
76. Ibid., 245.
77. Gützlaff, *Dong-Xiyang kao meiyue tongjizhuan,* 175.
78. Lindsay, *Report of Proceedings,* 4.
79. Xu, *Dazhong ji,* 67; Gutzlaff, *Journal of Three Voyages,* 331.
80. Xu, *Dazhong ji,* 80.
81. *YZDS,* 1:111, 117–20.
82. *QSL* DG, 36:378 (226.21a); *Shiliao xunkan,* 330 (619a–b).
83. *YZDS,* 1:127.
84. Inoue argues that officials and local scholars at Guangzhou had a common interest in opposing attacks on foreign trade by "statecraft" scholars like Bao Shichen (*Shindai ahen,* 85).
85. Yan, *Yangfang jiyao,* 1.11b–12a, 24.1a–43b.
86. Lin, *China Upside Down,* 89.
87. Inoue, *Shindai ahen,* 79–80.
88. Wang, *Ruan Yuan nianpu,* 581–82.
89. *RZH,* 2.1:766.
90. *Yapian zhanzheng shiqi sixiangshi,* 2.
91. Ibid., 3.
92. Xiao's essay (*RZH,* 2.1:767) dates to a period in which it was rumored but not yet certain (at least among the Chinese residents of Guangzhou), that the East India Company's trade monopoly would be revoked. He also refers to the publishing of prices current in Gützlaff's periodical, which as far as I am able to determine began with the DG13/10 (November 12–December 10, 1833) issue.
93. Li, *Wei Yuan shiyou ji,* 129.
94. Xiao, *Ji Yingjili, HGTZ2,* 4:1899–1949; *RZH,* 2.1:767 (as *Yingjili ji*); *Xiaofanghuzhai yudi congchao zaibubian,* 7, pt. 11.

95. *RZH*, 2.1:767.
96. Fang, *Kaopanji wenlu*, 263 (2.4a). Ye, of She county, Anhui, in 1831 (DG11) came to Guangzhou, where he composed his essay on England. His notice about newspapers, at the end of the text, may be a later addition.
97. Gützlaff in the DG13/12 (January–February 1834) issue of his magazine discussed newspapers, attributing their origins to Italy (see *Dong-Xiyang kao meiyue tongjizhuan*, 66). In 1833 Robert Morrison also described European newspapers in his *Zawen bian* (Morrison, *Memoirs of the Life and Labours*, 2:478). Ye's discussion of steamship mechanics resembles the content of the November–December 1833 issue of Gützlaff's *Magazine* (48).
98. *Yapian zhanzheng shiqi sixiangshi*, 2.
99. Bao, reprinted in *Yapian zhanzheng shiqi sixiangshi*, 4–5.
100. Ye, "Yingjilu-guo yiqing jilüe," in *Xiaofanghuzhai zaibubian*, 7, pt. 11:2–3; cf. variant reading in *RZH*, 2.1:790.
101. *Yapian zhanzheng shiqi sixiangshi*, 15.
102. Xiao, *Ji Yingjili*, *RZH*, 2.1:767.
103. Xiao, "Yuedong shibo lun," *HGTZ2*, 6:2794 (49. 2b); cf. variant reading in *RZH*, 2.1:775.
104. Ye, "Yingjili-guo yiqing jilüe," *Xiaofanghuzhai zaibubian* 7, pt. 11:2; *RZH*, 2.1:790.
105. Misra, *Central Administration*, 18–33.
106. *Shiliao xunkan*, 409–10 (21.765b–769b). According to Morse, Li Hongbin had replied to reports of the impending dissolution on January 16, 1831.
107. *Shiliao xunkan*, 450 (23.844b).
108. Xiao, *Ji Yingjili*, *RZH* 2.1:766; *HGTZ2*, 4:1901 (35.2a).
109. Xiao, *Ji Yingjili*, *HGTZ2*, 4:1905 (35.4a); *RZH* 2.1:767.
110. Xiao, *Ji Yingjili*, *HGTZ2*, 4:1905 (35.4a); *RZH* 2.1:767.
111. Ye, "Yingjili yiqing jilüe" *RZH*, 2.1: 787–92.
112. Yan, "Haifang yulun," *RZH*, 2.1:797.
113. Ye, "Yingjili-guo yiqing jilüe," *RZH*, 2.1:792.
114. Xiao, *Ji Yingjili*, *HGTZ2*, 4:1909 (35.6a/b); *RZH*, 2.1:768.
115. *Yue haiguan zhi jiaozhu ben*, 4.
116. *Guangdong haifang huilan* (38.62a).
117. *Yue haiguan zhi jiaozhu ben*, 453–65 (23).
118. Liang, *Haiguo sishuo*, 132; Fang, *Kaopanji wenlu*, 265 (11.8a).

Chapter Seven

1. Fairbank, "Creation of the Treaty System," 10.1:215.
2. On the Opium War, see Chang, *Commissioner Lin*; Fay, *Opium War*; Waley, *Opium War through Chinese Eyes*; Wakeman, *Strangers at the Gate*; Polachek, *Inner Opium War*; Mao, *Tianchao de bengkui*.
3. Chang, *Commissioner Lin*, 92–94.
4. Yu, *Yu Zhengxie quanji*, 3:279.
5. *CBYWSM* DG, 414:24 (2.1b).

6. *CBYWSM* DG, 414:73 (4.31a).
7. *YZDS*, 1:470.
8. *YZDS*, 1:279
9. *Lin Zexu quanji*, 3:44. Item dated to first ten days of DG18/5 (June 22–July 1, 1838).
10. Ibid., 7:261 (letter of DG20/11/29).
11. *RZH*, 2.1:824–25.
12. Yuan was known as "Shaow-Tih" (xiao De). According to Hunter, he left Penang for Malacca around 1825, having studied at the "Roman Catholic school" and knowing Latin. Before that year, when a Catholic Free School teaching English opened in Penang, the only Catholic education available was the General College, founded in 1808 by La société des Missions étrangères de Paris to train seminarians. Hunter reported "rumors" that Yuan was a Catholic convert (*Bits of Old China*, 260–63). A Chinese document described him as a man of Nanhai county, but ancestrally from Ba county, Sichuan, who knew Latin. It does not mention an official rank (*Lin Zexu quanji*, 10:370–71). Xiao Lingyu's 1832 *Ji Yingjili* stated that "the Directorate of Astronomy has a person who writes Latin, selected and sent by the Guangzhou maritime customs" (*HGTZ2*, 35.2b), possibly Yuan. No official rank is mentioned.
13. Liang Tingnan dated the text of this letter to between March 15 and April 13, 1839 (DG19/2), fitting Hunter's chronology (*Yifen wenji*, 26–27). It was reprinted at the end of May in the *Chinese Repository* (8:9–12), which stated that it "was permitted to obtain circulation among the people, in the same manner as many official documents commonly do, about three months since."
14. Huang Juezi, *Huang Juezi zoushu*, 48–49.
15. *Yapian zhanzheng*, 453; cited in Waley, *Opium War through Chinese Eyes*, 27.
16. *Lin Zexu quanji*, 3:135.
17. Hunter, *Bits of Old China*, 262.
18. Liang, *Yifen wenji*, 26.
19. Wu, "Liang Tingnan nianpu jianbian," 85.
20. *Lin Zexu shujian*, 46; *Lin Zexu quanji*, 3:190.
21. On Liang Zhi, see McNeur, *China's First Preacher*, 36, 40, 67–68, 82–83 (quotation on 82).
22. Smith, *Chinese Christians*, 52–54.
23. If the 1839 dating of "almost thirty years ago" is correct, Wen could have worked with Marshman in Bengal and appeared to be an "old man" (*CR*, 8:77, June 1839).
24. Britton, *Chinese Periodical Press, 1800–1912*, 31–32. Smith identifies him as Ah Lum or William Alum (*Chinese Christians*, 57).
25. Hill found on Lin's staff a young man who "had been in London for nearly eight years along with the late Mr. Elphinstone. He speaks English remarkably well, much better, indeed, than any Chinese whom I have ever met with" (*CR*, 8:483, Jan. 1840). This description does not match any of Lin's four known translators, and may refer to Rong Lin.

26. *Lin Zexu shujian*, 46.
27. Ibid., 174.
28. Ibid.
29. *Lin Zexu quanji*, 10:214.
30. Mao, *Tianchao de bengkui*, 116–19.
31. *Lin Zexu quanji*, 7:164.
32. Gulick, *Peter Parker*, 88.
33. *CR*, 8:76 (June 1839).
34. *CR*, 9:647 (December 1840).
35. Gulick, *Peter Parker*, 90.
36. Fay, *Opium War*, 180–95.
37. Greenberg, *British Trade*, 110.
38. Chang, *Commissioner Lin*, 75, 104.
39. *YZDS*, 1:596.
40. Sasaki, *Yapian zhanzheng qian Zhong-Ying jiaoshe wenshu*, 148.
41. *YZDS*, 1:515.
42. *CR*, 8:485 (January 1840). Hill was a passenger on the bark *Sunda*, wrecked in October 1840.
43. *YZDS*, 1:644–45.
44. Liang, *Yifen wenji*, 25.
45. Fay, *Opium War*, 180–210.
46. Lai, *Lin Zexu nianpu xinbian*, 322.
47. Lin's claim that "her uncle divided out enfeoffments to the outer ports" suggests the role of the prime minister. Perhaps Lin regarded Lord Melbourne's peerage as implying a literal family relationship (*YZDS*, 1:674).
48. *YZDS*, 1:674.
49. *YZDS*, 1:673–75.
50. *YZDS*, 1:744.
51. *YZDS*, 2:128–29.
52. Mao, *Tianchao de bengkui*, 114–19.
53. *YZDS*, 2:210.
54. *YZDS*, 2:355.
55. *YZDS*, 2:393.
56. Murray, *Encyclopædia of Geography*, 2:343.
57. *Lin Zexu quanji*, 10:9. Note that Britain proper is "London," while "England" represents the overall imperial structure.
58. *YZDS*, 2:125–27.
59. Scott, *Narrative of a Recent Imprisonment*, 46. Yi-li-bu memorialized on DG20/9/2 that he had captured six Indians who were buying supplies near Dinghai; presumably Scott met these men in Ningbo (*YZDS*, 2:412–13).
60. *CR*, 9:646–48 (Dec. 1840). Lin mentions these Indians in a memorial of DG20/7/19 (August 16, 1840), *YZDS*, 2:279. Stanton's narrative does not mention them.
61. *YZDS*, 2:423–24.

62. *YZDS*, 2:405.
63. Waley, *Opium War through Chinese Eyes*, 239–41.
64. Wei, *Yingjili xiaoji, RZH* 2.1, 905–906; *HGTZ1*, 35.21a–22b.
65. *YZDS*, 3:434.
66. Lai, *Lin Zexu nianpu xinbian*, 403.
67. Yu-qian, *Yu Jingjie gong yishu*, 950 (12. 65b).
68. *Yapian zhanzheng*, 5:499.
69. Scott, *Narrative of a Recent Imprisonment*, 74–75.
70. Ibid., 115.
71. *YZDS*, 5:195.
72. Hunter, *Bits of Old China*, 21–31.
73. *YZDS*, 2:413.
74. *Yapian zhanzheng*, 5:499.
75. *YZDS*, 5:196.
76. *YZDS*, 5:222.
77. *YZDS*, 5:330.
78. Davis, *China, During the War*, 220.
79. Ibid., 224.
80. *CBYWSM* DG, 415: 421–22 (56.16b–17b).
81. *YZDS*, 5:783.
82. *Yapian zhanzheng*, 4:216.
83. *CBYWSM* DG, 415:502–3 (59.47b–49a).
84. Dikötter, *Discourse of Race*, 10, 16–17.
85. Wyatt, *Blacks of Premodern China*, 42.
86. Wakeman, *Strangers at the Gate*, 17.
87. The *Zhigong tu* referred to "black devil slaves" from "islands overseas" who served the Portuguese and Dutch (*Huang Qing zhigong tu*, 73). The *Guangdong tongzhi* reproduced this description (*GDTZ*, 675:733; 330).
88. Cf. Wyatt's finding that "the Chinese construct of blackness exhibited great elasticity" (*Blacks of Premodern China*, 9).
89. On events in Taiwan, see Yen, *Taiwan in China's Foreign Relations, 1836–1874*, 28–43, and Polachek, *Inner Opium War*, 185–203.
90. Morse, *International Relations of the Chinese Empire*, 1:293.
91. *QSL* DG, 38:489 (359.23a–24b); Yao, *Dongming zougao*, 32–36.
92. Gully, *Journals*, 27.
93. Ibid., 97.
94. Shili should also refer to Singapore.
95. Yao Ying, *Dongming zougao*, 64–67.
96. *CBYWSM* DG, 415:46–47 (19b–21a).
97. *YZDS*, 5:55.
98. Yao, *Dongming zougao*, 69–70.
99. Ibid., 96, 128.
100. Ibid., 127, 133–34.
101. Ibid., 123–34. Polachek summarizes Yao's views on the strategic significance

of India (*Inner Opium War*, 200–3), and argues that the "Bengali" revolt mentioned in Yao's letters in 1842 was connected to the Gurkha requests for assistance. While in Taiwan Yao did not explicitly refer to the Gurkhas, and the "Bengali" revolt was likely connected to coastal rumors about the British defeat in Afghanistan.

102. Yao, *Dongming wenji, wen houji*, 1512:546–47 (7.7b–8a).

103. *Lin Zexu quanji*, 10:188–95 (original article in *Canton Press*, October 12, 1839).

104. Ibid., 10:215.

105. Ibid., 10:229–32 (original in *Canton Press*, January 18, 1840). "Chinese Tibet" (*Zhongguo Xizang*) renders the English "Chinese Empire in Thibet." The Chinese phrase "I think China sees that we are sending out troops as we please" (*xiang Zhongguo kan wodeng xi suibian chubing*) is a mistranslation of the original "Can it be suppose [*sic*] that China views with indifference such an army in motion from our possessions?" (a reference to the Afghan campaign).

106. Rose, *Nepal*, 95–101.

107. Mengboo, *Xizang zoushu*, 89–96 (3); FHA JJC LFZZ, reel 573:676–77 (DG20/10/3, rescripted DG20/11/7).

108. He-ning, *Xizang fu*, 666 (26a–b).

109. Petech, "Dalai-Lamas and Regents of Tibet," 388.

110. Mengboo, *Xizang zoushu*, 197–200 (3).

111. *YZDS*, 3:298–99.

112. FHA JJC LFZZ, reel 571:12–14 (Memorial, Qi Gong, DG21/4/24, rescripted DG21/5/28).

113. Mengboo, *Xizang zoushu*, FSN, juan 18, memorial DG21/9/6.

114. Fisher et al., *Himalayan Battleground*, 45–54.

115. *Qingdai Zangshi zoudu*, 1:219.

116. Ibid., 1:220.

117. Ibid., 1:218–21.

118. Bello, *Opium and the Limits of Empire*, 180–90.

119. *YZDS*, 1:675–77.

120. *YZDS*, 2:3–7.

121. *QSL DG*, 38:129 (338.4a–b).

122. *QSL DG*, 38:203–4 (342.6b–7a).

123. *Li Xingyuan ri ji*, 1:96 (cited in Bello, *Opium and the Limits of Empire*, 200n61).

124. *QSL DG*, 33:463 (26.20b).

125. *CBYWSM DG*, 415:268 (49.6b).

126. Yao, *Dongming zougao*, 124, 128.

127. Liang, *Yifen wenji*, 40–41.

128. For these events, see Hopkirk, *The Great Game*, 230–77.

129. *YZDS*, 5:294–95.

130. *CBYWSM DG*, 415:308–9 (51.1a–2b).

131. *CBYWSM DG*, 415:306–7 (50.39b–40b).

132. Yao, *Dongming wenji, wen houji*, 1512:547–48 (7.9a–10a).

133. Ibid., 1512:550 (7.14a).

134. Lawson, *East India Company*, 106; Keay, *Honourable Company*, 362–63; Greenberg, *British Trade*, 26; quotation on sepoys (1827), cited in Peers, *Between Mars and Mammon*, 87.

Chapter Eight

1. Chinese scholars have generally celebrated Wei as a pioneer of new information about the West. Leonard has published a revisionist study arguing that Wei was primarily restoring earlier "traditions" from pre-Qing contact with maritime Asia (Nanyang) (*Wei Yuan*, 204). In 1992, James Polachek advanced a reading of the *Haiguo tuzhi* as basically a polemical document (*Inner Opium War*, 195). My own view of these three interpretations will be given below.

2. Leonard, *Wei Yuan*, 11–31; Hummel, *Eminent Chinese*, 2:850–52.

3. On their compilation and publication see Huang, *Wei Yuan nianpu*, 227, 223–24.

4. *RZH*, 2.1:863–68.

5. Zheng, *Zhouju suozhi*, 1–2.

6. Wang, *Haiwai fanyi lu*.

7. *RZH*, 2.1:858–62.

8. *KYJX*, 1:147, 150 (5.1a, 2b).

9. Liu, "Cong 'Yutu kaolüe' dao 'Yinghuan zhilüe,'" 65.

10. Liang, *Haiguo sishuo*.

11. *HGTZ1*, 13.1a.

12. Wang, *Wei Yuan nianpu*, 51.

13. In the first, 50-juan (chapter) printing of 1844, Wei devotes juan 13 to annotating Murray's description of India, but juan 17 and 18 to a study of India's historical geography.

14. *HGTZ1*, juan 13 (East, South, and Central); juan 17–19. Two additional juan deal with "West India," indicating Asian countries west of the subcontinent, such as Persia and Judea.

15. *HGTZ1*, 13.2a–b. English names as given in Murray, *Encyclopædia of Geography*, 344–45.

16. Wang, *Wei Yuan nianpu*, 21, dates their meeting to 1823; Shi, *Yao Ying nianpu*, 64, to 1826. On the social and intellectual context of this period, see Polachek, *Inner Opium War*, 66–73.

17. *KYJX*, 1:150 (5.2b).

18. Shi, *Yao Ying nianpu*, 52.

19. *KYJX*, 1:147 (5.1a).

20. *KYJX*, 1:147 (5.1a). See also Polachek, *Inner Opium War*, 185–93.

21. For his earlier research, see Yao, *Shixiao lu*, 101–4; for Denham, see *KYJX*, 1:3 (preface).

22. *KYJX*, 1:3 (preface).

23. Shi, *Yao Ying nianpu*, 275–345. Yao's preface states that the *Kangyou jixing* was composed between 1844 and 1846, but entries for particular dates were later

revised. For instance, an essay in the record of his 1845 travels refers to the *Haiguo tuzhi* in 60 juan, although the edition Yao possessed in 1845 must have been the 50-juan edition of 1844, not the 60-juan second edition of 1847 (*KYJX*, 1:147 [5.1a]). Yao told a correspondent, probably in late 1847, that he had "greatly developed and [re]organized my book, removing extraneous portions and expanding and correcting it" (*Dongming wenji, wen houji*, 1512:561 [8.19b]). Shi, *Yao Ying nianpu*, 322–24.

24. *HGTZ1*, 13.38a.
25. *KYJX*, 1: 88–91 (3.2b–4a).
26. *KYJX*, 1:236–37 (8.3b–4a).
27. *KYJX*, 1:275 (8.4b).
28. *KYJX*, 2:301 (10.1a), cf. Yao's hand copy of Verbiest's map, 2:580–81 (16.25b–26a).
29. *KYJX*, 2:301–302 (10.1a–b).
30. Wei, *Shengwu ji*, 402:275 (5.36a).
31. *KYJX*, 1:152–53 (5.3b–4a).
32. Wei, *Shengwu ji*, 3rd ed., 160 (5).
33. *KYJX*, 1:147 (5.1a).
34. *HGTZ2*, 6:2615 (46.2a).
35. Xu, *Yinghuan zhilüe*, 6 (author's preface).
36. For instance, Yao's map of the countries below Tibet completely ignores the peninsular shape of continental Southeast Asia, although this is presented on other maps he includes (*KYJX*, 2:646–47 [16.58b–59a]).
37. *HGTZ2*, 1:165 (2.preface).
38. *HGTZ2*, 1:166–69 (2, 2b–3a). Cf. Li, *Yuantian tushuo*; Zhuang, *Da Qing tongshu* (ch. 6, n41–42).
39. *HGTZ2*, 1:173 (2, 5a); cf. Aleni, *Zhifang wai ji jiaoshi*, 23.
40. *KYJX*, 2:612–13 (16.41b–42a).
41. For an example, see *HGTZ2*, 1:193 (2.15a).
42. *KYJX*, 2:580–81 (16.25b–26a).
43. *HGTZ2*, 1:187–89 (2.12a–13a).
44. *KYJX*, 1:147 (5.1a).
45. *KYJX*, 1:147 (5.1a)
46. *HGTZ2*, 1:193 (2.15a).
47. *HGTZ2*, 2:710 (13.17b).
48. *HGTZ2*, 2:750 (13.37b).
49. Wei remarked: "[As for] how it differs from books on maritime countries by the men of the past, I observe: those all discussed the West using people from China; this, however, discusses the West using people from the West" (*yi Xiyangren tan Xiyang ye*) (*HGTZ2*, 1:5 [preface]).
50. *HGTZ2*, 6:2613–31 (46.1a–10a).
51. Wei argued that Buddhist references to cardinal directions were relative, whereas Verbiest misinterpreted them as absolute.
52. *KYJX*, 1:276 (9.5b).

53. See, for example, Xu, *Yinghuan zhilüe*, 74–75.
54. Ibid., 2 (prefaces).
55. *HGTZ1*, 1.39a–b; *HGTZ2*, 1:109–10 (1.38a–b).
56. *HGTZ2*, 1:165 ("Yuantu hengtu xu").
57. *HGTZ1*, 13.preface 1a–b; *HGTZ2*, 2:671–72 (13.preface 1a–b).
58. *HGTZ1*, 13.preface 1a–b; *HGTZ2*, 2:671–72 (13.preface 1a–b).
59. *HGTZ1*, 13.1b–2a; *HGTZ2*, 2:672–73 (13.1b–2a).
60. Wei, *Shengwu ji*, 1st ed., 402:272–73 (5.32b–33a).
61. Ibid., 402:275 (5.37b).
62. Ibid., 402:275–76 (5.37b–39a).
63. Yu, *Xiyu kaogu lu*, 2:845–46 (16b: 22a–b).
64. *KYJX*, 1:89–90 (3.3a–b); Liang, *Yifen wenji*, 112–13 (4).
65. Wei, *Shengwu ji*, 1st ed., 402:275–76 (5.38a–39a).
66. Kanda, "'Seimuki' zakkō," 332.
67. Wei, *Shengwu ji*, 1st ed., 402:268 (5.43b).
68. Wei, *Shengwu ji*, 3rd ed., 169–72 (6).
69. Wang, *Wei Yuan dui Xifang*, 151.
70. Wei, *Shengwu ji*, 1st ed., 402:276–79 (5.40a–46a). This article, attributed to the *Aomen yuebao*, appeared in the July 25, 1840, *Canton Press*. The original refers to:

> the magnificent [Russian] embassy which is now threading its way . . . to Pekin, to give heart to the Chinese, in the approaching struggle with England . . . to organize Eastern Asia against us, through means of its Lord Paramount, the Emperor of China. . . . The Russians have studied the affairs of India to little purpose, if they have not learned, that the most effectual mode of bringing down the Nepaulese on our plains, is by a mandate from Pekin.

The Chinese translation in Wei's work is truncated and faulty, reading: "We now hear that a Russian envoy has started from Pitege for China via Tartary, who will certainly provoke the Chinese to fight England, and who desires to get Beijing to issue an edict to the Burmese [sic] causing them to come attack. We don't know when the envoy will be able to arrive at Beijing."

71. Wei, *Shengwu ji*, 1st ed., 402:278 (5.43b–44b).
72. Ibid., 402:294 (6.29a–b); my italics.
73. Ibid., 402:294 (6.29b).
74. Ibid., 402:294 (6.29b).
75. Ibid., 402:276 (5.39a).
76. *QSL QL*, 21:821 (1031.16a).
77. Hummel, *Eminent Chinese*, 1:90–92; Polachek, *Inner Opium War*, 147; Zhao and Wu, "Aomen tusheng Puren Hanxuejia Majishi yu 'Xinshi dili beikao,'" 132.
78. Chen Li was able to meet Wei Yuan in Guangdong in 1847 (some sources erroneously give 1849), which he stated was "a number of years" (*shunian*) after writing his objections to Zhang Weiping (*RZH*, 2.1:1008–10). Thus, Chen probably read Wei's book very shortly after it was issued (in 1844) (Huang, *Wei Yuan nianpu*, 151).
79. *RZH*, 2.1:1008–10.
80. Xu, *Yinghuan kaolüe*, 73.

81. Ibid., 73–76; Xu, *Yinghuan zhilüe*, 236–37.
82. Fang, *Qing Xu Songkan xiansheng Jiyu nianpu*, 84.
83. *CBYWSM* DG, 416:163 (75.38b–39a).
84. *CBYWSM* XF, 416:546 (15.6a–b).
85. Yapp, *Strategies of British India*, 15.
86. *CBYWSM* XF, 417:530–33 (47.16b–22a).
87. Feng, *Jiaobinlu kangyi*, 49.
88. For instance, Fairbank terms Wei's *Haiguo tuzhi* "a many-faceted pioneer effort to get a new focus on the problems posed by international trade and Western gunboats," albeit "often misinformed" ("Creation of the Treaty System," 219). Huang Liyong is typical of Chinese authors in lauding Wei as a pioneer who "opened his eyes and saw the world" (*kaiyan kan shijie*) (*Wei Yuan nianpu*, 1).

Conclusion

1. Lamb, *British India and Tibet*, 57–64.
2. *CBYWSM* XF, 416:287 (1.5b–6a).
3. Lamb, *British India and Tibet*, 61.
4. *Qingdai Zangshi zoudu*, 296–97; edict in response, *CBYWSM* DG, 416:155 (75.23a).
5. Huc, *Souvenirs d'un voyage dans la Tartarie*, 2:41-42.
6. See Chapter 4, Note 32, for the relationship between *phe-reng* and *phyi-gling*.
7. *Qing zhong-qianqi*, 3:1314.
8. *CBYWSM* DG, 416:163 (75.39a).
9. *CBYWSM* DG, 416:176–77 (76.14a–15a).
10. *CBYWSM* DG, 416:195 (77.11a–b).
11. *CBYWSM* DG, 416:265–66 (77.31a–32a).
12. *Qingdai Zangshi zoudu*, 297–99.
13. *CBYWSM* DG, 416:206 (77.32a).
14. Horowitz, "Central Power and State Making," 84.
15. On these reforms, see Yoon, "Grand Council," and Halsey, "State-Making."
16. Hsü, "Great Policy Debate," 212–28.

Bibliography

Archives

British Library, Asia, Pacific & Africa Collections (formerly Oriental and India Office Collections)
First Historical Archives (Beijing), *Junjichu, Lufu zouzhe* 軍機處, 錄副奏摺
First Historical Archives (Beijing), *Junjichu Manwen lufu zouzhe* 軍機處, 滿文錄副奏摺
National Palace Museum (Taipei), *Junjichu dang* 軍機處檔

Published Materials

Agoston, Gabor. "Information, Ideology, and Limits of Imperial Policy: Ottoman Grand Strategy in the Context of Ottoman-Habsburg Rivalry." In *The Early Modern Ottomans: Remapping the Empire*, eds. Virginia H. Aksan and Daniel Goffman (New York: Cambridge University Press, 2007):75–103.
Alder, Garry. *Beyond Bokhara: The Life of William Moorcroft, Asian Explorer and Pioneer Veterinary Surgeon, 1767–1825* (London: Century Publishing, 1985).
Aleni, Giulio [Ai Rulüe 艾儒略]. *Zhifang wai ji jiaoshi* 職方外紀校釋, ed. Xie Fang (Beijing: Zhonghua shuju, 2000).
Allsen, Thomas T. *Culture and Conquest in Mongol Eurasia* (Cambridge, UK: Cambridge University Press, 2001).
Aomen lishi ditu jingxuan 澳門歷史地圖精選 (Beijing: Huawen chubanshe, 2000).
Aris, Michael, ed. and trans. *'Jigs-med-gling-pa's "Discourse on India" of 1789: A Critical Edition and Annotated Translation of the "lHo-phyogs rgya-gar-gyi gtam brtag-pa brgyad-kyi me-long"* (Tokyo: International Institute for Buddhist Studies of ICABS, 1995).
Athar Ali, M. "The Evolution of the Perception of India: Akbar and Abul Fazl." In Athar Ali, *Mughal India*:109–18.
———. *Mughal India: Studies in Polity, Ideas, Society, and Culture* (New Delhi: Oxford University Press, 2006).
Baddeley, John F. *Russia, Mongolia, China*. 2 vols. (London: Macmillan, 1919).
Bagchi, P. C. "Ancient Chinese Names of India." *Monumenta Serica* 13 (1948):366–75.

Bagrow, Leo. "The First Russian Maps of Siberia and Their Influence on the West-European Cartography of N. E. Asia." *Imago Mundi* 9 (1952):83–93.

Bamzai, P. N. K. *Culture and Political History of Kashmir*, vol. 2, *Medieval Kashmir* (New Delhi: M D Publications, 1994).

Bartlett, Beatrice S. *Monarchs and Ministers: The Grand Council in Mid-Ch'ing China, 1723–1820* (Berkeley: University of California Press, 1991).

Bawden, Charles, trans. *The Mongol Chronicle Altan Tobči* (Wiesbaden: Otto Harrassowitz, 1955).

Baxun wanshou shengdian 八旬萬壽盛典, SKQS, 661.

Bayly, C. A. *Empire and Information: Intelligence Gathering and Social Communication in India, 1780–1870* (Cambridge, UK: Cambridge University Press, 1996).

———. "The First Age of Global Imperialism, c. 1760–1830." *Journal of Imperial and Commonwealth History* 26 (1998):28–47.

Bello, David A. *Opium and the Limits of Empire: Drug Prohibition in the Chinese Interior, 1729–1850* (Cambridge, MA: Harvard University Asia Center, 2005).

Ben-Dor Benite, Zvi. *Dao of Muhammad: A Cultural History of Muslims in Late Imperial China* (Cambridge, MA: Harvard University Asia Center, 2005).

Benoist, Michel [Jiang Youren 蔣友仁]. *Diqiu tushuo* 地球圖說, XXSKQS.

Bernard, Henri. "Les Éstapes de la Cartographie scientifique pour la Chine et les Pays Voisins." *Monumenta Serica* 1/2 (1935): 428–77.

Bla-ma bTsan-po. *A Tibetan Religious Geography of Nepal*, ed. and trans. Turrell Wylie (Rome: Instituto italiano per il Medio ed Estremo Oriente, 1970).

Bogle, George. *Bhutan and Tibet: The Travels of George Bogle and Alexander Hamilton, 1774–1777*, ed. Alastair Lamb (Hertingfordbury, UK: Roxford Books, 2002).

Britton, Roswell S. *The Chinese Periodical Press, 1800–1912* (Shanghai: Kelley & Walsh, 1933).

Broc, Numa. *La Géographie de la Renaissance, 1420–1620* (Paris: Les Éditions du C.T.H.S., 1986).

Brook, Timothy. "The Early Jesuits and the Late Ming Border: The Chinese Search for Accommodation." In *Encounters and Dialogues: Changing Perspectives on Chinese-Western Exchanges from the Sixteenth to Eighteenth Centuries*, ed. Xiaoxin Wu (Sankt Augustin: Monumenta Serica, 2005):19–38.

Buglio, Ludovico [Li Leisi 利類思]. *Xifang yaoji* 西方要紀 (Ji'nan: Qi Lu shushe chubanshe, 1997).

Burke, Peter. *A Social History of Knowledge: From Gutenberg to Diderot* (Cambridge, UK: Polity, 2000).

Bysack, Gaur Dás. "Notes on a Buddhist Monastery at Bhoṭ Bágán." *Journal of the Asiatic Society of Bengal* 59/1 (1890):50–99.

Cai Tinglan 蔡廷蘭. *Hainan zazhu* 海南雜著 (Taipei: Taiwan yinhang, 1959).

Cammann, Schuyler. "The Panchen Lama's Visit to China in 1780: An Episode in Anglo-Tibetan Relations." *Far Eastern Quarterly* 9/1 (1949):3–19.

———. *Trade Through the Himalayas: The Early British Attempts to Open Tibet* (Princeton, NJ: Princeton University Press, 1951).

Chandra, Lokesh, ed. *Sanskrit Texts from the Imperial Palace at Peking in the Man-*

churian, Chinese, Mongolian, and Tibetan Scripts, Part 1 (New Delhi: Institute for the Advancement of Science and Culture, 1966).

Chang, Hsin-pao. *Commissioner Lin and the Opium War* (New York: W.W. Norton, 1964).

Chase, Hanson. "The Status of the Manchu Language in the Early Ch'ing" (PhD diss., University of Washington, 1979).

Ch'en, Kenneth. "Matteo Ricci's Contribution to, and Influence on, Geographical Knowledge in China." *Journal of the American Oriental Society* 59/3 (1939): 325–59.

———. "A Possible Source for Ricci's Notices on Regions near China." *T'oung Pao*, second series 34/3 (1938):179–90.

Chen Kesheng 陳克繩. *Xiyu yiwen* 西域遺聞 (Taipei: Wenhua shuju, 1968).

Chen Lunjiong 陳倫烱. *Bianhai quanjiangtu* 邊海全疆圖 (Tōyō Bunko II-11-L-56), 1790.

———. *Haiguo wenjian lu* 海國聞見錄 (Taipei: Taiwan sheng wenxian weiyuanhui, 1996).

———. *Haiguo wenjian lu* (1793).

Chen Shenglin 陳勝粦. "Lüelun Yao Ying kaiyan kan shijie de sixiang zhuzhang" 略論姚瑩開眼看世界的思想主張. In *Lin Zexu yu yapian zhanzheng lungao (zengdingben)* 林則徐與鴉片戰爭論稿（增訂本）(Guangzhou: Zhongshan daxue chubanshe, 1990):332–50.

Chen, Songchuan. "An Information War Waged by Merchants and Missionaries at Canton: The Society for the Diffusion of Useful Knowledge in China, 1834–1839." *Modern Asian Studies* (2011):1–31.

Chen Zehong 陳澤泓. "Zhu 'Yuantian tushuo,' jian chaodou gaotai—Qingdai zixue chengcai de tianwen xuejia, Daoshi Li Mingche" 著 "圜天圖說" 建朝斗高台—清代自學成材的天文學家,道士李明徹. *Guangdong shizhi* 廣東史志 4 (1994):73–76.

Chouban yiwu shimo 籌辦夷務始末, XXSKQS.

Chu, Pingyi. "Trust, Instruments, and Cross-Cultural Scientific Exchanges: Chinese Debate over the Shape of the Earth, 1600–1800." *Science in Context* 12/3 (1999):385–411.

Cišii [Qi-shi-yi 七十一]. *Xiyu zongzhi* 西域總志 (Taipei: Wenhai chubanshe, 1966).

Cooper, Randolf G. S. *The Anglo-Maratha Campaigns and the Contest for India: The Struggle for Control of the South Asian Military Economy* (Cambridge, UK: Cambridge University Press, 2003).

Cordier, Henri, ed. "Les Correspondants de Bertin, Secrétaire d'État au XVIIIe siècle." *T'oung pao* 18 (1917):295–379.

Courant, Maurice. *L'Asie Centrale aux XVIIe et XVIIIe siècles: empire kalmouk ou empire mantchou?* (Lyon: A. Ray, 1912).

The Chinese Repository (Canton: Printed for the Proprietors, 1832–1851).

Crane, Nicholas. *Mercator: The Man Who Mapped the Planet* (London: Weidenfeld & Nicolson, 2002).

Da Ming yitong zhi 大明一統志 (Xi'an: San Qin chubanshe, 1990).
Da Qing yitong yutu 大清一統輿圖 (Beijing: Quanguo tushuguan wenxian suowei fuzhi zhongxin, 2003).
Da Qing yitong zhi 大清一統志 1st ed.
Da Yingguo renshi lüeshuo 大英國人事略說 (Malacca: Ying-Hua shuyuan, 1832).
Dai Xueji 戴學稷. *Yapian zhanzheng renwu zhuan* 鴉片戰爭人物傳 (Fuzhou: Fujian jiaoyu chubanshe, 1985).
Dai, Yingcong. "A Disguised Defeat: The Myanmar Campaign of the Qing Dynasty." *Modern Asian Studies* 38/1 (2004):145–89.
Das, Sarat Chandra. *Tibetan-English Dictionary* (New Delhi: Adarsh, 2008).
Das Gupta, Ashin. "India and the Indian Ocean in the Eighteenth Century." In *The World of the Indian Ocean Merchant, 1500–1800: Collected Essays of Ashin Das Gupta*, ed. Uma Das Gupta (New Delhi: Oxford University Press, 1992):188–224.
Davies, C. Collin. "Aḥmad SHāh Durrānī." *Encyclopedia of Islam, Second Edition*. http://referenceworks.brillonline.com/entries/encyclopaedia-of-islam-2/ahmad-shah-DUM_0189 (accessed March 26, 2012).
Davis, John F. *China, During the War and Since the Peace* (London: Longman, Brown, Green, and Longmans, 1852).
———. *A Vocabulary, Containing Chinese Words and Phrases Peculiar to Canton and Macao, and to the Trade of the Those Places.* (Macao: Honorable Company's Press, 1824).
D'Elia, Pasquale M. "Recent Discoveries and New Studies (1938–1960) on the World Map in Chinese of Father Matteo Ricci SJ." *Monumenta Serica*, 20 (1961):82–164.
Dikötter, Frank. *The Discourse of Race in Modern China* (Stanford, CA: Stanford University Press, 1992).
Diskalkar, D. B. "Tibeto-Nepalese War, 1788–1793." *Journal of the Bihar and Orissa Research Society* 19/4 (1933):355–98.
Dorofeeva-Lichtmann, Vera. "Where Is the Yellow River Source? A Controversial Question in Early Chinese Historiography." *Oriens Extremus* 45 (2005–2006):68–90.
Dpal-ldan ye-shes [Panchen Lama III]. *Der Weg nach Śambhala (Śamb'alai lam yig)*, ed. and trans. Albert Grünwedel (Munich: Verlag der Königlich Bayerischen Akademie der Wissenschaften, 1915).
du Halde, J.-B. *Description géographique, historique . . . de l'empire de la Chine et de la Tartarie chinoise . . .* (Paris: P. G. Lemercier, 1735).
Edson, Evelyn. *The World Map, 1300–1492* (Baltimore: Johns Hopkins University Press, 2007).
Elliott, Mark C. "The Limits of Tartary: Manchuria in Imperial and National Geographies." *Journal of Asian Studies* 59/3 (2000):603–46.
———. "Whose Empire Shall It Be? Manchu Figurations of Historical Process in the Early Seventeenth Century." In *Time, Temporality, and Imperial Transition: East Asia from Ming to Qing*, ed. Lynn A. Struve (Honolulu: University of Hawai'i Press, 2005):31–72.

Elman, Benjamin A. *A Cultural History of Civil Examinations in Late Imperial China* (Berkeley: University of California Press, 2000).

———. *From Philosophy to Philology: Intellectual and Social Aspects of Change in Late Imperial China*, 2nd ed. (Los Angeles: UCLA Asian Pacific Monograph Series, 2001).

———. *On Their Own Terms: Science in China, 1550–1900* (Cambridge, MA: Harvard University Press, 2005).

Elverskog, Johan. *Our Great Qing: The Mongols, Buddhism and the State in Late Imperial China* (Honolulu: University of Hawai'i Press, 2006).

Encyclopedia of the Chinese Overseas, ed. Lynn Pan (Cambridge, MA: Harvard University Press, 1999).

Enoki Kazuo. "Researches in Chinese Turkestan during the Ch'ien-lung 乾隆 Period, with Special Reference to the *Hsi-yü-t'ung-wên-chih* 西域同文志." In *Studia Asiatica* (Tokyo: Kyuko-Shoin, 1998):442–74.

———. "Tsung-lê's Mission to the Western Regions in 1378–1382." In *Studia Asiatica* (Tokyo: Kyuko-Shoin, 1998):546–52.

Fairbank, John K. "The Creation of the Treaty System." In *Cambridge History of China* 10.1 (Cambridge, UK: Cambridge University Press, 1978):213–263.

———. "A Preliminary Framework." In *The Chinese World Order: Traditional China's Foreign Relations*, ed. John K. Fairbank (Cambridge, MA: Harvard University Press, 1968):1–19.

———. *Trade and Diplomacy on the China Coast: The Opening of the Treaty Ports, 1842–1854* (Stanford, CA: Stanford University Press, 1969).

Fairbank, John K., and S. Y. Teng. "On the Ch'ing Tribute System." *HJAS* 6/2 (1941):135–246.

Fang Dongshu 方東樹. *Kaopanji wenlu* 攷槃集文錄, *XXSKQS* 1497.

Fang Hao 方豪. *Zhong-Xi jiaotong shi* 中西交通史 (Changsha: Yuelu shushe, 1987).

Fang Wen 方聞, ed. *Qing Xu Songkan xiansheng Jiyu nianpu* 清徐松龕先生繼畬年譜 (Taipei: Taiwan shangwu yinshuguan, 1982).

Farquhar, David M. "The Origins of the Manchus' Mongolian Policy." In *The Chinese World Order: Traditional China's Foreign Relations*, ed. John K. Fairbank (Cambridge, MA: Harvard University Press, 1968):198–205.

Fay, Peter Ward. *The Opium War, 1840–1842* (Chapel Hill: University of North Carolina Press, 1997).

Feng Chengjun 馮承鈞. *Xiyu diming (zengdingben)* 西域地名(增訂本) (Beijing: Zhonghua shuju, 1980).

Feng Guifen 馮桂芬. *Jiaobinlu kangyi* 校邠廬抗議 (Shanghai: Shanghai shudian chubanshe, 2002).

Fisher, Margaret W. et al. *Himalayan Battleground: Sino-Indian Rivalry in Ladakh* (New York: Praeger, 1963).

Fisher, Michael H. *Indirect Rule in India: Residents and the Residency System, 1764–1858* (Delhi: Oxford University Press, 1991).

Fletcher, Joseph. "China and Central Asia." In *The Chinese World Order: Traditional*

China's Foreign Relations, ed. John K. Fairbank (Cambridge, MA: Harvard University Press, 1968):206–24.

———. "The Naqshbandiyya in Northwest China." In *Studies on Chinese and Islamic Inner Asia*, ed. B. F. Manz (Aldershot, UK: Variorum, 1995).

Flint, Valerie J. *The Imaginative Landscape of Christopher Columbus* (Princeton, NJ: Princeton University Press, 1992).

Foltz, Richard. "Uzbek Central Asia and Mughal India: Asian Muslim Society in the 16th and 17th Centuries" (PhD diss., Harvard University, 1996).

Fort William–India House Correspondence vol. 17 (Delhi: Manager of Publications, Government of India, 1955)

Foss, Theodore N. "A Western Interpretation of China: Jesuit Cartography." In *East Meets West: The Jesuits in China, 1582–1773*, eds. Charles E. Ronan and Bonnie B. C. Oh (Chicago: Loyola University Press, 1988):209–51.

Fracasso, Riccardo. "Shan hai ching 山海經." In *Early Chinese Texts: A Bibliographical Guide*, ed. Michael Loewe (Berkeley, CA: Society for the Study of Early China, 1993):357–67.

Fuchs, Walter. *Der Jesuiten Atlas der Kanghsi Zeit: China und die Aussenlaender* (Beijing: Catholic University, 1941).

———. "Materialien zur Kartographie der Mandju-Zeit." *Monumenta Serica* 1/2 (1935):386–427 and 3 (1938):189–231.

———. *The "Mongol Atlas" of China* (Peiping: Fu Jen University: 1946).

Fujian tongzhi 福建通志 (Taipei: Huawen shuju, 1968).

Funakoshi Akio 船越昭生. *Sakoku Nihon ni kita "Kōkizu" no chirigakushiteki kenkyū* 鎖国日本にきた「康熙図」の地理学史的研究 (Tokyo: Hōsei dagaku shuppankyoku, 1986).

———. "Zai Ka Iezusu kaishi no chizu sakusei to sono eikyō ni tsuite" 在華イエズス会士の地図作成とその影響について. *Tōyōshi kenkyū* 東洋史研究 27/4 (1969):506–25.

Fuyuan dajiangjun Yun-ti zougao 撫遠大將軍允禵奏稿 (Beijing: Quanguo tushuguan wenxian suowei fuzhi zhongxin, 1991).

Gaubil, Antoine. *Correspondance de Pékin, 1722–1759* (Geneva: Droz, 1970).

Greenberg, Michael. *British Trade and the Opening of China, 1800–42* (Cambridge, UK: Cambridge University Press, 1951)

Grevemeyer, J.-H. *Herrschaft, Raub und Gegenseitigkeit: Die politische Geschichte Badakhshans, 1500–1883* (Weisbaden: Harrassowitz, 1982).

Gu Hanyu changyongzi zidian 古漢語常用字字典 (Beijing: Shangwu yinshuguan, 2000).

Guangdong haifang huilan 廣東海防彙覽.

Guangdong tongzhi 廣東通志, Daoguang edition, *XXSKQS*; Yongzheng edition, *SKQS*.

Gudai Nanhai diming huishi 古代南海地名彙釋, ed. Chen Jiarong et al. (Beijing: Zhonghua shuju, 1986).

Gugong suocang Hendusitan yuqi tezhan tulu 故宮所藏痕都斯坦玉器特展圖錄 (Taipei: Gugong bowuyuan, 1983).

Gujin tushu jicheng 古今圖書集成 (Taipei: Wenxing shudian, 1964).
Gujin tushu jicheng Fangyu huibian Bianyidian 古今圖書集成方輿彙編邊裔典 (Chengdu: Sichuan minzu chubanshe, 2002).
Gulick, Edward V. *Peter Parker and the Opening of China* (Cambridge, MA: Harvard University Press, 1973).
Gully, Mr. *Journals Kept by Mr. Gully and Capt. Denham during a Captivity in China in the Year 1842* (London: Chapman and Hall, 1844).
Guo Deyan 郭德焱. *Qingdai Guangzhou de Basi shangren* 清代廣州的巴斯商人 (Beijing: Zhonghua shuju, 2005).
Guochao qixian leizheng chubian 國朝耆獻類徵初編 (Taipei: Wenhai chubanshe, 1966).
Gutzlaff, Charles [Karl Gützlaff]. *Journal of Three Voyages Along the Coast of China* (London: Frederick Westley, 1834).
Gützlaff, Karl [Ai-Hanzhe 愛漢者]. *Dong-Xiyang kao meiyue tongjizhuan* 東西洋考每月統記傳 (Beijing: Zhonghua shuju, 1997).
Guy, R. Kent. *The Emperor's Four Treasuries: Scholars and the State in Late Ch'ien-lung Era* (Cambridge, MA: Harvard University Press, 1987).
Halsey, Stephen R. "State-Making and Strategic Knowledge in the Late Qing: The Case of the Chinese Telegraph Administration" (unpublished paper, presented at the Annual Meeting of the Association for Asian Studies, San Diego, March 2012).
Handbook of Christianity in China, vol. 1, ed. Nicolas Standaert (Leiden: Brill, 2001).
Hanji quanwen ziliaoku 漢籍全文資料庫 (Taipei: Zhongyang yanjiu yuan jisuan zhongxin, 2000).
Hanyu da cidian 漢語大詞典 (Shanghai: Hanyu da cidian chubanshe, 1997).
Harris, George L. "The Mission of Matteo Ricci, S.J.: A Case Study of an Effort at Guided Culture Change in the Sixteenth Century." *Monumenta Serica* 25 (1966):1–168.
Heissig, Walther. *The Religions of Mongolia* (Berkeley: University of California Press, 1980).
He-lin 和琳. *Wei-Zang tongzhi* 衛藏通志, *XXSKQS* 683.
Henderson, John B. *The Development and Decline of Chinese Cosmology* (New York: Columbia University Press, 1984).
———. *Scripture, Canon, and Commentary: A Comparison of Confucian and Western Exegesis* (Princeton, NJ: Princeton University Press, 1991).
He-ning 和寧. *Xizang fu* 西藏賦 (Chengdu: Sichuan minzu chubanshe, 2002).
Ho, Koon-piu 何冠彪. "Qingdai qianqi junzhu dui guan si shixue de yingxiang" 清代前期君主對官私史學的影響. *Hanxue yanjiu* 漢學研究 16/1 (1998):155–84.
Holzwarth, Wolfgang. "Change in Pre-Colonial Times: An Evaluation of Sources on the Karakoram and Eastern Hindukush Regions (from 1500 to 1800)." In *Karakoram-Hindukush-Himalaya: Dynamics of Change*, ed. Irmtraud Stellrecht (Cologne: R. Köppe, 1998):297–337.

Hopkirk, Peter. *The Great Game: The Struggle for Empire in Central Asia* (London: John Murray, 1990).

Horowitz, Richard S. "Central Power and State Making: The Zongli Yamen and Self-Strengthening in China, 1860–1880" (PhD diss., Harvard University, 1998).

Hostetler, Laura. *Qing Colonial Enterprise: Ethnography and Cartography in Early Modern China* (Chicago: University of Chicago Press, 2001).

Hsü, Immanuel C. Y. "The Great Policy Debate in China, 1874: Maritime Defense Vs. Frontier Defense." *HJAS* 25 (1964–1965):212–28.

Hu, Minghui. "Cosmopolitan Confucianism: China's Road to Modern Science" (PhD diss., University of California, Los Angeles, 2004).

Hu Wei 胡渭. *Yugong zhuizhi* 禹貢錐指, *SKQS* 67.

Hua Linfu 華林甫. *Zhongguo dimingxue yuanliu* 中國地名學源流 (Changsha: Hunan renmin chubanshe, 2002).

Huang Aiping 黃愛平. *Siku quanshu zuanxiu yanjiu* 四庫全書纂修研究 (Beijing: Zhongguo Renmin daxue chubanshe, 1989).

Huang Chin-shing. *The Price of Having a Sage-Emperor: The Unity of Politics and Culture* (Singapore: Institute of East Asian Philosophies, 1987).

Huang Juezi 黃爵滋. *Huang Juezi zoushu Xu Naiji zouyi hekan* 黃爵滋奏疏許乃濟奏議合刊 (Beijing: Zhonghua shuju, 1959).

Huang Liyong 黃麗鏞. *Wei Yuan nianpu* 魏源年譜 (Changsha: Hunan renmin chubanshe, 1985).

Huang Peiqiao 黃沛翹. *Xizang tukao* 西藏圖考 (Lhasa: Xizang renmin chubanshe, 1982).

Huang Qing zhigong tu 皇清職貢圖, *SKQS* 594.

Huangchao tongdian 皇朝通典, *SKQS* 642–43.

Huangchao wenxian tongkao 皇朝文獻通考, *SKQS* 632–38.

Huber, Toni. *The Holy Land Reborn: Pilgrimage & the Tibetan Reinvention of Buddhist India* (Chicago: University of Chicago Press, 2008).

Huc, Evariste R. *Souvenirs d'un voyage dans la Tartarie, le Thibet et la Chine pendant les années 1844, 1845 et 1846* (Paris: D'Adrien le Clere, 1850).

Hummel, Arthur, ed. *Eminent Chinese of the Ch'ing Period*. 2 vols. (Taipei: SMC Publishing, 1991).

Hunter, William C. *Bits of Old China* (Taipei: Chengwen Publishing, 1976).

———. *The 'Fan Kwae' at Canton before Treaty Days, 1825–1844* (Shanghai: Kelly & Walsh, 1911).

Indo-Chinese Gleaner (Malacca: 1817–1822).

Inoue Hiromasa 井上裕正. *Shindai ahen seisakushi no kenkyū* 清代アヘン政策史の研究 (Kyoto: Kyōto daigaku gakujutsu shuppankai, 2004).

Ishihama Yumiko 石濱裕美子. "Sennanahyakuhachijū nen no Panchen Rama, Kenryūtei kaiken no honshitsuteki igi" 一七八〇年のパンチェンラマ・乾隆帝会見の本質的意義. In *Chibetto Bukkyō sekai no rekishiteki kenkyū* チベット仏教世界の歴史的研究 (Tokyo: Tōhō shoten, 2001).

Ismail, Ibrahim bin. "Missionary Printing in Malacca, 1815–1843." *Libri* 32/3 (1982):177–206.

Isnard, Albert. "Joseph-Nicolas Delisle, sa Biographie et sa Collection de Cartes Géographiques à la Bibliothèque Nationale." *Bulletin de la Section de géographie* 30 (1915):34–164.
Jacob, Christian. "Mapping in the Mind: The Earth from Ancient Alexandria." In *Mappings*, ed. Denis Cosgrove (London: Reaktion Books, 1999):24–49.
Jaeschke, H. *A Tibetan-English Dictionary* (Delhi: Motilal Banarsidass Publishers, 1998 [1881]).
Jami, Catherine. "Imperial Control and Western Learning: The Kangxi Emperor's Performance." *Late Imperial China* 23/1 (June 2002):28–49.
———. *Les "Méthodes rapides pour la trigonométrie et le rapport précis du cercle" (1774): Tradition chinoise et apport occidental en mathématiques* (Paris: Collège de France, 1990).
Ji Yun 紀昀. *"Yueweicaotang biji" zhuyi* 《閱微草堂筆記》注譯 (Beijing: Zhongguo Huaqiao chubanshe, 1994).
Jiao Yingqi 焦應旗. *Xizang zhi* 西藏志 (Taipei: Wenhai chubanshe, 1966).
Jindai Zhongguo dui Xifang ji lieqiang renshi ziliao huibian 近代中國對西方及列強認識資料彙編 (Taipei: Zhongyang yanjiu yuan Jindaishi yanjiusuo, 1972).
Ju Deyuan 鞠德源. "Jiang Youren hui Kunyu quantu" 蔣友仁繪坤輿全圖. In *Zhongguo gudai ditu ji (Qingdai)* 中國古代地圖集 (清代), eds. Cao Wanru et al. (Beijing: Wenwu chubanshe, 1997):120–25.
Kanda Nobuo 神田信夫. "'Seimuki' zakkō" 「聖武記」雑考. In *Shinchō shi ronkō* 清朝史論考 (Tokyo: Yamakawa shuppansha, 2005):328–43.
Kangxi chao Hanwen zhupi zouzhe huibian 康熙朝漢文硃批奏摺彙編 (Beijing: Dang'an chubanshe, 1984–1985).
Kangxi jixia gewu bian yizhu 康熙幾暇格物編譯注 (Shanghai: Shanghai guji chubanshe, 1993).
Keay, John. *The Honourable Company: A History of the English East India Company.* (New York: Macmillan, 1994).
Kim, Hodong. *Holy War in China: The Muslim Rebellion and the State in Chinese Central Asia, 1864–1877* (Stanford, CA: Stanford University Press, 2004).
Kirkpatrick, William. *An Account of the Kingdom of Nepaul* (London: William Miller, 1811).
Kowalewski, J. E. *Dictionnaire mongol-russe-français* (Taipei: SMC Publishing, 1993).
Kuhn, Philip A. *Soulstealers: The Chinese Sorcery Scare of 1768* (Cambridge, MA: Harvard University Press, 1990).
Kuhn, Thomas S. *The Structure of Scientific Revolutions*, 3rd ed. (Chicago: University of Chicago Press, 1996).
Kuo'erka dang 廓爾喀檔 (Taipei: Chenxiangting qiyeshe, 2006).
Lai Xinxia 來新夏. *Lin Zexu nianpu xinbian* 林則徐年譜新編 (Tianjin: Nankai daxue chubanshe, 1997).
Lamb, Alastair. *British India and Tibet: 1766–1910*, 2nd ed. (London: Routledge & Kegan Paul, 1986).
Laufer, Berthold. "Loan-words in Tibetan." In *Sino-Tibetan Studies* (New Delhi: Aditya Prakashan, 1987).

Lawson, Philip. *The East India Company: A History* (London: Longman, 1993).
Lazich, Michael C. "The Diffusion of Useful Knowledge in China: The Canton Era Information Strategy." In *Mapping Meanings: The Field of New Learning in Late Qing China*, ed. M. Lackner and N. Vittinghoff (Leiden: Brill, 2004):305–27.
LeDonne, John P. *The Grand Strategy of the Russian Empire, 1650–1831* (New York: Oxford University Press, 2004).
Ledyard, Gari. "Cartography in Korea." *The History of Cartography* 2.2, eds. J. B. Harley and David Woodword (Chicago: University of Chicago Press, 1987):236–345.
Legge, James, trans. *The Chinese Classics: The Shoo King or The Book of Historical Documents* (Taipei: SMC Publishing, 2000).
Leonard, Jane Kate. *Wei Yuan and China's Rediscovery of the Maritime World* (Cambridge, MA: Council on East Asian Studies, 1984).
Leslie, Donald D., and Mohamed Wassel. "Arabic and Persian Sources Used by Liu Chih." *Central Asiatic Journal* 26 (1982):78–104.
Lettres édifiantes et curieuses: concernant l'Asie, l'Afrique, et l'Amérique (Paris: A. Desrez, 1843).
Levi, Scott C. *The Indian Diaspora in Central Asia and Its Trade, 1550–1900* (Leiden: Brill, 2006).
Lewis, Mark Edward. *The Construction of Space in Early China* (Albany: State University of New York Press, 2006).
Li Borong 李柏榮. *Wei Yuan shiyou ji* 魏源師友記 (Changsha: Yuelu shushe, 1983).
Li, G. Roth. *Manchu: A Textbook for Reading Documents* (Honolulu: University of Hawai'i Press, 2000).
Li Mingche 李明徹. *Yuantian tushuo* 圜天圖說 (Beijing: Beijing chubanshe, 1997).
Li Ruohong. "A Tibetan Aristocratic Family in Eighteenth-Century Tibet" (PhD diss., Harvard University, 2002).
Li Xiaocong 李孝聰. *Ouzhou shoucang bufen Zhongwen gu ditu xulu* 歐洲收藏部分中文古地圖敘錄 (Beijing: Guoji wenhua chuban gongsi, 1996).
Li Xingyuan 李星沅. *Li Xingyuan riji* 李星沅日記 (Beijing: Zhonghua shuju, 1987).
Li Zhaoluo 李兆洛. *Lidai dilizhi yunbian jinshi* 歷代地理志韻編今釋, *XXSKQS*.
——— . *Yangyizhai wenji* 養一齋文集 (1878).
Liang Jiabin 梁嘉彬. *Guangdong shisanhang kao* 廣東十三行考 (Guangzhou: Guangdong renmin chubanshe, 1999).
Liang Tingnan 梁廷枏. *Haiguo sishuo* 海國四說 (Beijing: Zhonghua shuju, 1993).
——— . *Yifen wenji* 夷氛聞記 (Beijing: Zhonghua shuju, 1985).
Liangchao yulan tushu 兩朝御覽圖書 (Beijing: Zijincheng chubanshe, 1992).
Lin, Man-houng. *China Upside Down: Currency, Society, and Ideologies, 1808–1856* (Cambridge, MA: Harvard University Press, 2006).
Lin Zexu quanji 林則徐全集 (Fuzhou: Haixia wenyi chubanshe, 2002).
Lin Zexu shujian (zengdingben) 林則徐書簡(增訂本) (Fuzhou: Fujian renmin chubanshe, 1985).

Lindsay, H. H. *Report of Proceedings on a Voyage to the Northern Ports of China* (London: B. Fellowes, 1833).
Ling Tingkan quanji 凌廷堪全集 (Hefei: Huangshan shushe, 2009).
Lipman, Jonathan N. *Familiar Strangers: A History of Muslims in Northwest China* (Seattle: University of Washington Press, 1997).
Liu Guanwen 劉貫文. "Cong 'Yutu kaolüe' dao 'Yinghuan zhilüe'" 從《輿圖考略》到《瀛環志略》. In *Xu Jiyu lunkao* 徐繼畬論考 (Taiyuan: Shanxi gaoxiao lianhe chubanshe, 1995):63–83.
Liu Jielian 劉介廉 [Zhi 智]. *Tianfang zhisheng shilu* 天方至聖實錄 (Taipei: Guangwen shuju, 1975).
Lombard-Salmon, Claudine. "Un Chinois a Java (1729–1736)." *Bulletin de l'École Française d'Extrême-Orient* 59 (1972):279–318.
Lomi [Luo-mi 羅密]. *Menggu Bo'erjijite shi zupu* 蒙古博爾濟吉忒氏族譜. In *Beijing tushuguan cang jiapu congkan minzujuan* 北京圖書館藏家譜叢刊民族卷, eds. Guo Youling et al. (Beijing: Beijing tushuguan chubanshe, 2002):323–669.
Lu Ciyun 陸次雲. *Bahong yishi* 八紘譯史 (Beijing: Zhonghua shuju, 1985).
Lü Jianfu 呂建福. "Fojiao shijieguan dui Zhongguo gudai dili zhongxin guannian de yingxiang" 佛教世界觀對中國古代地理中心觀念的影響. *Journal of Shaanxi Normal University* (Philosophy and Social Sciences Edition) 陝西師範大學學報 (哲學社會科學版), 34/4 (July 2005):75–82.
Luk, Bernard Hung-kay. "A Study of Giulio Aleni's *Chih-fang wai chi* 職方外紀." *Bulletin of the School of Oriental and African Studies* 40/1 (1977):58–84.
Luo Yuejiong 羅曰褧. *Xianbin lu* 咸賓錄 (Beijing: Zhonghua shuju, 2000).
Ma Dexin 馬德新. *Chaojin tuji* 朝覲途記 (Yinchuan: Ningxia renmin chubanshe, 1988).
Ma Jie 馬揭 and Sheng Shengzu 盛繩祖. *Wei-Zang tuzhi* 衛藏圖志 (Taipei: Wenhai chubanshe, 1970).
Ma Junliang 馬俊良. *Yugong tushuo* 禹貢圖說 (Beijing: Beijing chubanshe, 1997).
Ma Zhu 馬注. *Qingzhen zhinan* 清真指南 (Ningxia: Qinghai renmin chubanshe, 1989).
Macartney, George. *An Embassy to China: Being the Journal Kept by Lord Macartney during his Embassy to the Emperor Ch'ien-lung, 1793–1794*, ed. J. L. Cranmer-Byng (London: Longmans, 1962).
Mann Jones, Susan, and Philip A. Kuhn. "Dynastic Decline and the Roots of Rebellion." In *Cambridge History of China* 10.1 *Late Ch'ing, 1800–1911, Part 1*, eds. Denis Twitchett and John K. Fairbank (Cambridge, UK: Cambridge University Press, 1978):107–62.
Mao Haijian 茅海建. *Tianchao de bengkui: Yapian zhanzheng zai yanjiu* 天朝的崩潰:鴉片戰爭再研究 (Beijing: Sanlian shudian, 2005).
Mao Ruizheng 茅瑞徵. *Huang Ming xiangxu lu* 皇明象胥錄 (Taipei: Huawen shuju, 1968).
Markham, Clements R., ed. *Narratives of the Mission of George Bogle to Tibet and of the Journey of Thomas Manning to Lhasa* (New Delhi: Cosmo Publishing, 1989).

Marshman, J. *Elements of Chinese Grammar* (Serampore: Mission Press, 1814).
McDermott, Joseph P. *A Social History of the Chinese Book: Books and Literati Culture in Late Imperial China* (Hong Kong: Hong Kong University Press, 2006).
McNeur, George H. *China's First Preacher, Liang A-fa, 1789–1855* (Shanghai: Kwang Hsueh Publishing House, 1934).
Medhurst, Walter H. *English and Chinese Dictionary*. (Shanghai: Mission Press, 1847).
Mei Wending 梅文鼎. "Lun Huihui li yu Xiyang li tongyi" 論回回曆與西洋同異, *Lixue yiwen* 曆學疑問, in *Meishi congshu jiyao* 梅氏叢書輯要 (Longwen shuju, 1888):46.4a.
Mengboo [Meng-bao 孟保]. *Xizang zoushu* 西藏奏疏 (Taipei: Guangwen shuju, 1978).
———. *Xizang zoushu* FSN (Academia Sinica, Fu Sinian Library, A 925.375 233).
Mian dang 緬檔 (Taipei: Chenxiangting qiyeshe, 2007).
Miles, Steven B. *The Sea of Learning: Mobility and Identity in Nineteenth-Century Guangzhou* (Cambridge, MA: Harvard University Asia Center, 2006).
Millward, James. "'Coming on to the Map': 'Western Regions' Geography and Cartographic Nomenclature in the Making of Chinese Empire in Xinjiang." *Late Imperial China* 20/2 (Dec. 1999):61–98.
Milne, William [Bo'aizhe 博愛者]. *Chashisu meiyue tongjizhuan* 察世俗每月統記傳 (Malacca, 1820).
Ming shi 明史, *SKQS*.
Mish, John L. "Creating an Image of Europe for China: Aleni's *Hsi-Fang Ta-Wen* 西方答問, Introduction, Translation, and Notes." *Monumenta Serica* 23 (1964):1–87.
Misra, B. B. *The Central Administration of the East India Company, 1773–1834* (Manchester: Manchester University Press, 1959).
Miyazaki Ichisada 宮崎市定. "Nanyō o Tō-Seiyō ni wakatsu konkyo ni tsuite" 南洋を東西洋に分つ根拠に就いて. *Miyazaki Ichisada zenshū* 宮崎市定全集 (Tokyo: Iwanami shoten, 1991–1994), 19:257–77.
———. "Rōgashū koku to Rōgasu koku" 狼牙脩国と狼牙須国. *Miyazaki Ichisada zenshū* (Tokyo: Iwanami shoten, 1991–1994), 19:278–316.
Moorcroft, William. "A Journey to Lake Mánasaróvara in Ún-dés, a Province of Little Tibet." *Asiatick Researches* 12 (1818):380–536.
Moorcroft, William, and George Trebeck. *Travels in the Himalayan Provinces of Hindustan and the Panjab; in Ladakh and Kashmir; in Peshawar, Kabul, Kunduz, and Bokhara: 1819–1825*, ed. H. H. Wilson (New Delhi: Munshiram Manoharlal, 2005).
Morgan, David. "Persian Perceptions of Mongols and Europeans." In *Implicit Understanding: Observing, Reporting, and Reflecting on the Encounters between Europeans and Other Peoples in the Early Modern Era*, ed. Stuart B. Schwartz (Cambridge, UK: Cambridge University Press, 1994):201–17.
Morrison, Eliza. *Memoirs of the Life and Labours of Robert Morrison*. 2 vols. (London: Orme, Brown, Green, and Longmans, 1839).

Morrison, Robert. *A Dictionary of the Chinese Language, In Three Parts* (Macao: Honorable East India Company's Press, 1815–23).

———. *A Memoir of the Principal Occurrences during an Embassy from the British Government to the Court of China in the Year 1816* (London: Hatchard, 1820).

———. *A View of China for Philological Purposes* (Macao: East India Company's Press, 1817).

———. *Xiyou diqiu wenjian lüezhuan* 西遊地球聞見略傳 (1819).

Morse, H. B. *The Chronicles of the East India Company Trading to China, 1635–1834*. 4 vols. (Oxford: Clarendon Press, 1926–1929).

———. *International Relations of the Chinese Empire*. 2 vols. (Taipei: Book World Co., 1966).

Mosca, Matthew W. "Empire and the Circulation of Frontier Intelligence: Qing Conceptions of the Ottomans." *HJAS* 70/1 (2010):147–207.

———. "Qing China's Perspectives on India, 1750–1847" (PhD diss., Harvard University, 2008).

Mou Runsun 牟潤孫. *Lun Qingdai shixue shuailuo de yuanyin* 論清代史學衰落的原因. In *Haiyi zazhu* 海遺雜著 (Hong Kong: Zhongwen daxue chubanshe, 1990):69–76.

Mukherjee, B. N. "Chinese Ideas about the Geographical Connotation of the Name Shen-tu." *East and West* 38 (Dec. 1988):297–303.

———. *The Foreign Names of the Indian Subcontinent* (Mysore: Place Names Society of India, 1989).

Mungello, David E. *Curious Land: Jesuit Accommodation and the Origins of Sinology* (Stuttgart: Franz Steiner Verlag, 1985).

Munis, Shir Muhammad Mirab, and Muhammad Riza Mirab Agahi. *Firdaws al-Iqbāl: History of Khorezm*, trans. and annotated by Yuri Bregel (Boston: Brill, 1999).

Muroga, Nobuo, and Kazutaka Unno. "The Buddhist World Map in Japan and Its Contact with European Maps." *Imago Mundi* 16 (1962):49–69.

Murray, Hugh. *Encyclopædia of Geography*. 3 vols. (Philadelphia: Lea and Blanchard, 1839).

Nair, P. Thankappan, ed. *Calcutta in the 18th Century: Impressions of Travellers* (Calcutta: Firma KLM, 1984).

———. *Calcutta in the 19th Century: Company's Days* (Calcutta: Firma KLM, 1989).

Needham, Joseph. "Geography and Cartography." In *Science and Civilisation in China*, vol. 3 (Cambridge, UK: Cambridge University Press, 1959):497–590.

Newby, L. J. *The Empire and the Khanate: A Political History of Qing Relations with Khoqand, c. 1760–1860* (Leiden: Brill, 2005).

Ng, Chin-keong. *Trade and Society: The Amoy Network on the China Coast, 1683–1735* (Singapore: Singapore University Press, 1983).

Norman, Jerry. *A Concise Manchu-English Lexicon* (Seattle: University of Washington Press, 1978).

Ong-Tae-Hae [Wang Dahai]. *The Chinaman Abroad; An Account of the Malayan Archipelago, Particularly of Java*, trans. W. H. Medhurst (Shanghai: Mission Press, 1849).

Onuma Takahiro 小沼孝博. "1770 nendai ni okeru Shin-Kazafu kankei—tojiyuku Shinchō no seihoku henkyō" 1770年代における清-カザフ関係—閉じゆく清朝の西北辺疆. *Tōyōshi kenkyū* 69/2 (2010):1–34.
Oxford Dictionary of National Biography. Ed. H. G. C. Matthew and Brian Harrison. (Oxford: Oxford University Press, 2004).
Park, Hyunhee. "The Delineation of a Coastline: The Growth of Mutual Geographic Knowledge in China and the Islamic World from 750 to 1500" (PhD diss., Yale University, 2008).
Parker, Geoffrey. *The Grand Strategy of Philip II* (New Haven, CT: Yale University Press, 1998).
Peers, Douglas M. *Between Mars and Mammon: Colonial Armies and the Garrison State in India, 1819–1835* (London: Tauris Academic Studies, 1995).
Perdue, Peter C. "Boundaries, Maps, and Movement: Chinese, Russian, and Mongolian Empires in Early Modern Central Eurasia." *International History Review* 20.2 (June 1998):263–86.
———. *China Marches West: The Qing Conquest of Central Eurasia* (Cambridge, MA: Harvard University Press, 2005).
Petech, Luciano. *China and Tibet in the Early XVIIIth Century: History of the Establishment of Chinese Protectorate*, 2nd ed. (Leiden: Brill, 1972).
———. "The Dalai-Lamas and Regents of Tibet: A Chronological Study." *T'oung Pao*, second series 47/3–5 (1959):368–94.
———. "The Missions of Bogle and Turner according to Tibetan Texts." *T'oung Pao* 39 (1950):330–46.
———. "Notes on Ladakhi History." *Indian Historical Quarterly* 24/3 (1948):213–35.
Pfister, Louis. *Notices Biographiques et Bibliographiques sur les Jesuites de l'Ancienne Mission de Chine, 1552–1773* (Shanghai: Catholic Mission Printery, 1932 [1976 reprint]).
Pingding Zhunga'er fanglüe 平定準噶爾方略, SKQS.
Polachek, James M. *The Inner Opium War* (Cambridge, MA: Council on East Asian Studies, Harvard University, 1992).
Pomeranz, Kenneth. *The Great Divergence: Europe, China, and the Making of the Modern World Economy* (Princeton, NJ: Princeton University Press, 2000).
Poppe, Nicholas. "Renat's Kalmuck Maps." *Imago Mundi* 12 (1955):157–59.
Postnikov, Aleksey V. "The Russian Navy as Chartmaker in the Eighteenth Century." *Imago Mundi* 52 (2000):79–95.
Pritchard, Earl H., ed. "Instructions of the East India Company to Lord Macartney on His Embassy to China, 1792–4, Pt. III." *Journal of the Royal Asiatic Society* 4 (1938):495–509.
Ptak, Roderich. "Yuan and Early Ming Notices on the Kayal Area in South India." In *China's Seaborne Trade with South and Southeast Asia (1200–1750)* (Aldershot, UK: Ashgate, 1999):137–56.
Putaoya Dongbota dang'anguan cang Qingdai Aomen Zhongwen dang'an huibian 葡萄牙東波塔檔案館藏清代澳門中文檔案彙編 (Macao: Aomen jijinhui, 1999).

Qian Qianyi 錢謙益. "Shijia fangzhi bian" 釋迦方志辨. *Muzhai youxue ji* 牧齋有學集, *XXSKQS* 1391.

Qin Guojing 秦國經 and Liu Ruofang 劉若芳. "Qingchao yutu de huizhi yu guanli" 清朝輿圖的繪製與管理. In *Zhongguo gudai ditu ji (Qingdai)*, eds. Cao Wanru et al. (Beijing: Wenwu chubanshe, 1997):71–78.

(*Qinding*) *Da Qing yitong zhi* (欽定)大清一統志 2nd ed., *SKQS* 474–83.

Qinding Huangyu Xiyu tuzhi 欽定皇輿西域圖志, *SKQS* 500.

Qinding Kuo'erka jilüe 欽定廓爾喀紀略 (Beijing: Quanguo tushuguan wenxian suowei fuzhi zhongxin, 1992).

Qinding Liao Jin Yuan sanshi guoyujie, Yuanshi yujie, 欽定遼金元三史國語解, 元史語解, *SKQS* 296.

Qinding Siku quanshu zongmu 欽定四庫全書總目 (Taipei: Taiwan shangwu yinshu, 1983).

Qinding tongwen yuntong 欽定同文韻統, *SKQS* 240.

Qing [= *Huangchao*] *jingshi wenbian* 清 [皇朝] 經世文編 (Beijing: Zhonghua shuju, 1992).

Qing Neiwufu Zaobanchu Yutufang tumu chubian 清內務府造辦處輿圖房圖目初編 (Beijing: Guoli Gugong bowuguan wenxian guan, 1936).

Qing shi gao 清史稿 (Beijing: Zhonghua shuju, 1977).

Qing shi lu 清實錄 (Beijing: Zhonghua shuju, 1985).

Qing shi lu 清實錄. In *Hanji quanwen ziliaoku* 漢籍全文資料庫 (Taipei: Zhongyang yanjiuyuan jisuan zhongxin, 2000).

Qing zhong-qianqi Xiyang Tianzhujiao zai-Hua huodong dang'an shiliao 清中前期西洋天主教在華活動檔案史料 (Beijing: Zhonghua shuju, 2003).

Qingdai waijiao shiliao 清代外交史料 (Beijing: Gugong bowuyuan, 1932).

Qingdai Zangshi zoudu 清代藏事奏牘 (Beijing: Zhongguo Zangxue chubanshe, 1994).

Qinggong Neiwufu Zaobanchu dang'an zonghui 清宮內務府造辦處檔案總匯 (Beijing: Renmin chubanshe, 2005).

Rachewiltz, Igor de, trans. *The Secret History of the Mongols: A Mongolian Epic Chronicle of the Thirteenth Century* (Leiden: Brill, 2004).

Randles, W. G. L. "Classical Models of World Geography and Their Transformation Following the Discovery of America." In *Geography, Cartography and Nautical Science in the Renaissance* (Aldershot, UK: Ashgate Variorum, 2000):5–76.

Rao Zongyi 饒宗頤. *Rao Zongyi ershi shiji xueshu wenji* 饒宗頤二十世紀學術文集 (Taipei: Xinwenfeng chuban, 2003).

Rawski, Evelyn S. "The Qing Formation and the Early-Modern Period." In *The Qing Formation in World-Historical Time*, ed. Lynn A. Struve (Cambridge, MA: Harvard University Asia Center, 2004):207–41.

Ray, Haraprasad. *Trade and Diplomacy in India-China Relations: A Study of Bengal during the Fifteenth Century* (New Delhi: Radiant Publishers, 1993).

Regmi, D. R. *Modern Nepal* (Calcutta: Firma K. L. Mukhopadhyay, 1975).

Regmi, Mahesh C. *Kings and Political Leaders of the Gorkhali Empire, 1768–1814* (Hyderabad: Orient Longman, 1995).

Ricci, Matteo [Li Madou 利瑪竇]. *Il Mappamondo cinese del p. Matteo Ricci, S.I.*, ed. and trans. Pasquale M. d'Elia (Rome: Biblioteca apostilica Vaticana, 1938).

———. *Qiankun tiyi* 乾坤體義, *SKQS* 787.

Richardson, H. E. *Ch'ing Dynasty Inscriptions at Lhasa* (Rome: Istituto italiano per il Medio ed Estremo Oriente, 1974).

Rizvi, Janet. "The Trans-Karakoram Trade in the Nineteenth and Twentieth Centuries." *Indian Economic and Social History Review* 31/1 (1994):27–64.

Rose, Leo E. *Nepal: Strategy for Survival* (Berkeley: University of California Press, 1971).

Rowe, David Nelson. *Index to Ch'ing Tai Ch'ou Pan I Wu Shi Mo* (Hamden, CT: Shoestring Press, 1960).

Rozycki, William. *Mongol Elements in Manchu* (Bloomington: Indiana University, Research Institute for Inner Asian Studies, 1994).

Rudolph, Jennifer. *Negotiated Power in Late Imperial China: The Zongli Yamen and the Politics of Reform* (Ithaca, NY: Cornell University East Asia Program, 2008).

Ruggieri, Michele, and Matteo Ricci. *Dicionário Português-Chinês*, ed. John W. Witek, S.J. (Lisbon: Biblioteca Nacional Portugal, 2001).

Sadakata, Akira. *Buddhist Cosmology: Philosophy and Origins*, trans. Gaynor Sekimori (Tokyo: Kosei Pub., 1997).

Saguchi Tōru 佐口透. *Jūhachi-jūkyū-seiki Higashi Torukisutan shakaishi kenkyū* 18–19世紀東トルキスタン社会史研究 (Tokyo: Yoshikawa Kōbunkan, 1963).

Salmon, Claudine. "Wang Dahai and His View of the 'Insular Countries' (1791)." In *Chinese Studies of the Malay World: A Comparative Approach*, ed. Ding Choo Ming et al. (Singapore: Eastern Universities Press, 2003):31–67.

Sarkar, Jadunath. *Fall of the Mughal Empire* (Bombay: Orient Longman, 1964–1972).

———. *A Study of Eighteenth Century India* (Calcutta: Saraswat Library, 1976).

Sasaki Masaya 佐々木正哉, ed. *Yapian zhanzheng qian Zhong-Ying jiaoshe wenshu* 鴉片戰爭前中英交涉文書 (Taipei: Wenhai chubanshe, 1976).

Satō Hisashi 佐藤長. *Chūsei Chibetto shi kenkyū* 中世チベット史研究 (Kyoto: Dōhōsha, 1986).

Schwartzberg, Joseph E. "Cosmographical Mapping." In *The History of Cartography*, 2.1, eds. J. B. Harley and David Woodward (Chicago: University of Chicago Press, 1992):332–87.

Scott, John Lee. *Narrative of a Recent Imprisonment in China after the Wreck of the Kite* (London: Dalton, 1841).

Sen, Tansen. *Buddhism, Diplomacy, and Trade: The Realignment of Sino-Indian Relations, 600–1400* (Honolulu: University of Hawai'i Press, 2003).

Shakabpa, Tsepon W. D. *Tibet: A Political History* (New Haven, CT: Yale University Press, 1967).

Shapin, Steven. *A Social History of Truth: Civility and Science in Seventeenth-Century England* (Chicago: University of Chicago Press, 1994).

Shi Liye 施立業. *Yao Ying nianpu* 姚瑩年譜 (Hefei: Huangshan shushe, 2004).

Shiliao xunkan 史料旬刊 (Taipei: Guofeng chubanshe, 1963).

Sichuan tongzhi 四川通志, 2nd ed. (Chengdu: Bashu shushe, 1984).

Simon, Walter, and Howard G. H. Nelson. *Manchu Books in London: A Union Catalogue* (London: British Museum Publications, 1977).
Sivin, N. "Copernicus in China." *Studia Copernicana* 6 (1973):63–122.
SKQS = (*Yingyin Wenyuange*) *Siku quanshu* (景印文淵閣) 四庫全書 (Taipei: Taiwan shangwu yinshuguan, 1983–1986).
Smith, Carl T. *Chinese Christians: Elites, Middlemen, and the Church in Hong Kong* (Hong Kong: Hong Kong University Press, 2005).
Smith, Carl T., and Paul A. Van Dyke. "Muslims in the Pearl River Delta, 1700–1930." *Revista de Cultura* 10 (2004):6–15.
Smith, Richard J. "Mapping China's World" In *Landscape, Culture, and Power in Chinese Society*, ed. Wen-hsin Yeh (Berkeley: Institute of East Asian Studies, 1998):52–109.
Stary, Giovanni. "An Unknown Chapter in the History of Manchu Writing: The 'Indian Letters' (*tianzhu zi* 天竺字)." *Central Asiatic Journal* 48/2 (2004):280–91.
Stein, Aurel. *Serindia: Detailed Report of Explorations in Central Asia and Westernmost China* (Delhi: Motilal Banarsidass, 1980–1983).
Struve, Lynn A. *The Ming-Qing Conflict, 1619–1683: A Historiography and Source Guide* (Ann Arbor, MI: Association for Asian Studies, 1998).
Subrahmanyam, Sanjay. "On the Window That Was India." In *Explorations in Connected History: From the Tagus to the Ganges* (New Delhi: Oxford University Press, 2005):1–16.
Sungyūn [Song-yun 松筠]. "Suifu jilüe" 綏服紀略. In *Zhenwu shiyi* 鎮撫事宜 (Taipei: Huawen shuju, 1969).
———. *Xizhao tulüe* 西招圖略 (Taipei: Huawen shuju, 1969).
Suzuki Chūsei 鈴木中正. *Chibetto o meguru Chū-In kankeishi: Jūhasseiki nakagoro kara jūkyūseiki nakagoro made* チベットをめぐる中印関係史：十八世紀中頃から十九世紀中頃まで (Tokyo: Hitotsubashi shobō, 1962).
Teng, Emma Jinhua. *Taiwan's Imagined Geography: Chinese Colonial Travel Writings and Pictures, 1683–1895* (Cambridge, MA: Harvard University Asia Center, 2004).
Texuan cuoyao meiyue tongjizhuan 特選撮要每月紀傳 (Batavia).
Thackston, Wheeler M. *The Baburnama: Memoirs of Babur, Prince and Emperor* (New York: Modern Library, 2002).
Thampi, Madhavi. *Indians in China, 1800–1949* (New Delhi: Manohar Publishers, 2005).
Tulišen [Tu-li-shen 圖理琛]. *Kōchū Iikiroku* 校注異域録: *Tulišn's I-yü-lu* (Tenri: Tenri daigaku, 1964).
Turner, Samuel. *An Account of an Embassy to the Court of the Teshoo Lama* (New Delhi: Asian Educational Services, 1991).
Unno Kazutaka 海野一隆. "Tō Jakubo oyobi Shō Yūjin no sekaizu ni tsuite" 湯若望および蔣友仁の世界図について. In *Tōzai chizu bunka kōshōshi kenkyū* 東西地図文化交渉史研究 (Osaka: Seibundō, 2003).
Uspensky, Vladimir. "The Previous Incarnations of the Qianlong Emperor." In *Tibet, Past and Present: Tibetan Studies I*, ed. Henk Blezer (Leiden: Brill, 2002):215–28.

Van Gulik, Robert H. *Siddham: An Essay on the History of Sanskrit Studies in China and Japan* (Nagpur: International Academy of Indian Culture, 1956).
Verbiest, Ferdinand [Nan Huairen 南懷仁]. *Kunyu tushuo* 坤輿圖說, *SKQS*, 594.
Wakeman, Frederic, Jr. "Drury's Occupation of Macau and China's Response to Early Modern Imperialism." *East Asian History* 28 (2004):27–34.
———. *Strangers at the Gate: Social Disorder in South China, 1839–1861* (Berkeley: University of California Press, 1966).
Waley, Arthur. *The Opium War through Chinese Eyes* (Stanford, CA: Stanford University Press, 1958).
Waley-Cohen, Joanna. *The Sextants of Beijing: Global Currents in Chinese History* (New York: W. W. Norton, 1999).
Walravens, Hartmut. "Father Verbiest's Chinese World Map (1674)." *Imago Mundi* 43 (1991):31–47.
Wang Chaozong 王朝宗. *Haiwai fanyi lu* 海外番夷錄 (Beijing: Suliuxuan, 1844).
Wang Dahai 王大海. *Haidao yizhi jiaozhu* 海島逸誌校注, ed. Yao Nan and Wu Langxuan (Hong Kong: Xuejin, 1992).
Wang Gungwu 王賡武. "'Haiguo wenjian lu' zhong de 'Wulaiyou'" 《海國聞見錄》中的 "無來由." In *Dongnan-Ya yu Huaren: Wang Gengwu jiaoshou lunwen xuanji* 東南亞與華人:王賡武教授論文選集 (Beijing: Zhongguo youyi chubanshe, 1986).
Wang Jiajian 王家儉. *Wei Yuan dui Xifang de renshi ji qi haifang sixiang* 魏源對西方的認識及其海防思想 (Taipei: Guoli Taiwan daxue wenxueyuan, 1964).
———. *Wei Yuan nianpu* 魏源年譜 (Taipei: Zhongyang yanjiu yuan Jindaishi yanjiu suo, 1981).
Wang, Jianping. *A Glossary of Chinese Islamic Terms* (Richmond, UK: Curzon, 2001).
Wang Qianjin 汪前進. "Kangxi, Yongzheng, Qianlong sanchao quanguo zongtu de huizhi" 康熙, 雍正, 乾隆三朝全國總圖的繪製. In Wang Qianjin and Luo Ruofang, *Qing ting san da shice quantu ji* 清廷三大實測全圖集 (Beijing: Waiwen chubanshe, 2007).
———. "Qianlong shisanpaitu dingliang fenxi" 乾隆十三排圖定量分析. In *Zhongguo gudai ditu ji (Qingdai)* 中國古代地圖集 (清代), eds. Cao Wanru et al. (Beijing: Wenwu chubanshe, 1997):113–19.
Wang, Xiangyun. "Tibetan Buddhism at the Court of Qing: The Life and Work of lCang-skya Rol-pa'i-rdo-rje (1717–86)" (PhD diss., Harvard University, 1995).
Wang Zhangtao 王章濤. *Ruan Yuan nianpu* 阮元年譜 (Hefei: Huangshan shushe, 2003).
Wang Zhongmin 王重民. *Lenglu wensou* 冷廬文藪 (Shanghai: Shanghai guji chubanshe, 1992).
Washington, George. *The Writings of George Washington from the Original Manuscript Sources, 1745–1799* (Washington, DC: U.S. Gov't Print. Off., 1931–1944).
Wei Yuan 魏源. *Haiguo tuzhi* 海國圖志, 1st ed. (Guwei tang, 1844).
———. *Haiguo tuzhi*, 2nd ed. (Taipei: Chengwen chubanshe, 1967).
———. *Shengwu ji* 聖武記, 1st ed. *XXSKQS* 402.

———. *Shengwu ji*, 3rd ed. (Taipei: Shijie shuju, 1962).
Wenxian congbian 文獻叢編 (Taipei: Guofeng chubanshe, 1964).
Wilkinson, Endymion P. *Chinese History: A Manual* (Cambridge, MA: Harvard University Asia Center, 2000).
Williams, S. Wells. *A Syllabic Dictionary of the Chinese Language*. (Shanghai: American Mission Press, 1874).
Wills, John E., Jr. "Contingent Connections: Fujian, the Empire, and the Early Modern World." In *The Qing Formation in World-Historical Time*, ed. Lynn A. Struve (Cambridge, MA: Harvard University Asia Center, 2004):167–203.
———. *Embassies and Illusions: Dutch and Portuguese Envoys to K'ang-hsi, 1666–1687* (Cambridge, MA: Council on East Asian Studies, Harvard University, 1984).
———. *1688: A Global History* (New York: Norton, 2001).
———. "Tribute, Defensiveness, and Dependency: Uses and Limits of Some Basic Ideas about Mid-Qing Dynasty Foreign Relations." *American Neptune* 48/4 (1988):225–29.
Wood, Herbert. "England, China, and the Napoleonic Wars." *Pacific Historical Review* 9/2 (1940):139–56.
Wu Baoxiang 吳寶祥. "Liang Tingnan nianpu jianbian" 梁廷枏年譜簡編. *Foshan kexue jishu xueyuan xuebao (Shehui kexue ban)* 佛山科學技術學院學報 (社會科學版) 20/4 (2002):82–88.
Wyatt, Don J. *The Blacks of Premodern China* (Philadelphia: University of Pennsylvania Press, 2010).
Wylie, Alexander. *Memorials of Protestant Missionaries to the Chinese* (Taipei: Ch'eng-wen Publishing Company, 1967).
Xiao Tenglin 蕭騰麟. *Xizang jianwen lu* 西藏見聞錄 (Beijing: Quanguo tushuguan wenxian suowei fuzhi zhongxin, 2003).
Xiaofanghuzhai yudi congchao zaibubian 小方壺齋輿地叢鈔再補編 (Taipei: Guangwen shuju, 1964).
Xie Qinggao 謝清高. *Hailu jiaoshi* 海錄校釋 (Beijing: Shangwu yinshuguan, 2002).
Xining fu xinzhi 西寧府新誌 (Xining: Qinghai renmin chubanshe, 1988).
Xiyu dili tushuo zhu 西域地理圖說注, ed. Ruan Mingdao (Yanji: Yanbian daxue chubanshe, 1992).
XXSKQS = *Xuxiu Siku quanshu* 續修四庫全書 (Shanghai: Shanghai guji chubanshe, 1995–1999).
Xu Dishan 許地山, ed. *Dazhong ji* 達衷集 (Taipei: Wenhai chubanshe, 1974).
Xu Jiyu 徐繼畬. *Yinghuan kaolüe* 瀛環考略 (Taipei: Wenhai chubanshe, 1974).
———. *Yinghuan zhilüe* 瀛環志略 (Shanghai: Shanghai shudian chubanshe, 2001).
Xuanzang 玄奘. *Da Tang Xiyu ji* 大唐西域記 (Taipei: Sanmin shuju, 1998).
Yan Congjian 嚴從簡. *Shuyu zhouzi lu* 殊域周咨錄 (Beijing: Zhonghua shuju, 1993).
Yan Ruyi 嚴如熤. *Yangfang jiyao* 洋防輯要 (Beijing: Zhishi chanchuan chubanshe, 2011).

Yao Ying 姚瑩. *Dongming wenji, wen houji* 東溟文集文後集, *XXSKQS*.
———. *Dongming zougao* 東溟奏稿 (Taipei: Taiwan yinhang, 1959).
———. *Kangyou jixing* 康輶紀行 (Taipei: Guangwen shuju, 1969).
———. *Shixiao lu* 識小錄 (Hefei: Huangshan shushe, 1991).
Yapian zhanzheng 鴉片戰爭 (Shanghai: Shenzhou guoguang she, 1954).
Yapian zhanzheng dang'an shiliao 鴉片戰爭檔案史料 (Shanghai: Shanghai renmin chubanshe, 1987).
Yapian zhanzheng shiqi sixiangshi ziliao xuanji 鴉片戰爭時期思想史資料選輯 (Beijing: Zhonghua shuju, 1963).
Yapp, M. E. *Strategies of British India: Britain, Iran, and Afghanistan, 1798–1850* (Oxford: Clarendon Press, 1980).
Yee, Cordell D. K. "Taking the World's Measure: Chinese Maps between Observation and Text." In *The History of Cartography*, 2.2, eds. J. B. Harley and David Woodward (Chicago: University of Chicago Press, 1994):96–127.
———. "Traditional Chinese Cartography and the Myth of Westernization." In *The History of Cartography*, 2.2, eds. J. B. Harley and David Woodward (Chicago: University of Chicago Press, 1994):170–202.
Yen, Sophia Su-fei. *Taiwan in China's Foreign Relations, 1836–1874* (Hamden: Shoe String Press, 1965).
Yin Guangren 印光任 and Zhang Rulin 張汝霖. *Aomen jilüe jiaozhu* 澳門記略校注, ed. Zhao Chunchen (Macao: Wenhua sishu, 1992).
Yingshi Majia'erni fang-Hua dang'an shiliao huibian 英使馬戛爾尼訪華檔案史料彙編 (Beijing: Guoji wenhua chuban gongsi, 1996).
Yoon, Wook. "The Grand Council and the Communication Systems in the Late Qing" (PhD diss., Yale University, 2008).
You Tong 尤侗. *Ming shi Waiguo zhuan* 明史外國傳 (Taipei: Xuesheng shuju, 1977).
———. *Waiguo zhuzhi ci* 外國竹枝詞 (Beijing: Zhonghua shuju, 1991).
Yu Fushun 於福順. "Qing Yongzheng shipai 'Huangyutu' de chubu yanjiu" 清雍正十排《皇輿圖》的初步研究. *Wen wu* 文物 12 (1983):71–75, 83.
Yu Hao 俞浩. *Xiyu kaogu lu* 西域考古錄 (Taipei: Wenhai chubanshe, 1966).
Yu-qian 裕謙. *Yu Jingjie gong yishu* 裕靖節公遺書 (Taipei: Wenhai chubanshe, 1969).
Yu Zhengxie 俞正燮. *Yu Zhengxie quanji* 俞正燮全集 (Hefei: Huangshan shushe, 2005).
Yuan shi 元史 (Beijing: Zhonghua shuju, 1976).
Yuan shi, *SKQS* 292–95.
Yuding yinyun chanwei 御定音韻闡微, *SKQS* 240.
Yue haiguan zhi jiaozhu ben 粵海關志校注本 (Guangzhou: Guangdong renmin chubanshe, 2002).
Yule, Henry, and A. C. Burnell. *Hobson-Jobson: A Glossary of Colloquial Anglo-Indian Words and Phrases* (London: Routledge & Kegan Paul, 1985).
Yunggui [Yong-gui 永貴] and Suldei [Su-er-de 蘇爾德]. *Xinjiang Huibu zhi* 新疆回部志 (Beijing: Beijing chubanshe, 2000).

Yuzhi Manzhu Menggu Hanzi sanhe qieyin Qingwenjian 御製滿珠蒙古漢字三合切音清文鑒, *SKQS* 234.
Yuzhi shiji 御製詩集, *SKQS* 1302–11.
Yuzhi wenji 御製文集, *SKQS* 1301.
Zhang Hai 張海. *Xizang jishu* 西藏紀述 (Taipei: Chengwen chubanshe, 1968).
Zhang Yushu 張玉書. *Waiguo ji* 外國紀 (Shanghai: Shanghai shudian, 1994).
Zhao Lifeng 趙利峰 and Wu Zhen 吳震. "Aomen tusheng Puren Hanxuejia Majishi yu 'Xinshi dili beikao'" 澳門土生葡人漢學家瑪吉士與《新釋地理備考》. *Ji'nan xuebao (Zhexue Shehui kexue ban)* 暨南學報 (哲學社會科學版) 28/2 (2006):131–36.
Zheng Guangzu 鄭光祖. *Zhouju suozhi* 舟車所至 (Taipei: Zhengzhong shuju, 1962).
Zhongguo difangzhi zongmu tiyao 中國地方志總目提要 (Taipei: Sino-American Publishing Co., 1996).
Zhongguo diyi lishi dang'an guan suocun Xizang he Zangshi dang'an mulu, Man Zang wen bufen 中國第一歷史檔案館所存西藏和藏事檔案目錄 (滿藏文部分) (Beijing: Zhongguo Zangshi chubanshe, 1999).
Zhongguo Yisilan baike quan shu 中國伊斯蘭百科全書 (Chengdu: Sichuan cishu chubanshe, 1994).
Zhonghua guditu zhenpin xuanji 中華古地圖珍品選集 (Harbin: Ha'erbin ditu chubanshe, 1998).
Zhou Ailian 周靄聯. *Xizang jiyou* 西藏紀遊 (Beijing: Zhongguo Zangxue chubanshe, 2006).
Zhou Kai 周凱. *Xiamen zhi* 夏門志 (Taipei: Taiwan yinhang, 1961).
Zhu Heling 朱鶴齡. *Yugong changjian* 禹貢長箋, *SKQS* 67.
Zhu Siben 朱思本 and Luo Hongxian 羅洪先. *Guang yutu* 廣輿圖 (Taipei: Xuehai chubanshe, 1969).
Zhuang Jifa 莊吉發. "Guoli gugong bowuyuan diancang 'Dazangjing' Manwen yiben yanjiu" 國立故宮博物院典藏"大藏經"滿文譯本研究. *Qingshi lunji* (3) 清史論集 (三) (Taipei: Wenshizhe chubanshe, 1997):1–96.
———. *Qing Gaozong shiquan wugong yanjiu* 清高宗十全武功研究 (Taipei: Guoli Gugong bowuyuan, 1982).
Zhuang Tingfu 莊廷尃. *Da Qing tongshu zhigong wanguo jingwei diqiushi* 大清統屬職貢萬國經緯地球式, 1794 (Library of Congress G3200 1794.Z5).
Zürcher, Erik. *The Buddhist Conquest of China: The Spread and Adaptation of Buddhism in Early Medieval China*, 3rd. ed. (Leiden: Brill, 2007).
———. "Xu Guangqi and Buddhism." In *Statecraft & Intellectual Renewal in Late Ming China: The Cross-Cultural Synthesis of Xu Guangqi (1562–1633)*, ed. Catherine Jami et al. (Leiden: Brill, 2001):155–169.

Index

Abd al-Qadir Khan, 142
Abdul Latif, 185, 189, 190
Acharya, 134, 140, 142, 152, 157, 158, 185, 261
Aden, 38
Afghans and Afghanistan, 22, 73, 74–75, 77–82, 91, 218, 337n33, 338n47, 338n52; and Badakhshan, 75, 77, 86–87; on court survey map, 106–8, 116; and Moorcroft mission, 190; and the Opium War, 259, 266–67, 290–92, 360n101
Agha Mehdi, 186–89
Agra, 115, 116
Ahmad Shah Durrani, 75, 78–83, 85, 86, 127, 337n33, 338n47, 338n52
Alamgir II, 78, 79, 81, 338n53
Aleni, Giulio, 208, 212, 213, 284, 285; geographic names used by, 36, 48, 50, 51, 117, 217, 282; viewed by early and mid-Qing scholars, 41–42, 125
Ali Gawhar. *See* Shah Alam II
Almeida, J. B., 168–70, 179
Aman, 242, 243
Amar Singh Thapa, 179
ambans, 127, 130, 135–36, 145, 157, 172–75, 307; during Anglo-Nepal War, 176–78, 180, 183; during the Opium War, 260, 261, 263, 264; discussed in post-Opium War period, 290–91, 297
America. *See* United States
Amin Khwaja, 82, 107
Amursana, 1, 2, 9, 293, 296
Anavatapta, 28, 29, 63
Andijan and Andijanis, 105, 109, 188, 265, 338n47
Anstruther, Peter, 250, 251, 273, 274, 287, 291
Anville, Jean-Baptiste d', 114, 116, 120, 122, 343n67–69, 344n72; compared with Ji Yun, 45–46; and "Enetkek," 339n80

Aomen jilüe, 56, 201, 225
Aqsu, 109
Arigūn, 78, 107
Assam, 259
Awadh, 140, 146, 152, 219, 276

Badakhshan, 75–80, 82–83, 85–87, 92, 108, 109, 265
Bajong, 136–38
Bal-po. *See* Nepal
"Ban'gala" (Bengal), 126
"Banggala" (Bengal), 58, 218
"Banggela" (Bengal), 49, 65, 217, 219, 221
"Baoshe" (Persia), 55
Bao Shichen, 216, 223–26, 231, 240, 242, 243
Bartlett, Beatrice S., 7
Baxun wanshou shengdian, 80
Bayly, Christopher, 196, 329n2
Bengal, 19, 81, 127, 128, 143, 173, 202, 242; on court survey map, 115, 117, 126; discussed in post-Opium War writings, 278, 279, 283, 297, 298; East India Company activity in, 1, 127, 148, 163, 164; in Kangxi and Yongzheng-era geography, 54–56, 58; Panchen Lama and, 130–35; in pre-Qing geography, 37, 48, 49; in Protestant geography, 216–22; in Qianlong-era geography, 63, 65, 95, 137, 139, 140, 143, 149–54; rumored unrest in, 266–68, 290; seen by Qing as a site of opium production, 206, 216, 244, 246, 249, 251, 257, 288–91; source of personnel for British, 170, 249, 250, 252, 254, 256. *See also* Acharya; "Ban'gala"; "Banggala"; "Banggela"; "Gangjiao"; "Mingjiaoliao"; "Mingyala"; "Minya"
Benoist, Michel, 113, 119–24, 210
Bering, Vitus, 121

Bhim Sen Thapa, 260, 263
Bhutan and Bhutanese, 62, 129, 130, 133–36, 218, 264; and Manning journey, 172–74; and Qing-Gurkha War, 139, 140, 142, 144
"black foreigners," 170; perceived during Opium War, 251, 252, 253, 254, 255, 256, 257, 268
Bodh Gaya, 29, 91, 129, 132
Bogle, George, 79, 129–31, 134, 135, 139
Bolor, 77, 79, 86, 109, 338n45
Bombay, 245, 251, 254, 257, 262, 276, 288, 291; described in Guangdong, 1800–1838 period, 204–7, 216, 219, 222; in pre-Qianlong geographic writing, 53, 56
Borgi, 145, 158, 348n80
Botelho, William, 242
Bridgman, Elijah, 242, 244
Bstan-'dzin-dpal-'byor, 142
Bu Dingbang, 251, 254
Bukhara, 74, 86, 185, 187, 189, 190, 265, 338n52
bureaucracy, Qing: compared to British India, 196–97; constraints on commentary by, 3, 14, 200, 233 306; involvement in mapmaking, 101–26; modes of intelligence gathering, 12–14, 191–98, 269. *See also* Grand Council
Burhan al-Din, 76, 77, 86, 108
Burma, 124, 179, 193, 227, 259, 300, 330n23; on maps, 38, 113; relations with Qing in Qianlong-era, 9, 99, 194; in Wei Yuan's writing, 20, 288, 293–294 297
Burut, 76, 83, 86, 107

Cai Tinglan, 214
Cai Xin, 54
Calcutta, 185–87, 202, 206, 216–18, 261, 262, 307, 351n39; contact with during Qing-Gurkha War, 142, 143, 145, 146; and Manning journey, 170–74; perceived in post-Qing-Gurkha War period, 152, 153, 156–58; seen from Tibet before 1788, 128–33, 135. *See also* "Galigada"; "Jialajida"; "Jialeguda"; "Jialiquda jing"
Canada, 205
Cantonese, geographic vocabulary in, 34, 56, 155, 166, 217, 232, 262, 350n14
cartography. *See* court survey maps; maps
Caspian Sea, 105–6, 114, 117, 292, 341n22, 342n55, 343n68
Chaibasa, 152
Chen Fengheng, 274

Chen Kesheng, 63
Chen Li, 292, 296, 297, 300
Chen Lunjiong, 42, 54–56, 201–3, 208, 280, 282, 283; consulted in 1820–1838 period, 208, 231, 242; cited in post-Opium War period, 274, 276; geographic nomenclature of, 165; map of, 211, 213, 282
Chen Mao, 54
Cheng-de, 136
Cheng Hanzhang, 224
Cheng Xunwo, 54, 202, 207
Chinese Monthly Magazine, 215
Chinggis Khan, 48, 58, 61, 90, 91, 288, 336n169
Chitral, 75, 86
Cišii, 84, 85, 98, 100, 274
Columbus, Christopher, 44
Cornwallis, Charles, 136, 137, 141–46, 148, 151, 154, 155, 193
"country trade," 85, 164–66
court survey maps, 101–5, 211–12; and Jesuit world maps, 118–24; Kangxi and Yongzheng editions, 103–07, 111, 211, 342n55; Qianlong edition, 107–14; representation of India on, 114–18. *See also* Benoist, Michel; He Guozong; Mingghatu, Yun-lu

Dahūngga, 255–57, 277
Dalai Lama, 136, 139, 141, 148, 177, 261; and the Bogle embassy, 130; and the Manning journey, 171, 172, 174
Daljit Gir, 142–44, 153, 156–58, 347n66
Da Qing yitong zhi, 34, 35, 62, 90, 94–96, 105, 203, 217
Davis, John F., 244, 307, 308, 350n17
Dawachi, 107
Da Xitian (India), 63
Da Yingguo renshi lüeshuo, 219, 220
Deboo, 107, 108
Delhi, 78–84, 88, 163, 179, 185, 190, 260; and court survey map, 115, 117; mentioned by Panchen Lama, 132, 134
Delhi Padshah, 62, 152, 156–59, 169, 184; mentioned during and after Opium War, 261, 262, 278, 290; mentioned in Tibet before 1794, 135, 140, 142, 143, 145, 146, 348n80
Delisle, Guillaume. *See* Ilse, Guillaume de l'
Deng Tingzhen, 240, 242, 250
Denham, Captain, 255, 257, 266, 274, 277, 280–82

INDEX

Dhaka, 115, 343n68
dharani, 72, 88
Dikötter, Frank, 254
"Dili (bacha)." *See* Delhi Padshah
Ding Gongchen, 213, 214
Diqiu tushuo, 120, 210
Directorate of Astronomy, 109–11, 119, 211, 358n12
Dong-Xiyang kao, 208
Drury, William, 170
Duncan, Jonathan, 140–42
Dundas, Henry, 149, 150
Dutch, 54, 56, 59, 147, 163, 164, 166, 202, 203, 214, 288, 293, 360n87

East India Company, English, 127–32, 134, 163–67, 169–71, 173, 220, 268; expansion, 1–2, 9, 63, 306, 349n119; and Macartney embassy, 148, 151; mentioned by Lin Zexu, 247, 250; mentioned by Wei Yuan, 251; and Moorcroft mission, 184–85; during Qing-Gurkha War, 137, 141, 146; strategy compared to Qing, 192, 193, 195, 196; understood in Guangzhou in 1830s, 223, 228, 230, 356n92
Eldengge, 86
Elliot, Charles, 244–46, 248–49
Elman, Benjamin A., 33
Elverskog, Johan, 60
Encyclopædia of Geography. See *Sizhou zhi*
"Enetkek" (India), 60–63, 88–91, 133, 279, 283; identified with Hindustan, 146, 348n85; origin of term, 48, 89, 339n80
Enoki Kazuo, 118
En-te-heng-e, 265
Entian, 267, 269
Erdeni-yin tobči. See *Menggu yuanliu*
Erya, 28
Espinha, Joseph d', 107, 110, 112, 113, 119

Fairbank, John K., 5–6, 8, 238, 329n3, 330n13, 365n88
Fan Shouyi, 53, 335n132
Fang Dongshu, 231, 268
Fanglüe guan, 112, 120
Fang Wei, 94, 95, 96
Farangi, 19, 130, 139, 152, 158, 181, 185, 306; first use in Tibet, 133–35, 346n32. *See also* Phe-reng; Pileng
Faxian, 29, 42, 63, 95
Feng Guifen, 300, 301
Fisher, Michael, 195

Flint, Valerie, 44
foreign policy, 2–6, 8, 21, 296, 301, 310; shift toward, 14, 197, 200, 303–5, 309; and Wei Yuan, 20, 271, 272, 286, 295
foreign geography, studied in China: compared to European practice, 43–47; post-Opium War changes, 272–86; practice of in Kangxi and Yongzheng reigns, 25–26, 32–43, 46–66; practice of in pre-Qing China, 26–32; as a pre-paradigmatic science, 39–40, 44, 286. *See also* yan'ge; maps
France and the French, 185, 216, 299, 300, 307; and court cartography; 119–21, 126 342n44, 343n69, 344n72; ports in India, 56; Wei Yuan proposes alliance with, 287–88, 292, 296, 298–99
French and Napoleonic Wars, 9, 163, 167–68, 170, 199
Fridelli, Ehrenbert, 105, 110, 340n9
frontier policy, 2–5, 87, 164, 174, 258, 309, 310; comparison of with British Indian strategy, 190–99; factors supporting, 11–14, 21, 159, 174, 269, 304–6; factors undermining, 232, 233, 273; Wei Yuan's shift from, 272, 295, 296
Fucanggan, 137, 157
Fude, 76, 77, 107–9
Fuheng, 112, 122, 137
Fujian, 84–85, 223–26, 232, 335n145, 335n146; distinctive geographic worldview, 15, 54; dominant source of coastal geography, 201, 202
Fuk'anggan, 182–84, 193, 289, 290, 349n121; contact with British India from Tibet, 139, 140, 142–45; influence on later geographers, 156–59, 261, 278, 348n80; and Macartney mission, 147–49, 151, 153, 154
Fu-zhu-long-a, 256

Gabet, Joseph, 307
Galdan Tsereng, 86, 341n14
"Galigada" (Calcutta), 142, 148, 152, 153, 157, 159, 262. *See also* Calcutta
Ganges River, 28, 63, 115, 116, 122, 123, 343n69
Gang-ga-le-ta-ze-xi, 152, 156
"Gangjiao" (India and its ports), 159, 196, 205, 230, 232, 237, 240–42, 269; identified as "India," 155, 217, 218, 226, 227, 246–46; origins of term, 165–67, 350n14
Gaohou mengqiu, 274

392   INDEX

Gartok, 185, 186, 308
Gaubil, Antoine, 53, 105, 106, 110, 119, 121, 341n14
geographic agnosticism, 18, 26, 43, 46, 65, 159; and court cartography, 102, 118, 123, 124; decline of, 209, 210, 272, 280, 285
geography, studied in China. *See* foreign geography
George III, King, 128, 151, 154–56, 166, 182, 193, 290
"Geshita" (coastal southern India), 56–57, 211
Ghalib Jang, 79
Giking, 168, 169, 351n28
Goa, 49, 56, 167, 204, 206, 212, 354n17
Gogeisl, Anton, 112, 119
Gombojab, 61
Gong Zizhen, 241
gosains, 129, 130, 134, 140, 142, 185 *See also* Purangir, Daljit Gir
Gouvêa, Alexandre de, 168
governor-general of British India, 128, 139, 148, 154, 181–83, 186, 278, 308; title found in Qing sources, 142, 143, 155, 181, 187, 190, 216. *See also* Hastings, Warren; Cornwallis, Charles; Wellesley, Richard
Grand Council, 69, 70, 126, 147, 194, 221, 298; and coordination between frontiers, 12, 99, 156, 160, 164, 195–97, 269, 309; and mapping, 112
"grand strategy," 11
"Great Game," 9, 21, 185, 292, 299
Great Western Ocean. *See* Western Ocean
Greenberg, Michael, 245
Guangdong, 34, 85, 128, 166, 194, 223–27, 290, 303; connected to Tibet, 152, 153, 261, 262, 264; growth of study of foreign geography in, 201–3, 207, 208, 211, 214, 231; trade with India, 63, 84, 138, 143, 190. *See also* Guangzhou; opium
Guangdong haifang huilan, 231
Guangdong tongzhi, 51, 201–9, 215, 217, 222, 355n23, 360n87; cartography in, 211, 212, 214; legacy of, 225, 231, 232, 242
Guangzhou, 85, 183, 188, 189, 298, 308, 350n14, 356n84; growth of study of foreign geography in, 201, 203, 207–9, 215–18, 221–29, 231; India as seen from, before Opium War, 155–56, 159, 169, 171; India as seen from, during Opium War, 245, 246, 248, 250, 252, 260, 261, 264–67; Indian merchants in, 53,
126–28, 164–67; Lin Zexu in, 241–48; and the Macartney embassy, 147–49, 151, 155; and Siam, 194–95; viewed from Tibet, 134, 143, 144, 171–74; in Wei Yuan's strategic plan, 289, 296. *See also* Guangdong
Gujin tushu jicheng, 36, 38, 62, 99
Gulab Singh, 259, 263, 264, 306
Guo Deyan, 165
Guo Guichuan, 242
Gurkhas. *See* Nepal
Gützlaff, Karl, 214, 218–22, 259, 356n92, 357n97
Guy, R. Kent, 94

Haidao yizhi, 202
Haiguo jilan, 208
Haiguo jiwen, 208, 240
Haiguo tuzhi, 274, 276–78, 286, 288, 303, 363n23, 365n88; reception of, 285, 296, 299, 362n1
Haiguo wenjian lu, 42, 54–56, 201, 203, 208, 213, 225, 242
Hailu, 222, 231, 249, 275, 283, 355n23; legacy of, 225, 240, 242, 276; production of, 207–7
Haipu, 260, 261
Hallerstein, Augustin, 110, 112, 113, 119, 121
Hastings, Warren, 129–34
He Guozong, 104, 107, 110, 112, 121, 122, 125, 210
He-lin, 138, 144, 146, 147, 154, 157
Henderson, John B., 33, 333n80
"Hendusitan" (Hindustan), 90, 92–94, 98, 113, 151, 152, 279; and Protestant geographers, 218–19
He-ning, 157, 261, 278, 279
Hešen, 138, 150, 151, 153, 157
Hindu Kush, 288, 293
Hindustan, 19, 54, 71, 73, 307, 337n33, 338n47, 348n80; on the court survey map, 108, 109, 117; described by Chinese Muslims, 58, 59; described in gazetteers from Xinjiang, 83–85; and Macartney embassy, 151, 152, 155; and Moorcroft mission, 187–91; and Opium War, 264, 265; and Protestant geographers, 216–22; understood by Qianlong, 76–83, 87–96, 98–100, 132, 145, 152; understood in Tibet before 1790, 132–35, and Wei Yuan, 279, 283, 288, 289, 292
Hindustan jade, 84, 92, 93

Homann, Johann, 106, 341n22
"Hongmao" (European), 56, 147, 151, 152, 202, 205, 254; mentioned in Tibet, 138–40, 148, 158, 159
Hong merchants, 213, 224, 226, 228, 241, 262
Hong Taiji, 1, 61
Hormuz, 38
Hou Xian, 95
Hu Wei, 28, 333n61
Huangchao jingshi wenbian, 223
Huangchao wenxian tongkao, 77
Huang Juezi, 226, 239–41, 243
Huang Qing zhigong tu, 203, 348n82, 360n87
Huangyu Xiyu tuzhi, 96, 112, 113
Huc, Régis-Evariste, 307
Hui. *See* Muslims, Chinese
Hulumosi (Hormuz), 38
Hunter, William C., 165, 241, 242, 252, 358n12, 358n13
Hūturi, 174, 176, 177

Ignat'ev, Nikolai, 300
Iliyang, 242–44, 258, 261, 268
Imad al-Mulk, 78, 79, 338n41, 338n53
Imperial Household Department, 111, 112, 168
India: names for in pre-Qing China, 47–49; as seen from the Chinese coast, 164–70, 201–31, 237–58; as seen from Tibet, 127–47, 157–59, 171–84, 260–64; as seen from Xinjiang, 73–93, 184–91, 264–65; usage of name in this book, 21–22. *See also* Bengal; Hindustan
information order, 3–4, 329n2
injilī (Christian), 188, 189
Inoue Hiromasa, 223, 356n84
Isle, Guillaume de l', 106
Isle, Joseph-Nicolas de l', 121, 345n91
Izzat-ullah, Mir, 185–90, 264, 265

Jagannath Temple, 140
Jahanabad. *See* Delhi
Jalafuntai, 298–300
Jalalabad, 266, 267
Jambudvipa, 116, 123, 126, 132, 179, 284; introduced by Buddhist geography, 28–29; used by Mongols, 60; used by Qianlong, 89, 117
Jami, Catherine, 104
Jaohūi, 76, 108, 342n37

Jardine, William, 240
Jartoux, Pierre, 110
Jaunpur, 58, 91, 95
Java, 163, 166, 202, 215, 216, 256, 335n145, 335n146
Jesuits: and court survey maps, 103–4, 107, 109, 114–16, 118–26, 210–14, 222, 279–82; introducing European world maps 31–32, 53. *See also* Aleni, Benoist; *Kunyu tushuo*; Ricci, Verbiest
"Jiaga'er" (India), 88, 180, 182, 196, 278, 279, 347n54, 348n80; emergence of term in Chinese, 62, 64; mentioned by Fuk'anggan, 139–40, 143, 145; in post-Gurkha War geography, 157–59
"Jialajida" (Calcutta), 266
"Jialeguda" (Calcutta), 216
"Jialiquda jing" (Calcutta), 218
Jiang Fan, 205, 209, 213, 222, 224, 225, 280
Jiang Tingxi, 111
Jiang Youxian, 166
Jiaying, 205, 206, 216, 226, 354n20, 355n23
"Jibin," 96, 340n94
'Jigs-med-gling-pa, 134, 135, 146, 159, 349n121
Ji Yingjili, 225
Ji Yun, 45–46, 286
Jumla, 139, 140
Junghar Mongols, 85, 113, 156, 293, 303, 330n23, 341n14; and court survey maps, 104–7, 113; invasion of Tibet, 61–62, 65, 128; policy used by Qing against, 8–11, 160, 192, 258; Qing conquest of, 1, 73, 75, 76
Junjichu. *See* Grand Council

Kabul, 259, 266, 267
Kanda Nobuo, 292
Kandahar, 80, 266
Kangxi emperor, 6, 29, 53–55, 72, 237, 293, 343n69; and mapping, 103–6, 111, 115, 120, 122, 123, 335n141; and Tibetan geography, 62–63
Kangyou jixing, 277–79, 284, 362n23
kaozheng ("evidential research"), 33, 39, 41, 89, 92, 98, 211, 222; and *Siku quanshu* project, 95–96
Karakoram Mountains, 73–74, 77, 81, 83, 85, 164, 186
Kashgar, 75, 76, 80, 83–86, 99, 259, 306; on court survey map, 105, 107, 108; 117, 118; and Moorcroft mission, 186–90

Kashmir and Kashmiris, 62, 127, 263, 279, 308, 336n172, 340n94; Afghans and, 75–76, 78, 79, 81–82; connecting Xinjiang to Hindustan, 74, 84, 91; and Moorcroft mission, 186–91; and Opium War, 252, 259, 265–66; trading to Tibet, 129, 158, 186

Kathmandu, 129, 136, 140–42, 152, 175, 177, 345n2; Company resident in, 183; Kirkpatrick in, 146; Yan Tingliang in, 138

Kazakhs, 87, 107, 112, 284

Keriya, 108

Ke-shi-ke, 183

Khoqand, 76, 77, 83, 86, 108, 109, 258, 305

Khotan, 76, 107–09

Khwaja-i Jahan, 76–78, 86, 108, 337n31

Kidd, Samuel, 216

Kirghiz, 76, 83, 86, 107

Kirkpatrick, William, 146, 148

Kišan, 243, 249, 307, 308

Kögler, Ignace, 110

Kuch Bihar, 129

Kuhn, Philip, 197

Kuhn, Thomas, 39, 45, 286

Kumaon, 140, 180

Kunlun, 29, 73, 76, 89, 92, 93

Kunyu quantu, 92, 109, 120, 121, 342n44, 344n69

Kunyu tushuo, 31, 42, 46, 53, 203

Kuo'erka jilüe, 157

Ladakh, 74–79, 81, 83, 164, 306, 308, 337n20; conquered by Gulab Singh, 258, 263, 264; on court survey map, 115, 116; and Moorcroft mission, 185–91;

Lahore, 78, 79, 83, 184, 263

Langyaxu/Langyaxiu, 34–36

lascars, 250–52, 255

Lcang-skya khutughtu Rol-pa'i-rdo-rje, 72, 77, 108, 130, 131

Leh. *See* Ladakh

Lewis, Mark E., 27

Lhasa, 62, 133–36, 139, 141–46, 180, 196; and Bogle mission, 130; and Manning journey, 172–74; and missionaries in, 63, 134, 307. *See also ambans*

Li Hongbin, 166, 167, 241, 357n106

Li Hongzhang, 309

Li Mingche, 211, 212

Li, Ruohong, 130

Li Shiyao, 166

Li Xingyuan, 265

Li Zemin, 30

Li Zhaoluo, 206–9, 213, 222, 240, 275, 354n20

Liang Fa, 242

Liang Tingnan, 231, 242, 246, 274, 290, 358n13

Liang Zhi, 242, 243

Lifan yuan, 241

Lin Zexu, 237–51, 259, 266, 276, 292, 298, 299; and Wei Yuan, 273, 275, 291

Lindsay, Hugh Hamilton, 220, 221

Liu Ruofang, 112

Liu Tongxun, 112

Liu Zhi, 57–59

Lu Ciyun, 36, 40–41, 58

Lu Kun, 167, 228, 231, 241

Luk, Bernard H. K., 50

Luo Hongxian, 38, 44

Luzon, 166, 212, 214, 252, 253, 288

Ma Dexin, 57

Ma Junliang, 38, 44

Ma Laichi, 57

Ma Zhu, 30, 59, 65

Macao, 56, 128, 152, 153, 173, 201, 211, 225; during French Revolutionary and Napoleonic Wars, 163, 167–71, 249; and the Opium War, 244, 254, 260, 267; in Wei Yuan's strategic plan, 288; Xie Qinggao in, 205, 354n20

Macartney, George, 146–57, 159, 160, 163, 167, 168, 344n81

Madras, 170, 206, 216, 219, 276, 288, 335n137; and the Opium War, 245, 246, 249, 250, 262

Mailla, Joseph de, 110

Maitland, Frederick, 246

Malacca, 30, 48, 163, 215, 216, 241, 242, 358n12

Malwa, 219, 246

Manasarowar, Lake, 28, 115, 185, 343n68, 343n69

Manchu script, in Qing scholarship, 72–73

Manning, Thomas, 171–75, 196, 351n41, 351n45

Mao Haijian, 244, 248

Map Bureau, 111

maps: compared in geographic research, 211, 213, 280; limitations of, 32, 37–39, 279–80; in post-Opium War research, 279–86. *See also* court survey maps; Jesuits

Marathas, 135, 163, 204, 206, 207, 283,

338n41, 348n80; as rivals of Afghans, 78, 80, 82, 184
Marjoribanks, Charles, 219
Marques, José Martinho, 275, 296
Marshman, Joshua, 186, 242, 351n41, 353n93, 358n23
Mecca, 30, 37, 38, 57
Medhurst, Walter, 216, 350n14, 350n17, 354n6
Mei Wending, 52
Mengboo, 260, 261
Menggu yuanliu, 91
Mercator, Gerardus, 45
Milne, William, 215, 216
Mingghatu, 104, 107, 108, 110, 112, 113, 121, 125
"Mingjiaoliao" (Bengal), 202
Ming shi, 41, 50, 51, 58, 95, 96, 203, 213; description of Ceylon, 35
"Mingyala" (Bengal), 206
Ming yitong zhi, 35, 37, 217
Ming Žen, 79, 338n47
"Minya" (Bengal), 56, 65
Mongols, views on India, 60
Moorcroft, William, 185–91, 196, 264, 265, 353n90
Morrison, Robert, 204, 213, 215–19, 350n14
"Mowo'er" (Mughal), 48, 54, 92, 117, 123, 159, 169, 279, 283
Mughals and Mughal empire, 75, 80, 106, 127, 150, 163, 337n33, 349n119; mentioned by Catholic missionaries, 48, 49, 58, 117, 123, 169, 279; seen from Tibet, 62, 132, 134, 135, 140, 152; in Small Western Ocean, 54; understood by Qing in Qianlong period, 71, 78, 81, 88. *See also* Delhi padshah, Hindustan
Murray, Hugh, 249, 273, 275, 276, 362n13
Muslims, Chinese: views on India, 57–59
Mustang, 264

Napier, William, 223, 228
Neiwufu. *See* Imperial Household Department
Nepal, 62, 129, 134–46, 164, 193, 219, 300; diplomacy with the Qing, 137–42, 146, 175–84, 258–64, 305–7; and *Guangdong Tongzhi* project, 212–13; influence on the Macartney mission, 147–56; invasions of Tibet, 135–38; in Wei Yuan's writings, 279, 286–94, 296–97
Nerbudda, 255, 256

Newby, Laura, 87
newspapers and books, foreign-authored: in Chinese translation, 225; missionary authored, 215–22; translated by Lin Zexu, 242–43, 247, 259, 266; used after the Opium War, 274, 292, 293, 307. *See also* Murray, Hugh; *Sizhou zhi*
"Niegajinna," 260–62, 269
Ningbo, 220, 250–52, 273, 359n59
Niyas (Niyaz) Bek, 81, 82, 85
Nizam al-Mulk, 79, 331n48
Nuckajoo, 187

Office of Military Archives, 112, 120
Onuma Takahiro, 87
operational geography, genre of, 16, 88, 98–99
opium, production and trade, 226, 256–58, 263–65, 268, 296, 350n24; origins studied by Qing scholars, 200, 202, 206, 216, 238–42, 244–49; pre-1839 growth of trade in, 165, 223–24; Qing efforts to combat trade in, 167, 168; Wei Yuan's views on, 251, 288–89
Opium War, 213, 231, 233, 237–58, 268–70, 330n12; involves Inner Asia, 258–68; response to by Qing scholars, 271, 280, 285, 289, 296, 298, 300, 303; response to by Wei Yuan, 273, 274, 276, 278, 286–87, 291

Pamir Mountains, 73–75, 77, 85, 91, 95, 96, 284
Pan Shicheng, 274
Panchen Lama, Third, 79, 129–37, 139, 141, 177, 346n43
Panipat, 80, 82
Parker, Peter, 244–46
Parrenin, Dominique, 110
Parsis, 165, 166, 227
Patna, 129, 246
Penang, 202, 226, 241, 256, 358n12
Perdue, Peter C., 9
Pereira, André, 110
Petech, Luciano, 134
Peter the Great, 106, 343n69
Phe-reng and variants, 134, 135, 159, 346n32
Pho-lha-nas, 128
"Pileng," 139–47, 156–60, 170–2, 185, 196; during Anglo-Gurkha War, 175–83; during Macartney embassy, 148, 152–54; during Opium War, 260–4, 269;

"Pileng" (*continued*)
  discussed by Wei Yuan, 273, 278, 279, 290, 291; discussed by Xu Jiyu, 297–98; origins of term, 139, 307, 348n76. *See also* Phe-reng; Farangi; Calcutta
"Piluo-guo" (Bengal), 63, 65
place-names: as a basis for analysis, 17–18, 33–37, 47, 70, 94; integration of by Wei Yuan, 272, 275, 276, 302; used on maps, 117, 281, 282, 283. *See also* yan'ge
Poirot, Louis de, 138
Polachek, James, 6, 360n101, 362n1
Pondicherry, 56, 204
Prithvi Narayan Shah, 129
Punjab, 74, 88, 127, 163, 184, 187, 263, 265; Afghans in, 78, 80, 83; British conquest of, 306–8
Purangir, 130–32, 134, 142, 347n66

qalandar, 84, 85, 339n64
Qi Gong, 261, 262, 267, 268
Qi Shaonan, 34, 35, 51, 65
Qian Daxin, 210
Qian Qianyi, 30
Qianlong emperor: and cartography, 107–6; patronage and control of official scholarship, 69–73; strategic perspective of, 193–98, 289–95; views on Indian geography, 79–83, 87–100, 130–133, 155–56
Qiao Renjie, 149, 150, 153, 154
Qin Guojing, 112
Qing shi gao, 77
Qing shi lu, 52, 108
Qintian jian. *See* Directorate of Astronomy
Qi-ying, 254, 298, 307, 308

Rajendra Bikram Shah, 260
Ran Bahadur Shah, 176, 263, 348n75
Ranjit Singh, 185, 187, 306
Régis, Jean-Baptiste, 105, 110
Residents, East India Company, 183, 192, 193, 195, 196
Ricci, Matteo, 31, 49–51, 65, 117, 212, 282, 334n117
Ripa, Matteo, 105, 111, 351n39
Rocha, Felix da, 107, 110, 112, 113, 119, 121
Rong Lin, 243, 370n25
Rose, Leo, 145
Ruan Yuan, 201, 202, 204, 205, 207–14, 354n14; comment on Gangjiao, 218; description of Arab merchants, 166; gazetteer of, consulted, 239, 242; and Xiao Lingyu, 224–25
Russia, 7–10, 212, 241, 266, 277, 279, 306; in court cartography, 105, 106, 117, 121, 124, 340n13; and "Great Game," 21, 192; in Jalafuntai's proposal, 296, 298, 299, 300, and Moorcroft mission, 185, 186, 189; transcription of, 34; in Wei Yuan's strategic thinking, 286–89, 291–94, 301, 364n70
"Ryga-gar." *See* Jiaga'er

Saicungga, 180–84, 193
Samarkand, 38, 96
Sanskrit, 47, 72–73, 93, 94, 100
scholastic geography, genre of, 16, 88
Select Committee of the East India Company at Canton, 167, 169, 204, 218, 219, 223, 228; and Macartney embassy, 148, 155
"Senba." *See* Sikhs
sepoys, 21, 206, 250, 252–54, 266, 268, 269; in occupation of Macao, 170, 249. *See also* "black foreigners"
Shah Alam II, 78, 80, 81, 163
Shahjahanabad. *See* Delhi
Shah Niyaz Khan, 185, 186, 189
Shanhai jing, 27, 41
Shapin, Steven, 40
Shengwu ji, 273, 278, 279, 286, 290–92
Shi ji, 27, 47, 331n1
Siam, 42, 167, 194, 195, 212, 288, 293, 294, 297, 298
Sichuan, 136, 138, 158, 171, 174, 176, 215, 217, 259, 277, 278, 358n12
Sichuan tongzhi, 158
Sikhs, 80, 83, 263, 265, 276, 306–8
Sikkim, 144, 172, 176, 181, 264
Siku quanshu, 92, 94–97, 100, 113, 125, 201, 203, 211
Siku quanshu zongmu tiyao, 41, 42, 43, 95, 123
Singapore, 163, 216, 222, 224, 225, 229, 255, 256
Sinju, 82
Sizhou zhi, 273, 275, 276, 279, 281
Small Western Ocean. *See* Western Ocean
Song Qiyuan, 251, 252
Srinagar, 140
statecraft scholarship (*jingshi*), 14, 15, 199, 223, 224, 226, 228, 356n84; and Wei Yuan, 273
Staunton, George Leonard, 151

INDEX 397

Staunton, George Thomas, 155, 351n45
Su Tingkui, 267
Šuhede, 119
Sukh Jiwan, 78, 79, 81
Su-leng-e, 168
Sultan Khwaja, 82, 338n47
Sultan Shah, 77–79, 85–87
Sumeru, Mt., 28, 29, 31, 89, 284
Sun Shiyi, 138, 143, 157, 158
Sungyūn, 157, 175, 184, 277, 278, 303
Surat, 53, 56, 117, 204, 205, 344n72
Sutlej River, 117, 163, 180, 187
Suzuki Chūsei, 132, 184, 348n76

Taiwan, 53–55, 137, 220, 250, 251; Yao Ying on, 201, 255–58, 268, 274, 277
Taksin, 194, 195, 294
Tashilhunpo, 129, 130, 136, 137
Tengyue, 289
"Tianfang" (Mecca), 38
"Tianzhu" (India), 56, 58, 62, 96, 227, 232, 253, 333n94; and "Enetkek," 60; in *Guangdong tongzhi*, 217–19; used before the Qing period, 47–49; used by Protestant geographers, 219, 221, 222; used by Qianlong, 89, 146
"Tianzhu wu Yindu kao'e," 89, 117
Tibet, 72–75, 127–31, 133–60, 169–86; and British conquest of Punjab, 305–8; in court survey maps, 104, 108, 115, 126; influence on Qing views of India, 60–64, 88–93, 128, 132–35, 138–47, 258–64; in Wei Yuan's strategic thinking, 288–91; Yao Ying on, 276–79. *See also* Nepal; Lhasa; *ambans*
"Ti-ling pa-ca." *See* Delhi Padshah
Tipu Sultan, 150, 151, 351n29
Tongwen yuntong, 72
Trebeck, George, 187
tribute system, 5, 178, 179, 184
Tulišen, 60, 117, 340n13
Turner, Samuel, 131, 139, 171

Ulungga, 187, 189, 190
United States, 195, 203, 287, 288, 292, 296, 299, 300
Utg'ali Bargišuwara Khan, 90
Uzbeks, 75, 78, 86

Varanasi, 129, 132, 140, 176, 246
Verbiest, Ferdinand, 58, 104, 109, 120, 212; and *Kunyu tushuo*, 31, 42, 46, 53, 203; and post-Opium War geography, 279–82, 284, 363n51
Victoria, Queen, 241, 246, 247
Vladislavich, Sava, 105, 106, 341n22

Waiguo dili beikao, 275
Wakeman, Frederic, 254
Wang Chaozong, 274
Wang Dahai, 166, 202, 207, 214, 274, 276
Wang Qianjin, 113, 343n58
Wang Wentai, 274
Wang Wenxiong, 149, 150, 153, 154
"Wangjiaola" (Bengal), 54, 56, 335n146
"Wangmai" (Bombay), 56–57
Washington, George, 195
Wei Yuan, 240, 301–4, 308; and Anstruther, 250–251, 273; and geographic research, 271–79; and mapping, 279–86; strategic perspective of, 286–95; reception of his work, 296–301
Wei-Zang tongzhi, 157
Wei-Zang tuzhi, 157
Wellesley, Richard, 163, 207
Wen Wenbo, 242
"Wendusitan" (Hindustan), 90, 94, 98, 113, 211
Western Ocean, 35–36, 49–59, 62–65, 174; mentioned during Macartney embassy, 147, 151–52, 155, 157; mentioned during Qing-Gurkha War, 138, 140, 143, 158; used at Guangzhou in 1800–1838 period, 212, 217, 218, 227; used in pre-Qing period, 31, 38
Wills, John E., Jr., 6
worldviews, geopolitical, 11–18, 160, 222–32, 269, 286–301
"Woya" (Goa), 56
Wu-cheng-ge, 83, 84
Wu Lai, 30
Wu Lanxiu, 205–8, 231
Wu Xiongguang, 169, 170
Wuyingdian printer, 112
Wyatt, Don, 254, 360n88

Xianbin lu, 38, 41
Xiao Lingyu, 224, 225, 227–31, 358n12
Xiao Tenglin, 62, 65
Xie Qinggao, 205–8, 213, 222, 231, 249, 276
Xi-en, 253
"Xilan(shan)" (Ceylon), 34, 35, 36
"Xilong" (Ceylon), 54
"Xilun" (Ceylon), 36

Xi-ming, 177, 178, 179, 181, 182, 183
"Xindusitang" (Hindustan), 58, 59
"Xiyang." *See* Western Ocean
Xiyu kaogu lu, 290
Xiyu tuzhi. See *Huangyu Xiyu tuzhi*
Xiyu wenjian lu. See Cišii
Xizang fu, 157, 261, 279
Xizang zhi, 157
Xizhao tushuo, 157
Xu Chaojun, 274
Xu Jiyu, 272, 274, 281, 285, 297, 298
Xuanzang, 29, 30, 36, 42, 47, 93

Yamuna River, 115, 116, 122
Yan Congjian, 35, 38
Yan Ruyi, 223
Yan Sizong, 229–31, 247
Yan Tingliang, 138, 139, 143, 147, 148
Yang Bingnan, 205, 354n20
Yang Yingju, 194
Yangcūn, 169, 173, 174
yan'ge, 33, 36, 64–65, 73, 88, 96; technique used by Wei Yuan, 272, 275, 280, 283, 285, 301
Yangfang jiyao, 223
Yao Ying, 276–85, 288, 290; on Taiwan, 201, 255–58, 266, 268, 274
Yao Zutong, 225
Yapp, Malcolm, 192
Yarkand, 71, 75–84, 86, 99, 259, 263–65; and court cartography, 107–9, 117, 118; and Moorcroft mission, 184–90
Ye Mingchen, 2, 298
Ye Zhongjin, 225–27, 229–31, 247, 357n96
Yi Kezhong, 225, 231
Yi-jing, 252, 253, 266
Yi-li-bu, 250, 252, 359n59
"Yindi" (Hindī), 84, 187, 265, 306, 308
"Yindu" (India), 58, 267, 276, 278, 279, 283, 308, 334n96; equated with "Gangjia," 227, 232, 246, 269; origins of, 47–48; used by Protestant geographers, 216–19; used in Qianlong period, 88, 89, 92, 92, 96
"Yin(g)diya," 48–50, 117, 123, 217
Yinghuan zhilüe, 272, 274, 297
"Yingjili" (England/English), 166, 213, 221, 240, 250, 265, 307, 308; and Moorcroft mission, 187–90; relationship to "Pileng," 19, 147–48, 159, 183

Yingjili xiaoji, 251, 273
Yin-xiang, Prince, 105–7
Yi-shan, 243, 265, 267, 268
Yiyu suotan. See Cišii
Yongle Emperor, 91, 95
You Tong, 35, 51
Yu Fushun, 106, 341n25
"Yu gong," 27–28, 126
Yu Hao, 290
Yu Zhengxie, 240
Yuan Dehui, 241, 242, 358n12
Yuan Taizu. *See* Chinggis Khan
Yuantian tushuo, 211
Yue haiguan zhi, 201, 231, 242
Yu-kun, 242
Yunggui, 83, 84
Yun-lu, Prince, 110, 112, 113, 120–22, 125
Yunnan, 28, 57, 62, 194, 289, 293, 299, 300; proximity to India, 106, 219, 221
Yu-qian, 248, 251, 253
Yutu fang. See Map Bureau

Zakharov, Ivan Il'ich, 299
Zeyilan (Ceylon), 36
Zhang Hai, 62
Zhang Weiping, 296, 364n78
Zhang Xie, 208
Zhang Yushu, 61
Zhao Jinxiu, 171–74
Zheng Guangzu, 274
Zheng He, 31, 34, 37, 52, 282, 289; in Qianlong-period scholarship, 42, 51, 92, 95
Zheng-rui, 150, 153
Zhifang wai ji, 31, 41, 42, 208, 213, 217, 282, 284
Zhou Ailian, 158
Zhouche wenjian lu, 205, 213, 225, 354n19
Zhouju suozhi, 274
Zhu Gui, 155, 156
Zhu Siben, 30
Zhuang Tingfu, 211, 213, 280–82
Zhuguo jiyou, 158
Zhwa dmar, 136, 142, 346n43, 348n79
Zongli Yamen, 21, 309
Zongmu tiyao. See Siku quanshu zongmu tiyao
Zou Yan, 27, 31–32, 284, 285
Zuo Zongtang, 309

Lightning Source UK Ltd.
Milton Keynes UK
UKHW010852120519
342513UK00002B/456/P